Johnny Noyes

D1606427

Sung Dynasty Uses of the *I Ching*

Reading the I Ching in the Pine Shade, Liu Sung-nien (active A.D. 1190–1224)
Source: Collection of the National Palace Museum, Taipei, Taiwan, Republic of China

Sung Dynasty Uses of the *I Ching*

Kidder Smith, Jr., Peter K. Bol,
Joseph A. Adler, and Don J. Wyatt

PRINCETON UNIVERSITY PRESS

PRINCETON, NEW JERSEY

Copyright © 1990 by Princeton University Press
Published by Princeton University Press, 41 William Street,
Princeton, New Jersey 08540
In the United Kingdom: Princeton University Press, Oxford

Library of Congress Cataloging-in-Publication Data

Sung Dynasty uses of the I ching / Kidder Smith, Jr. . . . [et al.].
p. cm.
Includes bibliographical references.
1. I ching. 2. China—Intellectual life—960–1644. I. Smith,
Kidder, 1944– .
PL2464.Z7S895   1990   299'.51282—dc20   89-24084

ISBN 0-691-05590-4

This book has been composed in Linotron Sabon

Princeton University Press books are printed on acid-free paper,
and meet the guidelines for permanence and durability of the
Committee on Production Guidelines for Book Longevity of the
Council on Library Resources

Printed in the United States of America by Princeton University Press,
Princeton, New Jersey
10 9 8 7 6 5 4 3 2 1

Contents

Preface   vii

Introduction   3

CHAPTER ONE
The *I Ching* Prior to Sung   7

CHAPTER TWO
The Sung Context: From Ou-yang Hsiu to Chu Hsi   26

CHAPTER THREE
Su Shih and Culture   56

CHAPTER FOUR
Shao Yung and Number   100

CHAPTER FIVE
Ch'eng I and the Pattern of Heaven-and-Earth   136

CHAPTER SIX
Chu Hsi and Divination   169

CHAPTER SEVEN
Sung Literati Thought and the *I Ching*   206

APPENDIX
The Fu Hexagram   237

Glossary   255

Bibliography   259

About the Authors   267

Index   269

Preface

THE *I Ching* IS so protean that over the last three thousand years of Chinese history it has occasioned hundreds of commentaries,[1] thousands of essays,[2] tens of thousands of citations,[3] and, we may surmise, millions of conversations. Sung dynasty (960–1279) *I Ching* studies are rife and renowned, for that text drew in every important thinker of the eleventh century and many of the twelfth.[4] This book examines how four influential figures of the Sung used the *I Ching* or *Book of Change* to address profound issues of human values. We are engaged in three interrelated pursuits. First is the historical study of a text: how the *I* was understood by particular people at a particular time. Second is the case studies of our four thinkers, Su Shih (1037–1101), Shao Yung (1011–1077), Ch'eng I (1033–1107), and Chu Hsi (1130–1200). Third, we suggest that in their diversity these four men reveal a commonality of goal and method within Sung literati thought. Here I will briefly discuss each of these aspects in turn.

We study the *Book of Change* historically. That is, we demonstrate how each of our four subjects brought a set of specific historical questions to bear on the *I*. In doing so, we seek to show how a classic was appropriated by later thinkers, how a single text could be taken to mean many different things, and what it is about the *I* that made it so significant to literati of the Sung. Our book is not a history of the Sung *I*—its schools, commentators, and texts.[5] Rather it is a study of the *I* in history.

---

[1] See, for example, Yen Ling-feng, *I-ching chi-ch'eng* (Complete collection on the *Book of Change*) (Taipei: Ch'eng-wen, 1975), which contains nearly two hundred commentaries but is by no means a complete repository of extant works. Many other commentaries have, of course, been lost.

[2] Over two thousand of these were extant in the seventeenth century. See Larry Schulz, *Lai Chih-te (1525–1604) and the Phenomenology of Change* (Ann Arbor: University Microfilms, 1982), p. 3, for a brief discussion. A quick perusal of scholars' literary collections (*wen-chi*) reveals that many include at least one short piece on the *I*.

[3] We possess records from as early as 603 B.C.E. in which people quote a phrase or more from the *I*. See the discussion of the *Tso-chuan* in chapter 1.

[4] In addition to the works studied here, see, for example, the writings of Fan Chung-yen (989–1052), Hu Yüan (993–1059), Ou-yang Hsiu (1007–1072), Chou Tun-i (1017–1073), Ch'en Hsiang (1017–1080), Ssu-ma Kuang (1019–1096), Chang Tsai (1020–1077), Wang An-shih (1021–1086), et al. For full citations and brief discussions of these and other works see Wang Chi-hsi, *Pei-Sung I-hsüeh-k'ao* (An investigation of Northern Sung *I Ching* studies) (Taipei: M.A. thesis, Taiwan Normal University, 1978).

[5] For that see Wang Chi-hsi, *Pei-Sung I-hsüeh-k'ao* and Imai Usaburō, *Sōdai ekikyō no kenkyū* (Researches on the Sung dynasty *I Ching*) (Tokyo: Meiji, 1958).

Our four literati thinkers are important for several reasons. Each was convinced that he understood the true nature of heaven, earth, and humanity. Each found in the *I Ching* evidence for believing that people who were socially and politically involved in a changing world could have a constant moral foundation. Their explanations were persuasive to many of their contemporaries and members of later generations. Their *I Ching* writings defined the principal issues that later students of the *I* would debate. Each, however, had a distinct view of the book. Su Shih saw it as evidence that an integrated human order ultimately depended on individual creativity. Shao Yung believed that *I Ching* images and numerology ordered the processes of an integrated universe. Ch'eng I took the *I* as a tool whereby literati might learn to act correctly in a world always threatened by selfishness and corruption. Chu Hsi used it in divination to realize the mind of the sages.[6]

Finally, we seek to demonstrate certain commonalities of Sung literati thinking, as well as its considerable diversity. Our four men shared with many of their contemporaries a commitment to arrive at the one real foundation for all values, to set out the method for doing so, and, as sages, to realize those values in the day-to-day conduct of life. While all of them used the *I* in these projects, each recognized that texts—even so remarkable a text as the *Book of Change*—were merely representations of values whose origins lay elsewhere. The *I* was a means for gaining access to those values. As such it must ultimately be transcended once that access was realized.

Work by other scholars has been of great benefit to us. The translations of James Legge and Richard Wilhelm introduced the *I Ching* text to one hundred years of Western readers.[7] Iulian Shchutskii, working in the Soviet Union during the early 1930s, explored questions of origin and development of the text and its commentaries.[8] Arthur Waley was the first European to read the *I* in light of the critical scholarship of men like Li Ching-ch'ih and Kao Heng.[9] Wing-tsit Chan continues to make Sung li-

---

[6] Certain figures have been left out of our discussion. Most notable are Chou Tun-i and Chang Tsai, though in many respects Shao Yung and Ch'eng I raise issues that are functionally similar. We make no mention of the considerable Taoist interest in the *I*. We have also omitted any reference to popular usage, though we may imagine that Shao Yung had enormous influence on their later practices, especially those that used the *I* to predict the future.

[7] James Legge, *The Yi King* (Oxford: Clarendon Press, 1892); Richard Wilhelm, *I Ging: Das Buch der Wandlungen*, 2 volumes (Jena, 1924); English translation by Cary F. Baynes, *The I Ching or Book of Changes* (Princeton: Princeton University Press, 3d edition, 1967). Both Legge and Wilhelm drew essentially on Ch'eng I's and Chu Hsi's traditions of the *I*.

[8] Iulian K. Shchutskii, *Researches on the I Ching*, translated by William L. MacDonald and Tsuyoshi Hasegawa with Hellmut Wilhelm (Princeton: Princeton University Press, 1979), a translation of materials written between 1928 and 1935.

[9] Arthur Waley, "*The Book of Changes*," *Bulletin of the Museum of Far Eastern Antiq-*

terati thought accessible to English speakers in a remarkable series of translations.[10] Yet while the *I* is perhaps the work of East Asian culture best known in the United States, it is rarely treated as a historical document. A pioneering exception is an article by Chi-yun Chen that demonstrates the political uses to which three Han dynasty (206 B.C.E.–220 C.E.) writers put the *I*.[11]

Like Chen, we have studied the *Book of Change* in its historical contexts. Rather than arguing that it transcends human culture or contains a timeless wisdom, we have examined its specific use by specific people. Thus we do not speak of the "real meaning" of the book, nor of the intrinsic meaning of a hexagram, as the meaning of each has varied enormously from user to user. At the same time, we are interested in why certain interpreters have dominated most of their successors. Our approach is therefore at odds with that of Richard Wilhelm in his translation and studies of the *I*. Wilhelm set out, like his Chinese teachers, to define the *I Ching* once and for all. Because his is the most influential of European-language translations, and because our translations often differ from his, we have in every case referred the reader to his text, cited as "W/B" (for Wilhelm and his English translator Cary Baynes) with the page number of the Princeton University Press third edition. In the case of hexagram names we have provided the Wilhelm/Baynes version in square brackets if it differs from our own, e.g., "hexagram #3 Chun (Sprout [Difficulty at the Beginning])."

We have followed the common practice of citing Chinese texts by *chüan* (i.e., chapter) and page number. Thus, a reference of the form *Erh-Ch'eng chi* 21A.269 indicates *chüan* 21A, page 269. A citation of *Hsi-tzu-chuan* B8 refers to part 2, section 8 of that work. The idiosyncratic pagination of the *Su Tung p'o chi* necessitates references of the form 2.5.29.110, indicating volume, *ts'e*, *chüan*, and page numbers.

Figures 3, 4, 5, and 7 in chapter 4 are taken from Fung Yu-lan, *A History of Chinese Philosophy*, Vol. II: *The Period of Classical Learning*,

---

uities 5 (1933), pp. 121–42. The article owes much to the pioneering work of Li Ching-ch'ih published during the 1920s and 1930s. See bibliography for full citations of Li's and Kao's work.

[10] See especially his translation of Chu Hsi's and Lü Tsu-ch'ien's *Chin-ssu-lu* as *Reflections on Things at Hand* (New York: Columbia University Press, 1967).

[11] "A Confucian Magnate's Idea of Political Violence: Hsün Shuang's Interpretation of the *Book of Changes*," *T'oung Pao*, series 2, 54 (1960), pp. 73–115. For a listing of Western-language materials on the *I*, see Hellmut Wilhelm, *Parerga*, no. 2, *The Book of Changes in the Western Tradition: A Selected Bibliography* (Seattle: Institute for Comparative and Foreign Area Studies, University of Washington, 1976) and *Zhouyi Network* 2 (1987), pp. 3–14. There is, of course, a voluminous amount in Chinese on the *I*. However, very little of it, even among recent work, asks historical questions. Correspondingly, few of these studies are cited here.

trans. Derk Bodde (Princeton: Princeton University Press, 1953), with the kind permission of Princeton University Press.

Each of us has worked closely with the others' chapters. The introduction is by Kidder Smith and Peter Bol. Chapter 1, on the early uses of the *I*, is by Kidder Smith. Chapter 2, on Ou-yang Hsiu and the Sung context, is by Peter Bol. Chapter 3, on Su Shih, is also by Peter Bol. He would like to thank Susan Bush, Ronald Egan, Michael Fuller, Neil Katkov and Stephen Owen for reading and commenting upon an early draft. Chapter 4, on Shao Yung, is by Kidder Smith and Don Wyatt. They would like to thank Anne Birdwhistell and John Henderson for their useful comments. Chapter 5, on Ch'eng I, is by Kidder Smith, who appreciates the careful reading given to it by John Ewell. Chapter 6, on Chu Hsi, is by Joseph Adler, who thanks Tu Wei-ming, Robert Gimello, Chi-yun Chen, and Richard Lynn for their helpful suggestions on an earlier version. Chapter 7 is by Kidder Smith, drawing on many conversations with Peter Bol; Joseph Adler wrote the materials on Chu Hsi. We would all like to express our deep appreciation to Wing-tsit Chan for many useful suggestions on translation and to Irene Bloom and Hoyt Tillman for their insightful remarks on the entire manuscript. Finally, our gratitude to Pete and Joanne Miller for their discerning indexing, to Wendy Chiu for her scrupulous copyediting, and to Margaret Case for her support throughout.

k.s.

Sung Dynasty Uses of the *I Ching*

Introduction

IN THE COURSE of the eleventh and twelfth centuries, China experienced one of the greatest transformations in its history. Sung dynasty thinkers laid the basis for later practices of moral philosophy, social organization, political theory and aesthetics. This book studies four men who had particular influence on Sung intellectual culture—Su Shih, Shao Yung, Ch'eng I and Chu Hsi. These men sought to define the relationship between the natural world of heaven-and-earth (*t'ien-ti*) and the world of human values. Each, in varying ways, saw heaven, earth, and humanity as an integrated field, in which values existed naturally. Knowing this natural unity, men would have a foundation on which to bring order to all under heaven. Each man, in varying ways, found the *I Ching* central to his project.

Sung society differed profoundly from its T'ang (618–906) antecedents. To understand the urgency of these men's work, we need first of all to ask briefly what their society had become, what social group they belonged to, why they sought a new basis for human values, and why the *I Ching* was so pertinent to their concerns.

Sung not only reunified China in the 960s, it removed from power men who had become militarily and fiscally independent of the central authority during the previous era, replacing them with officials selected by, sent from, and answerable to the court and emperor. Thus, what had been the rule of local strongmen was transformed into a single, well-organized, centralized, civil bureaucracy. Eliminating the primary cause of over a century's disorder, Sung created conditions for three centuries of growth. Agricultural production steadily increased. Technological and marketing innovations, an expanding population, developing urban centers, economic exchange freed of many restrictions that had been imposed by T'ang—all these led to greater wealth, spread over more regions and shared by more of the population than ever before. This wealth created resources that allowed new men to establish their families as members of the elite, especially men of commercial origin or from previously marginalized areas like the south. The revolution in economic production coincided with a revolution in the production of cultural materials—that is, with the invention of printing. The laborious and expensive hand-copying of manuscripts had encouraged scholars to specialize in a single text. Now many books became easily accessible, enormously expanding the potential for intellectual synthesis and innovation.

We can best understand the elite of this new society by contrasting them with their T'ang predecessors, aristocrats belonging to or allied with large, powerful and longstanding lineages based particularly in the north China plains. These men had supplied high officials to the empire since before T'ang itself came to power. Their claim to service thus rested on a pedigree independent of the state. However, the military conflicts that preceded Sung put an end to these lineages, as warfare devastated their economic base, familial networks, and the state on which they depended, and as warlords sought military or administrative skills without reference to class origins.

Both T'ang and Sung elite were landowners, and many served in the national bureaucracy as officials. As the chief educated group, they saw themselves as the holders of traditional culture. The crucial difference between them is the extent to which the Sung elite can be defined by their success in the imperial civil service examinations. By this measure the state itself institutionalized the primary mechanism by which one might seek and claim elite status. These exams tested the mastery of traditional cultural forms, especially the ability to compose in regulated styles and the memorization of canonical texts. This meant that for the first time in its history, China was governed by men whose qualifications for office were measured first in cultural and intellectual terms. The traditional name for this elite is *shih*. We translate that word as "literati" to reflect its predominantly cultural content.

Passing the final level of exams at the palace assured one of government appointment and thus the exercise of a small portion of the imperial power. In sharing its power in this manner Sung believed that they had chosen men who would look to the integrity of the state and the interests of the whole. Undoubtedly this was often true, as the various figures discussed in this book attest. In particular, through the first century of Sung rule, literati seem to have welcomed and abetted the state's centralized authority. Yet they might not always act in the interest of the whole. Ch'eng I stridently attacked literati as ambitious and self-serving, complaining that they did not seek to know *tao*. Though he was more fervent in his critique than the other three men we address, the substance of his analysis is echoed in their writings, and in the writings of others.

Ch'eng's dissatisfaction with prevailing literati values reflects a larger disjunction that had been developing between social, political and economic practices, on the one hand, and cultural identities on the other. In the former realm, T'ang institutions had generally been superseded. Yet T'ang cultural models still prevailed publicly well past the start of the eleventh century. Sung, however, had no aristocratic lineages that could be assumed to act as repositories of tradition—where the external forms of culture were uninterruptedly maintained, where ritual, etiquette, and style were practiced in a manner worthy of emulation. Such issues were not simply matters of private taste, for political power to shape society and the lives of both elite and commoners was at stake.

By the mid-eleventh century, the uneasiness about culture in general and cultural values in particular was obvious. In the 1030s Fan Chung-yen (989–1052) and Ou-yang Hsiu (1007–1072) had called for a major reconstruction of literati political practice, challenging the notion that received traditions were a sufficient grounding to literati values. The four men we treat here were passionately involved in the ensuing debates. The issues they raised were worked through slowly and painfully, from the 1030s to the death of Chu Hsi in 1200. We can identify three sets of questions that they, with other literati, sought to answer. These questions are the ground on which our book is built, and we believe that they afford the best means for seeing the commonalities and differences within Sung literati thought, and for developing a sense of the whole.

The first question concerns a new basis that would guide men in the creation of an integrated human society, one dedicated to benefiting all. Literati recognized that the inevitability of historical change meant a discontinuity between past and present forms. Where, then, could a constancy be found? Was the history of the Han (206 B.C.E.–220 C.E.) or T'ang empires the proper model, if it were flexibly applied? Should Sung base itself on the age of the sages that Confucius (551–479 B.C.) had struggled to transmit to his time? Was the basis instead inherent in the nature of the world—in heaven-and-earth—if one knew how to read it? (If the latter were the case, then what was the relevance of the preceding two thousand years of historical and cultural experience?) Or could the source itself never be directly known?

Related to these is the second set of questions: What is human nature? Are literati primarily social actors? Bearers of cultural tradition? Or do all human beings share something essential with heaven-and-earth? What, in other words, might human beings aspire to? Can they compare themselves with the sages of antiquity? Can individual literati establish themselves in the present as morally autonomous from political authority—yet remain responsible to the whole of society?

Third, whatever the basis, by what manner of *hsüeh* (study, learning) does one obtain access to it? Can one rely on cultural traditions, as transmitted by family, schooling or government service? Do texts convey the sages' wisdom from the past? If so, which texts? Can the mind apprehend values directly by contemplating the things of the world? Or does the mind itself contain primordial wisdom that can be tapped by the proper practices?

Why did men with these concerns turn to the *Book of Change*? One simple answer is that the *I Ching* had for centuries been intimately linked with related issues of heaven, earth, and humanity. Those who sought a universal grounding for values might turn naturally to such a model, especially one that claimed to encompass everything in heaven-and-earth. But there are many other reasons for its usefulness, which will emerge over the course of this book.

Chapter 1 introduces the *I Ching* text. More than the other Classics, the *I* has its particular language and hermeneutic protocols. This chapter presents these and other matters that Sung literati took for granted. It proceeds by discussing issues put to the *I* text from earliest times through the T'ang, whose version was the received text in Sung. Chapter 2 addresses the Sung intellectual context, beginning with the work of Ou-yang Hsiu, who more than anyone determined the questions that would be discussed in the mid-eleventh century. It also introduces the four central figures of our book. Chapters 3 through 6 are devoted to individual thinkers. Su Shih, while in many ways the heir of Ou-yang, went well beyond him in what he would consider relevant to the literati search for values. Shao Yung, though thirty years Su's senior, raised concerns about heaven-and-earth that only attained a wide audience in the period of Su's majority. Ch'eng I regarded Shao's morality as perfect yet proposed an alternative understanding of the pattern of heaven-and-earth. Chu Hsi found a solution to these eleventh-century issues that was considered conclusive by many Chinese through the remainder of the imperial period. In the final chapter we turn to the commonalities of Sung literati thought and to the particular qualities of the *I Ching* that made it so useful to these and other literati thinkers.

CHAPTER ONE

The *I Ching* Prior to Sung

LITERATI in Sung China made claims about the *Book of Change* that should give us pause. Ch'eng I remarks:

> There is not a single thing that those who made the *I* did not conjoin, from the obscure and bright of heaven-and-earth to the minute subtleties of the various insects, grasses and trees.[1]

His slightly older contemporary Chou Tun-i (1017–1073) asks rhetorically:

> How is the *I* the source of only the Five Classics? It is the mysterious abode of heaven, earth and the spiritual forces.[2]

Shao Yung built his philosophical framework from elements he found in and around the *I Ching*. Su Shih claimed that

> Those who are enlightened bring its *tao* (way) into practice. For them there is neither coming in nor going out. There is neither inside nor outside. They "flow through the six line-places [of the hexagrams]," and wherever they go "it is fortunate." Even acting as a sage is possible for them.[3]

And Chu Hsi, quoting one of the Appendixes to the *I Ching*, remarks:

> "The *I* discloses things, completes affairs, and encompasses the *tao* of all under heaven."[4] This is the general purpose of the *I*.[5]

Clarifying this, he says:

> "To disclose things and to complete affairs" means to enable people to divine in order to understand good and ill fortune and to complete their undertakings. "To encompass the *tao* of all under heaven" means that once the hexagram lines are set, the *tao* of all under heaven is contained in them.[6]

These claims challenge modern readers. How can the *I Ching* contain the *tao* of everything under heaven? How can this text do, or mean, so

---

[1] *Erh-Ch'eng chi* (The collected works of the two Ch'eng brothers) (Peking: Chung-hua, 1981), *Wai-shu* 7.394, i.e., *chüan* 7, p. 394 of the *Wai-shu*.

[2] *T'ung-shu* (Writings comprehending [the *Book of Change*]), section 30.

[3] *Su Shih I-chuan*, 8.182, quoting the *Hsi-tz'u-chuan* B8.

[4] *Hsi-tz'u-chuan* A10.

[5] *Chu-tzu yü-lei* 66, p. 2575.

[6] *Chou-i pen-i* 3:13b.

many things? While we may never fully share the convictions of Sung literati about these matters, we can begin our own investigation of their claims by asking questions from four familiar perspectives: What is the text of the *I Ching*? What were its origins? How was it first used? By what methods was it later interpreted? In this way we will move gradually from the *I* as a readily identifiable set of words to something more problematic, engaging, and powerful.

What is the text?   In this sense we can define the *I Ching* as a closed system, consisting of sixty-four hexagrams and the texts in Chinese that are associated with them. These hexagrams, or six-lined figures, are composed of solid (yang —) and/or broken (yin ——) lines, one atop the other, for example ☰ or ☷. Since each line can be either broken or solid, and since there are six line-places, sixty-four hexagrams can be formed.

Each hexagram has a name. The two examples given above are Ch'ien (Primal Yang [The Creative])[7] and Fu (Return), the first and twenty-fourth in the sequence. Others are Chun (Sprout [Difficulty at the Beginning]), Shih (Army), T'ai (Peace) and, the last hexagram, Wei-chi (Not Completed [Before Completion]). Each hexagram also has a hexagram statement (*t'uan* or *kua-tz'u*) associated with it.[8] That for Ch'ien reads "*yüan heng li chen.*" The original meaning of these words when the *I* was composed over the early centuries of the first millennium B.C.E. was perhaps "Initial receipt: profitable to divine," indicating that the *I* could be usefully consulted.[9] But at least as early as the third century B.C.E. this phrase was reread as four qualities: "primal, successful, beneficial, upright."[10] These words have since been combined and interpreted in various ways. Some have directed this phrase of the *I* away from matters of divination. This rereading represents one of several steps in transforming a specialized divination text into a "classic" (*ching*) that might eventually support the interest of Sung China's most creative moral thinkers.

The hexagram statement for Fu has changed relatively less in meaning,

---

[7] Hexagram names in brackets are the English renderings in Cary F. Baynes's translation of Richard Wilhelm's German translation of the *I*, *The I Ching or Book of Changes.*

[8] What is called "The Judgment" in Wilhelm/Baynes.

[9] For an extended discussion of the reading of *heng* as "receipt" and *chen* as "to divine," which revises earlier work by Kao Heng based on oracle bone evidence, see Edward Shaughnessy, *The Composition of the Zhouyi* (Ann Arbor: University Microfilms International, 1983), pp. 124–33. This phrase, *mutatis mutandum*, appears in a dozen hexagrams.

[10] See the *Tso-chuan*, Hsiang 9, 564 B.C.E., which is reproduced nearly verbatim in the *Wenyen*, Wing Seven of the *I Ching* (what Wilhelm/Baynes call the "Commentary on the Words of the Text"). For Ch'eng I's remarks on these as the beginning, growth, continuation and completion of things, see his *I-chuan* (Taipei: Shih-chieh, 1972), p. 3.

though its interpretations have also varied, as subsequent chapters will show. It reads:

> Return. An offering.
> In going out and coming in there will be no illness.
> A friend will come without misfortune.
> He will turn around and go back on his way (*tao*).
> He will come and return in seven days.
> Favorable for having somewhere to go.[11]

These are typical of the hexagram statements. As Arthur Waley has suggested, they contain concrete fragments of late Shang or early Chou life, as well as prognostication phrases like "without fault" or "beneficial whatever one does."[12]

Each line of the hexagram also has a text associated with it; these are called line statements (*yao-tz'u*). Their language is similar to that of the hexagram statements. For example, the first or bottom line statement of the Ch'ien hexagram reads:

> Hidden dragon. Do not act.

The second:

> One sees a dragon in the field. It is beneficial to see the great man.

The fifth line statement of Fu reads:

> Nobly returning, without repentance.

The sixth or top line:

> Confused return. Ill fortune. There are calamities and errors. If one were to set troops in motion, it would end in great defeat, bringing ill fortune to the country's ruler. Even in ten years one could not correct it.

The line statements have usually been understood as representing variations on the central theme of the hexagram. Readers, however, have construed the precise nature of this relationship in various ways. The basic text of the *I Ching* consists of no more than these six-line hexagram configurations, the hexagram names, hexagram statements, and line statements. (The other parts of the *I* will be discussed below.)

[11] Translation, with slight modification, from Richard Alan Kunst, *The Original "Yijing": A Text, Phonetic Transcription, Translation, and Indexes, with Sample Glosses* (Ann Arbor: University Microfilms International, 1985), p. 287. Kunst's translation attempts to reconstruct the *I* at the time of its origin.

[12] Arthur Waley, "The Book of Changes," *Bulletin of the Museum of Far Eastern Antiquities* 5 (1933), pp. 121–42.

What were its origins? There is general agreement that the *I* originated as a book of divination around the late second/early first millennium B.C.E. Stalks were cast and somehow counted, leading to an eventual prognostication. It has been thought that the *I* came from the Chou people, who conquered Shang in the mid-eleventh century B.C.E. Indeed, the most common way of referring to the text in the immediately succeeding centuries was as the *Chou I*, the *Change of Chou*.[13] The Shang practiced divination by reading cracks in bones. However, some form of divination by counting seems to have developed well before the end of that dynasty. Research in China over the last decade has addressed forty-odd examples of three- and six-numeral groupings, found as part of inscriptions on late Shang and early Chou oracle bones and bronzes.[14] The association with oracle bones suggests divination; several of the inscriptions accompanying the number groupings make this connection explicit. One text on a bronze vessel reads: "*Shih* [scribe-diviner] Yu Fu made this treasured precious vessel. Divined: 7–5–8."[15] The *I* may well have grown out of these practices. However, no clear stages of development have been demonstrated. In particular, no Chinese texts have been found that resemble the hexagram and line statements of today's *I Ching*.[16]

Recently, two American researchers have developed arguments originally suggested by Chinese scholars on the origin and structure of the hexagram and line statements. Both agree that the *I* underwent a process of editing by scribe-diviners (*shih*) in the early centuries of the first millennium B.C.E. But one view stresses the multiple nature of its sources, while

[13] See the *Tso-chuan*, where the entries from 672 to the mid-sixth century always refer to it as such. Note however that since the second century C.E. it has been suggested that "Chou" refers not to the Chou people but instead means "global," in the sense of "complete and comprehensive." See Willard Peterson, "Making Connections: 'Commentary on the Attached Verbalizations' of the *Book of Change*," *Harvard Journal of Asiatic Studies* 42.1 (1982), p. 116.

[14] See Chang Cheng-lang, "Shih-shih Chou ch'u ch'ing-t'ung-ch'i ming-wen chung ti I-kua," *K'ao-ku hsüeh-pao* (1980) 4, pp. 403–15 (an English translation, "An Interpretation of the Divinatory Inscriptions on Early Chou Bronzes," appears in *Early China* 6 [1980–1981], pp. 80–96); David N. Keightley, "Was the *Chou-i* a Legacy of Shang?" paper presented to the Association for Asian Studies, Chicago, April 1982; and Chang Cheng-lang, "Mien-shu 'Liu-shih-ssu kua' pa" (Postscript to the Silk Manuscript of *The Sixty Four Diagrams*), *Wenwu* (1984) 3, pp. 9–14.

[15] Keightley, "Was the *Chou-i*," p. 3.

[16] That text has been largely stable since about the early centuries C.E.; see Ch'ü Wan-li, *Han shih-ching Chou-i ts'an-tzu chi-cheng* (Taipei, Commercial Press, 1961). About a dozen short passages of today's *I Ching* are attested to in the *Tso-chuan*, dating to the fourth century B.C.E. and deriving from earlier material. For a discussion, see Hellmut Wilhelm, "*I-ching* Oracles in the *Tso-chuan* and *Kuo-yü*," *Journal of the American Oriental Society*, 79.4 (1959), pp. 275–80 and Kidder Smith, "*Zhouyi* Divination from Accounts in the *Zuozhuan*," *Harvard Journal of Asiatic Studies* 49.2 (forthcoming, 1989).

the other emphasizes the internal logic imparted by its editors.[17] Writing for the first, Richard Kunst states that the *I* is a collection of "brief, unconnected notes compiled as an aid to diviners who were already familiar with the subject matter."[18] More specifically, "It came into existence as an orally transmitted, organically evolving anthology of omens and their prognostications, popular sayings, historical anecdotes, and wisdom about nature, which were assembled into a manual around a framework of hexagrams and their solid or broken lines by diviners relying on the manipulation of yarrow stalks to obtain oracles."[19] This theory has the explanatory virtue of making it unnecessary to account for seemingly unrelated line statements within a single hexagram.[20] Expressing the other view, Edward Shaughnessy argues that the *I* "represents the conscious composition of an editor or editors."[21] For example, the line statements of hexagram #52 Ken (Stopping) refer, with one exception, to the parts of the body from feet to head, and the six lines of hexagram #24 Fu unexceptionally describe a "return" that is beautiful, repeated, sincere or confused.

As this research continues, the early history of the *I* will eventually emerge with greater clarity. As it does, however, it will diverge more and more from Sung views of how and why the *I* began. Sung writers received, sometimes skeptically, the tradition that the *I* was the product of four sages: the legendary hero of culture Fu-hsi; King Wen and the Duke of Chou (founders of the Chou dynasty); and Confucius.[22] Certain modern scholars might study the origins of the *I* so as to better understand the worldview of late Shang and early Chou. Sung scholars, however, like some other modern readers, studied it as evidence of sagely wisdom in the context of their own search for universal values. Thus as historians we may be separated from Sung figures not merely by a different set of facts but by a fundamentally different set of questions. What these earlier questions were, and how the *I* was made to speak to them, are the subjects of the subsequent sections.

How was it first used? We possess a few glimpses of early readers consulting the *I Ching* about matters of great personal and political im-

---

[17] Developing the ideas of Kao Heng and Li Ching-ch'ih, respectively. See Kao's *Chou-i ku-ching t'ung-shuo* (Peking, 1958) and Li's *Chou-i t'an-yüan* (Peking, 1978).

[18] In private communication.

[19] *The Original Yijing*, Abstract, p. 1.

[20] See hexagrams #2, 6, 9, etc.

[21] *The Composition of the Zhouyi*, p. 175.

[22] Though traditions vary, it was generally held that Fu-hsi devised the eight trigrams, King Wen the hexagram statements, the Duke of Chou composed the line statements, and Confucius wrote the Appendixes or "Ten Wings."

portance: battles and rebellions, aristocratic marriages, sons and heirs, etc. These come from the *Tso-chuan*, a history of the Spring and Autumn period (722–481 B.C.E.) that was itself assembled in the late Warring States.[23] They demonstrate the extent to which the meaning of the *I* has always changed as the needs and applications of its users changed. Taken together they also suggest the process through which the *I* evolved into a text that Han authorities were persuaded to canonize in 136 B.C.E.

The *Tso-chuan* shows people struggling to make sense of an extremely difficult text. Indeed, in a number of cases interpreters get into arguments over its proper reading.[24] We may recognize some of their other reactions as well: uncertainty, frustration, occasional dismissal—but primarily respect for the text. It is clear from these accounts that use of the *I* was fully integrated with other institutions of Spring and Autumn culture. When, for example, a ruler of the state of Ch'i seeks an auspicious prognostication to sanctify his incestuous marriage, a battle of interpretation ensues that draws upon current moral and religious practices, social expectations, and the ministerial right to criticize, involving as well court politics and a ruler's intimidation of his diviners.[25] Thus using the *I* text for prognostication did not produce a simple answer from a transcendent source but was instead conditioned by these sorts of social pressure.

The *Tso-chuan* material also shows how the *I* developed from a divination text into a book through which major moral issues could be addressed.[26] The nature of this process is suggested by the case of Nan-k'uai, who in 530 B.C.E. plots a rebellion against his ruler. Consulting the *I Ching*, he obtains the fifth line statement of hexagram #2 K'un, which reads "Yellow skirt, primally auspicious." Greatly encouraged, he shows this to a friend, without mentioning his intentions. The friend replies: "I have studied this. If it is a matter of loyalty and fidelity, then it is possible. If not, it will certainly be defeated. . . . If there is some deficiency [regarding these virtues], although the stalkcasting says 'auspicious,' it is not."[27]

Thus Nan-k'uai's improper purpose renders his whole prognostication invalid. His friend's fundamental assumption is that an act's moral qualities determine its consequences. The *I* will advise on which of several

---

[23] It is generally assumed that the *Tso-chuan* was put together from existing traditions around the late fourth or early third century B.C.E. See Barry B. Blakeley, "Notes on the Reliability and Objectivity of the Tu Yü Commentary on the *Tso Chuan*," *Journal of the American Oriental Society*, 101.2 (1981), p. 209 n. 17. The *Tso* contains approximately two dozen references to the *I*, dating from 672 to 485 B.C.E. On the use of the *Tso-chuan* as a source for the early use of the *I*, see Kidder Smith, "*Zhouyi* Divination."

[24] See, for example, the story of Mu Chiang (Hsiang 9, 564 B.C.E.) and the two cases discussed below.

[25] Hsiang 25, 548 B.C.E.

[26] For a stimulating account of this development, see Yü Tun-k'ang, "Ts'ung *I Ching* tao *I-chuan*," *Chung-kuo che-hsüeh* 7 (1982), pp. 1–27.

[27] Chao 12.

equally proper courses of action is best, but only something that is already moral can ever be "auspicious." Here we see how developments in sixth-century moral-cosmological thinking change not only the interpretation of a particular line statement of the *I* but also the very tasks to which the text could be directed. (Nan-k'uai, by the way, disregards this analysis, and within a year he is dead.)

In the case of Nan-k'uai we can see a perennial tension between two views of what determines future events, human action or a fate decreed by heaven. Nan-k'uai believes the *I* will give him knowledge of the latter. His friend, however, insists that humanity and heaven—the latter both as fate and as the source of morality—are not so set apart. The *I*, then, in giving information about heaven, also speaks of human actions. As we will see, Sung literati also used the *I Ching* in their attempts to redefine that relationship.

The *Tso-chuan* also gives evidence of a use for the *I* that stands outside formal divination. This is to cite its hexagram or line statements in conversation, much as one might cite any well-known text. Here, in contrast to those uses in which the *I* is valued for its access to heaven, it is valued as a part of the human cultural tradition, whose evidence it preserves. Thus in 513 B.C.E. a historian cites the *I* as proof that men of yore once tended dragons.[28]

More strikingly, in 603 B.C.E. a youth confides his political ambitions to the prince of Cheng. Later the prince remarks: "Covetous and without virtue—it's in the *Chou I* at the top line of Feng hexagram [#55]. He will not get beyond that." This line statement of Feng in today's *I Ching* reads in part, "He locks his door . . . and for three years he is not seen. Inauspicious." And indeed, the *Tso-chuan* reports that "after a year the people of Cheng killed him."[29] Here a prediction is made without stalks being cast. Thus the *I* moves farther still from its origin in a formal ritual context. Such usage depends on the text being so widely known that the prince of Cheng can invoke a particular statement simply by noting its place in the Feng hexagram. Toward the end of the Spring and Autumn period this method of using the *I* becomes increasingly common. In the sixth and fifth centuries B.C.E. we find people citing it in suasion, in medical prognosis, and even to help analyze the outcome of a battle.[30] Thus the *I* becomes used in ways that increasingly resemble other contemporary texts.

By what methods was it interpreted? How does one move from mute hexagrams and laconic texts to meaning? The earliest surviving accounts

28 Chao 29.
29 Hsüan 6.
30 Hsiang 28, Chao 1, Hsüan 12.

to answer this in a systematic way are known as the Ten Wings (*shih-i*). These consist of seven texts in ten sections dating from the late Warring States and early Han (third and second centuries B.C.E.). Though only three of these will be discussed below (marked with an asterisk), it will be useful to set out all seven in table format here.

However they may differ, all Wings begin with the unstated assumption of the *I*'s coherence, both as text and as change. Not only is the *I* itself coherent, it reproduces in certain ways the coherence of heaven-and-earth. Thus the questions posed in the late Warring States differ in an important way from those of the late Spring and Autumn. Seventh- and sixth-century B.C.E. readers attempted to determine the meaning of individual lines, usually deliberating specific courses of action.[31] The Wings however set out to understand the *I* as the system of heaven-and-earth. Thus the text becomes useful for structuring thought about the present, not just as a tool to know the future.

The first of the Ten Wings we will examine is the *T'uan-chuan*, or "Commentary on the hexagram statements."[32] As its name suggests, the *T'uan-chuan* usually begins by quoting and glossing the text that is attached to the hexagram. Regarding hexagram #24 Fu, it says:

"Return. Successful." The firm comes back.

In acting, proceed (*hsing*) with compliance so that "going out and going in are without distress. Friends come and it is without fault."

Wing	Chinese Title	Translated Title [W/B]
1 & 2*	T'uan-chuan	Commentary on the Hexagram Statements [Commentary on the Decision]
3 & 4	Hsiang-chuan	Commentary on the Images [The Image]
5 & 6*	Hsi-tz'u-chuan	Commentary on the Attached Verbalizations [Appended Judgments/Great Treatise]
7	Wen-yen	Elegant Words [Commentary on the Words of the Text]
8*	Shuo-kua	Remarks on the Trigrams [Discussion of the Trigrams]
9	Hsü-kua	The Ordered Hexagrams [The Sequence]
10	Tsa-kua	The Miscellany of Hexagrams [Miscellaneous Notes]

[31] See Smith, "*Zhouyi* Divination."
[32] Wilhelm/Baynes's "Commentary on the Decision," Wings 1 and 2.

"Reverting and returning to *tao*; in seven days comes the return": the heavens proceed (*hsing*).

"It is beneficial whatever one does": the firm grows. Does not Fu make apparent the mind (*hsin*) of heaven-and-earth![33]

In explaining each phrase, these glosses provide a context in which to read hexagram statements. This context is moral ("proceed with compliance") and cosmic ("the mind of heaven-and-earth"). Indeed, the implication is that moral behavior parallels cosmic processes, and that the pattern of both can be found in the *I*. Thus human behavior and heavenly movement are described with the same word, *hsing* (act or proceed).

Combining these, the *T'uan-chuan* for hexagram #30 Li (Attachment/ Brightness [The Clinging, Fire]) remarks:

Li is "attachment." The sun and the moon are attached to the sky. The various grains, grasses and trees are attached to the earth. The double brightness [of Li] is attached to correctness and so transforms and completes all under heaven.

The soft [second line] is attached to the centrally correct and is therefore "successful."

And the *T'uan-chuan* for hexagram #60 Chieh (Regulations [Limitation]), quoting the hexagram statement, says:

"Harsh regulations cannot be upright": their *tao* (way, course) will be exhausted. He is joyful so as to direct a dangerous situation. He takes his position according to regulations. He is centrally correct so as to penetrate.

Heaven-and-earth are regulated and so the four seasons are realized. If [the ruler] regulates by means of his institutions, he will not hurt property nor harm the people.

While the *T'uan-chuan* describes the moral universe it sees reflected in the texts of the *I*, it also seeks to demonstrate how the line configurations of the hexagrams imply the accompanying texts, with their prognostications of "inauspicious" or "no fault." The *T'uan-chuan* never explicitly defines the rules that govern these relationships, but we can readily infer several, three of which are especially prominent.

The first rule combines centrality (or the Mean, *chung*) with a traditional division of the hexagram into lower and upper trigrams, or three-line figures. In such a view, the second and fifth lines of the hexagram, being in the middle of their respective trigrams, possess the virtue of centrality, thus tending toward auspiciousness. The second rule concerns

[33] Note that the translation of the excerpts from the hexagram statement that appear here differs from that cited earlier. There we saw Richard Kunst's reconstruction of its original meaning. Here it is translated as the author(s) of the *T'uan-chuan* seem to have understood it.

"correctness" (cheng), in which the odd-numbered lines are solid and the even broken. This apparently derives from the fact that the solid line is written with the same mark as the Chinese numeral one, and the broken line requires two marks. Thus the *T'uan-chuan* generally declares that odd-numbered solid lines and even-numbered broken lines are auspicious, and that even-numbered solid lines and odd-numbered broken lines are not. The second lines of the Chieh and Li hexagrams are broken; thus both these lines are "centrally correct." Third, a relationship of "responsiveness" (*ying*) is possible between corresponding line places in the two trigrams (1–4, 2–5, 3–6). If the first line of a hexagram is solid and the fourth broken, or vice versa, they are responsive, which is generally auspicious.[34]

Yet the *T'uan-chuan* authors were not fully successful in demonstrating the coherence of the *I*. However consciously the text may have been composed, there are still prognostications of "auspicious" or "regret" or "nothing that is not beneficial" that such rules cannot readily explain. The *I* is, after all, not so consistent or easily governed. Furthermore, these rules are necessarily incomplete. Take, for example, a broken fifth line. It is central, but not correct. What if it "responds" to a solid second line, which is also central and incorrect? What additional rules, if any, does an interpreter invoke in these circumstances? At this point the *I*, like heaven-and-earth, escapes any simple explanation and reverts to being somewhat mysterious. What is more, even if the *T'uan-chuan* demonstrates a certain consistency to the *I*, its texts must still be applied to the user's current situation. As we have seen from the *Tso-chuan*, this process may be enormously complex. Thus the *T'uan-chuan* does not solve the matter of interpretation. It only refines and extends the route the interpreter must take. And thus one must still read the texts in a partially new way each time he or she consults the *I Ching*.

We have already encountered the tradition of viewing the hexagram as composed of a lower and an upper trigram. Since the trigrams each have three lines, broken or solid, there are eight possible trigram configurations. Many of these have a proper name—that is, a name that uniquely indicates that trigram and does not equally stand for some other word in Chinese (as "Fu" also means "return" in ordinary usage). For example, the trigram with three solid lines is called Ch'ien, like the hexagram with six solid lines, and the trigram with a solid line between two broken lines is called K'an [W/B The Abysmal/Water]. These names are attested to in

---

[34] For a more systematic treatment of these relationships, see section two of Wang Pi (226–49), *Chou-i lüeh-li*. A French translation with accompanying Chinese text is Marie-Ina Bergeron, *Wang Pi, Philosophe du non-avoir* (Taipei/Paris: Ricci Institute, 1986).

the *Tso-chuan*, as are a set of qualities associated with each trigram. One of the Ten Wings, the *Shuo-kua*,[35] records these qualities—the element, virtue, season, animal, bodily part, etc., that characterize each of the eight. Thus with K'an are associated water, danger, winter, pig and ears. The *Shuo-kua* says of it:

> K'an is water, ditch.
> It is lying concealed, crookedness, bow, wheel.
> In regard to humans, it is increased worry, heart disease, earache.
> It is the trigram of blood; it is red.
> In regard to horses it is a lovely back, high spirits, lowered head, thin hooves, shambling gait.
> In regard to carriages, it is many defects.
> It is penetration, moon, thief.
> In regard to trees, it is the strong and pithy.

The *Shuo-kua* also examines the trigrams structurally, naming Ch'ien and K'un, with all solid or all broken lines, the "parents" of the other six, which are then termed elder, middle, or younger son or daughter.

Trigrams, then, are not merely components of hexagrams. They are orientations to a dozen or more "fields" within heaven-and-earth that range from cosmic positioning (north) to earache, heart disease, and family structure, touching on plants and animals along the way. A user of the *I* can assign everything in heaven-and-earth to one of the eight trigrams. Through the set of trigram interrelationships he can also relate that thing to all other things. Sung literati thus inherited a tool with a phenomenal power to order the world.

These symbolic associations of each of the eight trigrams are known as "the images" or *hsiang*. So fundamental are they to the *I* and its workings that an early definition reads "The *I* is images."[36] Here we will examine three applications of the images, two from the mid-seventh century B.C.E. and one from the second century C.E. In the seventh century *I* divination was almost always interpreted in reference to the trigram images.[37] Thus in the *Tso-chuan* account of an approaching battle, we see an auspicious

---

[35] "Explanations of the Trigrams," Wilhelm/Baynes's "Discussion of the Trigrams."

[36] *Hsi-tz'u-chuan* B3. K'ung Ying-ta, editor of the orthodox T'ang edition of the *I*, also opens his General Preface with this definition; see *Chou-i cheng-i* (Ssu-pu pei-yao ed.), p. 1. Both these texts are discussed below.

[37] And decreasingly after that. See Smith, "Zhouyi Interpretation." Most interpreters in the imperial period hold that the trigrams were in fact created first and later doubled to become hexagrams. See, *inter alia*, K'ung Ying-ta's "Shu ch'ung kua," the second introductory essay to his *Chou-i cheng-i*. For arguments that the hexagram probably came first, see Sherman Hsiao-hai Chu, "*Chou I* chi-ko chi-pen wen-t'i ti t'i-ts'e," *Tsinghua hsüeh-pao* n.s. 16.1–2 (December 1984).

prognostication made because "The lower trigram of [hexagram #18] Ku is wind, its upper mountain. . . . We bring down their fruit and take their possessions [like a wind sweeping over a mountain]."[38] These two associations—wind and mountain—have remained the best-known qualities of the trigrams in question until today. In another example, a divination official, obtaining the line statement "Behold the light of the state," remarks:

> K'un is earth. [The trigram] Sun is wind. Ch'ien is heaven. Wind becoming heaven above the earth [means] mountain. If the treasures of the mountain are illuminated by the light of heaven, then he will rule the earth. Therefore it says, "Behold the light of the state."[39]

One function of the *Shuo-kua* seems to have been to collate and standardize these associations.[40] Han dynasty interpreters then combined and recombined these standard images via mathematical operations upon the hexagram structure. This school of *I Ching* interpretation is known as *hsiang-shu* or "image and number." "Number" here refers to the systematic generation of new tri- and hexagram relationships out of the originating hexagram. For example, the negative counterpart of hexagram #24 Fu, with its solid first line and five broken lines above, is hexagram #44 Kou, with a broken first line and five solid lines above. Because of this relationship, a thorough examination of Fu entails an examination of Kou. When this method is taken to its logical conclusion, all hexagrams can be formally related to each other in various ranks of intimacy. Specific manipulations define the various possibilities—inversion, alterations of specific lines, reading the "nuclear trigrams" (lines 2–3–4 and 3–4–5), etc.[41]

Hsiang-shu practice scrupulously relates each element of the hexagram configuration or text to images and number. For example, we have seen that the top line statement of Fu reads:

> Confused return. Misfortune. There are calamities and errors. If one were to set troops in motion, it would end in great defeat.

[38] Hsi 15, 645 B.C.E.

[39] Chuang 22, 672 B.C.E.

[40] This appears to parallel the syncretic systematization of diverse lore that John Henderson has shown lies at the root of much of the Han correlative thinking that soon followed the assembling of the *Shuo-kua*. See his *Development and Decline of Chinese Cosmology* (New York: Columbia University Press, 1984), especially "Origins of Correlative Thought in China," pp. 28–46.

[41] For a concise exposition of these and other Han methods, see Ch'ü Wan-li, *Hsien-Ch'in Han Wei I-li shu-p'ing* (Taipei: Student Books, 1975 [1940]), pp. 77–149.

Yü Fan (ca. 164–233), the most highly developed and thoroughgoing of Han *hsiang-shu* practitioners, remarks:

> When the fifth line changes to its correct situation, it is K'an,[42] which is "calamities and errors." The third line returns to the situation appropriate to its position and embodies the image of [hexagram #7] Shih(Army).[43] Therefore "if one were to set troops in motion," yin would rebel and not comply.[44] [The upper trigram] K'un is "death" and "burial." K'an is "flowing blood." Therefore "it will end in great defeat."[45]

This passage is extremely dense: Yü Fan is not creating a narrative but is revealing the hidden connections on which the *I* relies to produce meaning. In every case these revelations involve him in complex structures and relationships that derive primarily from the *Shuo-kua*. Thus the generalized military disaster imagery of the sixth line statement of Fu is here redefined specifically in terms of the trigram qualities of K'an and K'un and the hexagram Shih. This may appear to us as arbitrary manipulation, but its purpose is surely just the opposite. Instead of reading the line statement as a metaphor to be applied any way an interpreter sees fit, one reads it as entries in a code book. The free play of the texts is restrained by the precise connection "number" makes to the other trigrams. The implication of this precision is a world in which everything that exists and everything that happens is knowable and necessary. Thus the relationship between heaven-and-earth and humanity is not the vague parallelism of the *T'uan-chuan* but is instead calculable by *hsiang-shu* methods.

We have thus far examined two ways in which the Wings construe the relationship of the *I* with heaven-and-earth. The *T'uan-chuan* seeks to explain how a configuration of lines expresses fundamental parallels between heaven-and-earth and humanity, so as to establish moral guides for human practice. The *Shuo-kua* seeks to show how all things of heaven, earth, and humanity form categories defined by the eight trigrams of the *I*, and thus can be known and ordered. But only the *Hsi-tz'u-chuan*, Wings 5 and 6, argues that this is so because the *I* is a model of heaven-and-earth. For this reason the *Hsi-tz'u* was the most influential of the Ten Wings in Sung times, and is the last that we will consider here.[46]

[42] Since the fifth line is odd, it should be solid, not broken. With a solid fifth line, the upper trigram changes from K'un to K'an.

[43] Like Fu, the Shih hexagram contains only one solid line, which is in the second place. Yü Fan means that when the third, broken line of Fu moves down to the very bottom of the hexagram, pushing up the former first and second lines, the new hexagram formed is Shih.

[44] Following the sense of the first line statement of Shih.

[45] As preserved in Li Ting-tsuo, *Chou-i chi-chieh* (*I Ching chi-ch'eng* ed., vols. 9–10), p. 275.

[46] "Commentary on the Appended Texts." It is also known as the *Ta-chuan* (Wilhelm/

As Willard Peterson has shown, the *Hsi-tz'u* connects the various referents of the term "*I*" that we have encountered so far: a means of divination, a written text, and change itself. That is, it integrates the *I* as a technique of knowing, as a cultural relic transmitted by human sages, and as processes of heaven-and-earth. Peterson identifies four claims made by the *Hsi-tz'u* authors that advance these points:

> The first major claim of the "Commentary on the Attached Verbalizations" is that the technique, for which the rest of the *Change* is the written repository, duplicates relationships and processes at work in the realm of heaven-and-earth. The second major claim is that these relationships and processes are knowable, and the knowledge is the basis for efficacious action in the realm of human society (p. 85).
>
> We can know by means of the words in the *Change*, and we can be guided by their counsel—this is the third major claim of the "Commentary." . . . For making all of this more explicit to us, we are indebted to sages, from whom we have inherited the text known as the *Change* (p. 94).
>
> In the fourth section of the "Commentary on the Attached Verbalizations" the three major claims established in the preceding sections are drawn together to show that following the *Change* is more potent than any other way of conducting oneself in the world. The sentences move continuously, and ambiguously, between change in the realm of heaven-and-earth, the technique and text of the *Change*, which was made accessible by sages, and the superior man who accepts the guidance of the *Change* to optimize his "well-fortuned" conduct among the change in all-under-heaven (p. 99).

These are all Sung concerns as well: the grounding of knowledge in heaven-and-earth, the constancy of change, the *I* as a unique mode of access to knowledge under such conditions of change, and the role of the sages in transmitting the means of this access. Often the *Hsi-tz'u-chuan* makes claims about the *I* similar to those of the Sung literati cited at the beginning of this chapter. Here are several such passages, which set topics we will explore in later chapters.

The *Hsi-tz'u* begins by establishing that heaven-and-earth is indeed the true field of the *I* as a book, and *I* as change.

Heaven is honored, earth humble: Ch'ien and K'un are set![47]

Baynes's "Great Treatise") or the "Great Appendix." The best study of this text is Willard Peterson, "Making Connections: 'Commentary on the Attached Verbalizations' of the *Book of Change*," *Harvard Journal of Asiatic Studies* 42.1 (1982), pp. 67–116, to which the following discussion is much indebted. See also Gerald Swanson, "The Concept of Change in the *Great Treatise*," in *Explorations in Early Chinese Cosmology*, ed. Henry Rosemont, Jr. (Chico: Scholars Press, 1984), pp. 67–93.

[47] That is, the first two hexagrams. *Hsi-tz'u-chuan* A1.

is stored is surely not the images. The words are born from the images, which are stored in the words. Thus what is stored is surely not the words. . . .

If the meaning exists in "vigor" (chien), why do you need a horse? If the meaning exists in "compliance" (shun), why do you need a cow? If the lines are joined in indicating compliance, what need for K'un to be a cow? If the meaning responds to vigor, what need for Ch'ien to be a horse? And if you fix the horse as Ch'ien, when you investigate the hexagram text, then you have a horse but no Ch'ien.[57]

Essay 1 discusses the issue of a single unifying idea for each hexagram.

What is the hexagram statement? It discusses in a unified fashion the substance of a hexagram and illuminates the ruling [factor] from which it comes. . . . Therefore cite the hexagram name, and you have that which rules its meaning. Observe the hexagram statement, and more than half its intent [is present].[58]

By these means Wang Pi was able to free the I from the specialists' calculations, calendrical or otherwise, and create it as a literary text that educated men could use in almost any area of their concern—metaphysical, personal, political, etc. Indeed, without the level of abstraction that Wang makes available, most Sung readings of the I could not occur. Furthermore, Wang claims that wu, generally translated "non-being," stands tranquilly behind the multiplicity of change and movement. This view was extremely influential in Sung, and Ch'eng I, for example, explicitly attacked the following passage, in which Wang sets it out:[59]

Fu means "reverting to the root."[60] Heaven-and-earth take the root to be their heart/mind. Whatever moves [at some point] ceases and is tranquil. Tranquility is not the opposite of movement. Speech ceases and it is quiet. Quiet is not the opposite of speech. In this way, although heaven-and-earth are great—they richly contain the myriad things, thunder moves, the winds revolve, with a myriad transformations—silence and utter nothing (wu), these are their root. In this way when movement ceases amidst the earth, then is the heart/mind of heaven-and-earth apparent. If they take being as their root, then the different categories [of things] could not preserve their existence.[61]

Wang's was established as the officially sanctioned commentary on the I under T'ang; thus it also became the received text of the I Ching in Sung.

Ku-chu shih-san-ching (Ssu-pu chi-yao ed.), Chou I, 10.8b (p. 64). Cf. Hellmut Wilhelm, Change, Eight Lectures on the I Ching (New York: Harper, 1964), pp. 87–88.
Ku-chu shih-san-ching, 10.1b (p. 61). Cf. Wing-tsit Chan, A Source Book in Chinese Philosophy (Princeton: Princeton University Press, 1963), p. 318.
See, for example, Erh-Ch'eng chi, 2A.16, as well as Ch'eng's commentary on the Fu hexagram.
Quoting the T'uan-chuan.
Commentary to the T'uan-chuan, Ku-chu shih-san ching, 3.4b (p. 19).

This somewhat obscure statement is slightly clarified by two other passages:

Heaven-and-earth establish their places, and the I proceeds in their midst.[48]

The I is on a level with heaven-and-earth.[49]

This being so, men should base their understanding and action upon it:

When the superior man is at rest, he observes its images and contemplates its texts. When he acts, he observes its changes and contemplates its prognostications.[50]

It is in this context that the Hsi-tz'u discusses the sagely creation of the I. The same passage states:

The sages established the hexagrams and observed the images. They added texts to it and so illuminated the auspicious and inauspicious.

And in section A12:

The sages set up the images so as to exhaust the meaning. They established the hexagrams so as to exhaust the circumstances [of true] and false.

In these and related statements the Hsi-tz'u gives a picture of the I's origins that differs considerably from that painted by twentieth-century researchers. In the Hsi-tz'u view, the I derives from the sages' ability to perceive the orderly nature of heaven-and-earth as it was manifested all around them. Thus it remarks:

In antiquity when Pao-hsi [Fu-hsi] ruled all under heaven, he looked up and observed the images in heaven, he looked down and observed the patterns on earth, and he observed how the markings on birds and beasts were appropriate to their locales. Nearby he took it from his body, at a distance he took it from objects. Thereupon he initially made the eight trigrams.[51]

Thus the I is the record of sagely insight into the regularities of heaven-and-earth, including birds, bodies, and celestial patternings. Sung writers then are speaking from a tradition formalized in the Hsi-tz'u-chuan when they claim, like Chu Hsi, that "once the hexagram lines are set, the tao of all under heaven is contained in them."[52]

Since the Hsi-tz'u, the most important texts to Sung I Ching studies have been the short commentary and essays of Wang Pi (226–249). His

[48] A5.
[49] A3.
[50] A2.
[51] B2.
[52] Chou-i pen-i 3:13b.

ideas have been so thoroughly absorbed into subsequent Chinese and Western understandings of the *Book of Change* that on first glance they are nearly invisible. It is useful, therefore, to note three Han traditions of the *I* out of which he developed, in addition to the work of Yü Fan already discussed above. The first of these is the "official school" of the Imperial Academy, where in the late first century B.C.E. scholars like Ching Fang and Meng Hsi used the *I Ching* in conjunction with court astronomy and the calendar.[53] Their best-known innovation was the establishment of correspondences between the hexagram configurations and time units of the year. Thus, each month was correlated with a hexagram, beginning with #24 Fu (one yang line below five yin lines), moving next to #19 Lin (two yang lines below four yin lines), and continuing as yang increases from the bottom to the top of the hexagram.[54] This practice treats the hexagrams as abstract markers, based on the formal mathematical relationships between their lines. Hexagram #24 Fu is significant because its hexagram configuration can be seen as the first in a progressive series, not because its hexagram and line statements all discuss some aspect of "return." Indeed, such an approach ignores the hexagram and line statements entirely. Its purely structural concerns will become the basis for Shao Yung's work on the *I* in the eleventh century. In contrast, Yü Fan, for all his dependence on number, is scrupulous in addressing the texts. What both approaches have in common is a belief in precise correspondences between the realm of heaven-and-earth and that of humanity.

Wang Pi drew on two other Han traditions in his sharp reaction to these *hsiang-shu* treatments of the *I*. One was begun by a little-known figure named Fei Chih. According to the *Han-shu* (History of the Former Han), he "interpreted the book from the texts of the *T'uan-chuan*, *Hsiang-chuan* and *Hsi-tz'u-chuan* of the Ten Wings."[55] This seems to mean that he treated the Ten Wings as commentary speaking directly to the hexagram and line statements, rather than as material to be further manipulated in *hsiang-shu* style. This, of course, is what the authors of the Ten Wings seem to have had in mind in the first place. That this is noteworthy in Han times suggests the extent to which *hsiang-shu* types of question predominated over those that we have been ascribing to the au-

thors of the Wings. The other development from which proach grew was line-by-line commentaries (*chu*) on the *I* gan to appear by the second century C.E.[56]

Wang Pi combines line-by-line commentary with Fei Ch of the Ten Wings. This, as we will see, provides him with from which to attack the notions of correspondence tha calendrical use of the *I* and Yü Fan's method. In their pla two principles on which he claims the *I* is built. First, th text are not taken literally as objects but as symbolic re abstract qualities. He argues, for example, that the "dra of hexagrams Ch'ien and K'un connote "vigor" (*chien*) (*shun*), based on glosses that appear in the Wings. T usage the term "image" (*hsiang*) receives a new interp bols," in contrast to Yü Fan's use of the term as code ond, a hexagram is not a congeries of images but a si cept or "idea," "meaning" or "intent" (*i*), to whic related. His commentary therefore seeks to identify th cept for each hexagram. In Sung times this approac alternative to the *hsiang-shu* method. It was termed and pattern," in that it favored direct reading of the te minimal reliance on a mechanical indexing of trigra matical correlations.

Wang Pi sets out these principles in a set of six short essays called the *Chou-i lüeh-li* (Basic princ *Change*). Essay 4 addresses the matter of "images" lead to thinking in terms of types or categories (*lei*)

The words are that which clarify the images; obtai gets the words. The images are that which maintain t meaning, one forgets the image. Similarly, a trail is h you have the hare, you forget the trail. Traps are h you have the fish, you forget the trap. In this way, images, and images are the traps of meaning.

Because of this, one who stores up the words i images. One who stores up the images is not one w images are born from the meaning, which are stor

[53] On these writings, see Fung Yu-lan, *A History of Chinese Philosophy*, vol. 2, pp. 88–132 and Ch'ü Wan-li, *Hsien-Ch'in Han*, part 2, pp. 77ff.

[54] And then the similar growth of yin. This is attributed to Meng Hsi by the T'ang mathematician-monk I-hsing, as quoted in Fung, vol. 2, pp. 109–10. Meng's somewhat younger colleague Ching Fang then "allocated sixty of the hexagrams in such a way that each in turn had jurisdiction over the affairs of certain days. He regarded wind, rain, cold and heat as manifestations, for each of which prognostic omens exist." (*Han-shu*, as quoted in Fung, vol. 2, pp. 109–10).

[55] *Chüan* 88, quoted in Lin I-sheng, *Hu Yüan ti i-li i-hsüeh* (Taipei: Commercial Press, 1974), p. 6.

[56] Notably those by Cheng Hsüan (127–200), Hsün Sh 164–233). The surviving fragments of their commentari *Chou-i chi-chieh*. For a useful introductory study of these fucian Magnate's Idea of Political Violence: Hsün Shuan Changes," *T'oung Pao*, series 2, 54 (1960), pp. 73–115. Howard L. Goodman, *Exegetes and Exegesis of the Boo A.D.: Historical and Scholastic Contexts for Wang Pi* (International, 1985).

When the "*Cheng-i*" series (Correct meanings [of the Classics]) had been created in early T'ang, K'ung Ying-ta (587–648) used Wang's commentary as the basis for the *Chou-i cheng-i* (Correct meaning of the Book of Change).[62] In his introductory essays K'ung extends the sense of "image" developed by Wang into the primary mechanism by which the *I*, and the sage, know and act upon heaven-and-earth. His preface begins by adapting a definition of "*I*" that comes from *Hsi-tz'u-chuan* B3: "The *I* is images. The lines are models." He then argues that it is because the sage also possesses the *I*'s power of symbolic representation that he holds the power to know (by contemplation) and order (by setting categories):

The sage has [a way] to look up and contemplate, and to look down and inspect.[63] [Both the *I* and the sage] symbolize (*hsiang*) heaven-and-earth, and so nourish the various categories (*lei*) of things.

In the subsequent passage, K'ung goes on to identify the *I*, the processes of heaven-and-earth, and the sage-ruler with each other. If these proceed in order, then everything will function harmoniously. "Thus we know," he writes in another essay,

that the patterns (*li*) of the *I* are complete and include being and non-being. . . . The *I* is that whereby one makes decisions [in the realm of] heaven-and-earth, orders (*li*) human relations, and illuminates the *tao* of kings.[64]

No important *I Ching* commentators emerged between early T'ang and the Sung. Yet the mid-eleventh century saw a rush of new interest in the *I*. In addition to the men studied in this book, Fan Chung-yen, Hu Yüan, Chou Tun-i, Ch'en Hsiang, Ssu-ma Kuang, Chang Tsai and Wang An-shih all had significant writings on the *I Ching*.[65] In subsequent chapters, we will see why this might be so, and learn how the *Book of Change* was further developed by the four men whose *I Ching* writings we are investigating here.

[62] For a sketchy study of the Sung reception of the *Cheng-i*, see Imai Usaburō, *Sōdai eki-gaku no kenkyū*, pp. 14–29.

[63] Paraphrasing the *Hsi-tz'u-chuan* A3.

[64] *Chou-i cheng-i*, p. 3b.

[65] For a list of these and other Northern Sung writings, see Wang Chi-hsi, *Pei-Sung I-hsüeh-k'ao* (Taipei: M.A. thesis, Taiwan Normal University, 1978).

CHAPTER TWO

The Sung Context: From Ou-yang Hsiu to Chu Hsi

OU-YANG HSIU AND THE BEGINNING OF LITERATI INTELLECTUAL CULTURE

Our account begins with Ou-yang Hsiu (1007–1072), who, while neither the most sophisticated thinker nor the most skillful writer, was nonetheless the most broadly talented and influential figure before Chu Hsi. More than anyone, Ou-yang established the basic issues of Sung literati thought.[1] By the 1030s, when Ou-yang Hsiu was gaining fame for his learning and writing, Sung had already held unified control over north and south China for fifty years. Its institutions were deemed adequate by many. The civil administration had reasserted its authority over the military. The examination system had been dramatically expanded into the primary mechanism for official recruitment and the number of those schooling themselves in examination education was constantly increasing. The promise of the founding had been fulfilled. China was unified, internal threats to central authority were negligible, and the borders were generally peaceful. The examination system had proved to be an effective mechanism for drawing local elites to the state. It had gained credibility as a test of merit, and southern families especially had come to believe that acquiring the literary education to pass the examinations would ensure that their sons would be seen as literati and might well succeed in becoming officials.[2] From the perspective of those holding power at court, there was little cause for complaint.

Perhaps the examinations were too successful. Opportunities had not increased as the number of candidates had risen. In the first place, there was a limited number of civil offices to be had. Second, the system greatly

---

[1] For many of the citations from Ou-yang Hsiu's writings and for much of my understanding of his place in the eleventh century, I am indebted to Liu Tzu-chien, *Ou-yang Hsiu ti chih-hsüeh yü ts'ung-cheng* (Hong Kong: Hsin-ya, 1963) and the English version of the same, *Ou-yang Hsiu: An Eleventh-Century Neo-Confucianist* (Stanford: Stanford University Press, 1967); Teraji Jun, "O-yō Shū ni okeru tenjin sōkansetsu e no kaigi," *Hiroshima Daigaku Bungakubu kiyō*, 28.1 (1968), pp. 161–87; and Ronald C. Egan, *The Literary Works of Ou-yang Hsiu* (Cambridge: Cambridge University Press, 1984). My argument essentially follows Teraji's article.

[2] For an account of the examinations see John W. Chaffee, *The Thorny Gates of Learning in Sung China: A Social History of the Examinations* (Cambridge: Cambridge University Press, 1985).

favored the sons of high officials residing at the capital, many of whom could also gain rank directly by virtue of the positions of their relatives. In theory government office was open to those of greatest talent; in practice positions were filled by a group of highly successful bureaucratic families, anxious to see their progeny enter government service and quite content with the current state of affairs. Ou-yang Hsiu, a man from the south, had felt the effects of this: he had not been able to pass the examination until he gained entrée to one of the capital qualifying exams. Ou-yang spoke for many when, as a minor official in the 1030s, he joined in an attack on the court leadership. His accusation that the Chief Councillor, and by implication all those in power, had put their own family interests above the public good earned him a demotion but made him famous. Ou-yang's brilliance lay in his ability to treat what might have been reduced to a question of political in's and out's as the symptom of larger failings. The failure to promote and entrust responsibility to new men thus became a failure to seek men of true talent and virtue. An unwillingness to employ men of talent was an indication that the government was not intent on accomplishing great things but was content to muddle along as a second-rate dynasty.

Pressure increased on the court to bring in men with higher aspirations, and in 1043–1044, when the threat of a major border war led to the withdrawal of leading officials, they were given a chance. The emperor appointed Fan Chung-yen (989–1052) to a leading court position; Ouyang was one of several proponents of reform who joined Fan at court. Central to Fan's reform program were policies aimed at ensuring that in the future a bureaucratic role would be played by literati committed to using state power and institutions to take positive measures to benefit society as a whole. Fan proposed to restrict the right of high officials to secure official rank for their descendants and, at the same time, he set about to change the examination system.

The proposed examination reform gives us a clear sense of the new vision of learning. The existing system did represent a particular view of learning, of course; it tested literary skill and memorization. The prestigious "presented literatus" (chin shih) examination tested the ability to compose poetry according to exacting formal criteria and the ability to write prose essays, although prose seems to have figured only secondarily in grading. The "Various Fields" (chu k'o), abolished in the 1070s, tested memorization of various classics and knowledge of the official commentaries prepared in the early seventh century, T'ang ritual compendiums, or the first great histories. As Fan and Ou-yang recognized, this system stressed mastering received forms rather than the values those forms were intended to promote. Cultivating literary skill was more important than acquiring a moral purpose; training oneself to recite the great books and the old commentaries mattered more than asking what they could mean.

The general aim of the proposed changes was to encourage literati to be committed to ideal values and to recruit those who were. The proposal to require that local officials certify the "ethical conduct" (*te hsing*) of candidates illustrates this. More significant was the proposal to reverse the relative weight of poetry and prose sections of the exam in grading candidates. The reform position was clear: the point of education was to learn the ideal ways of governing. Therefore the initial decision to pass or fail was to be based on the intellectual quality of the prose essays, for only these allowed the candidates to expound their ideas on what the government ought to do to benefit society.[3]

The proposal to rate prose above poetry immediately aroused opposition. First, it redefined the goal of learning to stress developing ideas about what ought to be done, giving pride of place to those literati who criticized current policy and proposed reforms. As Fan explained in his reform memorial, "The *I Ching* says, 'When it is exhausted, change it. When it is changed it will continue. When it continues it will last long.' This expresses the pattern (*li*) of the world."[4] Second, it made the process of grading more subjective than ever before—examiners now had to judge the candidates' values—and it encouraged candidates to align their thinking with the political views of the chief examiners. The proposals would politicize learning, making its goal the critique of state policy and the proposal of reforms, and they would make politics more ideological. But the proposal was rescinded with the other reforms when Fan fell from power in 1044.

The reform proved that there was a nucleus of prominent officials who believed that learning's purpose was to establish ideal goals that could be realized through institutional action. The defeat of the reforms had consequences as well. By denying proponents of new learning significant roles in the formulation of policy, it encouraged them to direct their attention away from the court and emperor and appeal to the broader group of younger officials and examination candidates. It led, in short, to the creation of an intellectual culture among the literati that concerned itself with the connection between politics and morality and was highly critical of those in power at court. In the 1040s and 1050s a new generation of literati began to pursue this kind of learning and to write in the style of its leaders. Thus in 1057, when Ou-yang administered the exam-

---

[3] James T. C. Liu, "An Early Sung Reformer: Fan Chung-yen," in *Chinese Thought and Institutions*, ed. John K. Fairbank (Chicago: University of Chicago Press, 1957), pp. 105–31, esp. pp. 112–15. Fan Chung-yen, *Fan Wen-cheng kung cheng-fu tsou-i* A.6a–b, in *Fan Wen-cheng kung chi* (*Ssu-pu ts'ung-k'an* ed.).

[4] Fan Chung-yen, *Fan Wen-cheng kung cheng-fu tsou-i*, A.1b.

inations, there were enough candidates writing prose essays of the sort he
admired for him to carry out the reform of the 1040s on his own authority, at the examination itself, and to ignore the protests of those who
failed.

Through his own scholarship and literary writing, Ou-yang Hsiu did
more than any other figure to promote the new approach to learning. He
defined its intellectual problems for the next generation, and he demonstrated through his own work that antiquity could be taken seriously as
a source of answers. He went well beyond the traditional habit of using
antique ideals and models to criticize the present. In his essay "On the
Basis," written in 1042, he argued that the reestablishment of an integrated human order, such as was ascribed to antiquity, was the task of
the literati. From antiquity, he contended, literati could learn how to
guide social life and political institutions. If modern men understood the
true "basis" of the civilization of antiquity, he concluded, Sung government would free itself from the precedents of Han and T'ang history and
the Sung people would no longer need Buddhism for ethical guidance.[5] In
the 1050s Ou-yang restated the idea of a single, cultural source of values
capable of integrating the political and the social in his introduction to
the "Treatise on Rites and Music" for the newly revised *T'ang History*.

> Down to the end of the Three Dynasties [of antiquity] government issued from
> unity, and rites and music reached throughout the world. After the Three Dy-
> nasties government issued forth from duality, and rites and music became
> empty terms.

He explained this as follows: In antiquity "ritual" was made into the single basis for all aspects of life. The ritual forms of daily life were also the
forms through which the affairs of government were conducted and a
moral socio-political order maintained. Social life and work were defined
by ritual, and ethics were inculcated through the forms of life and work.
But when the Ch'in dynasty broke with past forms it became impossible
for all later rulers to return to the forms of antiquity. Instead they pursued
Ch'in policies in "governing the people," relying on administration, ju-
dicature, and the military, and ancient forms for "teaching the people,"
making ceremonial use of the old ritual forms and implements. "They
used the implements but did not know their intent. They had forgotten
the root but had preserved the branch." And Ou-yang concludes that
T'ang, although its ritual system was highly elaborated, "could not attain
the glory of the Three Dynasties; it preserved the forms (*wen*) but the

[5] Ou-yang Hsiu, *Ou-yang Hsiu ch'üan-chi* (rpt. Taipei: Shih-chieh, 1971), "Pen lun," pp.
411–13 (part 1), 121–24 (part 2–3). Partially translated in Wm. Theodore de Bary et al.,
Sources of Chinese Tradition (New York: Columbia University Press, 1960), vol. 1, pp.
386–90.

intent was not present in them. This is what is meant by 'rites and music became empty terms.' "[6]

The problem, Ou-yang noted in his introductions to the other treatises, was that historical change could not be ignored. If the forms of antiquity were resurrected in the present they would not produce the results they had in the past—the original "intent" would not be realized. But if modern men looked beyond the forms or, as we saw above, the particular rituals of antiquity, to see the intent and purpose those ancient forms were meant to achieve, they could make those purposes their own. Thus in the present, with institutions and social practices different from the past, "restoring antiquity" and matching the sages could only be achieved by using modern forms to realize the intents and purposes of antiquity. For example, if in antiquity the intent of ritual was to unite the political and the social in a single moral order, then scholars in the present could be like the ancients in sharing the intent of creating an integrated order. It was not necessary to replicate the ritual of the ancients.

Ou-yang's writings show that he conceived of this task in the broadest terms: the entire cultural tradition from antiquity to the present was to be taken into account and reevaluated. This sense of commitment to the past as the source of values went together with an intense self-consciousness that the present could no longer merely seek to maintain past traditions in a formal way. The past had authority, if properly understood, but received tradition as such had lost authority. Ou-yang's approach to the Classics, the textual source for any understanding of antiquity, exemplified the problem and the solution. "Between the time the Six Classics were burned by Ch'in and reappeared in Han the transmission through teachers was cut off and the texts became disorganized and error-ridden. Students were not able to recover their original authentic state and the exegetical studies of the various *Ju* flourished."[7] The exegetical tradition came into being because men no longer knew what the Classics really meant, in this view, yet the texts of the Classics themselves were not complete and the exegetical writings of the past were not reliable. In this manner the question of the significance and intentions of the Classics and the sages became open to debate and the grounds were set for an intellectual revolution.

We tend to assume, given the later role of the Classics in examinations, that literati had always grounded their thinking in them. But it is not clear that Sung literati took the Classics seriously as a source for thinking about transformative values before the new style of interpretation appeared.

[6] Ou-yang Hsiu and Sung Ch'i, *Hsin T'ang shu* (Peking: Chung-hua, 1975), 11.307–9. David S. Nivison, "Introduction," *Confucianism in Action*, ed. Nivison and Arthur F. Wright (Stanford: Stanford University Press, 1959), pp. 4–8.

[7] Ou-yang and Sung, *Hsin T'ang shu*, 57.1421.

The examination system, after all, gave little weight to prose essays, which might be written on themes drawn from the Classics, while holders of the less prestigious degrees in "various fields" merely memorized the texts and the received interpretations. Moreover, the officially sanctioned version of the Classics, the seventh-century K'ung Ying-ta edition, interpreted the Classics through pre-T'ang commentaries and subcommentaries. Ancient texts, as interpreted by scholars five hundred years past living in a period of political division, were not obviously inspiring. Ou-yang was one of several men who set out to show how literati could make the Classics directly relevant. His commentary on the *Classic of Poetry*, entitled the *Original Significance of the Poetry*, showed readers that it was possible to step around the exegetical tradition and even ignore problems in the organization of the Classic itself if they returned to the poems and read them as expressions of the poets' intents. The poems, he argued, were the work of very human men who were responding emotionally to the circumstances they faced. They could be understood through *jen ch'ing*, human responses to actual human circumstances. Understanding the poems directly was basic to grasping the purpose of the sage Confucius who had edited the collection: "Thus once we know the intents of the poets we will then have apprehended the purpose of the sage."[8] Confucius, Ou-yang argued, had used these poems, collected in the past, as models for the present of moral responses to human affairs. Ou-yang chose to think about morality from a historical rather than philosophical perspective. That is, he held that the norms for how men ought to feel about things were based on how men had felt about them in the past.

Ou-yang's solution to the problem of finding relevance in the Classics was simple yet radical. He read them in terms of "human affairs" (*jen shih*) and "human emotion" (*jen-ch'ing*). By doing so, he treated the *tao* of the sages as ways of acting that could be constant because they were based on the way men actually behaved and felt. Modern literati could thus learn from the sages how to act and write. As he explained to a student:

> In regard to learning, the superior man is concerned with behaving morally (*wei-tao*). To behave morally he must seek to know antiquity. After he knows antiquity and understands *tao*, then he practices it personally, applies it to affairs, and further manifests it in literary composition to express it, thus to gain the trust of later generations. His way of moral behavior is that which men such as the Duke of Chou, Confucius, and Meng K'o [Mencius] constantly practiced. His [ideas] for literary composition are those that are conveyed by the Six

[8] Ou-yang, *Shih pen i* (*Ssu-k'u ch'üan-shu chen-pen* ed.), 14.9a, "Pen mo lun."

Classics and have been found credible to the present. Their *tao* is easy to know and to model upon. Their words are easy to understand and to practice.[9]

There are other early Sung examples of making the Classics speak directly to the present that broke with the exegetical tradition to greater and lesser degrees. In fact, the precedents and models for this and much of what Ou-yang Hsiu represents had already been established during the late eighth and early ninth centuries by men like Han Yü and Liu Tsung-yüan, whose works were still widely read and debated. Sun Fu's (992–1057) commentary on the *Spring and Autumn Annals*, for example, went directly to the Classic itself to argue that Confucius, the accepted author of this work, had used his judgments of political affairs to establish two constant principles of government: the centralization of political authority and the defense of the political and cultural integrity of China against barbarian encroachment.[10] Sun used the "intent" of the sage to define the principles of government in the present. Sun even proposed that the official T'ang commentaries be set aside and new commentaries prepared.[11] Similarly Hu Yüan (993–1059), the record of whose oral teaching on the *Book of Change* we shall refer to later, gained fame as a teacher by demanding that students consider how principles found in the Classics could be applied to contemporary issues.

The idea of making antiquity speak to the present quickly became popular. It gave idealistic literati, men who wanted change and longed for a higher common purpose, a reason for learning and a cause for writing. Men who lacked official rank or came from families without literati traditions made reputations as literati through learning. For example, Li Kou (1009–1059) and Su Hsün (1009–1066), Su Shih's father, gained the attention of men like Fan Chung-yen and Ou-yang with writings that brought antiquity and the Classics to bear on modern issues. For these men "the way of the sages" was the way men involved in practical affairs had governed society and benefited the world. There was nothing mysterious or esoteric about a *tao* that could be seen as the path taken by men who used political power for the common good. There was nothing there that they could not do once they understood what it was. Thus Mencius, important to some for his claim that human nature is good, appeared to Ou-yang to have "only taught men to plant mulberries and raise chickens and pigs[;] he thought nurturing the living and sending off the dead was

[9] Ou-yang, *Ch'üan-chi*, p. 481, "Yü Chang hsiu-ts'ai ti-erh shu"; cf. Teraji, "O-yō Shū," p. 178.

[10] For a discussion of Sun Fu's commentary, see Alan Thomas Wood, "Politics and Morality in Northern Sung China: Early Neo-Confucian Views on Obedience to Authority" (Ann Arbor: University Microfilms, International, 1981), pp. 140–85.

[11] Liu Tzu–chien, *Ou-yang Hsiu*, p. 21.

the basis of the Kingly Way. . . . [T]he affairs [Mencius thought pertained to *tao*] were easy for men of the age to understand and approach."[12] Ou-yang was, in effect, treating sages as men like himself. "The words of the sages are not distant from human actualities (*jen ch'ing*)" and "The governance of Yao, Shun and the Three Kings was necessarily based on human actualities."[13]

The desire to see the sages as humans coping with universal human problems helps explain why Confucius was becoming the most important of all the sages. It was not hard to see Confucius as a Sung literatus. The *Analects* showed him to be a teacher responding to students, a man committed to learning from the past, a man anxious to serve rulers and make government moral but often disappointed by and in tension with political authority. Earlier sages had been kings and regents, but Confucius was a sage by virtue of his desire to understand the sages of antiquity and to establish a textual tradition that could guide others by editing the Classics. His character and values could be known. The Classics thus told Ou-yang, among other things, about Confucius as their editor: "In the *Poetry* we can see the mind of the Master, from the *Documents* we can know his judgments, with the *Rites* we can illuminate his models, with the *Music* we can grasp his virtue, with the *Change* we can examine his character, and in the *Spring and Autumn Annals* we can preserve his purpose."[14]

Human Affairs, Heaven-and-Earth, and Hsing-ming

By the 1050s Ou-Yang Hsiu's vision of learning had come to define the mainstream of the new intellectual culture; the practices of early Sung had lost their authority. Literati who made reputations for learning generally agreed that learning could guide them in transforming society and politics, that intellectual values should be independent of power at court, that the sages of antiquity and the Classics were sources of moral authority, and that antiquity, the sages and the Classics could be understood from the perspective of human affairs. This last matter was the most important, for thinking that the sages were "just like us" was essential to believing that modern men could act like the sages and transform Sung into an integrated human order. Yet this was also the most radical of propositions, one that had to be defended. For accepting it, Ou-yang knew, required setting aside other intellectual possibilities.

In Ou-yang's attack on the received understanding of the *Book of Change* we can see that Ou-yang was taking a stand on one of several

[12] Ou-yang, *Ch'üan-chi*, p. 482, letter to Chang.
[13] Liu Tzu-chien, *Ou-yang Hsiu*, p. 24.
[14] Ou-yang, *Ch'üan chi*, p. 410, "Tai Tseng Ts'an ta ti-tzu shu"; cf. Teraji, "O-yō Shū," p. 179.

important tensions in Chinese thought. Prior to Ou-yang's generation there was the Confucius of the *Analects* and the *Spring and Autumn Annals*, but there also was the Confucius of the *I Ching*. Ou-yang Hsiu set out to separate Confucius from the *I*. Denying that the Classic as received from the Han Dynasty was the Classic seen by Confucius, he insisted that "The ancient Classic of Confucius has been lost."[15] Further, he argued at length that the "Ten Wings" of the received text could not possibly be the work of the Sage.[16] This was entirely unorthodox. It contradicted the judgment of the official T'ang commentaries,[17] which had been followed by Hu Yüan in his teachings.[18] Because we do not think today that the *I* contains any material written by Confucius or that Confucius ever saw the work as we know it, the radicalness of Ou-yang's position is not immediately apparent. However, if we were to view Confucius from the perspective of issues in the *I*, we would have to argue that he was deeply absorbed with the *tao* of heaven-and-earth, that he subscribed to the yin-yang understanding of cosmic process, and that he looked to the relationship between heaven and man to define morality. We might well read the *Analects* in light of the more fully articulated natural-philosophical ideas found in the *Hsi-tz'u chuan*. In separating Confucius from the received *I*, Ou-yang was challenging such a view of Confucius and the *tao* of the sage.

Ou-yang Hsiu brought a "cultural-historical" perspective to bear on the Classics and thinking about morality. He argued against all those who believed that human affairs should be guided by "heaven's will," for example as evidenced through natural disasters and anomalies that many interpreted as signs of the moral failures of political authority. And he sought to turn scholars away from a concern with human nature and fate (*hsing-ming*), which for many meant the search for moral qualities that heaven had endowed in men or the ways in which heaven and nature had set the course for human life. Like the T'ang scholars whom he so admired, Ou-yang was concerned with government policy and the culture of the learned more than establishing that there were heaven-mandated norms of ethical conduct that all men should adhere to. He was convinced that government ought to further the general welfare and that to do this it had to formulate policies that took into account the patterns of actual

[15] Ou-yang, *Ch'üan chi*, p. 473, "Ch'uan I t'u hsü."

[16] Ou-yang, *Ch'üan chi*, pp. 568–71, "I t'ung-tzu wen," *chüan* 3; pp. 129–30, "I huo wen," second section; p. 1052, "*Hsi-tz'u* shuo." Ou-yang stated his views as early as 1037 in the "*I huo wen*" and reaffirmed his position twenty-five years later in "*Hsi-tz'u* shuo." For a more detailed account of Ou-yang's position see Shchutskii, *Researches*, pp. 65–71.

[17] *Chou I cheng-i*, introductory essays 6 and 7, in *Shih-san ching chu shu* (Peking: Chung-hua, 1980 reprint), pp. 10–11.

[18] Hu Yüan, as related by Ni T'ien-yin, *Chou I k'ou-i*, "Fa-t'i" 3a.

human behavior (*jen-li*) as evident through human affairs (*jen-shih*) and human emotional responses to affairs (*jen-ch'ing*). In other words, he believed it was possible to have a moral society based on how men actually behaved rather than ideas about how they ought to behave. Instead of establishing "order" by coercing the people into fitting particular forms of "good" behavior, the government should envision "order" as the situation achieved when the general interests and needs of the people were fulfilled. Ou-yang accounted for the integrated human order of antiquity on this basis. He thought the sages had acted according to such precepts, and he held that literati who intended to learn from the sages should as well. Ou-yang, however, saw that heaven-and-earth had traditionally provided an alternative basis for establishing social and political norms and that an appeal to heaven-and-earth had been used to buttress the claim that government's real task was to make men behave correctly rather than to reform policy in order to satisfy human interests.

Ou-yang's attack on those locating ultimate moral authority in the realm of heaven rather than man took numerous forms. A telling example is his critique, in 1040, of the traditional use of the cosmic five phases of change (*wu hsing*) by dynasties to claim possession of heaven's mandate (*t'ien-ming*) in legitimating their succession to the previous dynasty. Appealing to various auspicious signs associated with the "fire" phase succeeding the "wood" phase of Later Chou, for example, the Sung founder had adopted "fire" and the associated color red. Moreover, during the course of a dynasty, unusual natural events, from earthquakes to freakish births, were treated as signs of heaven's favor and disfavor and interpreted as judgments on the conduct of government.[19] Imperial Confucianism since the Han dynasty had supposed that heaven has ultimate authority over human affairs, and, further, that the way humans conduct government directly affects, for better and worse, the operation of heaven-and-earth, and thus the physical well-being of the people and agricultural prosperity of the state. The idea of "cosmic resonance" at the basis of this view supposed a correspondence between natural categories of human affairs and categories of heaven-and-earth, with aberrations in human categories stimulating aberrant responses from the parallel category in the otherwise regular operation of heaven-and-earth.[20] From this it followed that the task of a truly moral government was to establish a human order by keeping men in their natural categories of function and status.

[19] For a discussion of the role of the five phases or five agents in legitimation see Hok-lam Chan, *Legitimation in Imperial China: Discussions under the Jurchen Chin Dynasty (1115–1126)* (Seattle: University of Washington Press, 1984), pp. 19–48.
[20] For a more elaborate account of cosmic resonance see John B. Henderson, *The Development and Decline of Chinese Cosmology*, pp. 22–28.

But for Ou-yang Hsiu this appeal to heavenly authority to justify a fixed social order led men away from tending to practical affairs and considering what humans could accomplish. The sages, he claimed, did not appeal to cosmic cycles for legitimation; the Three Dynasties gained legitimacy by "apprehending the correctness of the world under heaven and joining all under heaven in unity, either through perfect fairness or great righteousness."[21] Ou-yang defined dynastic legitimacy entirely in terms of human accomplishment, and, at the same time, rejected the theory of portents and cosmic resonance as baseless speculation, in spite of the apparent reference to heavenly portents in Confucius's *Spring and Autumn Annals*.[22]

Ou-yang spelled out the larger issue and justified his own position in his new history of the Five Dynasties. If heaven could not be known, he argued, men had no choice but to make judgments on the basis of what could be known: human affairs.

> In the past Confucius wrote the *Spring and Autumn Annals* and included both heaven and man. In relating the "Basic Annals" [of these later rulers] I have written of man but have not written of heaven. How would I dare differ from the sage! Although the form (*wen*) is different, the intention is the same.
>
> Since Yao, Shun and the Three Dynasties, all cited heaven in undertaking affairs, and Confucius, in editing the *Poetry* and *Documents* did not remove [such references]. It must have been that the sage was not divorcing heaven from man, yet neither was he using heaven to examine man. If heaven were to be divorced from man, the *tao* of heaven would be ignored; if heaven were to be used to examine man, the affairs of man would be in doubt. Therefore he always preserved [references to heaven] but did not investigate [them]. Although the *Spring and Autumn Annals* records eclipses and changes among the planets, Confucius never said why they had happened; therefore none of his disciples had anything they could relate to later ages [about such matters].
>
> Thus is heaven in fact involved with man or is it not? I say, we do not know heaven, but we can seek guidance from the words of the sage. The *I* says, "Heaven's *tao* is to deplete the full and increase the modest, earth's *tao* is to change the full and continue the modest, the ghosts and spirits harm the full and benefit the modest, and man's *tao* is to dislike the full and like the modest."[23]
>
> This is the sage's ultimate judgment, his most detailed and clear, on the juncture between heaven and man. With regard to heaven-and-earth and the ghosts and spirits his choice of words takes into account that they cannot be known. What he can know is only man. . . . In the case of heaven-and-earth and the

[21] Ou-yang, *Ch'üan chi*, p. 414, "Cheng t'ung lun"; cf. Teraji, pp. 167–68.

[22] Teraji, pp. 162–67.

[23] From the *T'uan-chuan* of hexagram #15 Ch'ien (Modesty). Cf. W/B, p. 462.

ghosts and spirits he cannot know their minds. Thus he calculates [heaven-and-earth and the ghosts and spirits] as they are manifest in things. Therefore he relies on their visible traces to speak about them and [in the text of the *I*] talks about "depletion and increase, change and continuity, and harm and benefit." But man can be known. Therefore he directly speaks of [man's] emotional responses (*ch'ing*) and [in the text of the *I*] talks about "likes and dislikes" [only in this case claiming to know the mind that guides action]. The phrases he uses differ according to whether he knows or does not know, but when taken together they are no different from man [i.e., heaven-and-earth and man are alike in tending to the modest rather than the full].

Is [heaven] in fact involved with man or not? This is what is not known. It is because he does not know this that [the sage] constantly honors but keeps distant from [heaven]. But since there is no difference from man, he thus works only at improving our human affairs. Human affairs are heaven's intent. The *Book of Documents* says, "Heaven sees through our people's sight. Heaven hears through our people's hearing." It has never happened that man's mind was glad below while heaven's intent was angry above. It has never happened that the patterns of man were contravened below while heaven's *tao* was accorded with above. The king is lord of what is under heaven, nurtures the people, spreads virtue and carries out policies, in order to accord with man's mind. This is what is meant by 'serving heaven.'[24]

Ou-yang's desire to deny heaven-and-earth relevance in the search for values was not, of course, easily accepted. Even Hu Yüan, who did not subscribe to theories of human-cosmic interaction, still felt compelled to acknowledge parallelism between heaven-and-earth and man. Hu contended, for example, that the hexagrams and lines of the *I* contained "the *tao* of heaven-and-earth's continuity and change and the patterns (*li*) of the ten-thousand things' authentic and false responses," and further, that the "*tao* of change" was "the pattern (*li*) of heaven and man." He proceeded to define three parallels between the two realms:

Spoken of as heaven's *tao*: yin and yang change, completing the ten-thousand things; cold and heat change, completing the four seasons; light and dark change, completing night and day. Spoken of as human affairs: success and failure change, completing good and ill fortune; authentic and false change, completing benefit and harm; superior and lesser men change, completing order and chaos.

Now as a description of natural and historical process Hu's parallels work quite well. But this description of what "is" does not lead directly to conclusions about what "ought" to be. Political power could secure unceasing good fortune, benefit, and order only by choosing the success-

24 Ou-yang, *Hsin Wu-tai shih* (Peking: Chung-hua, 1974), 59.705–6.

ful, authentic, and superior man.[25] Hu could not rest content with the imitation of natural process. His explanations of the hexagrams follow this, setting out the struggle between good and bad in the realm of human affairs in order to show that the good can be constantly triumphant. He has kept a place for heaven-and-earth, as Ou-yang Hsiu has not, but only in name.

Ou-yang Hsiu recognized at least two other uses of the realm of heaven-and-earth that challenged his pragmatic focus on human affairs. The first, with strong roots in Wang Pi's commentary on the *I* and Han K'ang-po's exegesis of the *Hsi-tz'u-chuan,* saw the "spontaneity" or "naturalness" (*tzu-jan,* "so-by-itselfness") of cosmic process as the highest achievement of man. Hu Yüan's commentary notes this as well: "The *tao* of heaven-and-earth and the patterns of birth and completion are so-by-themselves." But, like Ou-yang, Hu finds little of value here for similar reasons: "no man is able to know their reality; we simply know [the patterns] are so-by-themselves."[26] An interest in spontaneous process could also lead to an interest in its origins in nothingness or non-being (*wu*) or the primal, undifferentiated unity that existed before things came into being, as Hu Yüan also notes disapprovingly.[27] As we might expect, Ou-yang objects strongly to those who pursued a mystic insight into primal origins at the expense of the practical matters he associated with the *tao* of the sages.

> When those who learn today do not deeply root themselves in this [sagely *tao*] they take pleasure in nonsense and think about the undifferentiatedness at the beginning of antiquity, holding the perfect *tao* to be without form. . . . [T]hey are concerned with lofty and far-reaching action and rely on nonsensical, useless theories. This is not what those who learn should put their minds to.[28]

The second, however, was of greater concern to Ou-yang: those who believed that the norms of heaven-and-earth process were also ethical norms for social process, and that these were endowed in human nature (and to some degree in all things) as *hsing* or "nature." Proponents of the *hsing-ming* (nature and destiny) theory argued that the duty of man is to act according to these innate ethical guides—and, implicitly, that the duty of government is to make sure men did. Liu Mu's numerological study of the *I,* for example, stated that man was born with the *hsing* of the five phases and that these corresponded to the five virtues of benevolence, righteousness, decorum, wisdom and good faith.[29] Such a view could eas-

---

[25] Hu Yüan, *Chou I k'ou i* (*Ssu-k'u ch'üan-shu chen-pen* ed.), "Fa t'i" 2a–b.

[26] Hu Yüan, *Chou I k'ou i,* "Hsi-tz'u" A.6a–b (i.e., *Hsi-tzu, chüan* A, pp. 6a–b).

[27] Hu Yüan, *Chou I k'ou i,* "Hsi-tz'u" A.2b–3b, A.35a, A.98b–99a.

[28] Ou-yang, *Ch'üan-chi,* p. 481, second letter to Chang hsiu-ts'ai.

[29] Liu Mu, *I-shu kou-yin-t'u* (*Ssu-k'u ch'üan-shu* ed.), A31.

ily imply that knowledge of history and culture were less important than diligent ethical conduct. Again, Hu Yüan includes this view in his commentary on the *I* in response to the *Hsi-tz'u chuan* statement: "What completes [the spontaneous natural *tao*] is *hsing*."

> "*Hsing*" is the *hsing* heaven endows. The *hsing* of heaven-and-earth is tranquil and inactive. That of which we do not know how it is so, but is so, is the heaven-and-earth *hsing*. However, the primal good *ch'i* is received by men, and all have a good *hsing* that is perfectly clear and unclouded, perfectly correct and undeviant, perfectly impartial and unselfish. The sage receives the complete *hsing* of heaven-and-earth. It is pure and unadulterated, firm yet not cruel. When he is happy, he is happy together with society; when he is angry, he is angry together with society. With benevolence he loves all men; with righteousness he orders all things. He continues the good *hsing* of all under heaven to complete his own *hsing*. Once he has completed his own *hsing*, he completes the *hsing* of the ten-thousand things. Once he has completed the *hsing* of the ten-thousand things, then he can participate in the *hsing* of heaven-and-earth. Thus what is able to continue the goodness of heaven-and-earth is the *hsing* of man.[30]

Hu Yüan's view that some men are capable of being entirely good and then helping others to become good as well served to justify his belief in activist attempts to improve society and transform human nature. His goals were not dissimilar from Ou-yang's, but he tried to find a place for ideas about human nature while Ou-yang, the author of the following passage, did not.

> I have been troubled by how many scholars today speak of *hsing* and therefore I always say, "Now *hsing* is not something scholars should be urgently concerned with. It is something the sages spoke of rarely." The sixty-four hexagrams of the *I* do not speak of *hsing*. What they speak of are the constant patterns of activity and tranquillity, success and failure, and good and ill fortune. The 242 years of the *Spring and Autumn Annals* do not speak of *hsing*. They speak of the veritable record of good and bad and right and wrong. . . . What the Six Classics transmit are all the human affairs that are most pressing for society. On these they speak in great detail, but *hsing* is not even mentioned once in a hundred instances . . . The fact that the "Doctrine of the Mean" says, "Heaven's decree is what is meant by *hsing*, guiding *hsing* is what is meant by *tao*," makes clear that *hsing* lacks constancy and there must be something to guide it. . . .
>
> If one asks, "Is *hsing* really not worth studying?" I say, *hsing* comes into being together with the physical body and is something all men have. Those who act as superior men simply cultivate their person and govern others. The

[30] Hu Yüan, *Chou I k'ou i*, "*Hsi-tz'u*" A.36b.

goodness and badness of *hsing* need not be investigated. If *hsing* were in fact good the person would still have to be cultivated and others governed. If *hsing* were in fact bad the person would still have to be cultivated and others governed. If one does not cultivate his person then even if he is a superior man he will be a lesser man.[31]

Ou-yang's sages were not "natural" sages who merely acted according to innate moral guides. They "learned and knew it;" they made mistakes and corrected their faults.[32] They were guided by what they had learned from the human past, not by innate qualities. For in Ou-yang's view innate qualities lacked particular moral character. They were merely the faculties humans possessed.

But the *I Ching* as traditionally understood justified all these interests. It treated processes of heaven-and-earth as models for human society; it contained a cosmogony that could be interpreted in terms of development from original non-being to being; and it had a place for *hsing*. In addition it supported a long and continuing tradition of numerological speculation and the practice of divination. Thus to argue both that the Classics should be read in terms of human affairs and that literati should follow the sages in taking human affairs, rather than the realm of heaven-and-earth, as the true basis for human judgment, Ou-yang Hsiu had to find a way around the *Book of Change* or alter the way it was understood. In short, he had to show that it did not excuse men from schooling themselves in culture and history in a search for knowledge of the constant patterns of human affairs.

In brief, Ou-yang Hsiu argued that the *I* as received contained only two layers that expressed the intent of sages. The first was the sixty-four hexagrams as revived by King Wen, founder of the Chou. The second was the *T'uan* and *Hsiang*, written by Confucius to make King Wen's intent clear. Both men, Ou-yang contended, had struggled to keep diviners from controlling the *I*.

> The sixty-four hexagrams were employed from antiquity. The theories of diviners from the Shang and Hsia Dynasties are to be seen in outline in the *Documents*. King Wen, confronting the chaos of [the Shang king] Chou, had a mind that worried about the world and a will that was concerned with ten-thousand generations, but he lacked the means to express them. He held that the hexagrams and lines had arisen from odd and even numbers, and that yin and yang had alternated and through interaction had completed patterns (*wen*). These contained within them the images of superior men and lesser men, advance and retreat, movement and tranquillity, and firm and soft as well as the patterns of

---

[31] Ou-yang, *Ch'üan chi*, p. 320, "Ta Li Hsu ti-erh shu."
[32] Teraji, p. 180. Cf. Ou-yang, *Ch'üan chi*, p. 327, third examination question.

order and chaos, rise and fall, success and failure, and good and ill fortune. Thus he used them to convey his words and named it the *I*. In later generations it was used for divination.

Confucius appeared at the end of Chou. He feared that King Wen's purpose would not be apparent to later ages and that the *I* would be exclusively employed for divination. He then wrote the *T'uan* and *Hsiang* and illuminated the meanings of the hexagrams. He always cited sages, superior men and kings as fitting its affairs and constantly spoke in terms of the four quarters, the myriad states, heaven-and-earth and the greatest of the ten-thousand things. It must have been that he was making clear [that the text] did not stop at divination. . . . Only then was the *I* ranked among the Six Classics. . . .

Now the texts of the six lines are divination phrases. The numbers of the "*ta yen*" (great expansion)[33] are a divination method. They had been used since antiquity. King Wen changed their phrases but did not change this method. Therefore I say that the "*ta yen*" is not an affair of King Wen. What are called the phrases [or verbal elaborations] have the images of superior man and lesser man, advance and retreat, movement and tranquillity, and firm and soft and the patterns of order and chaos, rise and fall, success and failure, and good and ill fortune. . . .

He who wishes to see King Wen's intent in creating the *I* will go far amiss if he leaves aside the phrases and holds fast to the divination method. All those who wish to be superior men will learn from the sages' words; those who wish to be diviners will learn from the "*ta yen*" numbers. The choice is up to you.[34]

Ou-yang also contends that contradictory theories preclude certain knowledge about the ultimate origin of the *I*, the role of Fu-hsi, the Ho-t'u (River Chart) and Lo-shu (Lo Diagram), and the eight trigrams. He allows that the Ten Wings contain interesting material, some of which may stem from the sages, but which must be corroborated by other Classics to be useful. Citing the prolixity of the Wings, the multiplicity of modes of expression they contain, and internal inconsistencies, he attributes the Wings to unknown and unreliable teachers.[35]

Ou-yang did, however, give an account of his understanding of the intent of about half of the hexagrams, noting what he did not understand at various points. His comments define what he sees as the particular human affair to which the hexagram speaks and the constant pattern of human activity the sages intended it to represent.[36] Thus Ou-yang

---

[33] See *Hsi-tz'u-chuan* A8.

[34] Ou-yang, *Ch'üan chi*, p. 129, "*I* huo wen," first section.

[35] Ou-yang, *Ch'üan chi*, pp. 568–70, "*I* t'ung-tzu wen," part 3; pp. 129–30, "*I* huo wen," part 2. For an account of some of Ou-yang's objections see Shchutskii, *Researches*, pp. 65–71.

[36] Ou-yang, *Ch'üan chi*, pp. 561–68, "*I* t'ung-tzu wen," parts 1 and 2.

brought the *I* into line with his vision of learning by acknowledging only parts of it as expressing the intents of the sages. This enabled him to deny that divination, which supposed that men could rely on the ghosts and spirits to know how to act, had any place in the sages' purpose. Yet Ou-yang also left a problem for the next generation. He had argued persuasively for a cultural-historical perspective in the search for values, but at the same time he had insisted that there were "patterns" and "constants" to human affairs that could serve as the basis for an integrated moral order among men. Thus some might well ask where these constants were to be found, what they were, and how they should be realized in practice.

Whether or not they were persuaded that heaven-and-earth and *hsing-ming* were irrelevant to understanding values, Ou-yang Hsiu and his generation had redefined the intellectual culture of the literati. Henceforth "learning" would always mean more than cultural refinement and being well-schooled in past traditions. For generations to come, learning would be the self-conscious search for the superior vantage point from which to view the whole, be it the whole of human affairs or the whole of heaven-and-earth and humanity, seeking values that were not limited by particular received traditions. An acceptance of the reality of historical change would be part of that search; for serious thinkers true values transcended fixed definitions and particular forms. Even if he could not identify them himself, Ou-yang persuaded others that there were constant or even universal patterns, principles, and intentions, and that men could, with their own minds, know these more fundamental constancies by examining things and affairs as they really were. This new approach to learning brought with it active attempts to come to terms with the real world, even when the purpose was to transform it. The great promise of learning was simply this: that through it literati would arrive at an integrated, coherent vision that would show the way to a harmonious unity of politics and morality, self and society. Through learning in this manner they would be able to reestablish a unity of public institutions and society, of political and moral values. The integrated, coherent vision they hoped to find through learning was to provide the basis for transforming Sung into an integrated, coherent order.

DISCOVERING THE SYSTEM: THE SECOND GENERATION

Two of the most influential political and intellectual leaders of the next generation illustrate the desire to find coherent visions and use the institutions of government to put them into effect. Ssu-ma Kuang (1019–1086) and Wang An-shih (1021–1086) began their official careers just as the reform movement of the 1040s was reaching its height. By the 1060s, both were seen as men of scholarly attainment, moral purpose, and integrity, and they were being offered important roles in the formulation of policy. Wang came to power first, under the new emperor Shen-tsung (r. 1067–1085), and launched a series of reforms aimed at transforming the bureaucracy and official recruitment, rationalizing local government, increasing agricultural production, guiding the commercial economy, integrating local society, raising government revenues, and strengthening the military.[37] The "New Policies," as they came to be called, created institutions that greatly expanded the role of the state at the expense of private interests. Within two years, officialdom had divided into irreconcilable factions of supporters and opponents.

During the 1070s Ssu-ma Kuang, in semi-retirement in Loyang, acted as the leader of the opposition to the New Policies. With Ssu-ma's arrival, Loyang, already home to Shao Yung, Ch'eng I, and several other opponents of the regime, became the center of conservatism. Ssu-ma himself had once been a reformer of sorts, having argued for well over a decade that political stability and social prosperity depended upon the rationalization of the bureaucracy, clearer definition of bureaucratic roles, and stricter standards in the administration of existing institutions.[38] But in contrast to Wang, who kept asking what more government could do and what initiatives officials should undertake, Ssu-ma had always concerned himself with how government should function and how bureaucrats should behave. For Ssu-ma the issue was not what more government should do, but how the existing institutions and unity of the dynasty could be maintained. On the death of the emperor Shen-tsung, Ssu-ma was recalled. Until his death in 1086 he strove tirelessly to abolish the New Policies and to limit the authority and activities of state institutions. The regime he led controlled the court until 1093; Su Shih became a leading minister; and Ch'eng I was summoned to serve as an imperial lecturer. Members of the new regime had disagreements with each other, as well as with the New Policies, and their new responsibilities made these even more apparent. It is fair to say that from the early 1070s until the Jurchens' capture of the capital in 1126 the literati, particularly those serving in office, were unable to establish any real consensus on political and intellectual issues of the day. The demotion and, in many cases, exile of opponents of the New Policies in the 1070s, the 1090s, and again in the first decade of the twelfth century only increased suspicion and hostility.

Wang and Ssu-ma, in spite of their obvious differences, both proceeded along the lines set out by Ou-yang Hsiu. Both brought the cultural-his-

[37] For an account of Wang An-shih and the reforms see James T. C. Liu, *Reform in Sung China* (Cambridge: Harvard University Press, 1959).

[38] On Ssu-ma Kuang's political theory see Anthony J. Sariti, "Monarchy, Bureaucracy, and Absolutism in the Political Thought of Ssu-ma Kuang," *Journal of Asian Studies* 32.1 (1972), pp. 53–76.

torical perspective to bear on the realm of "human affairs" in search of principles that could guide state and society in a changing world. For Wang An-shih these principles were to be found in the governance of the sages as related by the Classics. He explicitly used the ideal integrated order of antiquity to justify the reforms and define their goal. The Classics contained a perfect system, Wang argued, because the sages had coherent programs that integrated men into a unified social order where "morality was the same for all and customs were uniform." To guide the present, men had to grasp the intentions of the sages and adopt their principles for ordering society, as inferred from the specific policies and institutions the sages created to realize their intentions.

For Ssu-ma Kuang these principles were to be found in political history. Whether earlier men had understood it or not, Ssu-ma Kuang saw that there were certain principles for the organization of political power and the administration of government that, when followed, enabled a dynasty to establish itself and, when contradicted, led to the demise of the state. The sages had acted according to these principles and, to the extent they had been successful (and Ssu-ma found them relatively unsuccessful), Han and T'ang governments had as well. But while Wang's integrated system necessitated extending the role of the state, aiming at ending the distinction between public and private, Ssu-ma's stable socio-political order survived because it limited the scope of state power. Ssu-ma's state would be the one institution that could keep competing private interests in harmonious relationship to each other because, since it did not threaten any one interest, it was trusted by all to do only what was necessary to maintain a situation in which private interests could be harmoniously pursued. Both Wang and Ssu-ma believed that the correct functioning of state institutions was fundamental to order and prosperity. Both believed in a centralized bureaucratic system. And both believed that their political principles were also moral principles.[39]

Wang and Ssu-ma bridged the gap between Ou-yang Hsiu's idealistic rhetoric and the more pragmatic realities of his practice. In practice, Ou-yang left it to learned individuals to determine correct policy according to the occasion. Individuals accumulated knowledge and insight and made judgments according to the matter-at-hand. Ou-yang was neither programmatic or systematic, although he was usually consistent on larger issues. His concern was that policy should be based on how men actually

[39] For comparisons of Ssu-ma Kuang and Wang An-shih see Robert Hartwell, "Historical Analogism, Public Policy, and Social Science in Eleventh- and Twelfth-Century China," *American Historical Review* 76.3 (1971), pp. 690–727, and Bol, "Rulership and Sagehood, Bureaucracy and Society: An Historical Inquiry into the Political Visions of Ssu-ma Kuang and Wang An-shih," ACLS Workshop on Sung Dynasty Statecraft in Thought and Action, Scottsdale, Arizona, January 1986.

behaved, that it should accord with "human patterns" and satisfy human interests. He could be admired as a man, yet he did not provide a well-defined political program that others could join in supporting.

But Wang and Ssu-ma did have programs. They knew what had to be done and how it should be done. They integrated and reached conclusions that generated coherent sets of interrelated policies. Admirers of Ou-yang would have to be like Ou-yang themselves, while men persuaded by Ssu-ma and Wang could join in support of a particular program and find a place for themselves as part of it. Both men prepared writings that explained what they wanted to do. Wang's essays, his famous "Ten-Thousand Word Memorial" of 1057, his commentary on the "Great Plan" chapter of the *Documents*, and eventually the official commentaries on the *Poetry, Documents,* and *Institutes of Chou* and his *Explanations of Written Characters*, all served this purpose. For his part, Ssu-ma produced a series of well-known memorials, philosophical treatises, and important historical works, including the *Comprehensive Mirror in Aid of Government*, a chronology of Chinese history for the 1,362 years prior to the founding of Sung in 960. Both also wrote on the *Book of Change*.

It is certainly true that in their other writings Ssu-ma Kuang and, to a lesser extent, Wang An-shih made an effort to take into account the *tao* of heaven-and-earth and *hsing-ming*.[40] Yet in doing so, we might argue, both were illustrating Ou-yang Hsiu's claim that "Whether one uses the actualities of man (*jen ch'ing*) or draws inferences from the traces of heaven-and-earth and ghosts and spirits, there will be no difference."[41] That is, they made their theories about heaven-and-earth fit what they already had concluded about human affairs. However, the fact that they wanted to show that the principles they found in the realm of man were also operative in the realm of heaven-and-earth indicates that their audience had not been persuaded that heaven-and-earth and *hsing-ming* could be ignored.

We find confirmation of this in some of the examination questions

[40] See, for example, Ssu-ma Kuang's commentary on the *I*, Yang Hsiung's *T'ai hsüan*, and the *Lao tzu*, and Wang An-shih's commentary on the *Lao tzu*. However, they saw the unity of heaven and man somewhat differently. In power, and anxious to thwart attempts to use natural disasters to attack his policies, Wang denied that events in the realm of heaven were responses to human affairs; see Li T'ao, *Hsü tzu-chih t'ung-chien ch'ang-pien* (Peking: Chung-hua, 1986), 269.6597. On another occasion he argued that no real distinction between heaven and man could be made, although he reserved knowledge of how they were united for someone who had an understanding of the "spirits"; see *Lin-ch'uan chi* 62.660. Ssu-ma Kuang was much more forthright. In an essay on the *I* he responded to the question of whether the *I* concerned human affairs or heavenly affairs by insisting that there was one universal *tao* that worked through yin and yang and the five phases in the realms of man and of heaven equally; see *I shuo* (*Ssu-k'u ch'üan-shu chen-pen* ed.), 1a–b.
[41] Ou-yang, *Ch'üan-chi*, p. 562, "*I* t'ung-tzu wen."

asked by Tseng Kung (1019–1083), a student of Ou-yang Hsiu and an early friend of Wang An-shih. In one question Tseng poses the following problem. He notes that the *I* says that "The *tao* of heaven-and-earth is simple," "the goodness of simplicity matches perfect virtue," and "yet all patterns under heaven are apprehended." How, he asks, is this possible? The processes that bring the myriad things into being and sustain them appear to be infinitely complex; the achievement of understanding through the simple would seem not to fit with the realities of "human affairs."[42] Tseng's question was not entirely sympathetic, yet it reflected his sense that literati were looking for intrinsically simple principles guiding the operation of heaven-and-earth, and an intrinsically simple way of human knowing that would give ready insight into how things worked in the human world. This awareness of a widespread concern with holistic understanding reappears in a question Tseng wrote on the Six Classics. The essential thing about the Classics, Tseng states, is simply that they make it possible for "scholars to know how to accord with the patterns of *hsing-ming*, correct their minds and cultivate their persons, govern the state and society, fully realize the appropriate roles of heaven-and-earth and the ghosts and spirits, and comply with the *hsing* of the myriad things. But their words are not uniform and their intents are difficult to know."[43] The problem posed for the students is to explain in practical terms how they can accomplish these five goals.

Tseng, Wang, and Ssu-ma were at the center of the intellectual culture of their generation. But on the intellectual periphery, there were literati from well-established official families who sought to develop coherent understandings of heaven-and-earth and *hsing-ming* as a basis for answering the kinds of questions Tseng Kung posed. It is an indication of the changes yet to take place that Chu Hsi would later see these figures, who in their own times had rejected the cultural-historical perspective of the day, as the bearers of true learning. Chang Tsai (1020–1077), for example, used the yin-yang process of *ch'i* to describe the *tao* of heaven-and-earth and, on that basis, defined man's "heavenly *hsing*." Learning to be a sage, in his terms, meant training oneself to act according to this *hsing*, the essential principles of heaven-and-earth endowed in man. Chang also wrote a commentary on the *I*.[44] Like Chang, Chou Tun-i (1017–1073) took heaven-and-earth and *hsing-ming* as his starting point to speak to human affairs and the way of learning. His "Explanation of the Diagram of the Supreme Ultimate" eventually became the classic Neo-Confucian statement of cosmogony. In his *Comprehending the*

---

[42] Tseng Kung, *Tseng Kung chi* (Peking: Chung-hua, 1984), p. 762.

[43] Tseng Kung, *Tseng Kung chi*, p. 766.

[44] For a discussion of Chang Tsai's philosophy see Ira E. Kasoff, *The Thought of Chang Tsai (1020–1077)* (Cambridge: Cambridge University Press, 1984).

Book of Change (*I t'ung*), now known by the later title of *Book of Comprehending* (*T'ung shu*), we find statements such as these:

> Great is the Change, the source of *hsing-ming*.[45] The *Book of Change* is not only the source of the Five Classics; it is the deep and dark abode of heaven-and-earth and the ghosts and spirits.[46] The way of the sages is nothing other than absolute impartiality. Someone asked, "What does this mean?" I said, "Heaven-and-earth are simply absolutely impartial."[47]

In one sense, however, Chou Tun-i and Chang Tsai were truly the contemporaries of Wang An-shih and Ssu-ma Kuang. They tried to envision integrated orders based on simple principles that could serve as the foundation for social and political values. The difference, and it is an important one, is that Chou and Chang supposed that these principles were also innate to man as a creation of heaven-and-earth and were not conclusions drawn from historical experience or justified by cultural tradition.

Shao Yung, the subject of a following chapter, is another example of this effort. His great work, audaciously entitled *The Book of the Supreme Principles Ordering the World* (*Huang-chi ching-shih shu*), is a guide to seeing order in cosmic change, in accordance with the patterns of *hsing-ming*, cultivating the self, ordering the world, and setting all things in their proper place. For Shao, heaven-and-earth—not human affairs—is the starting point: "Only when man is able to know how the *tao* of heaven-and-earth and the myriad things is fully realized by man will he be able to fully realize [the potential of] the common people."[48]

Although Shao was born in 1011, making him a contemporary of Ou-yang Hsiu, he does not seem to have become intellectually prominent until the 1050s and 1060s, a period marked by the growing influence of the generation of Wang An-shih and Ssu-ma Kuang. This helps to account for Shao's eagerness to make his mark by establishing a systematic understanding of the cosmos and history that could generate norms for social and political practice. In contrast to the other men dealt with in this book, Shao did not come from a literatus family. What we know of his family was apparently provided by Shao himself, and much of what we know about Shao's intellectual career before he gained the attention of officials residing at Loyang is quite anecdotal. His great-grandfather is said to have been a military officer under the founding emperor, but the next two generations did not serve in government. Shao's father is said to have been schooled in the Classics and to have taught in his hometown in north

---

[45] Chou Tun-i, *T'ung shu*, section 1. In Wing-tsit Chan, *A Source Book in Chinese Philosophy*, p. 466, modified.

[46] *T'ung shu*, section 30. In Chan, *A Source Book*, p. 477, modified.

[47] *T'ung shu*, section 37. In Chan, *A Source Book*, p. 479, modified.

[48] Shao Yung, *Huang-chi ching-shih shu* (*Ssu-pu pei-yao* ed.), 5.7a.

China. In 1049 father and son moved to Loyang after having traveled extensively. It is not clear how we should account for Shao Yung's extensive travels with his father, given that his father was apparently not a civil official. Two possibilities suggest themselves, that his father had a military career of some sort or that he was a merchant.

Two biographies, both by men who knew him in Loyang, note that Shao Yung claimed he received "his learning" through scholarly transmission. They describe it as "using numbers to infer the cycles of heaven-and-earth and of yin and yang, and predicting their transformations."[49] It is said that in about 1035 Shao was taken under the tutelage of Li Chih-ts'ai (?–1045), the local subprefect, who spoke to him of learning about the "patterns of things (*wu-li*) and *hsing-ming*," who encouraged him to comprehend the Classics, and who gave him various diagrams and numerological methods for studying the *I* that had been popular at the capital.[50] In any case, Shao pursued his studies avidly and diligently. "Once he began to learn, he strongly admired the lofty and far-reaching, saying that the affairs of the former kings could be made to happen."[51]

In many of the stories that eventually appeared, Shao is an eccentric of the first order, a man whose appeal was both charismatic and practical: he could divine the future. Yet a more sober assessment suggests that Shao's appeal to his literatus friends and patrons—Chang Tsai, the Ch'eng brothers, Ssu-ma Kuang, and others—had less to do with his system than with the fact that he had devoted himself to learning rather than official success. Perhaps he was proof that "learning" could actually satisfy a man's desires, something that some successful officials wanted to believe but might have doubted. He did, without question, achieve a reputation in Loyang, for in 1061 and then again in 1069 he was recommended to the court as scholar-recluse and was offered official rank and even an appointment. He turned both down and remained in Loyang until his death in 1077. One of his biographers noted that when Shao "gave [his learning] to the world there were none who could understand it."[52] We should probably read this to mean that some of Shao's official patrons did not want to understand it. For although Shao's use of the *I Ching* for numerological speculation about heaven and man did not enter the main-

[49] This quotation is drawn from Fan Tsu-yü, *Fan T'ai-shih chi* (*Ssu-k'u ch'üan-shu chen-pen* ed.), 36.15a, "Kang-chieh hsien-sheng chuan." See also Ch'eng Hao, *Erh-Ch'eng chi*, pp. 502–4, "Shao Yao-fu hsien-sheng mu-chih ming." For a biographical study of Shao Yung and the various anecdotes concerning him see Don Juan Wyatt, "Shao Yung: Champion of Philosophical Syncretism in Early Sung China" (Ph.D. dissertation, Harvard University, 1984).

[50] See the accounts of Shao's studies with Li Chih-ts'ai in their biographies in the *Sung Dynastic History* (Sung shih), 428.12728 and 431.12824.

[51] Ch'eng I and Ch'eng Hao, *Erh-Ch'eng chi*, p. 503.

[52] Fan Tsu-yü, *Fan T'ai-shih chi* 36.15a.

stream of literati thought, in every generation there were men who studied his writings and methods. He represents a strand of thinking that remained part of the intellectual culture of the literati.

THE MORAL AUTONOMY OF THE INDIVIDUAL: THE THIRD GENERATION

Su Shih (1037–1101) and Ch'eng I (1033–1107) represent a third generation. It is common, at least since Chu Hsi's day, to stress the great differences between Su, a high-ranking official whose intellectual reputation cannot be detached from his literary accomplishments and official career, and Ch'eng, who spurned cultural accomplishment in favor of teaching his moral philosophy. However great these differences were, Su and Ch'eng together mark an important turning point in literati thought. Both men were concerned with the moral autonomy and intellectual independence of the individual literatus as one who lived in constant tension with political power and the institutional system. Even before the promulgation of Wang An-shih's New Policies, an event that prompted reflection on the intellectual basis of political differences, both men had shown a marked concern with how the individual should act. With the exception of a series of fifty essays Su wrote for the decree examination of 1061 (but later disowned), neither man gave serious thought to perfecting institutions as a means of transforming society or to defining the principles of a perfect institutional system. Assuming the coherence and fundamental unity of things, they asked instead how the individual could understand that coherence, make a personal connection to *tao*, and use that connection as a basis for independent yet socially responsible action.

Su and Ch'eng articulated and proposed resolutions to what was becoming a real tension in literati values: the desire to be part of the system without subordinating oneself to it. With hindsight we can see that they spoke to the emerging historical problem of the literati: the lack of opportunity for official careers. During the course of the eleventh century, the examination system, combined with the spread of local schools, had prompted increasing numbers of families to prepare sons for official careers and, with every generation, the number of young men from official families seeking office had increased as well. When the traditional assumption that a literatus was to serve could no longer be sustained, literati were forced to ask how they could remain literati, members of the socio-political elite, without office. The problem was heightened, but not fundamentally different, for those who, like Su, did have official careers but found that their opposition to Wang An-shih's New Policies kept them shut out of office during their best years. How could men remain politically and socially responsible, gain reputations, and influence others without positions of real authority? The interest in the moral autonomy of the individual so evident in the thinking of both men fit well with both the social changes and the political situation of the day.

But they also had substantial intellectual disagreements with the conclusions Wang and Ssu-ma had reached, that once men knew how the system ought to function, responsibility required that literati subordinate themselves to the need to maintain the integrity of the institutional structure. For each man, knowledge about how to act depended upon finding the "ruler within" that would enable him to respond flexibly to changing circumstance. It is not surprising that we find Su and Ch'eng giving particular attention to problems relating to individual knowledge and action: What does the individual possess innately? What is the role of learning from external sources? How can the individual maintain unity with *tao* while responding to changing circumstances? How does the man know that he is in unity with *tao*? This is not to deny, of course, that Su and Ch'eng approached the questions of their generation from very different perspectives.

By Su's own account he continued the general cultural and historical orientation of Ou-yang Hsiu, although Su also claimed that his ideas could describe the basic processes of heaven-and-earth and explain the true meaning of *hsing-ming*. He grew up in the Ou-yang tradition. His father, Su Hsün (1009–1066), was a self-taught man from Szechuan; Su Hsün and his brother were the first in their family to make the transition from farming and trade to acting as literati. Impressed by the reform leaders of the 1040s, anxious to be recognized by famous men as a true talent, Su Hsün eventually gained the attention of Ou-yang Hsiu through his writings, just as his two sons, Su Shih and Su Ch'e (1039–1112), were passing Ou-yang's famous examination of 1057. Four years later the brothers were invited to take the special decree examination for men of extraordinary promise, having been sponsored by Ou-yang Hsiu and Ssu-ma Kuang respectively. In short, Su Shih came from a family that had struggled to establish its credentials as literati and had done so by pursuing the new mode of learning and writing.[53]

Ch'eng I (1033–1107) did not have to work at gaining recognition as a literatus for himself or his family. He came from a truly notable northern family; his ancestors had already been serving in government during the Five Dynasties and had held leading positions in Sung. His father, Ch'eng Hsiang (1006–1090), having gained rank through privilege, postponed taking a post until he had seen to the education and marriage of family members in his care, and eventually rose so high in the bureau-

[53] Information on Su Hsün and Su Shih is drawn from biographies by George Hatch, *Sung Biographies*, ed. Herbert Franke (Wiesbaden: Franz Steiner Verlag, 1976), pp. 885–900 and 900–968, respectively.

cracy that official rank was given to five of his relatives.[54] Like his older brother Ch'eng Hao (1032–1085), Ch'eng I had been carefully trained for an official career. In the 1050s both had been placed in the State Academy (*Kuo-tzu chien*), the capital school reserved for the sons of high officials that regularly supplied a disproportionate number of successful candidates. But the Ch'engs did not gain their ideas of learning from men like Ou-yang Hsiu. In their teens they were sent to study with Chou Tun-i, and although it cannot be shown that they adopted Chou's philosophical ideas, they certainly came to share his philosophical orientation. Later they studied with their uncle Chang Tsai, and in the 1070s they knew Shao Yung in Loyang.

In contrast to his brother Ch'eng Hao, who graduated in 1057 with Su Shih, Ch'eng I failed the final palace examination in 1059 and chose not to pursue an official career. Instead he spent the next decade with his father at various posts. He settled in Loyang in 1072 when his brother, who had been rising rapidly in the bureaucracy, took a sinecure in Loyang rather than continue to serve under the New Policies regime, and he followed his brother in devoting himself to learning and teaching. In contrast to the Su brothers, the Ch'engs engaged in philosophical inquiry, seeking to understand the connections between heaven-and-earth, *hsing-ming*, and ethical values. Perhaps, in the Ch'engs' concern with ethics, we can see the assumption of a well-established family that the ethical conduct of social relations was more important than cultural accomplishment, the device so frequently used by those seeking to persuade others that they were indeed literati.

While Ch'eng I had been traveling with his father, Su Shih had been advancing in the bureaucracy. After passing the 1057 and 1061 examinations and taking a prefectural staff post, he passed the examination for appointment to an academic institute and appeared destined for a succession of ever higher capital posts. But he opposed the New Policies and, in 1071, left Kaifeng to serve in the prefectures, where he remained until his arrest for criticizing the court in 1079. Already a man of literary fame, Su's banishment to Huang-chou made him celebrated among opponents of the regime. With the change in government in 1085 came a series of court appointments, and he was given charge of the 1088 examinations. By 1085 Ch'eng had established a scholarly reputation, and he was summoned to court to lecture the emperor.

At court Su and Ch'eng were allied with mutually hostile factions. Ch'eng, the first casualty, was forced out in 1087 and returned to Loyang.

[54] See the biographies of Ch'eng Hao and Ch'eng I by Wing-tsit Chan, in *Sung Biographies*, pp. 169–79. For accounts of the family also see various writings by Ch'eng I, *Erh-Ch'eng chi*, pp. 645–60.

Two years later Su, having been attacked himself, temporarily withdrew to the prefectship of Hang-chou. The return of New Policies officials to power at court in 1093, when the youthful emperor began to rule in his own right, brought Su Shih's active career as an official to an end. In 1093 he held ministerial rank; by the end of 1094 he had been banished to the deep south. Ch'eng did not have an easier time. The court confiscated his land, forbade his teaching, and banished him to Szechuan in 1097. In 1100 the accession of a new emperor brought their release. Su died in 1101, but Ch'eng lived to see the beginning of a new and more vicious purge the next year. This time Ch'eng avoided banishment, but his writings were ordered destroyed, as were those of Su and his leading followers.

Both Su and Ch'eng had followers among the generation of literati who began their careers in the 1070s. These men defended and transmitted their ideas. Su's most noted followers believed that individual cultural accomplishment was still a worthy part of literati learning, while Ch'eng appealed particularly to those who believed in the reality of the moral nature. Both men attracted opponents of the New Policies regime, because they explained not only why the New Policies were misguided but also why achievements in learning were more important to being a responsible literatus than gaining official position. For officials who saw their careers being blocked by factional politics and who had lost (or never had) faith in political service as a means of achieving ideals, Su and Ch'eng exemplified alternative ways of establishing reputations. For the much larger group of examination candidates, whose chances of entering government were decreasing as the number of candidates increased, Su and Ch'eng provided justifications for acting as a literatus without serving in government.

The court's attack on the Su and Ch'eng groups went well beyond a desire to purge the bureaucracy of uncooperative administrators. At heart this purge was ideological. The New Policies were themselves based on the intellectual justifications provided by Wang An-shih's learning. Their success required intellectual unity: modes of learning that thwarted unity had to be eradicated. Ch'eng's claims for the primacy of individual moral transformation denied both that society could be transformed through institutional means and that men who did not "know *tao*" could effectively lead government. Su's claim that diversity in all fields was necessary to social unity similarly undercut the court's contention that unity depended upon uniformity. The differences were great. Wang, Su and Ch'eng offered three definitions of what was necessary to lasting social cohesion and political harmony. Wang's sage transformed society by creating a coherent, integrated institutional system; Ch'eng's did so by knowing and acting in accord with the moral norms inherent in self and things; Su's sage, a more nebulous figure, creatively responded to change by bringing into being new things that would serve as provisional guides for others.

CHU HSI: THE SOUTHERN SUNG RESOLUTION

In spite of their domination of the central government through the remainder of Northern Sung and their effectiveness in extending the state school system, by 1126 adherents of the New Policies had not yet succeeded in forcing a literati consensus on the ends and means of learning. The loss of the north to the Jurchens, the restoration of the dynasty in the south in the 1130s, and the decision to subsidize the Jurchens' Chin dynasty instead of mobilizing to recover the north gave New Policies opponents a new opportunity.

The loss of the north, the traditional base for all dynasties that had unified north and south, and the constant specter of the northern threat colored politics throughout the Southern Sung period. Their consequences were felt in intellectual culture as well, for political authority during the first decades of Southern Sung was associated with the New Policies and Wang An-shih's learning, even if the goal of institutional renewal was lost in the face of the exigencies of war. For some of those who believed that the nature of literati learning ultimately determined the fortunes of the state, it was clear that Wang An-shih's learning was responsible for the loss of the north and the policy of appeasement that blocked its recovery. Those who thought Wang's learning had led Sung astray thus faced the question of what literati ought to have valued in Northern Sung and which of the various intellectual alternatives Northern Sung offered they should follow. The process of sorting out the intellectual legacy of Northern Sung was largely finished by the end of the twelfth century, and literati who put their faith in the promise of moral cultivation had come to define the center of intellectual culture. Political activism and cultural accomplishment had lost much of their appeal to men who were personally concerned with *tao*. In short, Ch'eng I's issues had been accepted as the true concerns of learning.

Southern Sung literati could look back on Northern Sung and see how various hopes had been dashed. Ou-yang Hsiu's faith in the possibility of learning from history and culture had been tried, but it had not led to a lasting intellectual consensus. Wang An-shih had worked to unify, enrich and strengthen the state, but his measures had not prevented a military disaster. Su Shih's accommodation of diversity and literary creativity had not mobilized literati in defense of the state. There was, perhaps, nothing left to try except moral renewal. But the turn toward moral thought was certainly facilitated by the efforts of Chu Hsi (1130–1200).

Chu Hsi was the Ou-yang Hsiu of Southern Sung. His vision of learning replaced Ou-yang's at the center of creative thought. Chu's understanding of Confucianism, not Ou-yang's, defined how later ages would think of "Sung learning." By the end of his life Chu Hsi had become the most influential scholar of his times, despite the court's attack on his school as "false learning" in the 1190s. His influence did not depend on his bureaucratic career. During the half-century between his examination degree and his death, he held office for only nine years, almost all his posts being in local government, and spent only forty-six days at court (during which time he had three audiences with the ruler). Yet by the end of these fifty years he, with his students and allies, had succeeded in creating, outside of the government school system and examination education, the infrastructure of private academies, the corpus of texts, and the network of scholarly communities necessary to sustain a coherent program of education and cumulative scholarly tradition. He persuaded literati that true learning was a means of transforming the self into a moral person along a path directed at sagehood, and he provided them with the institutional and pedagogical means to accomplish this. He published critical editions of the writings of the Ch'eng brothers and their disciples' record of their oral teachings. He wrote commentaries on writings by Chang Tsai and Chou Tun-i. He prepared an anthology of quotations from Chou, Chang and the Ch'engs on the nature of learning and the various areas of literati responsibility. He wrote commentaries on the Classics and established the *Analects, Mencius, Great Learning*, and the *Doctrine of the Mean* as the *Four Books*, through which the essence of the Way of the sages could be understood. He commented extensively on past literary writing and wrote a commentary on Han Yü's literary collection. He prepared to write a revision of Ssu-ma Kuang's *Comprehensive Mirror in Aid of Government*, wrote historical accounts of the leading statesmen of Northern Sung, and concerned himself with family and community institutions.[55]

[55] For Chu Hsi's career and many of his principal works see biographies by Wing-tsit Chan, *Sung Biographies*, pp. 282–90 and Conrad M. Schirokauer, "Chu Hsi's Political Career: A Study in Ambivalence," in *Confucian Personalities*, ed. Arthur F. Wright and Denis Twitchett (Stanford: Stanford University Press, 1962), pp. 162–88. For Chu's critique of Su Shih and Wang An-shih see Bol, "Chu Hsi's Redefinition of Literati Learning," in *Neo-Confucian Education: The Formative Stage*, ed. Wm. Theodore de Bary and John Chaffee (Berkeley and Los Angeles: University of California Press, 1989). For Chu's work on the *Four Books* and the *Great Learning* in particular, see Daniel K. Gardner, *Chu Hsi and the Ta-hsüeh: Neo-Confucian Reflection on the Confucian Canon* (Cambridge: Harvard University, Council on East Asian Studies, 1986). Chu's position was assailed by other philosophically minded scholars, Lu Chiu-yüan being the most famous example, but also by men with historical and institutional interests, such as Ch'en Liang. On the latter, see Hoyt Cleveland Tillman, *Utilitarian Confucianism: Ch'en Liang's Challenge to Chu Hsi* (Cambridge: Harvard University, Council on East Asian Studies, 1982).

The increasing narrowness of Southern Sung intellectual culture, a sharp contrast to the diversity and openness of the eleventh century, was a sign that Chu Hsi's efforts to establish his vision of literati learning were succeeding. Chu Hsi's philosophical foundations—his understanding of heaven-and-earth and man's place in it—systematized ideas Ch'eng I and others had articulated. But Chu Hsi was much broader than the Ch'engs; not unlike Ou-yang Hsiu, he aimed to reevaluate the entire cultural tradition. With his erudition and breadth of interests he achieved what none of his intellectual predecessors had accomplished: he redefined the cultural history of China from antiquity to his own day on the basis of the new moral philosophy. Chu Hsi realized the larger intellectual goals Ou-yang Hsiu had envisioned. He established a lasting definition of literati learning that placed man in position to take responsibility for his world, to see the whole, and define the proper course of life by and for himself. But the tables had been turned on Ou-yang, for now the foundation of literati thought was in the realm of heaven-and-earth, and ideas about heaven-and-earth were used to define norms for human affairs. Heaven and man had been reconnected in a way that required individuals to cultivate themselves in order to realize heaven's decree; cosmic resonance had become a faint echo. We can see this final transformation in their different assessments of the *I Ching*. For Ou-yang the *I* was a work about human affairs; the sages had not cared about divination. Chu Hsi argued, however, that the sages had created the *I* for divination. The chapters to follow will illuminate different ways literati thought about the *I* and some of the ways the *I* was used in literati thinking. Perhaps they will also help us understand why, in the end, "human affairs" proved to be an inadequate foundation for the literati search for values.

CHAPTER THREE

Su Shih and Culture

VALUES, CULTURE, AND POLITICS

Su Shih, the Prefect of Hu, was arrested in the fall of 1079 for "slandering the court." Back in the capital a month later, he was jailed, tried, and found guilty. It is said that he was saved from execution only because the emperor himself interceded. In any event, at the end of the winter Su left for a five-year term of exile in Huang-chou, midway up the Yangtze toward Szechuan.

Su Shih left Huang-chou in 1084, his political views unchanged. He had, however, come to a deeper understanding of what he meant and why he was right. His commentary on the *Book of Change* was written during this exile. Though it is a commentary on the *I*, it is also Su Shih's account of himself, something that made it possible for others to "know him." But he saw it as more than either of these. Together with his commentaries on the *Analects* and *Book of Documents*, it was also meant to "correct the mistakes of past and present" and "bring benefit to the age."[1] Shortly before his death in 1101, returning from a second exile on Hainan Island in the distant south, he again spoke of the importance of this work: "Only when I regard these three books on the *Change, Documents*, and *Analects* do I feel this life has not been lived in vain. Nothing else is worth mentioning. . . ."[2]

Why did Su attach such importance to his commentaries on these three Classics, and particularly to his work on the *I Ching*? Why did he make a point of writing commentaries on the Classics while in exile? The answers to these questions turn out to be very closely related. At that time Su was seen by many, in the language of the day, as a "literatus of culture" (*wen shih*), a man famous for his accomplishments in the arts of prose, poetry, and calligraphy. He had been arrested, jailed, tried, and exiled because in literary pieces—mainly poems in this case—he had rid-

---

[1] *Su Tung-p'o chi (Kuo-hsüeh chi-pen ts'ung-shu* ed.) 4.11.4.15, "Yü T'eng Ta-tao." The dating of the commentary to Su's Huang-chou period follows his testimony to the elder statesman Wen Yen-po (1006–1097) in a letter from the period; see *Su Tung-p'o chi* 2.5.29.110, "Huang-chou shang Wen Lu-kung shu," noted in Tseng Tsao-chuang, "Ts'ung 'P'i-ling *I chuan*' k'an Su Shih ti shih-chieh kuan," *Ssu-ch'uan ta-hsüeh hsüeh-pao ts'ung-k'an* 6 (1980), pp. 59–60.

[2] *Su tung-p'o chi* 4.12.7.29, "Ta Su Po-ku."

iculed the court, its New Policies, and its goal of transforming society from above and unifying values and customs below. Writing commentaries allowed Su to demonstrate his seriousness: exiled from the center of political life he devoted himself to matters whose importance transcended the politics of the moment. He was not to be seen as a mere literary stylist or a superficial critic, good at writing snide comments but lacking a real alternative.[3] Su Shih said as much on finishing the commentary on the *I*: "Even if on reading you find nothing of value in it, it will still be enough to show that when forlorn I did not forget the *tao*, and when old I was able to learn."[4] And yet Su Shih stood out among leading intellectuals of the day because he saw real value in the various modes of individual cultural accomplishment others held to be irrelevant or even harmful to realizing *tao*. The ideas in his commentary on the *I Ching* help account for his continued involvement in literary and artistic pursuits and justify them as serious and useful enterprises.

This essay begins with an account of Su Shih the literary man, who relied on his literary fame to gain a hearing as a critic of the government. The objective here is to show that in the eleventh century "literary men" could still conceive of themselves as being at the center of intellectual culture. Su Shih certainly saw himself as one who was being intellectually responsible, and he wished others to see him that way as well. We shall then turn to his commentary on the *I* and see how he uses that text to address fundamental questions in the literati search for values. Finally we shall return to consider the implications of Su's understanding of the *I* for literary and artistic accomplishment.

Su Shih and Wen

For the convenience of introduction we have used "literary" to describe Su Shih. This is misleading. It is more useful, and historically more correct, to speak of Su as a man who defended the value of *wen* in general and the importance of individual accomplishment in various genres of prose, poetry, calligraphy, and painting as modes of engaging in *wen*. Some of Su's contemporaries assumed that those who devoted so much attention to literary and artistic pursuits were not serious about understanding fundamental values and thus were not being morally and intellectually responsible. In their terms someone who spent so much time "doing *wen*" (*wei wen*) was unlikely to be seeking *tao*. Su's commentaries

---

[3] James T. C. Liu notes this view when he writes in *Reform in Sung China* (Cambridge: Harvard University Press, 1959), p. 29, that ". . . in opposing the New Policies and in criticizing the northern conservatives at the same time, the moderates tended to be supercritics who had few constructive alternatives to offer."

[4] *Su Tung-p'o chi* 2.5.29.110, "Huang-chou shang Wen Lu-kung shu."

were evidence that he did, in fact, care about *tao*. We shall argue that one of Su's achievements was to explain how individual cultural accomplishment could be a real means of realizing *tao*. To see the importance of this we must first consider how it came about that concerns with *wen* and *tao* were in tension.

Wen was central to the intellectual culture of Sung literati well into the eleventh century. It connected politics, learning, and tradition. In politics Sung aimed to establish a civil (*wen*) order after a long period during which military interests were paramount. To do this it recruited its civil officials from among the literati, men who were schooled in the great texts of Chinese tradition. And it recruited them through an examination system that tested either the memorization of texts (various combinations of the Classics, the earliest histories, or ritual compendia) or composition in highly regulated forms of poetry and prose. In early Sung two ideas justified the use of a test of *wen* (literary composition) to identify men learned in *wen* (the textual tradition) to further *wen* (civil interests) in government. First, it was held that the socio-political order in the present should seek to approximate the greatest forms and models of the past (either of the Han and T'ang empires or antiquity). Second, it was thought that to accomplish this it was necessary to have as officials those most knowledgeable and adept at using past forms. The most prestigious examination required skill in literary composition: the ability to tie together references to past texts around the given theme and to fit what one had to say into a highly regulated traditional form. Its goal was to find men committed to formal traditions. The best candidates drew upon the textual tradition to construct a formally coherent, balanced composition, just as the Sung state sought to unify and organize the realm into a coherent political order drawing on the models of the past.

But, as we saw in chapter 2, these notions were challenged by men like Ou-yang Hsiu in the mid-eleventh century. They argued that good *wen* was more than a matter of formal culture, technical skill, and the ability to approximate past models, whether in writing or government. Their critique of the examination system and the "current style" had much to do with a central idea of Chinese poetics: "poetry speaks of the will" (*shih yen chih*). The proper function of the examination writing, they held, was to make accessible the ideas and values of the candidate. The surface or form of examination composition (the *wen*) should count for less than the moral ideas that gave the piece its coherent pattern or organization (the *li*). Similarly, they argued, the point of learning from the textual tradition was not to master its forms and models but to understand its *tao*. Although some took the *tao* of antiquity to be the forms of antiquity, the new generation of intellectuals argued that *tao* could be conceived of separately from the forms—as the principles and intentions that had guided the men of the past, which were articulated in their doctrines, or which gave structure to their institutions. The function of individual composition in the present thus should be to reveal the writer's apprehension of these integrating ideas. With this in mind some argued that the prose sections of the examination, which lent themselves more readily to the exposition of ideas, should count more than the poetry sections. This attitude had serious implications for thinking about government as well. Some argued, for example, that current policy should be guided not by the forms of the past but by the *tao* of antiquity. For such men continuity with the past was to be achieved by realizing in the present the principles inferred from past *wen*; the forms were not to be taken literally.

Ku wen, "ancient style prose," was the vehicle of these men. To some extent this mode of writing was a compromise between formalists and those who sought principles independent of their traditional expression. *Ku wen* essays, for example, gave considerable attention to rhetorical technique, drew upon the Classics, histories, and philosophical writings, and found classical precedents for their relatively unadorned and straightforward style of exposition. But *ku wen* also addressed ideas and values: essayists discussed how *tao* should be realized in the present in learning and politics. Under the tutelage of his father, an admirer of Ou-yang Hsiu, Su Shih first made his reputation through *ku wen*, writing fifty essays for the special decree examination of 1061.

By the time Su went into exile the view that *wen* was a vehicle for ideas, values, and principles had carried the day. But this doctrine had also set the ground for challenges to the centrality of *wen* in literati learning. Four challenges are particularly important for understanding Su Shih.

First, some believed that if the goal of studying the textual tradition was to learn principles and ideas, one needed only to study the texts with the correct ideas. Thus we find men narrowly defining "This Culture of Ours" (*ssu wen*) and "This Way of Ours" (*ssu tao*) as the texts and ideas of certain sages (as conveyed by the Classics) and the writings of a handful of later men (e.g., Mencius, Yang Hsiung, Han Yü). Similarly, Wang An-shih's new examination system required knowing only certain classics (and Wang's commentaries) and writing essays that explained how to realize their principles in the present. Ssu-ma Kuang, on the other hand, argued that the histories were just as vital. This narrowing of the texts considered worthy of study during Northern Sung was also manifested by a growing willingness to reject Taoism and Buddhism as sources of enduring ideas. We shall see that Su Shih's views made it unnecessary to define a narrow or orthodox tradition.

Second, the idea that good *wen* is morally serious prose led some to question the status of less formal sorts of literary endeavor. For most, the issue was not whether men should write occasional poetry or prose but whether such writing could be taken seriously in intellectual discourse and learning. Was writing that was personal, specific to the occasion, and lacking in normative statements worth the effort that was necessary to doing it well? Su Shih sought to explain why such casual forms, even though they demanded care and attention, could be compatible with a real moral concern. He also saw that calligraphy and painting could be justified in the same fashion.

Third, some held that if the point of learning *wen* was to understand and manifest normative values, the way a person acted was a far better indicator of his real values than what he wrote. Proposals to reform the examination system frequently included provisions for investigating the "ethical conduct" (*te hsing*) of the candidates. But by the 1080s some moral philosophers had already begun to argue that an education that required spending time mastering literary skills was actually detrimental to the moral development of the individual, for it turned his attention away from the personal embodiment of moral values toward finding the forms and techniques that would impress others. In Su's vision, however, the process that made individual cultural accomplishment of real value possible was also the basis for all moral action. Indeed, engaging in *wen* could be a form of moral action.

Fourth, as literati became increasingly concerned with understanding *tao*, some began to argue that the real basis for values was not, in fact, within the cultural-textual tradition at all. Men such as Shao Yung and the Ch'eng brothers argued that the principles that ought to guide human society were aspects of *tao* as the universal processes of heaven-and-earth (*t'ien ti*) and were innately endowed in man as part of heaven-and-earth. In this view the sages were models because they practiced these principles, but the principles did not depend on the sages, the achievements of antiquity, or human consciousness to be true. This was perhaps the greatest challenge to Su's belief in the value of cultural traditions. We shall see that his commentary on the *I* explains *tao*, human nature, and natural process in such a way that culture remained relevant and necessary.

For some literati during the last quarter of the eleventh century, Su Shih was living proof that the challenges to *wen* could be met. He provided them with a model, both by the way he acted as a man and by the way he wrote. Su Ch'e, Su Shih's younger brother, close friend and confidant, began his funerary biography of Su Shih with the statement: "This Culture of Ours has fallen; up to whom will those born later look?"[5] This was an extraordinary claim. It depicted Su Shih as the vehicle through which "This Culture of Ours," the cultural tradition of China itself, had

---

[5] *Su Tung-p'o chi* 1.2.0.41. The term *ssu wen* comes from *Analects* 9:5.

been continued in the present. Most of the biography recounts at great length Su Shih's career as a civil official and his rise to the highest levels of government, noting along the way that some had been surprised that a literary man could be such an able administrator. The piece closes with an intellectual biography of sorts. It discusses Su Shih's *wen*: his unique ability, his literary and artistic accomplishment, and his learning from and insight into great texts. Here we see that Su Ch'e's claim that his brother had continued "This Culture of Ours" in the present was grounded in his conviction that Su Shih had understood the ideas of the *wen* of the past.

With regard to *wen*, the Gentleman obtained [his special talent for] it from heaven. When young, he and I both took our father as our teacher. At first [my brother] liked the writings of Chia Yi and Lu Chih. In discussing order and chaos in past and present he did not speak emptily. But then he read the *Chuang tzu*. He said with a sigh, "Previously, when I perceived something of what was within me, my mouth was unable to put it into words. Now I have seen the *Chuang tzu* and grasped my own mind." Subsequently he produced [his three-part essay] "On the *Doctrine of the Mean*." He discussed the subtleties, none of which had been explained by men in the past.

He once said to me, "In my view among those who learn in today's world, only you can be ranked with me." But when he had been exiled to Huang-chou he shut his door and lived in seclusion. He raced on with brush and ink, and his *wen* underwent a complete transformation. It came to be like "a stream coming down in flood,"[6] and, overwhelmed, I was no longer able to keep up with him.

Our father read the *Book of Change* in his later years. When he had mused over the lines and images and apprehended the actual human experience of the actual circumstances of the firm and soft, far and near, happiness and anger, going with and going against in order to contemplate its language, the meaning [of the *Change*] all fell into place. His *Commentary on the Change* was not finished when illness overtook him, and he ordered the Gentleman to complete his work as he had intended. In tears [my brother] received that charge, and ultimately produced the completed work. Only then did the subtle language from a thousand years past become clearly understandable.[7] He further wrote *Explanations of the Analects*, in which he repeatedly brought out Master K'ung's concealed points in a timely way. At the very last, when he was living

[6] *Shih ching*, Hsiao ya, "T'ien pao." Arthur Waley, *The Book of Songs* (London: George Allen and Unwin Ltd., 1937), p. 125.

[7] It is not clear to what extent Su Hsün's work on the *I* was taken over by Su Shih; most take the commentary as a statement of Su Shih's ideas. Su Shih himself claimed that he first gained insights into the text on his own and "then following the learning of my late father, composed the *Commentary on the Change* in nine *chüan*." See *Su Tung-p'o chi* 2.5.29.110, "Huang-chou shang Wen Lu-kung shu."

on Hainan, he wrote his *Commentary on the Documents* to clarify through inference the learning of high antiquity which had been disrupted. Much of what he said had not been understood by former *Ju*.[8] Having completed the three books he placed his hand on them and sighed, "Even if the present age is still unable to trust [me], if there are superior men in the future they ought to understand me."

As for his occasional poems, laments, inscriptions, accounts, letters, memorials, expositions, and proposals, they generally surpassed those of others. There is the *Eastern Slope Collection* in 40 *chüan*, the *Later Collection* in 20, the *Memorials* in 15, the *Inner Rescripts* in 10, and the *Outer Rescripts* in 3 *chüan*. His poetry basically resembles that of Li [Po] and Tu [Fu]. Late in life he enjoyed T'ao Yüan-ming. His [works] rhyming to [those of] T'ao were almost complete, four *chüan* in all.

When young he liked calligraphy, and when old he did not tire of it. He said of himself that he did not match the men of Chin [in calligraphy] but that he had more or less come close to Ch'u [Sui-liang], Hsüeh [Chi], Yen [Chench'ing], and Liu [Kung-ch'üan] of T'ang.[9]

Su Ch'e casts his brother in a form which is not, I think, far removed from what Su Shih thought of himself. He was a literatus with a brilliant talent for *wen*—perhaps the greatest poet, calligrapher, and prose stylist of Sung—but he was also someone who had understood the foundations of the cultural tradition. Saying that Su understood "the learning of high antiquity which had been disrupted" implicitly challenged the claims the Ch'eng brothers made for themselves as the first since Mencius to have transmitted the *tao* of the sages. Su was neither narrow nor orthodox. He valued Chuang Tzu's relativism, yet he also drew on the idea of internal standards from the *Doctrine of the Mean*. Others could not match his creative talent, yet in his unique achievements he was indebted to his predecessors. Su Shih was not easy to imitate.

Su Shih's concern with *wen* and individual expression helps us understand his opposition to Wang An-shih's New Policies. As Su saw it, the division between him and the regime followed from a fundamental difference in understanding the nature of true values. Against Wang's belief that intellectual controls and uniformity were necessary if the literati were to act in concert, Su defended intellectual diversity. In 1086, after his return from exile and the fall of the New Policies government, Su wrote his follower Chang Lei (1054–1114):

[8] In its Sung usages, *Ju* is impossible to translate simply. Broadly speaking, it is anyone who argues for employing the models of the Classics or sage kings in contemporary politics. More narrowly it means someone who specializes in the Classics. Futhermore, Ch'eng I was in the process of redefining it to mean a true Confucian of his persuasion.

[9] *Su Tung-p'o chi* 1.2.0.49–50.

There has never been a decline in *wen-tzu* (literary writing) such as that of today. The source of this is really Mr. Wang. Mr. Wang's *wen* is not necessarily not good. The problem is that he likes to make others the same as himself. Ever since Confucius was unable to make others achieve the same benevolence as Yen Hui or the same courage as Tzu Lu, it has not been possible to move other people towards each other. Yet with his learning (*hsüeh*) Mr. Wang would make all under heaven the same. The beauty of the soil is the same in bringing things into being; it is not the same in that which is brought into being. It is only on barren, brackish soil that there are yellow reeds and white rushes far as the eye can see. This, then, is the sameness of Mr. Wang.

I recently saw Chang Tzu-hou, who said that the late emperor, at the end of his life, was very concerned with the vulgarity of *wen-tzu* and wished to somewhat alter the method for selecting literati [to serve as officials]; he simply never had the time for it. Those making proposals would restore to some extent poetry and *fu* (rhapsody) [in the examinations] and establish officials for the learning of the *Spring and Autumn Annals*. This is very fine. I am old. Whether those born later will still get to see the great whole (*ta ch'üan*) of past men depends on you . . . [and my other principal followers].[10]

For Su "vulgarity" in writing was uniformity. Good writing accurately revealed the individual character and ideas of the writer. Thus Wang An-shih's writing was good because it manifested the learning a particular man had developed, but when others imitated Wang—as the new examination system encouraged—individuated expression was lost and the quality of writing declined. Better, Su argues, to return to the old examination system, one that gave more weight to individuation and that strand of the textual tradition, represented by the *Spring and Autumn Annals*, that recognized that as circumstances changed, the appropriate response had to change as well. The correct is not uniform; diverse responses can spring from common soil. When Su speaks of the "great whole of past men" he suggests that all the individual possibilities represented by the past are aspects of a grander whole.

Su Shih cultivated the image of spontaneity and individuality in the face of widespread doubt that it was possible to be both responsible yet spontaneous or to maintain both a commonality of purpose and individuality. Some have read Su's famous comment on his own practice of *wen* as an exaggerated response to those who doubted:

My *wen* is like a spring with a ten-thousand-gallon flow. It does not care where, it can come forth any place. On the flatlands spreading and rolling, even a thousand miles in a day give it no difficulty. When it twists and turns about mountain boulders, it takes shape according to the things encountered—but [it]

---

[10] *Su Tung-p'o chi* 2.6.30.11, "Ta Chang Wen-ch'ien shu."

cannot be known. What can be known is that it will always go where it ought to go and stop where it cannot but stop, that is all. Even I am not able to understand the rest.[11]

Su's commentary on the *I* suggests that we should take this seriously, not just as a comment on his own writing, but as a statement about how men ought to be able to act.

Su Shih and the Book of Change

Su Shih's commentary on the *Book of Change*[12] speaks of *tao* and the universal process through which *tao* is brought into practice in the world of change. It is we as scholars looking back on his work who make the connections between the commentary and Su's life and circumstances. When Su Shih writes in a letter that "Even if on reading you find nothing of value in it, it will still be enough to show that when forlorn I did not forget *tao*, and in old age I was able to learn," he invites us to read the commentary as nothing more than a demonstration of his seriousness. We

[11] *Tung-p'o t'i-pa (Ts'ung-shu chi-ch'eng* ed.) 1.15, *Tzu p'ing wen.* At the time some used this claim to perfect spontaneity to deny that Su could be a model for others. In a memorial text for Su, his follower Ch'ao Pu-chih makes a point of referring to this text and insisting (not incorrectly) that Su was in fact "diligent." *Chi-le chi (Ssu-pu ts'ung-k'an* ed.) 61.469.

[12] The edition of the commentary followed is *Su-shih I chuan (Ts'ung-shu chi-ch'eng* ed.) in 9 *chüan.* I have benefited from several interpretations. Hou Wai-lu et al., *Chung-kuo ssu-hsiang t'ung-shih,* vol. 4, part 1 (Peking: Jen-min ch'u-pan-she, 1959), pp. 584–89, makes convincing comparisons between this commentary, Su Ch'e's *Lao-tzu chieh,* and several philosophical essays by Su's follower Ch'in Kuan. George Hatch's treatment of the commentary, the first Western account, is in *A Sung Bibliography,* ed. Yves Hervouet (Hong Kong: The Chinese University Press, 1978), pp. 4–9. The reevaluation of Su Shih and Chinese intellectual history now taking place in the People's Republic of China has resulted in numerous studies of Su Shih and at least two articles on his commentary: Tseng Tsao-chuang's 1980 article, noted above, and K'ung Fan, "Su Shih 'P'i-ling *I-chuan*' ti che-hsüeh ssu-hsiang," *Chung-kuo che-hsüeh* 9 (1983), pp. 221–39. The latter has many useful insights.

Although this commentary was originally Su Hsün's idea, Hatch finds little of Su Hsün in it. Chu Hsi, on the other hand, does, but blames what he perceives as Buddhist and Taoist elements on Su Shih; see citations in Wang Chi-hsi, *Pei-sung I-hsüeh k'ao* (M.A. thesis, Taiwan Normal University, 1978), p. 71. Precisely these elements are crucial to Su Shih's position, as Hou and Hatch note. For an account of Chu Hsi's critique of Su Shih and this commentary in particular, see Bol, "Chu Hsi's Redefinition of Literati Learning," in *Neo-Confucian Education: The Formative Stage,* ed. John Chaffee and Wm. Theodore de Bary (Berkeley and Los Angeles: University of California Press, 1989).

Ideas in this commentary appear also in Su's later commentary on the *Documents;* see Su's discussion of the "one" and the unity of the "mind of man" with the "mind of the way" in Hatch's account of that commentary in *A Sung Bibliography,* pp. 15 and 18 respectively. They are also compatible with many of the ideas found in Andrew March, "Self and Landscape in Su Shih," *Journal of the American Oriental Society* 86 (1966), pp. 377–96.

might, therefore, read the commentary only for what it tells us of Su's character. However, Su Ch'e's claim that with this work "the subtle language of a thousand years past became clearly understandable" suggests that it is also possible to read the commentary as a text intended to persuade readers to accept Su's views. I have taken this perspective and organized my account around three issues: (1) Su's explanation of how men ought to read the *I* as a practical guide to conduct, (2) his account of how men ought to conceive of *tao*, as something that exists independently of the book, in relation to the world of change, and (3) his description of how men can bring *tao* into practice for themselves. The last, the highest achievement of learning for Su, bears most directly on the practice of *wen*.

This three-part organization is suggested by Su's interpretation of a passage in the "Commentary on the Attached Verbal Elaborations" (*Hsi-tz'u-chuan*), the most philosophical of the "Ten Wings" of the *I*. The authors of this text distinguished between *I* as the name for a book and *I* as the name for that book's way or method (*tao*) of divination. Further, they held that this *tao* of divination was consonant with the *tao* of heaven, earth and man, that is, with the universal process of change in the world. This correspondence was vital to their argument that the book, with its sixty-four hexagrams, 384 lines, and various verbal elaborations, was the most important of all texts to know and learn from, for it justified their conclusion that through divination men could use the book to understand the changing world. Thus, as Willard Peterson translates, the authors of the "Appendix" wrote:

> Being the book that it is, the *Change* cannot be put at a distance. Being the way (*tao*) [of divining] that it is, it repeatedly shifts.[13]

But Su does not understand the *tao* of the *I* as divination, and he suggests at one point that divination is an "empty device" of mere utilitarian value.[14] Elsewhere, adopting Ou-yang Hsiu's position, he writes: "The *I* was the sages' means of fully expressing the variations of human emotion and actuality (*jen ch'ing*). It was not a means of seeking the spirits through divination."[15] He understands the passage above to mean that while one may not depart from the text of the *I* when using the book as a

---

[13] Willard J. Peterson, "Making Connections: 'Commentary on the Attached Verbalizations' of the *Book of Change*," *Harvard Journal of Asiatic Studies* 42.1 (1982), p. 81. *Hsi-tz'u-chuan* B7.

[14] *Su Shih I-chuan* 7.169, commenting on *Hsi-tz'u-chuan* A10. Note that Su does not hold to the paragraphing of the *Hsi-tz'u* found in standard texts. Citations of this section of his commentary include references to the *Hsi-tz'u-chuan* paragraphs (Harvard-Yenching Institute Sinological Index Series edition of the *I*) for convenience only. However, with the exception of several sentences regarding number (*Hsi-tz'u-chuan* A8 and A10), he does not rearrange the text.

[15] Su Shih, *Su Tung-p'o chi*, 4.12.72, "Wen: Kung-yang san-te wei shan."

guide to conduct, the book is separate from *tao*. The book is fixed and limited, while *tao* is neither limited nor fixed. This implies that to act truly in accord with *tao*, or to bring *tao* into practice, one cannot stick to the book. *Tao*, Su concludes, is "at a distance" or "far-off," and thus man's aim in learning is to reestablish a direct connection to it, unmediated by fixed concepts and texts. Men can take the book as a guide to daily practice, Su agrees, but ideally they will learn to embody and be guided by *tao* itself. His commentary on this section of the "Appendix" explains:

> Whenever it speaks of [the *I*] "as a book" it is referring to that which has already been created in forms and objects. The [*I* as a] book can be seen and pointed to and verbally transmitted. One should not seek afar [for its meaning], going beyond the written elaborations (*wen tz'u*). . . . [16] As for its *tao*, that is far-off.
>
> What cannot be put at a distance is the book, not the *tao*. One may not seek afar; therefore one accords with the verbal elaborations (*tz'u*) [in the book] and calculates [the outcome] toward which they point. [The statement] "In the beginning [follow its verbal elaborations]" is said to those who are not yet enlightened. When those who are not yet enlightened master this book, use its "measures for coming in and going out," investigate its "alarms inside and outside," perceive its "causes for anxiety and concern," and follow its "fixed rules," they can make few their errors.
>
> Those who are enlightened bring its *tao* into practice (*hsing ch'i tao*). [For them] there is neither coming in nor going out, there is neither inside nor outside. They "flow through the six places," and wherever they go "it is meet." Even acting as a sage is possible [for them]. . . . [17]

The *I* as a written work can serve men as a practical guide because it does have something to do with *tao*. Our first task is thus to consider how, in Su's eyes, the relation between the book and *tao* bears on interpreting the book as a guide to conduct, and what Su sees as the themes of its advice. When Su thinks of the book as a guide he has the sixty-four hexagrams and their hexagram and line statements in mind. A translation of his interpretation of the Fu hexagram (Return) is included in the appendix as an example. However, *tao* is "far-off." Su can say this on the basis of his views about how men can legitimately conceive of *tao*. Thus our second task shall be to examine his arguments in this regard, most of which are found in his commentary on the "Great Appendix," because they are fundamental to his claim that those who are enlightened bring *tao* into practice without sticking to the book. Su's account of how this can be

[16] Su distinguishes between *yen*, translated here as "saying," and *tz'u*, "verbal elaborations." In the first case language is used to express an idea directly and is intended literally; in the second case language is also used suggestively; the ideas are gotten across through tone and image as well as through direct expression.

[17] *Su Shih I-chuan* 8.182–83. *Hsi-tz'u-chuan* B8.

accomplished, largely found in his commentary on the "Great Appendix" as well, will be our third concern.

Reading for Practical Guidance

HOW TO READ THE BOOK

Why can the *I Ching* serve as a guide? Su explains that it was created in an attempt to make *tao* accessible to men. The various parts of the text are actually ever more elaborate attempts to describe *tao* and set forth what it implies for human conduct. In the following passage words in quotation marks appear in the text Su is discussing.

> Now the great whole of *tao* never had a name. The *I* actually "began" this [process of giving names to *tao*]. [The sages] bestowed the "name" [*I*] upon [*tao*]. But they thought the name was inadequate so they chose the "things" [i.e., yin and yang] as metaphors for the idea of [the name]. Then they thought these "things" were inadequate [to express the idea] so they "directly said" it. Then they thought "saying" it was inadequate so they defined [what they had said] through "verbal elaborations." Then it was complete. A "name" is a summary statement of what one has to "say." "Verbal elaborations" are detailed accounts of what one has to "say." . . . Now a "name" draws on what everyone knows in order to represent that which they do not know.[18]

Although the various layers adopt different modes of expression, they all serve a common purpose. The problem that necessitated these layers, however, was that "the great whole of *tao*" (*tao chih ta-ch'üan*) is extremely difficult to represent. It is something men "do not know." But the sages had ideas that could be represented and used to guide men. The layers of the book thus are attempts to more adequately represent these ideas and what they implied for human conduct. The authors were motivated by the fear that with time the more summary-like layers would become incomprehensible.

> The sages chose these "four images" to create the *I*. At that moment its images existed but not its "verbal elaborations"; they only guided men with the ideas [expressed by the images]. . . . The sages thought later ages would be incapable of understanding [the ideas in the images]. Therefore they "appended verbal elaborations" to "inform" [later ages] and "determined good and ill outcomes" to "differentiate" [the appended elaborations]. The sages worried about society profoundly.[19]

---

[18] *Su Shih I-chuan* 8.179. *Hsi-tz'u-chuan* B5. I have glossed "things" as yin and yang following the previous lines of commentary.

[19] *Su Shih I-chuan* 8.171. *Hsi-tz'u-chuan* A11.

It follows from this that if men use the book as a guide they can act in accord with the sages' ideas about *tao*.

Su's commentaries on the hexagrams explain what the sages had in mind for human conduct. But he is explaining layers of text that are representations of ideas. How does he know that he has understood what the sages meant? In a passage discussing Confucius's contribution to the text Su explains that the "images" (*hsiang*) originally referred both to the eight trigrams (and the things in nature they symbolized), out of which the hexagrams were formed, and to the individual lines (and the symbolic things and affairs associated with the lines of a particular hexagram). He then notes:

> "Image (*hsiang*) means 'to image' (*hsiang*)." To image is to speak about a semblance (*ssu*). The real substance [of image] has that which cannot be said. Therefore its semblance is used to inform. The enlightened discern the true through the semblance. The unenlightened, seeing the semblance of the semblance, go farther off everyday.[20]

Su is enlightened. He understands what the authors intended to accomplish. He reads the parts from the vantage of the whole and later elaborations from the vantage of the original idea. He contrasts his style of interpretation with an inductive, literalist approach that attempts to establish the coherence of the text as a whole by building from the meanings of the individual sentences. In the following passage he is commenting on examples of line interpretation in the *Hsi-tz'u-chuan*.

> Those who interpret a Classic ought to grasp it through the intent. This is not in the meanings of the sentences. If one [stays] within the meanings of the sentences, then unintegrated, convoluted theories [will result] and he may instead harm the intent of the Classic. Confucius discussed the *I* like this; scholars might well seek his starting point.[21]

For Su the particulars of text must be understood from the vantage of the intent that generated them all. Those who try to determine what the parts of the text mean by finding ad hoc explanations that make the parts consistent will misconstrue the text.

Su brings this approach to bear on his interpretations of the hexagrams. He begins with the idea of the hexagram as a whole and then understands the meanings of the six lines. In the case of the Fu hexagram (Return), the particular configuration of yin and yang—that is, one yang line "returning" beneath five yin lines—is the idea around which the meanings of the six lines are distinguished. Su explains this interpretive stance as follows:

[20] *Su Shih I-chuan* 8.175. *Hsi-tz'u-chuan* B3.
[21] *Su Shih I-chuan* 7.163. *Hsi-tz'u-chuan* A7.

One cannot look at a hexagram in terms of the line differences. . . . If one grasps its particular configuration of yin and yang, then the meaning of the six lines will be coherently connected (*kuan*). In interpreting each of the sixty-four hexagrams, I first seek out the starting point of its particular configuration of yin and yang. When I have grasped the starting point, then, when the rest is explained separately, everything agrees. I would claim that without ever having bored holes [i.e., forced the text] I have thread it together (*t'ung*).[22]

Understanding the parts from an idea of the whole, or variation and difference from a sense of underlying unity, is integral to Su's style of reading. Elsewhere he explains this relationship by saying that "the hexagram speaks of the character/nature (*hsing*), the lines speak of the emotional responses (*ch'ing*)" that arise as the nature responds to particular circumstances.[23] Su's point is that to account for the particulars one must understand that which gives rise to them, just as emotional responses are diverse effects of the single nature or character of the person responding.

For Su, the unity or coherence of the particulars are rooted in something so abstract that it cannot be fully and exactly defined. Su claims to "discern" it, and he sees the particulars as diverse manifestations of some fundamental unity. Thus it is not necessary to force the particulars into consistency and agreement to arrive at a conclusion about what they mean. The particulars are merely specific manifestations or expressions of the source whence they arose; they are not exhaustive. Thus it is unnecessary to fit them together into a single integrated system at a formal level.

It is certainly the case that Su's commentary focuses on larger issues without belaboring the details. He has a sense of the general structures or larger ideas he wants to get across. In this he is drawing a lesson from his own commentary.

> Those good at acting on the world do not demand that it must be a certain way. Were they to demand this, they would lose everything. . . . With regard to the "correct," the superior man merely makes whole its greater matters. There is an approach to making whole its greater matters: do not impose "must be" on the minor and the greater matters will be whole.[24]

Su's approach to reading is, we might say, a particular manifestation of his general idea about acting. We shall see below that the guides to con-

[22] *Su Shih I-chuan* 7.156. *Hsi-tz'u-chuan* A3. "Particular configuration of yin and yang" translates *ch'i*, following Su Shih's gloss on that term.

[23] *Su Shih I-chuan* 1.4, "Ch'ien." Su's use of the terms *hsing* and *ch'ing* in this regard will be examined later.

[24] *Su Shih I-chuan* 3.60. "Wu-wang (Innocence)."

duct he finds in the hexagrams are similar to the values that inform his reading.

HOW TO ACT ACCORDING TO THE *I CHING*

Su's concern with the problem of unity and coherence in reading is also at the center of his interpretation of what the hexagrams teach men who, "not yet being enlightened," must rely on the book to "make few their errors" in life. Taken together his comments reveal a social vision. They explain the root of disorder in society, the wrong response to the problem, and the true solution. His starting point is simple. Disorder, *luan*, arises from competition or struggle, *cheng*.[25] Men compete out of self-interest. They want others to recognize them as worthy and unique, to gain rewards, and, thus, to increase their self-esteem.[26] They believe besting others to be the only way to gain social recognition. In this situation the losers only think of imitating the winners, instead of judging how they should act by a more constant standard.[27] Such men are "blinded by things." That is, they equate their self-worth with the social rewards of rank, wealth and reputation. They refuse to believe that "within themselves they certainly have that which is correct" and make no effort to "develop it."[28] In modern terms we might say such men lack moral independence and autonomy, have not yet acquired a sense of self, or lack an individuated identity.[29] In a world where competition for relative advantage divides men, how should a responsible man act? Merely refusing to be involved is not an acceptable response, for by doing so one allows the sprouts of disorder to flourish.[30]

Responsible men will try to make it unnecessary for individuals to increase their self-worth by self-destructively competing with others. They will try to show men that they can have real value by acting in ways that promote social cohesion. Su sees the hexagrams as depicting two different ways of achieving this. The false approach is closely akin to what Su criticizes in Wang An-shih and the New Policies. Here men try to establish unity by setting a standard and demanding that all individuals conform, or in terms Wang admired, by "making morality the same and customs one" (*t'ung tao-te i feng-su*).[31] Men who try to do this are the political

[25] *Su Shih I-chuan* 1.11, "Chun (Difficulty at the Beginning)," 1.17 "Sung (Conflict)," and 6.147, "Chi-chi (After Completion)."

[26] *Su Shih I-chuan* 1.19–21, "Shih (Army)."

[27] *Su Shih I-chuan* 1.17–19, "Sung (Conflict)."

[28] *Su Shih I-chuan* 1.13, "Meng (Youthful Folly)."

[29] This is a theme in much of Su's occasional writing during the 1070s. For a discussion of some representative pieces see Bol, "Culture and the Way in Eleventh-Century China," pp. 211–22.

[30] *Su Shih I-chuan* 2.43–46, "Ku (Decay)."

[31] *Lin-ch'uan chi* (Shanghai: Chung-hua, 1959), e.g., 75.794, "Yü Ting Yüan-chen shu." *Locus classicus: Li chi,* "Wang chih."

versions of Su's bad readers: rather than understanding diverse parts as deriving from a fundamental unity, they try to force the parts to agree or individuals to measure themselves against a single fixed standard. Some try to move men toward unity by demanding that they follow a single leader. But, Su argues, the effort to "assemble others behind oneself" leads to factionalism and further struggle. "Moreover, the world has never been brought together by one [man] alone."[32] Some would have all others agree with them, thus establishing a way in which all men can be the same. It is not that men cannot be made to appear the same, Su notes, but "Can making others the same without obtaining their sincere agreement be called 'making others the same'?" And if men are not in sincere agreement, they cannot be trusted to follow the leader's model when they are in danger.[33] Shared motivations do not follow from the appearance of agreement. Achieving unity by demanding uniformity is not possible. "The sage is able to be always correct (*sheng-jen neng pi cheng*); he is not able to force the world to always follow (*pu-neng shih t'ien-hsia pi ts'ung*)."[34] In Su Shih's understanding of the hexagrams, social cohesion requires enabling individuals to figure out what is good by themselves and to act on that knowledge for themselves. Su allows that there can be forms of commonality, but he does not think there can be universal agreement on what is right specifically or that all men can sincerely unite behind a single leader.

There is an alternative to establishing social harmony by imposing uniformity from outside and above. For Su the hexagrams teach men that "within themselves they certainly have that which is correct"; they also show men the need to develop it.[35] Rather than establishing himself as a leader of men by competing for merit, the superior man will try to establish things that provide security for others, so that they will be free to develop themselves.[36] Rather than forcing others to realize their inner correctness, the superior man will wait until others truly want to realize it and then help them give it expression.[37] The sage rewards men according to the contributions they make by themselves; he does not rely on extraordinary rewards nor encourage men to compete for extraordinary merit.[38] He does not demand agreement from others, nor does he reject those who disagree; he joins with those who truly share the same motivation.[39] He is not afraid of problems, rather he is always attending to

[32] *Su Shih I-chuan* 5.108, "Ts'ui (Gathering Together)."
[33] *Su Shih I-chuan* 2.33, "T'ung-jen (Fellowship with Men)."
[34] *Su Shih I-chuan* 3.59, "Wu-wang (Innocence)."
[35] *Su Shih I-chuan* 1.13, "Meng (Youthful Folly)."
[36] *Su Shih I-chuan* 1.11–13, "Chun (Difficulty at the Beginning)."
[37] *Su Shih I-chuan* 1.13–15, "Meng (Youthful Folly)."
[38] *Su Shih I-chuan* 1.19–21, "Shih (Army)."
[39] *Su Shih I-chuan* 2.33–35, "T'ung-jen (Fellowship with Men)."

matters that can become problems. He does not wait until there is a present danger.[40] He does not try to make everyone correct. Instead he tries to see that the general order of things is correct and puts up with minor opposition.[41] He influences people, but he is able to have a "spiritual exchange" with them because he can forget his own particular interests.[42] Rather than trying to assemble all behind one, he recognizes that there are many groups, and tries to be the one who can accommodate all of them.[43] He is involved in society. "What one values in the sage is not that he is passive and unengaged with things. One values that he always enters into the realm of good and ill outcomes with things yet does not become disordered."[44] His aim is to help things find their own true course, rather than to seek to impose a course upon them. He helps things be themselves.

> Once the age is in good order, it is as a great river flowing down in its channel. When it becomes disordered, it overflows in all directions and cannot be stopped. It is not that water enjoys being like this. Rather, there must be something that goes against its nature. When it has flooded without cease, that which is going against it must decline and its nature will necessarily recover. Water will choose for itself where it will be at peace and return there. Those in antiquity who were good at governing never competed with the people. Instead they allowed them to choose for themselves and thereupon guided them to it.[45]

The kind of social unity Su finds depicted in the hexagrams of the *I Ching* allows for diversity within unity and change within continuity. Men who learn from the book correctly will act harmoniously in a world of diversity and change. But it is apparent from Su's interpretations of the hexagrams that the kind of man who can take the lead in keeping the world on course by helping things be themselves goes beyond external guides. He has access to another source of value. He has access to *tao*.

Tao

Tao exists independently of the *I Ching*, and the enlightened can bring it into practice without relying on the book. How, then, does Su Shih conceive of *tao*? He explains his ideas by taking up a number of issues we usually associate with philosophical thinkers of his day, men such as Shao Yung, Chou Tun-i, Chang Tsai and the Ch'eng brothers. Like them, Su asks how men should understand the relation between *tao* and the actual

---

[40] *Su Shih I-chuan* 2.43–46, "Ku (Decay)."
[41] *Su Shih I-chuan* 3.59–62, "Wu-wang (Innocence)."
[42] *Su Shih I-chuan* 4.75–77, "Hsien (Influence)."
[43] *Su Shih I-chuan* 5.107–10, "Ts'ui (Gathering Together)."
[44] *Su Shih I-chuan* 5.124, "Ken (Keeping Still)."
[45] *Su Shih I-chuan* 6.138, "Huan (Dispersion)."

things and affairs of this world of change. For Su this relationship can be understood as a "one and many" problem. Su assumes that the "many," the manifest diversity of things in the world, are fundamentally "one." They have a single origin and are participants in a unifying pattern or process. Su also recognizes that whatever constitutes this more fundamental unity is of a more abstract conceptual order than the specific things and events men can perceive directly. To speak of that which gives unity to changing things he sometimes uses the term *li*, by which he usually means the pattern or principle inherent in the way something operates or comes to be as it is. He does not give this term the philosophical importance it later gains in Ch'eng-Chu philosophy, yet he uses it in a manner that comes close to Ch'eng I's usage, for he speaks of the *li* of all things being one and of the innumerable *li* of specific things and affairs. (We should probably understand this in terms of a hierarchy of ever more inclusive categories: a specific bamboo has its *li*, as does a variety of bamboo, as does bamboo in general, as do all plants, as do heaven-and-earth; thus the *li* of the most inclusive category or "thing" includes the *li* of all other things.) But in many instances Su does not use the term *li*. This does not keep him, however, from pointing to the existence of organizing ideas, relationships, patterns of development, and so on that account for the variety of particular instances. This level of understanding is absolutely essential for those who aim to cope with a changing world, but Su is not always clear about the nature of such understanding. In some instances he supposes that it is a form of intellectual knowledge, subject to explicit explanation and definition, but in other instances (particularly as he approaches more abstract and inclusive levels) he suggests that such ideas can be "apprehended" (*te*) intuitively but not "known" (*chih*) intellectually.

The idea that fundamentally all things are one is a matter of faith, as Su recognizes. One assumes there is that which unifies, but all we see is change and variation at the level of specific things. The assumption of unity is crucial, however, because it makes it possible to believe that the goal of a harmonious social world has a real basis. Su does not want to accept the view that partial interests are the only possible basis for a socio-political order or that the best literati can hope for is to balance as many interests as possible. There were at least two possible consequences of presuming this fundamental unity that Su Shih avoids. The first was believing, with Wang An-shih, that the real interest of every thing is its function as part of the whole and that the function of every thing can be defined relative to all other things, in order to determine roles for all. Second, it was also possible to go in the other direction and believe, like Ch'eng I, that literati should seek to know the fundamental unity and respond to things according to the pattern (*li*) they found. For Ch'eng, literati had to cultivate their ability to see the pattern of their minds, for the pattern of the mind was at once the pattern of heaven, and it defined man's role in the universe.

Su's vision of the connection between the one and the many, or between *tao* and things, justified neither effort. Envisioning the world of things as open-ended makes it impossible to postulate a whole defined by its parts and thus to fix the roles of things relative to it. Treating the fundamental unity as an inexhaustible and mysterious source of variation makes the pursuit of philosophical knowledge of *tao* pointless. The following passage contains these two essential features of Su's position.

> All the *li* under heaven have always been one, but the one cannot be held fast. When [men] know they have never not been one but no one holds it [i.e., the one] fast, that is close to it. This is why the sages . . . made it clear that the firm and soft [i.e., yin and yang] and variation and transformation (*pien hua*) originally came from one, but through interaction arrive at infinite *li* . . . Now as for coming forth from one but reaching the infinite, when men observe this they think there are infinite differences. But when sages observe this . . . wherever they go it is one.[46]

First, Su denies that the "one," as the origin and unifying aspect of change, can be defined. One "knows" the many *li* are one but does not try to define what the one is or reduce it to fixed principles that can be applied universally. Second, the process of change, once engendered, is constantly unfolding, and the world is becoming ever more diverse. Men cannot suppose that what has already happened constitutes a perfect whole. They must be able to see the diversity, without supposing that it is merely meaningless differentiation, and envision the unity, without trying to define it.

Following the *Hsi-tz'u-chuan*, Su uses the term *sheng sheng* to refer to the fact that things are constantly coming into being.[47] In general he also accepts the view that constant generation proceeds through the interaction of opposites, for which the interaction of yin and yang is paradigmatic. However, the fact that things are generated according to a regular process does not mean that the things and affairs that come about are predetermined.

> Now firm and soft [i.e., yin and yang] interact (*hsiang t'ui*) and variation and transformation come into being. When variation and transformation come into being, the *li* of good and ill outcomes is not fixed.[48]

The process through which things arise is open-ended and indeterminate. On the other hand, although all arises from unity, the original unity disappears as change takes place and things are engendered. Once "one"

---

[46] *Su Shih I-chuan* 7.156. *Hsi-tz'u-chuan* A2.
[47] *Su Shih I-chuan*, 7.161, 7.166.
[48] *Su Shih I-chuan* 7.156. *Hsi-tz'u-chuan* A2.

gives rise to "two," we can see the two, but the original one recedes from view. Here is how Su explains the statement "Being present in heaven it becomes image, being present in earth it becomes form; variation and transformation have appeared."

Heaven and earth are one thing. Yin and yang are one vital force. In this case it [the one vital force] becomes image; in the other case it becomes form. Where it is present is different. Therefore saying "being present" makes clear that it is one. Image is the essential florescence of form expressed above; form is the bodily substance of image left below. Men see its [expression] above and [leavings] below and right away think it to be dual. How could they know it was never not one? From this perspective what the age calls variation and transformation has always come forth from one, but it is dual wherever it is present. From duality on [there are variations and transformations] beyond calculation.[49]

Once the process of change has begun it must continue. Su sees this as inevitable. At the same time he is careful to insist that continual generation and diversification is not "caused" or "directed." This is evident in his interpretation of the cosmology of the *Hsi-tz'u-chuan*. That text refers to a Supreme Ultimate giving rise to two principles (taken by most to refer to yin and yang). These in turn generate four images, which in turn give rise to the eight trigrams. Su interprets this passage somewhat differently:

Supreme Ultimate is prior to the existence of things. Now if there is a thing, there must be above and below [i.e., the two principles]. When there is above and below, there necessarily will be the four directions [i.e., four images]. When the separation between the four directions is established, the eight trigrams are brought about. This is a necessary development; there is nothing causing it to be so.[50]

After the fact we see a logical development. It is necessary but we cannot say that it was planned. Su thus takes a stand against the idea, found in some ancient texts (and in the *I Ching*), that there is some ultimate cause or directing agent that guides things. If Su were to suppose this he might conclude that men needed only to know the plan or the director. He argues instead that things operate according to their own principles; they are "so-by-themselves."

The rising and falling of the ten-thousand things through the four seasons are all [matter of] their being so-by-themselves (*tzu-jan*). Nothing directs them. But [the text] speaks of the high god (*ti*) because there is something there more subtle than things. This is their *shen* (spirit), but it is spoken of as the high god.[51]

[49] *Su Shih I-chuan* 7.153. *Hsi-tz'u-chuan* A1.
[50] *Su Shih I-chuan* 7.170. *Hsi-tz'u-chuan* A11.
[51] *Su Shih I-chuan* 9.191. *Shuo kua* 4.

Su grants that there must be something there that keeps the thing changing in its own fashion, but by using the term *shen* to refer to it he suggests that it cannot be known and defined. The *shen* has the same status as anything else that constitutes fundamental unity: we sense its presence behind its various manifestations, but we do not know it directly.

To describe his vision of how the one and the many are related Su occasionally uses metaphors having to do with water.[52] Water is the best metaphor for *tao* and the "virtue of the sages," Su claims, because it "has no constant form."[53] Water is constant and one—it remains water—yet it is always varying as it flows through the changing landscape. We can only perceive it through its particular variations. It allows Su to envision how "What the times calls change and transformation always comes from the one."[54] But water is not merely a metaphor. "Water exists at the juncture of non-being and being, beginning the separation from non-being and entry into being."[55] Water is not *tao*, but it is closer than any other thing to *tao* and illustrates how manifest diversity can still be one. Similarly Su uses the image of a river arising from a single source as a way of thinking about *tao*. Modern man lives "downstream," separated from the "source" (i.e., *tao*) by ever-increasing change. "The variations (*pien*) of *tao* and *te* are like the daily downward rush of the Yangtze and Yellow River. . . . The sages thought that when one stands at its endpoint he will not be able to see its whole and fathom all their variations."[56]

As long as the source of the river is not exhausted, the water will keep flowing. Su is, of course, interested in what it means to act in accord with *tao* as the one source. He sees that it is up to man to make the connection between the source of change and the actual situations of his downstream world. The sages saw this as well. "They feared that everyone would proceed along downstream and not know to return to their source (*tsung*). Therefore they treated what men did not understand as the inexhaustible [source]. [But having taught men that there was a source] they feared everyone would chase after the inexhaustible without cease. Therefore they referred to flourishing virtue as the ultimate limit."[57] The sages wanted men to understand that there was a fundamental unity and to act accordingly. However, to identify this unity in a manner that could be totally inclusive they had to point to it as something that was unknowable and thus conceptually inexhaustible. Doing this encouraged attempts to

---

[52] For more on the role of water in Su's thinking see Andrew March, "Self and Landscape in Su Shih," *Journal of the American Oriental Society* 86 (1966), pp. 377–96.

[53] *Su Shih I-chuan* 7.159. *Hsi-tz'u-chuan* A4.

[54] *Su Shih I-chuan* 7.153. *Hsi-tz'u-chuan* A1.

[55] *Su Shih I-chuan* 7.159. *Hsi-tz'u-chuan* A4.

[56] *Su Shih I-chuan* 9.189. *Shuo kua* 1.

[57] *Su Shih I-chuan* 8.177. *Hsi-tz'u-chuan* B3.

know what could not be known. Men could thus get stuck pursuing something they could not attain. Therefore to get men to pay attention to their social roles the sages defined models of conduct as the goal.

Now Su shares this disinclination to "know *tao*," and he also believes that men should be concerned with practice, rather than philosophical knowledge. But he does not argue that bringing *tao* into practice can be equated with the particular historical models of sages past (the "flourishing virtue" of the quotation). He wants to be a sage himself, and he thinks others should want to as well. As Su's description of his own writing suggests ("my *wen* is like a ten-thousand gallon spring"), bringing *tao* into practice ought to be something like being the river oneself. Later we shall examine Su's account of how men can accomplish this in their own lives.

Su ties together the ideas we have been discussing in his explanation of a passage that equates yin-yang processes with *tao*. For Su this is impossible. He explains the passage with the aim of showing that the authors did not intend this, but he also recognizes that this is exactly what others have understood. This leads him to discuss the fundamental error of using things that come from the unitary source to define the source, and he offers Mencius's account of human nature as a particular example of this error. We see here how Su uses a philosophical problem to reject the philosophical project. His interpretation begins by regrouping the sentences of the *Hsi-tz'u-chuan* so that the passage begins with a reference to what is beyond definition and then introduces yin and yang. The passage in the *Hsi-tz'u* reads:

Thus spirit has no bounds and change (*i*) has no substance. One yin and one yang [i.e., yin and yang in alternation] are what is meant by *tao*. That which continues it is good. That which completes it is the nature (*hsing*).[58]

Su's comments begin:

What kind of thing are yin and yang in fact? Even those with the aural and visual acuity of [Li] Lou and [Shih] Kuang[59] have never yet apprehended their semblance. When yin and yang interact (*chiao*), thereupon they bring things into being (*sheng wu*). When things come into being, thereupon there are images. When the images are established, yin and yang are hidden. All that can be seen are things, not yin and yang. But can one say that yin and yang are without existence? The most stupid know this is not so. How could things bring themselves into being? This is why one who, pointing to bringing things into being,

[58] *Hsi-tz'u-chuan* A4.
[59] Li Lou could see tiny distant objects, once finding a treasured pearl the Yellow Emperor had lost. Shih Kuang was a Spring and Autumn period music master, famed for being able to foretell the fortunes of a state from its music.

calls it yin and yang, and one who, not seeing their semblance, says they have never existed are both confused.[60]

Things come into being out of the *interaction* (or "intercourse") of yin and yang. It follows from this, Su contends, that things thus created cannot be equated with yin and yang themselves. He then explains why the text says yin and yang are what is meant by *tao*.

> The sages knew *tao* was difficult to speak of. Therefore they borrowed yin and yang to speak of it, saying "one yin and one yang are what is meant by *tao*." One yin and one yang is a way of saying yin and yang have not yet interacted and things have not yet come into being. There is no metaphor for the approximation of *tao* more exact than this. As soon as yin and yang interact they bring things into being. At first they make water. Water is the juncture of being and non-being. It begins to separate from non-being and enter into being. Lao Tzu recognized this. His words were: "The highest good is like water" and also "Water is close to *tao*."[61] Although the virtue of the sages can be spoken of with names, it cannot be circumscribed by one thing, just as is the case with water's not having constant form. This is the best of the good; it is "close to *tao*" but it is not *tao*. Now when water has not yet come into being and yin and yang have not yet interacted and through the whole expanse there is not a single thing, yet we cannot say that there is nothing there—this truly is the approximation of *tao*.[62]

Just as Su supposes that something brings things into being (yin and yang), so does he suppose that there is something prior to yin and yang (*tao*). But what is ultimately prior, the state in which the process of creation is latent, can only be described approximately through negation. It cannot be known and defined. No thing is it. It is plausible that Su takes the phrases "spirit has no bounds and change no substance" to refer to it. Yet men can gain insight into it even if they cannot define it. Su now shifts the focus of his explanation to the problem of using ideas about *tao* to define certain values as universal.

> Yin and yang interact and bring things into being. *Tao* and things connect and bring the good into being. When things come into being yin and yang are hidden. When the good is established *tao* is not apparent. Therefore it says, "That which continues it is good." As for "That which completes it is [man's] nature"—the benevolent see *tao* and call it benevolence, the knowing see *tao* and call it knowledge.[63] Now benevolence and knowledge are what the sages called "good." The good is the continuation of *tao*, but one may not refer to it as *tao*.

[60] *Su Shih I-chuan* 7.159.
[61] *Tao-te-ching*, chapter 8.
[62] *Su Shih I-chuan* 7.159.
[63] Here Su is inserting the immediately following lines of the "Appendix": "The benevo-

Su's transition from heaven-and-earth processes to the realm of human values takes place in the phrase "*tao* and things connect and bring the good into being." Things without consciousness of the human sort maintain their connection to *tao* and act spontaneously. This is possible through their inherent "nature," *li*, or *shen*. What happens as a result is by definition good because it is true to the nature of a thing.

For man this is possible, but it does not happen automatically. At the end of this entry in the commentary Su explains that there is an intimate connection between man's nature and *tao*. Su explained, in an earlier passage, that the sages never intended to be benevolent or righteous. Rather, they had the mind for feeling commiseration and the mind for making distinctions, and when they acted on something "these minds were manifested in things."[64] This is how "*tao* and things connect" in the realm of human values, as man brings what he possesses naturally to bear in his responses to events. However, this does not mean that *tao* or human nature can be reduced to certain of its past manifestations.

Su now takes aim at Mencius and ethical philosophy in general.

> Now one may, if one knows the son but not the man [i.e., father], see the man through [the son]. But one may not think that it is the man himself. Therefore it says "What continues it is good." If in learning *tao* one begins from its continuations, then *tao* will not be whole. In the past Mencius took the good to be [man's] nature and thought he had fully gotten it. After I read the *Change* I knew he was wrong. In regard to human nature Mencius apparently only saw its continuations. Now the good is an effect of the nature. Mencius did not reach the point of seeing the nature. Rather, he saw the effect of the nature and then took what he had seen to be the nature. The good in regard to the nature is like fire being able to cook things. May I, because I have not yet seen fire, point to all the cooked things in the world and regard them as fire? Cooked things are an effect of fire.[65]

Su has not denied the existence of this nature nor the possibility of insight into it, but he has rejected efforts to define it in terms of the particular effects that result when it is brought into contact with things. His closing remarks relate nature to *tao*:

> Dare one ask about the distinction between the nature and *tao*? I respond: one may speak of their approximations. The approximation of *tao* is sound. The approximation of the nature is hearing. Is it that there is sound and thereupon hearing or hearing and thereupon sound? These two—are they actually one or

lent see it and call it benevolence, the wise see it and call it wisdom, and the common people employ it daily without knowing."
[64] *Su Shih I-chuan* 7.154. *Hsi-tz'u-chuan* A1.
[65] *Su Shih I-chuan* 7.159–60.

actually two? Confucius said, "Man can broaden *tao*, it is not that *tao* can broaden man."[66] He also said, "[To have] the spirit and illuminate it depends upon the man."[67] The nature is that by which he is a man. Were it not for this he would have nothing with which to be completing *tao*.[68]

Thus man possesses already the innate ability to realize *tao* through his own practice. As he does so he extends *tao* further. He keeps the river flowing through him; he does not try to dam it up.

Finally, we should note that Su explains the creation of the *I Ching* in terms of his conception of the relationship between *tao*, change, and things. The *I* is not *tao*, but it begins from *tao*; it is a depiction of the process of change that brings things into being. It is, in short, evidence that the sages conceived of *tao* as Su Shih does, or that Su Shih does as the sages did.

> To exist through interaction (*hsiang yin*) is called continual coming into being (*sheng sheng*). Were there not coming into being there would be neither gain nor loss, neither good nor ill outcomes. At this moment [before coming into being] "change" (*i*) exists in its midst and no man sees it. Therefore it is called *tao* and it is not called "change."
>
> There is coming into being and there are things. Things interact, generate each other, and the variations of good and ill outcomes and gain and loss are fully present. At this moment *tao* is operating (*hsing*) in their midst but men do not know it. Therefore it is called "change" and it is not called *tao*.
>
> When the sages created the *I*, had they not set out something (*pu yu suo she*) they would not have had anything [to give form to] interaction in the realm of things and affairs, thus to fully express the variations of gain and loss and good and ill outcomes. That is why they set up Ch'ien on the basis of that which was firmest in the world and posited K'un on the basis of that which was softest in the world. When Ch'ien and K'un interacted, the variations of gain and loss and good and ill outcomes began to arise in all their complexity.[69]

The *I Ching* thus uses dual process to play out the changes that arise once things have come into existence. It is, Su suggests, a useful tool for men who must cope with a world of diversity and uncertainty but are unable to maintain a connection to *tao* and participate in the process of change spontaneously. It is a work for a fallen age.

> Now *tao* is only one, but the creation of the *I* necessarily proceeded through duality. [When there is] duality, then there will be inner and outer. When there

[66] *Analects* 15:29.
[67] *Hsi-tz'u-chuan* A12.
[68] *Su Shih I-chuan* 7.160.
[69] *Su Shih I-chuan* 7.161. *Hsi-tz'u-chuan* A5.

is inner and outer, then there will be good and bad. When there is good and bad, then there will be gain and loss. Confucius took the *I* to be the idea of a declining age and restored it in middle antiquity because it proceeded through duality. The one was for his own practice. Duality was to aid the people.[70]

This leads us back to the distinction with which we began this account of Su's commentary. Once men become conscious that the *I*, as a book, is merely an example of making a connection between *tao* and human affairs by playing out a process of change, they can put aside the book and learn to do it for themselves. How can they accomplish this?

Bringing Tao into Practice

Men who aim to bring *tao* into practice aim to be sages themselves and, like Confucius, act from a basis in unity to do things upon which others can rely. Sages act through duality in two senses. They bring things into being through the dual process of change, bringing opposites into interaction in the manner of the *Book of Change*. They also establish things that, because they are separate from the original unity, create a state of duality in which the things created and *tao* are separate.[71] This is the great paradox. Men bring *tao* into practice by bringing new things into being as they respond to things. They say things and do things others can observe. The others appreciate and learn from what has been and take these things as the good and imitate them. But the choice to value and imitate these good things men had created meant a loss of appreciation for *tao* as the ultimate source of value. Thus, action that brings *tao* into practice has the effect of creating things that separate men from *tao* and keep them from ever seeking unity with *tao* for themselves. Originating from a state of unity with *tao*, the sages' actions have real value. But true sages realize that their actions are always specific to the occasion; others see them as normative statements. Those who are enlightened act flexibly and responsively and thus bring *tao* into practice. In a colophon Su once made a distinction between the enlightened men and those who see only fixed principles:

> The learning that fathoms mystery (*hsüan-hsüeh*) and the learning that investigates principles (*i-hsüeh*) are one. When there are enlightened men in an age, the learning that investigates principles is all a "mystery." When there are unenlightened men, the learning that fathoms mystery is all "principles."[72]

[70] *Su Shih I-chuan* 8.180. *Hsi-tz'u-chuan* B5.

[71] For examples of these two uses of "duality" (*liang* and similar terms) see *Su Shih I-chuan* 7.156, 7.161, 7.168, 7.170, 8.180.

[72] *Tung-p'o t'i-pa* 1.10, "Pa Ching-ch'i wai-chi."

Su is "enlightened." He sees principles as part of mystery.

One who acts as a sage, and who has freed himself from the need to be guided by fixed principles, functions spontaneously and without calculation.

> If the superior man, in relation to *tao*, reaches unity and is not dualistic, like a hand functioning of itself, then he does not know why it is so yet it is so.[73]

He acts directly—there are no conscious ideas or norms mediating his relation to either *tao* or the affairs to which he responds. As Su notes: "reach unity and there is no I."[74] This means, Su explains, that he has no "mind" (*hsin*) of his own, that is, he is not acting out of a particular and partial interest. "Whatever has a mind of its own cannot attain unity, even if it wants to. If it has not attained unity it will lack trustworthiness. What lacks trustworthiness is hard to know and follow."[75] The sage maintains this state. "He is different from other men only in not having a mind."[76]

The sage achieves his worldly function through unity with *tao*: he does not have to rely on set ideas about how things should be. Thus he allows things to realize their own inherent *li*.

> If he has no mind and is one, and if he is one and is trustworthy, then every thing [to which he responds] will fully realize its heavenly *li* in life and death. Therefore the living do not credit him and the dying do not blame him. If there is neither blame nor credit, how could the sage not fully occupy his position at the center [of things]? But as soon as I have a mind among them, then things [under my influence] will be opportunistic and deviant and will not realize their *li* . . . , and even if I want to occupy my position it will not be possible.[77]

Through his actions the sage ensures that all things will be themselves. Su believes that there is a fundamental unity, that all things participate in it, and that if things are given no alternative but to be truly themselves, everything will be as it ought to be.

But men are not instinctively sages. They have consciousness, they act according to ideas about what they think is right, they are confused by the world of change, and they are afraid of letting themselves be themselves.

> Heaven-and-earth is of one *li* with man, yet a man is rarely able to resemble heaven-and-earth because things are able to blind him. Variation and transfor-

---

[73] *Su Shih I-chuan* 1.4, "Ch'ien."
[74] *Su Shih I-chuan* 1.4.
[75] *Su Shih I-chuan* 7.154. *Hsi-tz'u-chuan* A1.
[76] *Su Shih I-chuan* 7.155. *Hsi-tz'u-chuan* A1.
[77] *Su Shih I-chuan* 7.155.

mation disturb him, good and ill fortune distract him, and what he cannot know confuses him. Now if nothing blinds him, a man will certainly resemble heaven-and-earth.[78]

What can men do to get back on track? They could, given this formulation, decide that being a sage required cutting themselves off from things, in order to apprehend their unity with heaven-and-earth. Su does not accept this. Instead he argues that consciousness is a necessary part of becoming a sage.

We can distinguish three stages in Su's description of this process through which men can bring *tao* into practice and act as sages: (1) the acquisition of knowledge and skill, (2) the intuitive leap into a state of unity, and (3) the spontaneous response to things. Expressed in terms of Su's river analogy, the first stage is movement upstream toward the source, proceeding through understanding the variations and transformations that have already taken place; the second is attaining unity with the source; and the third is returning downstream to respond to things in a manner whose uncalculated spontaneity accords with the process of change. These stages are immediately connected in practice. Su has the individual moving back and forth constantly between knowledge, unity, and practice. We would be in gross error, and contradicting Su's own practice, were we to argue that he is encouraging men to spontaneous practice without knowledge and an intuition of unity.

The first stage requires gaining knowledge. For, "not yet knowing it fully, not yet seeing it completely, this is why he errs."[79] The knowledge Su is most interested in concerns that which lies behind the apparent variations. This brings him closer to the fundamental unity.

> That by which he comes to be on a par with heaven-and-earth is through being able to know the causes of dark and light, the explanations for life and death, and the situations of the ghosts and spirits.[80]

With this kind of knowledge one can extend from known instances to unseen instances within the same category.

> If one must have seen something before he knows, then what the sage knows will be little. Therefore the learning of the sage is to extend from what he has seen to what he has not seen.[81]

Getting to the *li* of something involves knowing how the thing works, knowing how to do it, and knowing what the possible responses to it are.

---

[78] *Su Shih I-chuan* 7.158. *Hsi-tz'u-chuan* A4.
[79] *Su Shih I-chuan* 7.158.
[80] *Su Shih I-chuan* 7.157. *Hsi-tz'u-chuan* A3.
[81] *Su Shih I-chuan* 7.157. *Hsi-tz'u-chuan* A4.

In most cases Su simply assumes that part of acquiring knowledge is mastering or training oneself in the appropriate techniques. Occasionally he says explicitly:

> To "get to the essence of principles" is to "fathom *li*." . . . Water will serve as an analogy for this. Knowing how one floats and knowing how one sinks, and in every case knowing the means to respond, is "getting to the essence of principles."[82]

But gaining knowledge of how something works and learning the techniques for responding to it are not the same as achieving unity with the source. For Su there is always something more that cannot be intellectualized. One must leap from intellectual knowledge into a state of unity with that which keeps the thing alive and changing. Attaining unity with *tao* is a term for this holistic intuition. Su also uses *shen* to refer to the mysterious factor at the heart of the matter.

> What *shen* does cannot be known. Contemplate variation and transformation and know it. The most essential and most changing of all things, and that by which the sage "fathoms the profound [i.e., *li*]" and "examines the seed [i.e., practice]," are brought to a conclusion with *shen* every time. Thus one knows that *shen* is everywhere present in the midst of variation and transformation. It is possible to know *shen* thereby, but it is not possible to point [to something] as *shen*.[83]

The aim of the intuitive apprehension is not to increase intellectual knowledge, but to be able to practice what he knows. The final stage is a return "downstream," as he responds to the changing world through action. His intuition of unity does not tell him what to do. Instead it allows him to act spontaneously, without self-consciousness, so that he and things each proceed further along their natural course.

> If one uses *shen* to bring knowledge into practice, the mind will not be sullied by things and affairs, and he will cause things to manage themselves without himself being involved.[84]

As a practical example of moving through these three stages Su uses swimming. In the following he is explicating a much discussed passage in the *Hsi-tz'u-chuan* that speaks of "getting to the essence of principles" and "entering *shen*." Su correlates this with a line from the "Explanations of Hexagrams" commentary: "Fathom *li* and realize *hsing* (the nature) in order to arrive at *ming* (destiny)."

[82] *Su Shih I-chuan* 8.177. *Hsi-tz'u-chuan* B3.
[83] *Su Shih I-chuan* 7.166. "Profound" and "seed" are glossed as "pattern" and "practice" by Su; see 7.167.
[84] *Su Shih I-chuan* 7.168. *Hsi-tz'u-chuan* A10.

To get the essence of principles is to fathom *li*. Entering *shen* is to realize *hsing* and arrive at *ming*. Fathom *li* and realize *hsing* to arrive at *ming*—but not only this. One [should] plan to "achieve practice." Water will serve as an analogy for this. Knowing how one floats and knowing how one sinks, and exhausting all the variations of water and in every case having the means to respond [to its variations] is getting to the essence of principles. Knowing floating and sinking and being one with [water], without [consciously] knowing it to be water, is entering *shen*. He who is one with it without [consciously] knowing it to be water will always be good at swimming, and how much more so when managing a boat! This is what is meant by achieving practice. When a good swimmer manages a boat, his mind is relaxed and his body is comfortable. What is the reason for this? His practice is beneficial and his person secure. When I have reached the point that my person is secure in a matter, then no thing will take my measure [i.e., control me] and virtue will accumulate.[85]

Swimming is a practical example of how men can act in accord with *tao* and stay afloat in the world of change. One must know about water and he must know how to swim, but whether he will be able to practice what he knows spontaneously in response to the variations he meets depends upon his ability to achieve a state of unity, where he is no longer conscious of any separation between self and water. He aims to stay afloat without having to force water to suit his personal interests against its own nature. When he "enters *shen*" he is arriving at the fundamental unity. He and water are part of the same universe by virtue of the unity of *li*, the existence of *hsing*, the activity of *shen*, and the presence of *tao*. Su, nevertheless, is not interested in explaining "how this is so;" it is sufficient to "know that it is so."

Up to this point we have pursued Su's account of how men can bring *tao* into practice in terms of the relationship between "self" (*wo*) and "things" (*wu*). We have noted that, for Su, moral action does not require calculating to satisfy fixed standards about how things ought to be. Some might argue that this approach can only serve to keep the world on course if the actor has cultivated a pure nature and transformed himself according to the sages' models. Su takes up the problem of inherent nature (*hsing*), emotional response (*ch'ing*) and destiny or decree (*ming*) in response to such ideas. He argues that men should transcend ideas about what they ought to be (i.e., what universal qualities are endowed in them as men) and simply let themselves be themselves. If they can achieve unity with their own nature, and stop trying to act according to what they think they ought to have in their nature, they will be on the right track. The nature with which the individual is endowed is connected to *tao*. But while all men have a nature, it is not the same for every man. Men are of

[85] *Su Shih I-chuan* 8.177. *Shuo kua* 1.

different sorts; they can try to train themselves to do what is thought good or bad, but they cannot remove that unique source of personality they possess as individuals. Nor can they define it. Instead, they should cultivate the ability to let their nature function spontaneously as they respond to things. Achieving this is the true meaning of *ming*.

Su debates these matters at the beginning of his commentary. He starts by noting that men are kept from truly discerning their *hsing* by their ideas about it.

> There are many discussing *hsing* and *ming* today. On this account I beg to try to speak about their general aspect. Men who spoke of *hsing* in antiquity did so in the manner of telling a blind man about something he had not discerned (*shih*). The blind man has never had sight. You wish to tell him about this thing but fear he will not discern it, so you use yet another thing to describe it. Now when you describe it with another thing, there is the other thing, it is not this thing. It is only because he has no sight that you have told him about the other thing, yet if he does not discern can you go on to befuddle him with more things?
>
> Superior men in the past worried that *hsing* was difficult to see. Therefore they used what could be seen to speak of *hsing*. Now to use what can be seen to speak of *hsing* is always [to be speaking of] the semblance of *hsing*.[86]

Rather than defining it as some thing, men should think of *hsing* as something that cannot be added to or reduced through calculated effort.

> The superior man cultivates his goodness every day to reduce his not-goodness. When the not-good dissipates day by day, something that cannot be gotten rid of is still there. The lesser man cultivates his not-goodness every day to reduce his goodness. When the good dissipates day by day, something that cannot be gotten rid of is still there. As for that which cannot be gotten rid of, [the sages] Yao and Shun could not add to it and [the evil] Chieh and Chou could not subtract from it. Must this not be *hsing*?

No matter how the person has chosen to act—it is a given for Su that in retrospect we can distinguish the obviously good and bad—each man has something that remains unaffected. *Hsing* exists in each man. We have already seen that Su denies that it can be called "good," but he does suppose that if men truly connect to it, whatever happens will be appropriate. The moral imperative, then, is that men make a connection to their *hsing* so that they can truly be themselves.

> On arriving at this [irreducible something that must be *hsing*], if the superior man employs this to practice *tao* then he will not be far from the sage. However, if there is the arriving at this and there is the employing of this, then his practice of *tao* will always be dualistic. Like a tool being employed by the hand, this is

[86] *Su Shih I-chuan* 1.3, "Ch'ien."

not as good as the hand functioning by itself. [In the latter case] no one knows why it is so, yet it is so.

Su has now made his basic distinction between those who rely on an intellectual understanding of the "one" to guide their action and those who act spontaneously and uncalculatedly from unity with the thing, or *tao*, or *hsing*. He goes on to explain that *ming* is actually a term for putting an end to this dualistic state by reaching *hsing* and letting it function of itself.

> When *hsing* reaches this [point of functioning of itself] it is called *ming*. *Ming* means "command." The ruler's command is called *ming* (decree). Heaven's command is called *ming* (destiny, fate). The coming [into practice] of *hsing* is also called *ming*. The coming [into practice] of *hsing* is not a decree or destiny. Lacking something with which to name it, we temporarily locate it [in the category of] *ming*. Death and life, ill and good fortune are all *ming*. Even if they had a sage's knowledge, none would know that by which they are so, yet they are so. When the superior man in relation to *tao* arrives at unity and is not dualistic, just as the hand functions by itself, neither does he know why it is so, yet it is so. This is why we temporarily locate it [in the category of] *ming*.

In contrast to those who understand *ming* as those moral qualities endowed in all men by heaven (which it is man's true "destiny" to realize), Su argues that *ming* is merely a term of convenience, used to refer to the spontaneous functioning of *hsing*. It follows, Su concludes, that there is no real difference between *hsing* and *ming*. In particular, Su denies that a distinction should be drawn between the heavenly and the human in man. Similarly, in contrast to those who saw human emotional responses (*ch'ing*) as a threat to realizing the nature and the root of evil in the world, Su argues that there is no real distinction between the *hsing* and *ch'ing*.

> *Ch'ing* are the movements of *hsing*. Go back upstream and arrive at *ming*. Go on downstream and arrive at *ch'ing*. There is nothing that is not *hsing*. Between *hsing* and *ch'ing* there is not a distinction between good and bad. When [*hsing*] is dispersed and does something then it is called *ch'ing*. Between *ming* and *hsing* there is not a discrimination between the heavenly and the human. When one arrives at its unity and there is no self, then it is called *ming*.[87]

The *hsing* is the nature of *tao* in the individual. To act in accord with *tao* he must achieve unity with his own nature and let it come into practice. He cannot define it as something, but he can let it unfold through its functioning as actual emotional responses to things. The visible expression of the nature is always specific: a particular reaction to a particular situation in the world of change. He sees aspects of his given nature, we might say,

[87] *Su Shih I-chuan* 1.3–4, "Ch'ien." The passage concludes by discussing the relationship between the hexagram and the six lines as the equivalent of that between *hsing* and *ch'ing*.

by seeing how he himself responds to things. But as long as he is convinced he is responding spontaneously, from a sense of unity with himself, he can be sure he is acting in concert with *tao*, to which he is connected by his *hsing*. By being himself, understanding things, and uniting the two, he is bringing *tao* into practice.

All men have *hsing* and can "hear" *tao*, but they act individually in specific situations. And, as Su's insistence on the importance of knowledge makes clear, what they are able to accomplish will be limited by what they know and the things they meet. From the perspective of fundamental unity, the character of each man is a unique thing that ought to be allowed to unfold by itself. It can do this only through functioning in actual circumstances. From the perspective of the individual, the *hsing* gives him unity and identity. Men can "hear" *tao* only through their own individual filters of acquired knowledge and given character. In effect, men "broaden *tao*" by realizing their differences in practice. A pluralistic world, where men act according to a universal process in various manners in response to things, is the only way men can keep *tao* flowing.

In a long passage at the end of his commentary Su goes back and ties together the various strands we have been discussing: the creation of the *Book of Change*, its value as a guide to conduct, the nature of *tao*, and the process of bringing *tao* into practice.

What are going with (*shun*) and going against (*ni*)? The variations of *tao* and *te* are as the daily downwards rush of the Yellow River and the Yangtze. Follow the [transformations] downstream to the "coming into being of the yarrow stalk," the "creation of numbers," the "establishment of the hexagrams," and the "coming into being of the individual lines," and then the actual circumstances (*ch'ing*) of all things are fully available.

The sages thought that if one were to stand at its end point he would not be able to discern its whole and exhaust its variations. Therefore they traced back upstream to go back to follow from its origin (*ch'u*).

Tao is what they bring into practice. *Te* is that which is completed by their practice. *Li* is that by which *tao* and *te* are so. *I* (principles) are the explanations of that by which they are so. If a superior man wishes to practice *tao* and *te*, but does not know the explanation of that by which they are so, then he does so as a slave to their names. If he is a slave to their names and is not secure with their real substance, then the big and the small and the first and the last will interfere with each other, and *tao* and *te* will not be in harmonious accord. Take, for example, a wooden doll automated by a spring: its hand rises and its foot goes out, its mouth moves and its nose follows. How unlike a man's own use of his body, where what moves, moves of itself, and what stops, stops of itself. It does not have to be adjusted or regulated before it works harmoniously and suitably. This is why the superior man esteems *hsing* and *ming*.

If he wishes to reach *hsing* and *ming* he must trace back up from that by which they are so. Now that by which [it is so that] he eats and drinks are hunger and thirst. These hardly enter from outside. Eating and drinking are things man does not depend on learning to be able to do. The "that by which they are so" is clear. Now if he examines it carefully, will there not be something that is never hungry or thirsty remaining there whence hunger and thirst came? At this point *hsing* can be seen. There is *hsing*. There is what is seen. He who is able to unify these two will then have arrived at *ming*. This is what is meant by "going against" [i.e., tracing back to the source].

Once the sages apprehended the *li* of *hsing* and *ming*, then, "going with," they went downstream in accord with it to fully realize all its variations. They followed one thing and doubled it [i.e., gave it a complementing opposite] to open the gate of continual generation. This is what is called "proceeding through the two to aid the practice of the folk."[88] Therefore they "combined the three fundamental forces" [i.e., ways of heaven, earth, and man] and established the "six places" [or six lines of the hexagram] to move in the midst of the "eight trigrams." "Heaven and earth, mountain and lake, thunder and wind, water and fire" [i.e., the things the eight trigrams image] variously intermingled with each other. Once they had fully realized the variations of these eight things, the actual circumstances of deviance and correctness, the auspicious and the ominous, regret and remorse, anxiety and concern, advance and retreat, and success and failure [that could be related to these configurations] could not be exhausted [i.e., the basic structures accommodated an infinite variety of possibilities]. This is what is meant by "going with."

Cut bamboo to make a flute. Hollow it out and blow into it. Even [the great musician] Shih K'uang was unable to fully realize the variations of harmony and descant, the measures of tone and rhythm. Now go back and seek it [i.e., the origin]. There are only five notes and twelve tones. At the origin of the five notes and twelve tones there is only whistling. At the origin of the whistling there is only silence. Did not those who made music in antiquity necessarily stand in the midst of silence?

Thus speaking [from the vantage of] *hsing* and *ming*, going with is going away from while going against is coming towards. Therefore [the text] says, "He who counts what is going away is going with, he who knows to come towards is going against." The sixty-four hexagrams and 384 lines are [the result of] having gone back to seek its source from a position at its end. "Therefore the *I* counts going against" [i.e., backwards].[89]

Playing the flute illustrates what it means to bring *tao* into practice; it is also an actual example of accomplishing this in practice. With this one instrument innumerable variations are possible. These variations have in

[88] *Hsi-tz'u-chuan* B6.
[89] *Su Shih I-chuan* 9.189–90. *Shuo kua* 1–2.

common the notes and tones, just as the *I Ching* has its trigrams, and *tao* its *li*. But to keep producing music—to keep music alive—men must keep producing new variations, and in doing so they are broadening music as they continue it. To accomplish this, however, they must work back to attain the common origin of variation and thence return to practice, just as the superior man seeks to reach that point in his own nature that is beyond desire, and the sages, reaching unity, created the *I Ching*. They must learn how to play the flute and they must understand the constancies of music, but to play spontaneously and bring new variations into being they must begin from an intuition of the origin.

What holds for music holds for culture generally and for prose, poetry, calligraphy and painting in particular. Cultural pursuits serve well to confirm Su's views. For in reading Su's commentary we may sometimes wonder whether he really can believe that the world will be better off when men act without aiming to satisfy fixed norms. In Su's ideal world, where men act spontaneously in response to changing circumstance and do not try to force uniformity on the actions of others, it is impossible to say what will take place. Yet Su is sure that what does take place will be appropriate. In literature and art this may well be so. These areas remain vital only if there is continual production and variation. Yet, when Su looks back at what he has done and others have done, cultural activities can appear to form a single continuous flow from past to present, and he may conclude that his task is to maintain the flow.

ENGAGING IN *WEN* AND BRINGING *TAO* INTO PRACTICE

In the *Book of Change* Su saw the sages playing out the process of change—from its origin in unity through duality to manifest diversity—to create the essential configurations of events (the hexagrams), to which men might refer to understand their own situation and calculate their response. But Su went beyond this to see the *I* as the Classic of classics, we might say, because it came closer than any other work to providing a paradigmatic model for the universal process of bringing *tao* into practice. His commentary on the *Documents* indicates that he saw the latter work as depicting the institutions that were brought into being as the ancients realized this universal process in response to changing historical circumstances. Su uses the *Documents* to argue that the socio-political order of antiquity was brought into being in the same manner as the *Book of Change*. This implies, we may note, that while it is socially useful to rely on traditional institutions, the truly enlightened will see that it is not necessary to stick to past models—just as they can transcend the *I* as a book.

Su's writings illustrate the breadth of his interests and his openness to the cultural tradition in all its diversity. At some level, everything man has done is an extension of *tao* and holds some interest. We do not find Su fixing a curriculum or defining an intellectual orthodoxy. However, this does not mean everything is equal. Su distinguishes those who are enlightened, and those who understand the process of responding to things, from the unenlightened, who seek uniformity of results and merely imitate past achievements. As he explains with reference to Wang An-shih, true unity lies in the ability to bring things into being. It should not be equated with uniformity in what is brought into being. Men who demand that all others be the same or adhere to fixed standards keep others from bringing *tao* into practice. They mistake the effects for the cause and universalize what was originally intended to be a specific response to a particular moment.

How does this bear on "engaging in *wen*" (*wei wen*) as a literati pursuit? The simple answer, as it emerges from Su's various comments on prose, poetry, calligraphy, and painting, is that *wei wen* is one way the individual can train himself to be constantly realizing universal process as he responds to things. These kinds of writing and painting as well are particularly appropriate for one who believes that *tao* can best be brought into practice by responding specifically to particular events in a world of change, for traditionally they were understood to be personal works for specific occasions. However, when we ask how this is possible and why literati should value these pursuits, the answer becomes more complicated.

The complexity arises from Su's desire to understand *wen* in two ways at the same time. In his first view he can see these four arts as media employed by the individual to express in fixed form his personal response to particular occasions. When Su takes this attitude, he tends to stress the content of a work, that is, what it reveals about the things or affairs to which the author is responding. For Su, we should recall, being able to respond requires truly understanding the thing one is confronting. He assumes that a written response tells us whether the author has truly apprehended the *li* or the "idea" (*i*) of something, for example. Because true understanding is also a sign of the author's ability to engage in the universal process—and revealing those ideas to others is a case of bringing something into being—it follows that the work also tells us something about the degree to which the author has cultivated this ability. If this view were taken absolutely, however, it could follow that the only reason to engage in *wen* would be to manifest one's ideas about things. The various genres of prose, poetry, calligraphy, and painting would not be necessary to accomplish the purpose. Saying what you mean directly would be adequate. Su does not reach this conclusion.

Su notes, of course, that getting profound ideas across is even harder than arriving at them in the first place. They are not things that can be simply stated. But ultimately he avoids the utilitarian conclusion that the arts are of value in communication because he has a second view of *wen*. Su insists that these media are "things" in themselves. They have real historical existence and they have their *li*. Prose, poetry, calligraphy, and painting are things in the same sense that bamboo, tea, and water are things. There is, however, a difference. Natural objects develop and change according to their own *li*, while these cultural traditions develop and vary over time only through human activity. To respond to affairs, Su argues, men must know the techniques of responding. The swimmer must know how to swim; the writer must know how to write. The point of uniting with water is that it allows one to use his techniques to respond spontaneously to change. If one chooses to respond through *wen*, he must have mastered the techniques of expressing what he has in mind; he can then employ them spontaneously to change. It follows, Su notes, that one who engages in universal process through *wen* will, without aiming to do so, bring works into being that extend the category in which he is composing through variation. This too tells Su about the man. Taking a historical perspective and seeing the work in terms of form, that is, in relation to the category of poetry or calligraphy, for example, Su can value the work as continuing the process of bringing things into being.

The history of culture as a history of cumulative change, in which later generations draw upon the works of past men and establish new variations, while (ideally) grounding themselves in the origins of tradition, may provide a more persuasive illustration of Su's vision of universal process than the workings of heaven-and-earth. In any case it is evident that Su conceives of prose, poetry, calligraphy, and painting as "things" and can evaluate an individual's works in these terms. It should be clear, however, that the process of responding to things is the origin of value for Su. Men should not calculate their actions according to ideas about desirable effects; they should act in accord with *li*. By the same token, writers should not write with the aim of innovation; they should write according to the *li* inherent in writing. Good effects follow from true action, and innovation results from true writing. After the fact the effects can be appreciated, but their goodness results from embodying process, not from calculation.

Su's ability to see all these levels at once—the unfolding of a category of *wen*, the ability to capture the idea of a thing in expression, and the revelation of individual character—is evident in the following colophon for a painting by the much admired T'ang painter Wu Tao-tzu:

> Those who know, create things. Those who are able, transmit them.[90] They were not completed by one man alone.

---

[90] This contrasts with Confucius's assertion in *Analects* 7:1 that "I transmit but do not innovate." Lau, trans., p. 87.

Regarding superior men in relation to learning and craftsmen in relation to crafts: having begun in the Three Eras and having passed through Han, when they reached T'ang [the things created through learning and transmitted through craft] were fully available (pei). Hence when poetry reached Tu [Fu] Tzu-mei, prose reached Han [Yü] T'ui-chih, calligraphy reached Yen [Chen-ch'ing] Lu-kung, and painting reached Wu [Tao-hsuan] Tao-tzu, then the variations of past and present and all possible affairs were fully available.

Wu Tao-tzu painted human figures as if catching a shadow with a lamp. He accepted what came and allowed what went as it suddenly appeared or went off the side; horizontal, slanting, level, and straight—all were reinforcing each other. He grasped the number of what was so-by-itself and was not off by a hair-tip. He put forth new ideas in the midst of rule and measure; he lodged subtle li outside of daring carelessness. In past and present there has been only one man of whom it can be said, "A traveling blade with room to spare, a swinging axe which makes the wind."[91] With other paintings I am sometimes unable to determine authorship, but when it comes to Tao-tzu, I know whether they are authentic or not at a glance.[92]

These traditions proceeded through cumulative change, becoming ever more elaborated and developed. The T'ang masters, Su comments elsewhere, synthesized the various achievements of the past while bringing the variations in calligraphy and poetry to the ultimate.[93]

In the case of Wu Tao-tzu, Su gives particular attention to the spontaneity with which he responded to things through painting. In the following account of "flying white" style calligraphy by Ts'ai Hsiang (T. Chün-mo) Su argues that bringing new variations into being requires first mastering the variations of the category "calligraphy" and arriving at their fundamental unity.

A thing [i.e., category] is of one li. If you have comprehended its idea, then you can do any part of it. Doctoring by specialty is the downfall of medicine. Painting by subject is the vulgarization of painting. The doctoring of [the great doctors of the past] Ho and Huan did not distinguish between young and old. The paintings of Ts'ao [Pa?][94] and Wu [Tao-tzu] did not select just men or just

[91] Chuang Tzu, The Complete Writings, trans. Burton Watson (New York: Columbia University Press, 1969), p. 269.

[92] T'i-pa 5.95, "Shu Wu Tao-tzu hua hou." Dated 1085.

[93] Su Shih, Ching-chin Tung-p'o wen-chi shih-lüeh (Peking: Wen-hsüeh ku-chi, 1957), 60.999, "Shu Huang Tzu-ssu shih-chi hou." Su notes that as a result men tended to regard the T'ang masters as the "source," and failed to see the need to go back and draw upon earlier achievements as well.

[94] Ts'ao Pa (fl. mid-eighth century) was famous for both his paintings of imperial horses and imperial ministers. See William Acker, Some T'ang and Pre-T'ang Texts on Chinese Painting (Leiden: E. J. Brill, 1954), vol. 2, p. 296. I thank Susan Bush for pointing out this

things [to paint]. It is acceptable to say that [the best painters and doctors] were strong in doing certain things, but it is unacceptable to say that they were able to do this but not able to do that. Those who do seal script today do not do clerk and running style as well, nor do they get to cursive style. It must be that they are not yet able to comprehend their idea. With the likes of Chün-mo [however] formal, running, cursive, and clerk styles are like the idea [also: are as he intends]. His remaining strength and extra intent are transformed into the "flying white" style. It can be cherished, but it cannot be learned. If he had not comprehended the idea, could it have been thus?[95]

Ts'ai produced unique works because he had mastered the various aspects of calligraphy as a thing and apprehended the fundamental unity of the thing. Note that Su describes the unique achievement as a transformation of something Ts'ai had within that he wanted to express. It happened to come out this way, and could come out this way because of Ts'ai's training and understanding, but it was not intended.

From the perspective of the larger task of learning to bring *tao* into practice, cultural pursuits are themselves of minor significance. Yet, precisely because they are "things" that can be used for this purpose, they have value to the individual. This attitude is brought out in Su's account of a monk who mastered the zither at age seven, calligraphy at eleven, poetry at fifteen (the unique phrasing of which brings paintings to mind), and then turned to studying the dharma. Now, Su points out, from the perspective of one who has attained *tao*:

> The sea of dharma of the Flower Garland is a "grass hut"—how much more so poetry, calligraphy and the zither. However, among those who learned *tao* in antiquity none entered from emptiness. Wheelwright Pien chiseled wheels and the hunchback caught cicadas [and, having done this all their lives, were regarded as being men of *tao*].[96] As long as they can develop their cleverness and skill with it, nothing is too humble. If [Monk] Tsung apprehends *tao*, then his lute-playing and calligraphy will both gain in strength, and his poetry even more. If Tsung is able to be like one mirror containing ten-thousand, then his calligraphy and poetry ought to be even more unique. I shall peruse them, taking them as an indicator of the degree to which Tsung has apprehended *tao*.[97]

Cultural pursuits are useful as means of "apprehending *tao*." Moreover, because engaging in them involves producing works that can be perceived directly, they provide others with a means of "apprehending how he is as

---

possibility. Other possibilities include Ts'ao Chung-ta of Northern Ch'i and Ts'ao Pu-hsing of Three Kingdoms Wu.

[95] *T'i-pa* 4.78, "Pa Chün-mo fei-pai."

[96] *Chuang Tzu, The Complete Writings*, pp. 152–53, 162, 199–200.

[97] *Ching-chin Tung-p'o wen-chi shih-lüeh* 56.913–15, "Sung Ch'ien-t'ang Tsung-shih Wen-fu shu."

a man" (te ch'i wei-jen), as Su sometimes puts it, and knowing the degree to which he has apprehended *tao*. But, again, the uniqueness of the work is an effect of the process, not the goal.

When Su does address the issue of appropriate goals for the individual who chooses to respond to things through writing, he speaks of the need to express one's understanding of the thing at hand. This is a simple formulation of that idea:

Confucius said, "Verbal elaborations simply get the point across" (tz'u ta erh i). Things certainly have this *li*. Not knowing it is the problem. If one knows it, the problem is not being able to get it across in speaking and writing. Verbal elaborations are simply what get this across. . . . Now I have looked over the ten essays you sent, beginning with Eastern Han. In all of them you consider the past in order to steer the present; you are interested in real practices for aiding the age; this is exactly what I have expected during my life from my friends and all superior men who learn *tao*.[98]

We see here two other points that bear on the value of writing. First, responding to affairs through writing is useful. It makes it possible for others to understand things that they have difficulty understanding. Second, in writing one can respond to an affair in the present by introducing one's understanding of other things in the past—the *li* is the same, though clarifying it is hard.

When the author has mastered the media of expression and truly understood his subject, he can express what he has in mind fluently. In the following letter, written at the end of his life, Su notes both the spontaneity of the *wen* and the ideas the author is getting across. He uses this occasion to argue that whether something deserves to be called *wen* depends on whether what the author has in mind is made clear, rather than on the "literary" quality of his expression.

I have thoroughly perused your letter and the poems, rhapsodies, and miscellaneous prose you sent. On the whole they are like moving clouds and flowing water. At the beginning there is no fixed substance, but they always go where they ought to go and stop where they ought to stop. The *wen* and *li* are so-by-themselves; the unrestrained attitudes come freely into being. Confucius said, "If it is said without *wen*, it will not go far."[99] He also said, "Verbal elaborations simply get the point across." When verbal elaborations stop at getting the intent across, they are suspected of not being *wen*, but this is not so at all. I doubt you will find one in a million who seeks out the subtlety of a thing—like

---

[98] *Ching-chin Tung-p'o wen-chi shih-lüeh* 47.797, "Ta Yü Kua shu"; citing *Analects* 15:41. In the *Analects, tz'u* is usually taken to mean words or language. I have rendered the term according to Su's usage. This letter is said to date from the Yüan-yu period.

[99] *Tso chuan* (Harvard-Yenching Institute Concordance ed.), p. 307, Hsiang 25/*fu* 2.

tying the wind or catching a shadow—and is able to make this thing be complete in the mind. How much less often is one able to make it be complete in speech and writing? This is what is meant by verbal elaborations getting the point across. When verbal elaborations reach the stage of being able to get the point across, then the *wen* cannot be exhausted.

Yang Hsiung liked to make his verbal elaborations difficult and deep in order to give an attractive appearance (*wen*) to his shallow and simple ideas. If he had said them straight out, then everyone would have known [they were shallow]. This is precisely what is meant by "insect carving." His *Supreme Mystery* [a book modeled on the *Change*] and *Exemplary Sayings* [in imitation of the *Analects*] are both of this ilk. Why did he only regret his rhapsodies? He carved insects all his life and, having only varied the melody, then called them Classics. Is this permissible? Ch'ü Yüan composed the "Li Sao." This further variation of the Feng and Ya [of the *Odes*] "can rival the sun and moon in brilliance."[100] May it be called "insect carving" because it resembles a rhapsody? If Chia I had gone to visit Confucius he would indeed have been welcomed, yet [Yang] disparages [his writing] as rhapsodies and treats [Ssu-ma] Hsiang-ju in the same class. Hsiung's ignorance was such in case after case. One can talk about it with those who know, though it is difficult to speak of it with the vulgar. I mention this since we have been discussing *wen*.

Ou-yang Hsiu spoke of *wen-chang* as being like pure gold and beautiful jade. The market has a fixed price. They (*wen-chang*) are not things that men can fix the value of with their talk.[101]

It is clear here that when Su speaks of "getting the point across" he is speaking of the more profound matter of attaining and expressing a holistic understanding of something. If a piece can accomplish this, it has real value, irrespective of the genre in which it is written. The value of a piece is not, ultimately, to be determined by social expectations about how it ought to be written or what kind of writing is serious.

Su is willing to extend this attitude to the subject as well, arguing that the quality of understanding has greater significance than the thing itself. He explains why this is so in his comment on Huang Ju's *Essential Record of Grading Tea*.

Things have divisions, but *li* has no bounds. Exhausting all distinctions in the world will not suffice to realize fully the *li* of one thing. If an enlightened man temporarily lodges [his intent, i.e., becomes one] with the thing in order to bring out its distinctiveness, then with the variations of one thing he can fully realize the bamboo of the southern mountains.

When those who learn peruse the ultimate [variations] of a thing and proceed

<hr />

100 *Shih-chi* 84.2482.
101 *Ching-chin Tung-p'o wen-chi shih-lüeh* 46.779–81, "Ta Hsieh Min-shih shu."

on the outside of things, then whatever they seek they will apprehend. Therefore Wheelwright Pien, who went on for seventy years and grew old chiseling
wheels, and Cook Ting, who advanced in *tao* through a craft, were selected [to
illustrate Chuang-tzu's disputation]. . . .

Who could examine the actualities of a thing in such a detailed way as this
[i.e., Huang Ju's grading of tea] except someone of perfect tranquillity who
sought nothing, who was empty within and did not leave [his intention] behind
[in the thing]?[102]

Huang's success in seeing deeply into the category tea, through temporarily lodging his intent with tea (i.e., becoming one with it), gives him insight into *li* that he can extend to other things, thus allowing him to suggest matters of broader meaning from the limited case of tea.

Su extended to painting his vision of writing and calligraphy as modes
of realizing universal process in responding to things, taking as his best
example the work of his cousin Wen T'ung (T. Yü-k'o). Here too we find
an appreciation for control of the medium, understanding things profoundly, and expressing what one has in mind spontaneously.

Once when I discussed painting, I said that men and animals, buildings and
utensils all have constant forms; as for mountains, trees, water, and clouds,
although they lack constant forms, they have constant *li*. If constant form is
lost, everyone knows it; when constant *li* is not right, even those who are versed
in painting may not know. Therefore, all those who make a reputation by de-
ceiving the age necessarily trust to what is without constant form.

However, the loss of constant form stops with what is lost and does not spoil
the whole. But if constant *li* is not right then you destroy everything. It is because the forms are without constancy that one must take care about the *li*. The
artisans of today may be able to fully realize the forms, but when it comes to
the *li*, unless one is a superior man of outstanding talent he will be unable to
discriminate.

In bamboo, rocks, and leafless trees, [Wen T'ung] Yü-k'o can truly be said to
have apprehended their *li*. Now they are alive and now dead; now they are
twisted and cramped, and now regular and luxuriant. Their roots and stems,
joints and leaves—sharp and pointed or veined and striated—have innumerable
variations and transformations. They are never once repeated, yet each fits its
place. They agree with heaven's creation and accord with human ideas. It must
be that an enlightened literatus has temporarily lodged with them. . . . Only
those who have insight into *li* and have deeply perused [these paintings] will
know that what I say is not wrong.[103]

[102] *Tung-p'o t'i-pa* 1.14, "Shu Huang Tao-fu P'in ch'ao yao-lu hou."
[103] *Ching-chin Tung-p'o wen-chi shih-lüeh* 54.874–75, "Ching-yin yüan hua chi." In Susan Bush and Hsio-yen Shih, trans., *Early Chinese Texts on Paintings* (Cambridge: Harvard
University Press, 1985), p. 220, with minor modifications.

Wen T'ung apprehended the underlying unity of the things he was painting and thus was able to bring them into being in their many variations.
Su's comments go well beyond painting; they are about thinking and acting in the present. In another account of how Wen T'ung paints bamboo
Su makes a similar point: depicting something accurately and spontaneously—bringing one's ideas into concrete manifestation—requires gaining a fundamental understanding of the thing as a whole.

> When bamboo first comes into being, it is only an inch-long shoot, but its
> joints and leaves are all there. It develops from [shoots like] cicada chrysalises
> and snake scales to [stalks like] swords rising eighty feet, because this develop-
> ment was immanent in it. Now when painters do it joint by joint, and add to it
> leaf by leaf, will this be a bamboo? Therefore, in painting bamboo one must
> first apprehend the complete bamboo in the breast. One takes up the brush and
> gazes intently. Then one sees what one wants to paint and rises hurriedly to
> pursue it, wielding the brush forthwith to catch what one has seen. Like a hare
> leaping and falcon swooping—if one hesitates it will be lost.
> Yü-k'o instructed me thus. I am not able to do so but [my] mind discerns
> how it is so. Now when the mind discerns how it is so but one is not able to do
> so, inner and outer are not one, and mind and hand are not in accord. This is a
> fault stemming from not learning. Therefore, all who have seen something
> within but are not adept at executing it, will, in everyday life, see something
> clearly for themselves but suddenly lose it when it comes to putting it into prac-
> tice. This is not only true with bamboo.
> [Su Ch'e] Tzu-yu composed the "Ink Bamboo Rhapsody" for Yü-k'o, and
> said, "Cook Ting merely cut up oxen, but the nourisher of life chose him [as an
> example]. Now when you, Master, make use of this bamboo here and I think
> you are one who has tao, am I wrong?" Tzu-yu had never painted; therefore he
> only grasped his intent. As for me, I have not only grasped his intent—I have
> grasped his method as well.[104]

The spontaneity with which Wen T'ung painted depended upon his having the idea full in his mind. But, Su points out, this is not enough to
accomplish the deed in practice. The acquisition of skill and technique is
just as necessary. Being able to practice what you know requires training.
Others may only see the intent behind the enterprise; Su has also grasped
the process that makes it possible.
Wen T'ung is an example of someone who has learned how to bring
tao into practice. Su's comments on his painting suggest how we should
understand Su's claim, in connection with Monk Tsung, that he can take
a man's cultural accomplishments as an indicator of the degree to which

---

[104] *Ching-chin Tung-p'o wen-chih chih-lüeh* 49.813–14, "Yün-tang-ku yen-chu chi." In
Bush and Shih, trans., *Early Chinese Texts on Painting*, pp. 207–8; slightly modified.

the individual has apprehended *tao*. Wen T'ung "has *tao*," in Su Ch'e's view. The works give particular manifestation to an ability that has universal significance. In Wen T'ung's case this is evident from the fact that his painting is simply a further extension of his "virtue" into practice.

> Yü-k'o's prose is the lees of his virtue, and Yü-k'o's poetry is the hair-tip of his prose. What is not fully expressed in the poetry overflows to become calligraphy; it is transformed to become painting. Both are what is left over from poetry. Those who appreciate his poetry and prose are increasingly few. Are there those who love his virtue as much as they love his painting? Alas.[105]

If, for Su, *tao* is the ultimate source of value, then bringing *tao* into practice through responding to things is man's means of realizing true values in the world. Ultimately people must trust the process; external standards are not a real alternative. Wen T'ung had the virtue, and so does Su Shih. He puts his trust in the process and is sure that whatever results will be appropriate:

> My *wen* is like a spring with a ten-thousand-gallon flow. It does not care where, it can come forth any place. On the flatlands spreading and rolling, even a thousand miles in a day give it no difficulty. When it twists and turns about mountain boulders, it takes shape according to the things encountered—but it cannot be known. What can be known is that it will always go where it ought to go and stop where it cannot but stop, that is all. Even I am not able to understand the rest.[106]

[105] Bush and Shih, *Early Chinese Texts on Painting*, p. 196; modified.
[106] *Tung-p'o t'i-pa* 1.15, *Tzu p'ing wen*.

CHAPTER FOUR

Shao Yung and Number

SHAO YUNG is best known for his use of number, inspired by the *Book of Change*, to build a world-system of enormous scale and complexity. Thus a contemporary noted that Shao "contemplated the growth and decline of heaven-and-earth, inferred the waxing and waning of sun and moon, examined the measure-numbers of yin and yang, and scrutinized the form and structure of firm and soft."[1] Somewhat less remarked on is the way this knowledge of heaven-and-earth was the means for Shao to address the issues of human nature and destiny (*hsing-ming*) that came to occupy literati thinkers from the 1030s on. Shao's numerology is one language in which to express the constant order he can define in heaven-and-earth. Knowing this order, he suggests, literati will recognize their ultimate identity with the ten-thousand things and so become sages. In this way they will be able to order society and give all human beings their fullest expression.

Shao shows literati their place in the world by setting out the increasingly profound levels of reality he sees ordering the things around him. These things (*wu*) then become his primary text. Yet there is one written document that can help people learn to read the world because it is structured in the same way as heaven-and-earth. This is the *I Ching*. This chapter addresses the nature of Shao's orders and their implications, and how these derive from the *Book of Change*. First we set out Shao's claims about men and things, especially the importance of "contemplating things" (*kuan-wu*). We then address the three major layers of order that Shao discerns in heaven-and-earth. Here we engage Shao in his familiar role of system-builder, diagram-maker, and interpreter of the *Book of Change*. In the conclusions we will see the extraordinary powers that come to literati who can genuinely contemplate the things of heaven-and-earth.[2]

---

[1] Chang Min, "Hsing-chuang lüeh," in Chu Hsi, *I-Lo yüan-yüan lu*, 5.3a. "Firm and soft" of course refer to the solid and broken lines of the *I Ching*.

[2] We rely primarily on Shao's magnum opus, the *Huang-chi ching-shih shu*, or *The Supreme Principles for Ordering the World* (or *for Ordering the Generations*) (*Ssu-pu pei-yao* edition). It is now in nine *chüan* with an introductory chapter. Shao worked on these materials throughout the 1060s and 1070s. The first four *chüan* consist largely of charts, some of which were probably added by later students and editors. The main section is called the *Kuan-wu p'ien*, "Pieces on Contemplating Things," and consists of *chüan* 5 through 8. *Chüan* 5 and 6 are the Inner Sections, as Shao himself arranged them, while *chüan* 7 and 8,

CLAIMS AND PROMISES

The aim of Shao's learning or *hsüeh* is to teach people to contemplate the things of the world (*kuan-wu*) the way a sage does. This may seem a secondary matter in attaining sagehood. But human beings are also things, and Shao claims that by seeing the true nature of things literati will consequently know the nature of heaven-and-earth and of themselves as well. This knowing is a function of a human mind (*hsin*) that is sensitive to all aspects of its environment. The sage extends these fundamental sensitivities until he can, with his single mind, observe the minds of the ten-thousand things. Just as his mind can represent the intentions of heaven, so can his mouth represent its words, and he can even participate in the creative activities of heaven-and-earth. Among men, he is one in a billion.[3] We will begin the discussion here by setting out human nature and the problems of subjectivity and selfishness. Then we will discuss Shao's commitment to *hsüeh* as the one way to overcome this condition. Finally, we will present the fruition of learning: an unsurpassable sagehood whereby one hears, sees, and knows every thing and thereby acts as heaven-and-earth.

Man is a thing (*wu*), like everything in heaven-and-earth. This is the ground for his sagehood. But most men do not see the world this way. Instead they confuse their relative reference points with reality. Shao says:

> If we contemplate the present from the perspective of the present, then it is called the present. If we contemplate the present from the perspective of the future, then it is called the past. If we contemplate the past from the perspective of the present, then it is called the past. If the past contemplates itself, then it is called the present.
>
> From this we know that the past is not necessarily the past and the present is not necessarily the present. It is all from my perspective in contemplating it.[4]

According to Shao, people normally take their subjective views as the standard for measuring all things. Archery provides a good example:

> Now, bows are certainly strong or weak. So if you have a bow and two men pull it, then the one with strength will think the bow weak. The one without

---

the Outer Sections, are probably edited by close students, including Shao's son Shao Po-wen. See Toda Toyosaburō, "Sho Yō to Sho Bobun," *Hiroshima Daigaku Bungakubu Gakuhō*, 1958.2, pp. 1–28.

[3] *Huang-chi ching-shih shu*, 5.5a–6a. Unless otherwise noted, all subsequent footnotes are to this text.

[4] 5.14b. This passage also lays the ground for Shao's concern with foreknowledge, to be discussed below. Compare 8B.34a, where Shao discusses two towers of equal height, such that someone standing on one notices only that he is level with someone on the other, ignoring that both are high in the sky.

strength will think the bow strong. Therefore the one with strength does not think that his own strength is overplenty but thinks the bow is weak, and the one without strength does not think that his strength is insufficient but thinks the bow is strong.[5]

Shao is concerned with the way these problems reveal the inadequacy of all our usual ways of knowing. Of course, we are likely to take the wrong perspective when we engage in such abstruse questions as the nature of time. But even with common objects like a bow we tend to look in the wrong place, projecting qualities onto the object rather than locating them in our subjectivity. Shao calls on us instead to contemplate things from the perspective of things, entirely transcending the subjective perspective. In doing so, he gives us our first hint of what sages do. We have given three translations of the first sentence, one literal and two interpretive.

1. If you do not me things, then you can thing things.
2. If you do not project your own subjectivity onto things, then you can treat them objectively.
3. If you do not confuse yourself with things, then you can treat them *qua* things.

The sage benefits things and is without a self.[6]

That is, if you do not take your personal reactions as the measure of things, then you will be able to see them as they are and bring them real benefit. Doing so requires thorough selflessness.

It will take the rest of this chapter to explain what it is to "thing things" and thereby find in them the order of all heaven-and-earth. We can begin, however, with Shao's demand that men go beyond the derivative qualities that arise from their own subjective responses (or particularities, *ch'ing*) and come to see the true nature (*hsing*) of both things and themselves.[7] This is a novel redefinition of a famous pair of terms. The following passage explains how it works:

> To contemplate things from the perspective of things is *hsing* (the nature). To contemplate things from the perspective of self is *ch'ing* (subjective responses). The nature is impartial and illuminated. Subjective responses are partial and dark.[8]

[5] 8B.34b.

[6] 8B.27b. In the same way one should also "rejoice in things from [the perspective of] things" (8B.26a).

[7] Both these terms are discussed in the glossary, where Shao's somewhat unusual usage is compared to that of other Sung figures.

[8] 8B.16a. Note the poem on this subject, "Hsing-ch'ing yin," in Shao's collected poetry, the *I-ch'uan chi-jang-chi* (*Ssu-pu ts'ung-k'an* ed.), 18.115b, which expresses the same ideas.

Hsing then refers to things' true nature, grounded, as we will see, in heaven-and-earth, that which the sage contemplates. If we do not confuse our clouded self-interests with the true nature of things, we will be nearly sages ourselves:

If you employ the self, then you will have subjective responses. Subjective responses [lead to] what is hidden, and what is hidden to dimness.

If you rely on things, then you will have the nature. The nature [leads to] what is spiritual (*shen*), and what is spiritual to illumination.[9]

Such is the promise that Shao holds out. Thus what began as a simple problem of contemplation turns out to be the heart of developing the sage's point of view.

Only *hsüeh* or learning will take us to that point:

[Someone] said: "There are ancients whose great accomplishments did not come from learning. Why must you say 'learning'?"

[Shao] said: "Chou Po and Huo Kuang[10] were able to accomplish great affairs. It was only because they lacked learning that they never fully realized goodness. If one is a man yet does not learn, he will not be able to illuminate the principles (*li*) [of things]. If he cannot illuminate principles, then he will hold fast to [individual] things without being able to interconnect (*t'ung*) them.[11]

In the following passage, Shao provides *hsüeh* with a new content. He is speaking in reference to Confucius's disciple Yen Hui, who alone was said to love learning.[12]

Yen Tzu did not stray, and when he got angry he did not err twice.[13] Straying, anger and twice erring are subjective responses. They are not the nature. If you do not arrive at the nature and destiny (*ming*), then it does not warrant being called a love of learning.[14]

Thus learning means to arrive at or perfect one's nature and destiny. Its progress should be endless and all-consuming: "Learning lies in not stopping. Therefore Wang T'ung (584–618) said, 'Just give your life to it.' "[15] It must also engender an attitude of great joy: "If learning does not arrive at delight, you cannot call it learning."[16]

Perfecting this learning brings enormous existential and practical con-

[9] 8B.27b.

[10] Famous ministers of the Western Han.

[11] 8B.39a. See the glossary for a discussion of the various ways the figures of this book use the term "*li*," and for the English equivalents appropriate to each.

[12] *Analects* 6:2.

[13] In reference to *Analects* 6:3 and *Hsi-tz'u-chuan* B4.

[14] 8B.31b.

[15] 8B.40a.

[16] 8B.39b.

sequences. Shao sets these out in the following passage, which concludes the inner chapters of the *Kuan-wu-p'ien*. He begins by discussing how the sage can accommodate every thing because he does not consider them from his subjective viewpoint. Instead he identifies with all things. In this way he can use the mind of the world as his own.

Now, the way a mirror is able to illuminate is that it does not conceal the forms of the ten-thousand things. Although this is so, the ability of a mirror not to conceal the forms of the ten-thousand things is not as good as the ability of water to unify the forms of the ten-thousand things.[17] Although this is so, the ability of water to unify the forms of the ten-thousand things is not as good as the sage's ability to unify the particularities (*ch'ing*) of the ten-thousand things.[18]

The way the sage is able to unify the particularities of the ten-thousand things is that he is able to contemplate in reverse (*fan-kuan*).[19] What is meant by contemplating in reverse is not contemplating things from the perspective of the self. What is meant by not contemplating things from the perspective of the self is contemplating things from the perspective of things. Since one can contemplate things from their perspective, then how can there be a self in their midst?!

From this we know that I am a man, and men are also me. Men and I are both things. This is how one can use all the eyes of the world as one's own eyes; there is nothing these eyes do not contemplate. One can use all the ears of the world as one's own ears; there is nothing these ears do not hear. One can use all the mouths of the world as one's own mouth; there is nothing these mouths do not say. One can use all the minds of the world as one's own mind; there is nothing these minds do not think about. . . .

To be able to do things that are most broad, far-reaching, elevated and great [like these acts of contemplating, hearing, speaking and thinking], and at its center not do a single thing (*wu-i-wei*), how can one not call it most spiritual and most sagely?

It is not only I who call it most spiritual and most sagely. The world calls it most spiritual and most sagely. It is not just one generation that calls it most spiritual and most sagely. "Knowledge does not go beyond this."[20]

These are Shao's claims and promises. If one learns to contemplate things, one can, with the sage, use the world's minds as one's own and

---

[17] Because water can adapt itself perfectly to them, both by accepting them into it and by molding itself into their shape, and then return to its original shape. Both the mirror and water reflect what is before them, but water does it in three dimensions and is neither fixed nor subject to breaking.

[18] Because the sage can accommodate and shape himself the way water can. He can also see the unity that underlies the disparateness of the ten-thousand things.

[19] That is, like the mirror and water, the sage reflects (*fan*) things without a distorting subjectivity. He thus contemplates them not from his own perspective but in reverse (*fan*), from the point of view of the things themselves. Shao explains this in the next lines.

[20] 6.26b, quoting at the end *Hsi-tz'u* B3.

act without action. The subsequent sections of this chapter will develop Shao's view of the orders of heaven-and-earth, that which the sage has insight into. We will need to ask ourselves as we progress: how is such systematic thought related to such marvelous contemplation?

ORDERS OF REALITY

Shao Yung uses the term *t'ai-chi* or "supreme ultimate" to stand for the unmoving source of all order and of every thing in heaven-and-earth. From *t'ai-chi* emerge, in turn, spirit, number, images, and things. This section discusses these orders of reality, and the next few paragraphs preview the more detailed arguments that follow.

Shao derives the term *t'ai-chi* from its single appearance in the *Hsi-tz'u-chuan*, which says "In the *I* there is *t'ai-chi*."[21] All things emerge from *t'ai-chi*. First comes spirit *(shen)*, inchoate and ineffable, the marvelous workings of the whole.[22] While spirit is inchoate, it is not chaotic. Its orderliness, however, is not susceptible to articulation. Instead it consists in the self-existing principles Shao calls "*li*." Number, the most fundamental order that *can* be articulated, in turn emerges from spirit and principles. Shao values number because it precisely expresses the relationships between key elements of heaven-and-earth.[23] He can also use it to order the past, structure the present, and predict the future. From number in turn emerge images. These are not only the four images of the *Hsi-tz'u-chuan* A11, but stages and categories in the creation of all things. Finally, things *(wu* or *ch'i)* themselves appear.

Two passages in the *Huang-chi ching-shih shu* set out this structure, though each is so compressed as to be nearly impenetrable on first encounter. Our translations preserve the laconic diction of the original, which we hope the following sections of this chapter will illuminate.

> That *t'ai-chi* does not move is its nature. It issues forth, then spirit. Spirit, then number. Number, then images. Images, then objects. Objects, then change. Again it returns to spirit.[24]

And:

[21] A11. The term *t'ai-chi* does not seem to have had much use until the eleventh century, when Liu Mu and Chou Tun-i also devote considerable attention to it.

[22] This use of "spirit" to create a residual category of ineffability is in keeping with previous and current discourse. See, for example, Graham, *Two Chinese Philosophers*, pp. 11–118. For a fuller treatment of Shao's usage, see Hou Wai-lu, *Chung-kuo ssu-hsiang t'ung-shih* (Peking: Jen-min, 1959), vol. 4a, pp. 529ff.

[23] In this he bears a surface similarity to Liu Mu, discussed in chapter 2. For an extended treatment of Ch'eng I's reactions to Shao's numerology, see chapter 7, "Sung Literati Thought and the *I Ching*."

[24] 7B.23b.

> T'ai-chi is one (unitary). Unmoving, it gives birth to two (duality, i.e., yin and yang). Duality, then spirit. Spirit gives birth to number. Number gives birth to images. Images give birth to objects.[25]

And so the world emerges from the unmoving, undifferentiated unity of t'ai-chi.

In the next sections of this chapter we will treat this emergence in inverse order, working our way back to t'ai-chi. We distinguish three levels on which Shao Yung articulates the orderliness of heaven-and-earth. These are images and objects, number, and spirit and principles. The next three sections are each addressed to one of these. Each level has a characteristic logic and form of organization, and each expresses the coherence of heaven-and-earth in a different way. Since these levels are also stages in the continual creation of the world, each level also governs the level above it. Images, for example, are an abstract and concise way of ordering the ten-thousand things. Yet prior to images is number, a still more abstract and powerful way of ordering images. In turn "the numbers of the world emerge from principles."[26] Thus, while "one can attain the images and numbers of heaven and thus [know things] by inference, the activities of spirit cannot be measured."[27] Only principles can represent the most subtle orderliness that exists at this level.[28]

"Contemplation" remains a key term. Indeed, we might take the concluding section of this chapter as an attempt to understand the following passage:

> Now, what is meant by contemplating things is not using the eye to contemplate them. It is not contemplating them with the eye but contemplating them with the mind. It is not contemplating them with the mind but contemplating them with principles (li).[29]

Images and Objects

Shao uses the term "images" (hsiang) to indicate the structure through which the multiplicity of heaven, earth, and the ten-thousand things emerges. He uses "objects" (ch'i) to indicate things (wu) in their material aspect, as they emerge at the last stage of that process. The term "image" derives from the Book of Change, where one of its meanings is defined in the same Hsi-tz'u passage that also mentions t'ai-chi:

[25] 8B.23a.
[26] 7B.19b.
[27] 8A.16b.
[28] Ibid.
[29] 6.26a.

In the *I* there is *t'ai-chi*. This gives birth to the two modes [of yin and yang]. The two modes give birth to the four images. The four images give birth to the eight trigrams (A11).

In keeping with that progression, images represent orderliness in two ways: they indicate the stages through which everything comes into being, and they mark the categories through which all things are interrelated. In this section we will examine them first as stages, then as categories. Finally we will see how stages and categories combine to allow Shao to know the unfolding of future events.

As Shao addresses the initial stages in the ten-thousand things' emergence from movement and stillness, he sets up the framework that will equally allow him to explain the categories to which they belong. These stages and categories are real, Shao claims; they are neither subjective (like *ch'ing*) nor are they merely conventional, man-made distinctions. Instead they derive from heaven-and-earth.

Heaven is born of movement (activity, *tung*). Earth is born of stillness (tranquillity, *ching*).[30] One movement and one stillness interact and the *tao* of heaven-and-earth is fully expressed in them.[31] Yang is born at the beginning of movement. Yin is born at the peak (*chi*) of movement. A yin and a yang interact and the functioning (*yung*) of heaven is fully expressed in them. The soft is born at the beginning of stillness. The firm is born at the peak of stillness. A firm and a soft interact and the functioning of earth is fully expressed in them.

What is great in movement is called the major yang. What is small in movement is called the minor yang. What is great in stillness is called the major yin. What is small in stillness is called the minor yin. The major yang is the sun. The major yin is the moon. The minor yang is the stars. The minor yin is the zodiacal spaces. Sun, moon, stars, and zodiac interact, and the substance (*t'i*) of heaven is fully expressed in them.

What is great in stillness is called the major softness. What is small in stillness is called the minor softness. What is great in movement is called the major firmness. What is small in movement is called the minor firmness. The major softness is water. The major firmness is fire. The minor softness is earth.[32] The minor firmness is stone. Water, fire, earth and stone interact and the substance of Earth is fully expressed in them.[33]

[30] In chapter 1 we saw Wang Pi posit a tranquillity that stood prior to action. While Shao's *t'ai-chi* is also silent and unmoving, on this level he treats both movement and stillness as equal terms.

[31] That is, the basic pair "movement and stillness" sets the possibilities for something so great as the *tao* of heaven-and-earth, which can still find its full expression within them. In the same way, other pairs of terms, set out below, set the possibilities for all further development.

[32] This earth of the four images is *t'u*. The earth of heaven-and-earth is *ti*.

[33] 5.1b.

This emergence proceeds through stages of division and redivision. Movement (heaven) and stillness (earth) give birth to yin, yang, firm and soft, that is, to the four images. These in turn redivide into major and minor aspects.

But the images also represent categories. Their major and minor aspects have physical correlates: the major yin is the moon, the minor firmness is stone, and so on with each of the other six. In subsequent passages of *chüan 5*, each of these eight in turn is identified with a basic element: the sun is heat, stone is thunder, etc.[34] Eventually finer and finer distinctions are made, and this classificatory process is repeated until a complex mechanism of stimulus/response and change/transformation accounts for the ten-thousand things of heaven-and-earth.[35] For example, Shao divides living things into animals and plants, classifies animals into those that fly and those that walk, and combines and recombines these categories to accommodate all other things. Even difficult cases find a place. A chicken is a flyer that walks.[36] Or: "Water's trees: the category of coral. Stone's flowers: the category of carbonate of soda."[37] Thus all things can be ordered on the model that Shao develops out of the *Hsi-tz'u* passage we have examined above. Shao's prose, of course, also reflects this parallelism and symmetry.

In this system "image" has both a narrow and broad meaning. Narrowly, it refers only to the four images that Shao derives from the *I Ching*. But broadly, all Shao's categories function as images, in that each provides a set of types within which further classifications can be established. Used in this way, the images create a vast matrix that includes every thing, so that knowing any thing, one can unerringly infer its relationship to every other thing. Thus *chüan 5* of the *Kuan-wu p'ien* correlates the four images with the seasons, with developmental stages, the Classics, political style and moral standards. Corresponding to the four seasons are the stages of birth, growth, harvest and storage. Tied to these are the four Classics,[38] which are linked with the four types of rulers,[39] each of whom rules the state by means of a particular virtue.[40] Because heaven-and-earth is so powerfully structured around fours, and because it is a unified order, Shao naturally finds that the human realm of texts, rulers and ethics is also clearly structured in that manner.

[34] 5.2a.
[35] 5.2b–3b.
[36] 8B.15a.
[37] 8B.13b.
[38] The *Books of Change, Documents, Poetry* and the *Spring and Autumn Annals*; 5.8a and 9a.
[39] Emperor, monarch, king, hegemon, conceived both historically and as types; 5.9b.
[40] *Tao*, virtue (*te*), effort and strength; 5.14a.

The images are simultaneously categories and stages. Thus they can also be used to look into the future. We will conclude this section by examining two passages that explain how this is so. The first is apparently simple but adumbrates the difficulties of the second. It states:

Each of the ten-thousand things has the sequence: *t'ai-chi*, two modes, four images, and eight trigrams. It also has the images of past and present.[41]

That is, every thing comes into being by following the bifurcations of the *t'ai-chi* sequence. But this sequence can be read in two directions.

The second passage suggests how this might be so. It is extremely dense, and its two points require some interpretation in advance. First, it distinguishes between the possibilities inherent in categories (*lei*) and the realization of these possibilities as substances (or bodies, *t'i*). For example, heaven and earth are the two categories that are born from the two modes, yin and yang. Yet their substances are set by the four images—since the sun and moon are the substances of heaven, and firm and soft the substances of earth. These four substances act as categories in their own turn, whereupon the eight trigrams set the next round of substances, and so on through the ten-thousand things.

Second, this sequence can also be read the other way. Though things always come into being in this order—what Shao calls their "birth order"—it is possible to follow time in the opposite direction—what Shao calls "going against the order of time (*ni*)." The former allows one to know the relationships between things; the latter leads to foreknowledge. The passage reads:

Yin and yang are born and divide into the two modes. The two modes interact and give birth to the four images. The four images interact and give birth to the eight trigrams. The eight trigrams interact and give birth to the ten-thousand things.

Therefore the two modes give birth to the categories (*lei*) of heaven-and-earth. The four images set the substances (bodies, *t'i*) of heaven-and-earth. The four images give birth to the categories of sun and moon. The eight trigrams set the substances of sun and moon. The eight trigrams give birth to the categories of the ten-thousand things. The doubled trigrams [i.e., sixty-four hexagrams] set the substances of the ten-thousand things.

Categories are the order of birth. Substances are the interaction of images. Inferences [of the future] by means of the categories must be rooted in [the order of] birth. Contemplation of the [relationships between synchronic] substances must derive from the images. Birth is about the future: one infers by "going against [the order of time] (*ni*)." Images are about what has already come about: one contemplates by "going along with [the order of time]

[41] 8B.9b.

(*shun*)." . . . Therefore time can be known by going against. Things must come into being by going with.[42]

These, however, are only the general principles of foreknowledge. Its specific calculations depend on number, whereby one follows the logic of the birth sequence "against" the direction of the normal flow of time and so can see what is about to unfold. These calculations are discussed in the next section.

Number

In the previous section we saw how Shao uses images to establish categories through which all things (*wu*) develop and are mutually related. He traces these categories back through sun, moon and rain to heaven-and-earth, yin and yang, and movement and stillness. He also employs their sequence to suggest how foreknowledge is possible. As compelling as this schema is, it is crude when compared to that of number, which can more precisely define the relationships of things, predict the future, and comprehend vast quantities of space and time. Intertwined with number are diagrams or *t'u*, which give concrete form to complex numerological relationships. Both are remarkable in their internal consistency and ability to systematize diverse kinds of information; both also depend greatly on materials derived from the *I Ching*.

In this space it will not be possible to address all of Shao's applications of number. Instead we will examine three representative arrangements: the *hsien-t'ien* or Preceding Heaven sequences, the Ho-t'u or Yellow River Chart, and a diagram of time that is generally understood as a cosmic calendar.[43] Each of these will bring us closer to Shao's sense of what it means to contemplate things.

---

[42] 8B.2b.

[43] Shao probably obtained both the *hsien-t'ien* arrangement and the Ho-t'u from his teacher Li Chih-ts'ai; see Michael Freeman's account of their time together in "From Adept to Worthy: The Philosophical Career of Shao Young [sic]," *Journal of the American Oriental Society*, 102.3 (1982), pp. 477–91. The diagrams' ultimate provenance may well have been Ch'en T'uan, an elusive figure from the very early Sung. (For a brief summary of what is known of Ch'en, see his biography by T. Araki in *Sung Biographies*, ed. Herbert Franke [Wiesbaden: Steiner, 1976], pp. 120–23.) Graham, *Two Chinese Philosophers*, pp. 152–53, provides a summary of the transmission stories, as does the *Sung-shih* biography of Shao (translated by Fung Yu-lan in *A History of Chinese Philosophy* [Princeton: Princeton University Press, 1952–1953], vol. 2, p. 453). Imai Usaburō, *Sōdai ekigaku no kenkyū* (Researches on Sung dynasty *I Ching* studies) (Tokyo: Meiji, 1958) bases his book on the "official" later interpretation of Chu Chen (1072–1138), from the latter's *Han-shang I-chuan*, but Imai's book contains nothing of consequence on Shao. Shao himself mentions the importance of Ch'en T'uan to his development. See for example the poetry analyzed by Matsukawa Kenji, *Sō-Min no shisō-shi* (Philosophical poetry of the Sung and Ming) (Sapporo:

We can begin with a passage that nicely bridges the concerns with images and objects that we have just explored.

> *T'ai-chi* having divided, the two modes (*liang-i*) were established. Yang rose and interacted with yin. Yin descended and interacted with yang. [Thus] four images were born.
>
> Yang interacted with yin, yin interacted with yang, and they gave birth to the four images of heaven.[44] The firm interacted with the soft, the soft interacted with the firm, and they gave birth to the four images of earth.[45] Thereupon the eight trigrams were realized (completed). The eight trigrams interacted, and afterwards the ten-thousand things were born therein.
>
> Thus one divides and makes two. Two divides and makes four. Four divides and makes eight. Eight divides and makes sixteen. Sixteen divides and makes thirty-two. Thirty-two divides and makes sixty-four. Therefore [the *Shuo-kua*, section 2] says, "Divide yin, divide yang, alternately use soft and firm. Thus the *I* has its six ranks[46] and attains its clarity."
>
> Ten divides and makes one hundred. One hundred divides and makes a thousand. A thousand divides and makes ten-thousand. It is like the way a root has a trunk, a trunk has branches, a branch has leaves. The bigger they are, the fewer they are. The finer they are, the more they are. Unite them and it makes one. Spread them out and they make ten-thousand. Because of this at Ch'ien it divides, at K'un it joins, at Chen it grows, at Sun it diminishes.[47] It grows and then divides. It divides and then diminishes. It diminishes and then joins.[48]

Three points need emphasis here. First, Shao is suggesting that the principles of the *Shuo-kua* and *Hsi-tz'u-chuan* can be more precisely and clearly represented by the number sequences 1–2–4–8–16–32–64 and 10–100–1000–10000 than they can by the texts themselves. Second, this numerical language makes both the hugeness and unity of its subject matter immediately apparent. At one extreme we have one, the single source of all, at the other ten thousand and they are as conjoined as the parts of a tree. Third, there is a simply learned pair of rules that governs this system: things develop by a cycle of division that is repeated and reversible, and, the corollary, as the number of things grows, their size decreases.

Hokkaido University Press, 1982), especially pp. 1–7. For a Ch'ing dynasty *summa* on these and other diagrams, see Hu Wei, *I-t'u ming-pien* (Illuminating and differentiating the *I Ching* diagrams) (Taipei: Kuang-wen, 1971).

[44] That is, the major and minor yin and yang, or sun, moon, stars and zodiacal space.

[45] That is, major and minor firm and soft, or water, fire, ground and stone.

[46] The "six ranks" would normally refer to the six lines of the hexagram, but here Shao takes them to mean the six divisions—to get from one to sixty-four—that he has been discussing.

[47] "Joining" is ascribed to K'un in *Hsi-tz'u* A5. The logic of this cycle comes from the *hsien-t'ien* arrangement, on which more presently.

[48] 7A.24b.

Thus we have two great things (heaven and earth), four large things (the four images), and ten-thousand small things like us. This is a powerfully compact conceptualization. In the next pages we will see how Shao applies it to the world.

Such a system is already familiar to us from Shao's use of the images, and the above passage begins to suggest how concisely number can represent its well-ordered nature. But Shao's most typical use of number is not the linear progression from 1 to 64 but rather the complex sets of relationship between numbers that constitute his diagrams. Here we will examine how he transforms that progression into what is known as the *hsien-t'ien* (preceding heaven) or Fu-hsi arrangement of the trigrams. Shao calls this sequence *"hsien-t'ien"* because he believes it existed prior to the creation of heaven. It is both temporally and logically prior, for heaven-and-earth goes through a cycle of birth and decay like all else, and the *hsien-t'ien* sequence orders them as well.[49]

As the reader may have already noticed, the 1–2–4–8–16–32–64 sequence derives from a passage in the *Hsi-tz'u-chuan* that we have already encountered:

> In the *I* there is *t'ai-chi*. This gives birth to the two modes. The two modes give birth to the four images. The four images give birth to the eight trigrams.[50]

Here are two graphic representations of the creation of the trigrams. Figure 1 is attributed to Shao himself.[51] But it is much harder to make out (even for someone who reads Chinese) than the version of it attributed to Chu Hsi, which we have therefore included as figure 2.[52]

The first thing we might notice is these diagrams' appealing symmetry. This aesthetic coherence has profound cognitive implications: it is much easier to understand how the diagram "works" by looking at it than by describing it. Indeed, we may be able to grasp how "number gives birth to images" almost at once, especially if we have had any exposure to the binary number system. By contrast, a narrative account might begin as follows: "As *t'ai-chi* divides and produces yin and yang, a process of bi-

---

[49] The term *hsien-t'ien* derives from a passage in the *Wen-yen* commentary to the Ch'ien hexagram: "He precedes heaven and heaven does not oppose him." But it has a number of other interesting referents with which Shao's usage resonates. Most significant is this passage in *Lao Tzu* 25: "Before heaven and earth were born, silent and empty. . . . Man models himself on earth, earth on heaven, heaven on *tao*, *tao* on self-so." (In the Taoist religion of T'ang times, Hsien-t'ien T'ai-hou is also the mother of Lao Tzu.)

[50] A11.

[51] In Huang Tsung-hsi's *Sung-Yüan hsüeh-an* (Case studies of Sung and Yüan scholars) (*Ssu-pu pei-yao* ed.), 10:21b.

[52] From his *I-hsüeh ch'i-meng* (Introduction to the study of the *I*), now preserved in his *Chou-i pen-i* (Original meaning of the *Chou-i*) (Taipei: Shih-chieh, 1968), p. 7. The relationship of these two versions is discussed in Fung Yu-lan, *History*, vol. 1, p. 454.

太柔　太剛　少柔　少剛　少陰　少陽　太陰　太陽
‐‐　━━　‐‐　━━　‐‐　━━　‐‐　━━

柔　剛　陰　陽
‐‐　━━　‐‐　━━

静　　　動
‐‐　　一動一静之間　　━━

Fig. 1. The *Hsien-t'ien* diagram
Source: *Sung-Yüan hsüeh-an* (*Ssu-pu pei-yao* ed.) 10.21b.

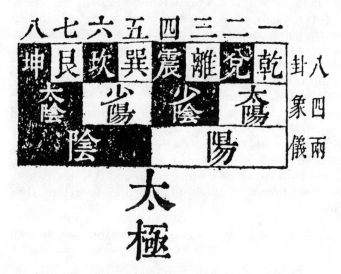

Fig. 2. The *Hsien-t'ien* diagram
Source: Chu Hsi, *I pen-i* (Shih-chieh), p. 7.

nary splitting is initiated that next produces four items, one of yang and yang, one of yang and yin, one of yin and yang, and one of yin and yin. These are related to each other. . . ."

Such diagrams allow Shao to classify and connect complex materials, thus clarifying their relationships and demonstrating the order of things that he is engaged in contemplating. Note, for example, that there is another ordering implicit in this diagram. If we assign the numeral 0 to each yang line and 1 to each yin line,[53] then the first trigram, Ch'ien, becomes 000; the second, Tui, 001; the third, Li, 010; the fourth, Ch'en, 011; and so on through the eighth, K'un, 111. Thus the trigrams are numbered in sequence from 1 to 8 in the binary number system, as Chu Hsi's superscript in figure 2 indicates.

To bring out the full implications of this ordering, we should note that the *hsien-t'ien* diagram can take a circular form as well. It is made by "lifting off" the two halves of the top line and rearranging them into a circle, so that trigrams 1 through 4 (beginning with Ch'ien on the extreme right and moving toward the center) drape down the left-hand side of the circle, and trigrams 5 through 8 (beginning with Sun at the left center and moving toward K'un at the extreme left) drape down the right side.

Numerous numerological relationships can be found in this circle. For example, if we examine the pairs of trigrams across it, assigning the number 1 to a yang line and the number 2 to a yin line,[54] then the total of each trigram pair is always 9. Similarly, if we number the trigrams in the square arrangement 1 through 8, as in this example, then the total of each cross-circle pair in the circular arrangement is also 9. But the importance of this diagram lies not only in its ability to present, simply and economically, complex relationships that would overwhelm a narrative account, but also in the variety of dynamics to which it can be applied. For example, the square diagram implies only one primary development, that of the emergence of the eight trigrams from the unitary *t'ai-chi*. The circle, however, can be used to indicate stages in both the cyclical growth and decline of yang or of yin. If we start in the lower left, at what we would call 7:30 if our circle were a clock face, we could trace the increasing presence of yang lines in the trigrams as we circled clockwise, reaching Ch'ien at 12:00. At 1:30, however, yang has already begun its decline, yin increases, and by 6:00 we have arrived at K'un. Then the process continues, as we move from K'un to 7:30 and yang begins its return. Thus *chüan 7B* begins:

> The *hsien-t'ien* diagram circles around the center. Going from the bottom up is called rising. Going from the top down is called descending. Rising is called

[53] In fact to follow *Hsi-tz'u* A10 we should do it the other way round, but one of the beauties of pure number is that "the other way round" is just a mirror image of itself.

[54] Following *Hsi-tz'u-chuan* A10.

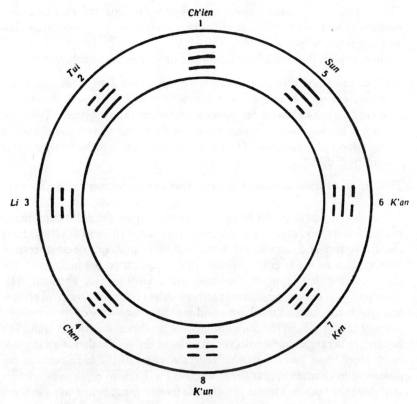

Fig. 3. The *Hsien-t'ien* diagram—circular
Source: Fung Yu-lan, *History of Chinese Philosophy*, vol. 2, p. 460.

giving birth [to yang]. Descending is called decline [of yang]. Therefore yang is born below and yin is born above.

By means of this the ten-thousand things are produced by inverse movement (*fan-sheng*). Yin gives birth to yang, yang gives birth to yin. Yin again gives birth to yang, yang again gives birth to yin [or "returns (*fu*) to give birth to . . ."].

By means of this it follows the circle and is inexhaustible.[55]

The circle is round, it is heaven, it is movement. As such the circular *hsien-t'ien* also introduces time and space. For example, Ch'ien, at the top, is both summer and south; Li, at the left, is spring and east, etc. Most of these trigram associations are not original to Shao. On the contrary, some derive from the *Shuo-kua*[56] and others from pre-Han and Han texts.[57]

[55] 7B.1a.
[56] For example, the principle of associating directions with trigrams. But note that the

Thus while Shao's associations may appear fanciful and eccentric to a modern reader, many of them are in fact scrupulously derived from classical sources.

Shao applies these to a host of cosmic processes in the following:

> Ch'ien and K'un fix the positions up and down. Li and K'an set the gates of left and right. They are the opening and closing of heaven-and-earth, the exit and entry of the sun and moon. Spring, summer, autumn, and winter; the dark, new, crescent and full moon; the lengthening and shortening of days and nights; the expansion and contraction of cosmic rotations—there is nothing that does not come from this![58]

That is, all of these activities can be expressed in terms of these four trigrams.[59]

The development of the *hsien-t'ien* diagram from the eight trigrams to the sixty-four hexagrams is important to the scope of Shao's system. Here too are square and circular versions. And every principle of organization that applied to the trigram version applies equally to the hexagram: the sequence, the development, the cross-circle pairings, etc. Thus the relationship of these two versions is further evidence for the powerful consistency of mathematical thinking—and for the consistency of the ten-thousand things that Shao contemplates with these diagrams' aid. The hexagram arrangement marks the months of the year rather than the seasons. Here Shao gives a graphic representation of the Han conception, discussed in chapter 1, that the hexagram Fu (Return) represents the first month of the year. With one yang line in its first place below five yin lines, Fu stands for the first return of yang to an all-yin situation. Of course in this instance the hexagram and line statements of Fu are completely irrelevant to Shao's considerations. When the sixty-four hexagrams are displayed in sequence, they constitute the rewriting of the hexagrams in the form we call the binary sequence from 0 to 63 that would so astound Leibniz when he learned of it through the Jesuits.[60]

---

particular associations of *Shuo-kua* 4 are those of the *hou-t'ien* or Succeeding Heaven diagram.

[57] Thus John Henderson remarks in *The Development and Decline of Chinese Cosmology*: "The classical sources of these various entities run almost the entire gamut of late-Chou and early-Han cosmological literature, ranging from the 'Great Plan' chapter of the *Documents Classic* to the *Ta-Tai li-chi* (The Elder Tai's *Record of Rites*)" of the first century C.E. (p. 125).

[58] 7A.26b.

[59] Note that these are the four trigrams that do not change (*pu-i*) when they are inverted—they remain the same whether read from the top down or the bottom up. See 7A.29b *et seq.* for Shao's treatment of this. They are also the four hexagrams that since Han times have been excluded so as to create the more manageable number 60 out of 64.

[60] For an account of this encounter, see David Mungello, *Leibniz and Confucianism: The Search for Accord* (Honolulu: University of Hawaii Press, 1977), especially pp. 62ff.

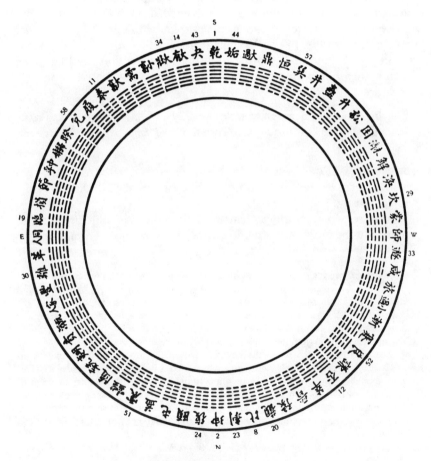

K'UN	KEN	K'AN	SUN	CHEN	LI	TUI	CH'IEN
GREATER YIN		LESSER YANG		LESSER YIN		GREATER YANG	
YIN				YANG			
SUPREME				ULTIMATE			

Fig. 4. The *Hsien-t'ien* diagram—hexagrams, square
Source: Fung Yu-lan, *History of Chinese Philosophy*, vol. 2, p. 459.

Fig. 5. The *Hsien-t'ien* diagram—hexagrams, circular
Source: Fung Yu-lan, *History of Chinese Philosophy*, vol. 2, p. 462.

Shao used number to obtain foreknowledge. In itself this was nothing unusual, and even someone like Ch'eng I, who otherwise disdained Shao's numerology, admitted to its efficacy.[61] The *hsien-t'ien* diagram was particularly useful in this regard. To understand Shao's application of it we should begin with this passage from *Shuo-kua* section 3:

> Heaven-and-earth fixed their positions. Mountain and pond circulated their *ch'i* [between each other]. Thunder and wind stirred each other. Water and fire did not reject each other. The eight trigrams interacted.[62]

This passage concludes with three sentences that are hard to translate, since they play on a pair of opposites, *"shun"* and *"ni,"* which we encountered at the conclusion of the previous section. *Shun* means "going along with" or "in sequence." *Ni* means "going against" but also "in advance," with the connotation of foreknowledge.[63] "Going along with it in sequence" indicates that one comes to know things in the order that they occur naturally. *Ni*, or "going against the direction of time," means reaching with the mind into the future, against the flow, and knowing things before the stream of time has brought them to us. Thus this passage concludes:

> Numbers going away are going in sequence (*shun*). Knowing what is to come is contrary motion (*ni*, in advance). Therefore the *I* "goes against" (*ni*) its numbers.[64]

The numbers in question are, for Shao, those associated with the two versions of the *hsien-t'ien* diagram, as the passages to be discussed below will demonstrate.

There are two more things that are useful to keep in mind as we try to understand the process of foreknowledge. First, we should recall the way yin and yang grow and decline as one goes around the *hsien-t'ien* circle

---

[61] See *Erh-Ch'eng chi*, p. 197, where Ch'eng affirms Shao's ability to predict the length of someone's life. See chapter 7 for further discussion of this relationship.

[62] Note that this passage identifies the eight trigrams by their associated images. These also derive from the *Shuo-kua*, which discusses them in section 4, immediately subsequent to this passage. Thus heaven stands for Ch'ien, fire for Li, etc. Pairs like "thunder and wind" (Chen and Sun) emerge from the "family system" of the eight trigrams described in chapter 1 of this book. Ch'ien and K'un are the parents. Chen and Sun are the eldest son and daughter, since the determinant single yin or yang line of each is in the trigram's first place. This pairing, though not its order, thus corresponds to the circular *hsien-t'ien* arrangement of Fu-hsi, wherein trigrams are matched across the circle by family ranking. However, the *hsien-t'ien* arrangement differs from the *Shuo-kua* family ranking in that the former, we could say, mixes the sexes: Chen, the eldest son, is followed by Li and Tui, the second and third daughters.

[63] For a pair of pre-Sung examples of this usage, see Morohashi, *Dai Kan-Wa jiten*, vol. 11, pp. 41d–42a.

[64] *Shuo-kua* 3.

clockwise from Ch'ien, through the decline of yang to K'un, and back to Ch'ien. In the following passage Shao refers to this as "revolving leftwards," which is the normal direction that time flows. Second, we should remember that if we look up at night to the pole-star, heaven also appears to revolve very, very slowly to the left.[65] Now, if one goes in the opposite direction, to the right, it is *ni*, "contrary motion" and "foreknowledge." This is how Shao uses the *Shuo-kua* passage:

> "Numbers going away are going in sequence": If you go in the same sequence as heaven, it's revolving leftwards, the trigrams that have already been produced. Therefore it says "numbers going." "Knowing what is to come is contrary motion (or 'in advance')'": If you go in the contrary direction from heaven, it's revolving rightwards, all the trigrams that have not yet been produced. Therefore it says, "knowing what is to come."
>
> Now, "the numbers of the *I*" are realized "in contrary motion." This one section directly illuminates the meaning of the [circular Fu-hsi] diagram, which is like knowing the four seasons in advance.[66]

Shao applies these principles once more in the following passage. It too will require some explanation.

> When yang is within yin, yang proceeds contrarily (*ni*). When yin is within yang, then yin proceeds contrarily. When yang is within yang, or yin within yin, then they both proceed in sequence (*shun*).
>
> These are true and perfect principles. They can be seen according to the diagram.[67]

The diagram in question is the circular version of the *hsien-t'ien*. Let us look first at the left-hand side of the circle. At 7:30 we find the Chen trigram with two yin but only one yang line. At 9:00 and 10:30, the trigrams have two yang lines. By 12:00 we have reached Ch'ien, with all yang lines. This then is the yang side of the circle. On the right-hand or yin side we see, correspondingly, the increase of yin lines from 1:30 until 6:00. In both cases the motion is clockwise. This is *shun*, "going along in the normal sequence," as yang grows within yang's side of the circle and yin within yin's.

Now, one may also go in the opposite direction. Here one follows the progressive growth of yang from 4:30 to 3:00 to 1:30 to 12:00. Because the developmental sequence that Shao attributes to this diagram takes the

---

[65] Thus Chang Tsai writes: "Heaven revolves leftwards; [the celestial bodies,] occupying positions in its midst, follow it. Being slightly slower, they [appear to] move to the contrary, in a rightward direction." From *Cheng-meng* (Correcting ignorance), 11.9, in Ira Kasoff, *The Thought of Chang Tsai* (Cambridge: Cambridge University Press, 1984), p. 56.

[66] 7A.24a.

[67] 7A.33b.

clockwise growth of yang and yin as natural, this motion constitutes going in a contrary direction. Because the circle implicitly describes the pattern of normal growth and decline, this is also going contrary to natural time: it is going into the future.

If we understand this in conjunction with Shao's conception of images as both categories and substances, we see that we can apply his system of images and number as easily to foreknowledge as we can to classifying anything that already exists. The fundamental ordering is the same in both cases, after all. Presumably, if we contemplated things (*kuan-wu*) unimpeded by our usual selfish preoccupations, we could not only determine the particular category into which their image places them but equally understand their coming into being. That is, we could know what will develop next.[68]

The second diagram we need to examine is the Ho-t'u or Yellow River Chart. As opposed to the *hsien-t'ien-t'u*, which addresses the trigrams, the Ho-t'u deals purely in numbers, though these necessarily include the numbers associated with the trigrams. Traditionally the Ho-t'u was said to have emerged from the Yellow River—there is one brief reference to it in *Hsi-tz'u-chuan* A11. Later traditions saw it emblazoned on the flank of a horse or dragon-horse. The Ho-t'u was the subject of much discussion from Han times on.[69] However, no versions of it date any earlier than Shao Yung, who may be said therefore to be its originator for the late imperial period.[70] Even the depictions of it we do possess are not indisputably from Shao's hand; the figure that follows, from Chu Hsi, is nevertheless consonant with Shao's descriptions.

[68] We say "presumably" because there is no record that Shao explains the process in this way. Later accounts, like his apocryphal *Mei-hua I-shu*, provide a complex numerological technique of generating hexagrams, etc. But we do not know whether Shao himself ever employed such methods.

We have not discussed the *hou-t'ien-tu*, the Succeeding Heaven diagram. Here Shao's treatment of the *I* materials resembles the standard structural analyses of K'ung Ying-ta, Ch'eng I or even Su Shih. For example, he says, "Fu's following [hexagram #23] Po illuminates how order is born from chaos. . . . Oh the times, oh the times!" (7B.18a). And: "Yang moves in its midst, without a hair's separation—this is the meaning of Fu" (7B.18b). For a discussion of the *hou-t'ien*, see 7B.11a–25b, called by Shao's editors "The Images and Numbers of the *Hou-t'ien*."

[69] These matters are discussed in John Henderson, *The Development and Decline of Chinese Cosmology*, pp. 82–87. On p. 84 Henderson mentions various associations of the Ho-t'u with the eight trigrams advanced by K'ung An-kuo (ca. 156–74 B.C.E.), Liu Hsin (ca. 46 B.C.E.–23 C.E.) and Ma Jung (79–166).

[70] Though the Ho-t'u is mentioned in various pre-Sung texts, no one knows today what form it took. For a survey of the Ho-t'u, especially in and around the T'ang, that manages to avoid mentioning Shao, see Michael Saso, "What Is the *Ho-t'u?*" *History of Religions* 18 (1978), pp. 399–416. Shao's treatment of the Ho-t'u became in turn the *locus classicus* for all later discussions. One can pull out cases of this quite at random. Much of the utility of the Ho-t'u lies in the new applications that later figures devised for it. See, for example, Hu Wei, *I-t'u ming-pien*.

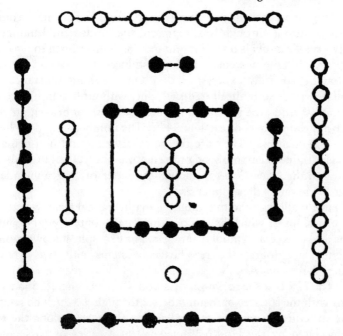

Fig. 6. The Ho-t'u
Source: Chu Hsi, *I pen-i* (Shih-chieh), p. 6.

The Ho-t'u consists of the numbers 1 through 10 arranged in four concentric squares. The odd numbers are represented by white circles, the even by blackened circles. The inner square is 5 surrounded by the second square, which is 10. Surrounding that are 1, 2, 3, and 4. The outer square consists of 6, 7, 8 and 9. Each of these is placed just outside the number which it is five more than, that is, 6 is just below 1, 7 is just above 2, etc.[71]

This diagram incorporates at least two bits of number lore that may be unfamiliar to us, though Shao's audience surely took them for granted. The first derives from the *Hsi-tz'u-chuan*:

Heaven is 1, earth 2, heaven 3, earth 4, heaven 5, earth 6, heaven 7, earth 8, heaven 9, earth 10.[72]

The second bit of lore is the *Hsi-tz'u*'s association of the numbers 6, 7, 8, and 9 with the yin or yang lines of the hexagram. Six stands for an old (*lao*) yin line that is about to change into its opposite; seven is a young

[71] For a brief exposition of these sets of four numbers, see 7A.6b. Graham, *Two Chinese Philosophers*, pp. 155–56, briefly discusses Liu Mu's use of these two sets.
[72] A10. Shao quotes this passage verbatim in 7A.15a.

(*shao*) yang line that will not change; and so on.[73] For Shao Yung the numbers from one through four represent the fundamental numbers of the universe: "*T'ai-chi* is one. Without moving it gives birth to two. Two, then spirit."[74] "One movement and one stillness interact and the *tao* of heaven-and-earth fully expresses it."[75] "One, without substance, is to symbolize what is so-by-itself (*tzu-jan*); one, without function, is to symbolize *tao*."[76] And "the substance-numbers (*t'i-shu*) of heaven are 4. . . . The substance-numbers of earth are 4."[77] The numbers 5 and 10 lie outside these sequences: "They are the poles of being and non-being (*yu-wu*)."[78] Thus, in its emphasis on only eight numbers, the Ho-t'u is compatible with the *hsien-t'ien-t'u*, though the latter of course includes the number 5 and omits the number 9.[79]

The Ho-t'u allows Shao to establish a mathematical framework within the relationships of which he can position many contemporary counting systems and powerful symbolic numbers. For example, his own concerns with ones and fours; the ten heavenly stems and twelve earthly branches;[80] the *Shuo-kua*'s association of 3 with heaven and 2 with earth;[81] the *Hsi-tz'u*'s association of 3 and 5 with change;[82] Shao's own concern with the squares of the numbers 2 through 9, which he relates to various structural aspects of the *I Ching*[83]—these are among the topics accommodated by the Ho-t'u framework in a series of passages that Shao's later editors called "The Complete Numbers of the Ho-t'u, Heaven and Earth."[84] The sources of this number lore include the *Hsi-tz'u-chuan*, Yang Hsiung (53 B.C.E.–18 C.E.), Tung Chung-shu (ca. 179–104 B.C.E.), and a host of other Han figures, as if Shao had set out to demonstrate the importance of number to most classical figures important to the eleventh century. Thus the diagram functions as a matrix wherein disparate numerological phenomena, representing a multitude of processes, relationships, and points of view, can be successfully integrated, and myriads of disparate things successfully contemplated.[85]

---

[73] A8. See 7A.6b-8a for Shao's extensive treatment of this ancient theme.

[74] 8B.23a.

[75] 5.1a.

[76] 7A.1a, which develops these ideas at some length.

[77] Ibid. Cf. 7A.23a, where the Ming commentator Huang Yüeh-chou explains that this indicates the way that four things, like eye, ear, nose, and mouth or sun, moon, stars, and zodiacal spaces, are unified in a single face or a single cosmos.

[78] 7A.6b.

[79] 7A.6b makes this connection explicit. Cf. Chu Hsi's *I-hsueh ch'i-meng* for a more complete discussion.

[80] Treated in 7A.13a.

[81] Section 1, treated in 7A.13b.

[82] A9, treated in 7A.15a.

[83] 7A.15a.

[84] This is 7A.1a through 24a, the first pages of the *Wai-p'ien*.

[85] We have not discussed the Lo-shu (Lo River writing), the companion piece to the Ho-

To conclude this section we will address Shao's famous set of cyclic markers. These are the generation (*shih*), which is thirty years long; the revolution (*yün*), which is twelve generations or 360 years; the epoch (*hui*), thirty revolutions or 10,800 years; and the cycle (*yüan*), twelve epochs or 129,600 years. (For an excerpt from one of the charts setting out this system, see figure 7.) As is well known, Shao believes that the universe goes through 129,600-year cycles of birth, growth, decay and death.[86] Thus it is generally assumed that these cyclic markers are the elements of a cosmic calendar. Such a view is reinforced by Shao's extension of these markers to smaller and smaller time units, where they indicate a year, the year's twelve months, the months' thirty days, their twelve hours, and their thirty double-minutes.[87]

This is no ordinary calendar. It is true enough that Shao derives the numbers 12 and 30 from the twelve months that make up an approximate year and the thirty days that make up an approximate month. But surely Shao is not suggesting that a month has exactly thirty days or a year twelve months. (Already by Han, Chinese astronomers had approximated the number of days in a year to be 365¼.) Indeed, at one point he argues that a month really has forty days, but that it discards one decade, just as a season is really four months long but discards one month.[88] Furthermore, there are cases where Shao uses these figures loosely, at one point speaking of one hundred years as if it might be equivalent to three generations.[89]

But it is Shao's other ways of extending these cyclic markers that reveal his intentions as numerological, that is, symbolic, rather than mathematical. In one instance he argues for the correspondence of the four cyclic markers to the "four images" of sun, moon, stars and zodiacal space we encountered in the previous section.[90] In another he correlates the cyclic markers with the four seasons. Within each season are the subcycles spring-summer-autumn-winter. Thus Shao can speak of sixteen periods, the "spring of spring," the "summer of spring," the "autumn of spring," the "spring of winter" and so on.[91] Here he also attributes a moral dimension to the cosmic process of birth and decay. It is thus easy for him,

t'u. It is the magic square of three. See Schuyler Cammann, "The Magic Square of Three in Old Chinese Philosophy and Religion," *History of Religion* 1 (1961), pp. 37–80, and John Henderson, *The Development and Decline of Chinese Cosmology*, pp. 82–87 and 125–26.

[86] For a clear exposition, see Fung Yu-lan, *A History of Chinese Philosophy*, vol. 2, pp. 469–74. The Sung dynasty takes place part way into the seventh epoch, just past the peak, which occurred at the time of Yao.

[87] 6.11b.

[88] Parallel with the way the diviner discards one of the fifty stalks when prognosticating with the *I*. See 7A.9a for this argument.

[89] 6.16a.

[90] 6.11a.

[91] 6.14a.

Sun Cycle	Moon Epoch	Star Revolutions	Zodiacal Generations	Years	Hexagram	Events
1st (*Chia*)	1st (*Tzŭ*)	1-30	1-360	1-10,800	24 ䷖	
	2nd (*Ch'ou*)	31-60	361-720	10,801-21,600	19 ䷒	
	3rd (*Yin*)	61-90	721-1,080	21,601-32,400	11 ䷊	Star Revolution 76 (*Chi*): Beginning of creatures
	4th (*Mao*)	91-120	1,081-1,440	32,401-43,200	34 ䷡	
	5th (*Ch'en*)	121-150	1,441-1,800	43,201-54,000	43 ䷪	
	6th (*Ssŭ*)	151-180	1,801-2,160	54,001-64,800	1 ䷀	Star Revolution 180 (*Kuei*); Zodiacal Generation 2,157: Rule of Yao
	7th (*Wu*)	181-210	2,161-2,520	64,801-75,600	44 ䷫	Dynasties of Hsia, Yin, Chou, Ch'in, Two Han, Two Chin, Three Kingdoms, N. & S. Dynasties, Sui, T'ang, Five Dynasties, Sung
	8th (*Wei*)	211-240	2,521-2,880	75,601-86,400	33 ䷠	
	9th (*Shen*)	241-270	2,881-3,240	86,401-97,200	12 ䷋	
	10th (*Yu*)	271-300	3,241-3,600	97,201-108,000	20 ䷓	
	11th (*Hsü*)	301-330	3,601-3,960	108,001-118,800	23 ䷖	Star Revolution 315 (*Wu*): Ending of Creatures
	12th (*Hai*)	331-360	3,961-4,320	118,801-129,600	2 ䷁	

Fig. 7. Table of Cosmic Chronology
Source: Fung Yu-lan, *History of Chinese Philosophy*, vol. 2, p. 471, derived from Shao Po-wen's account contained in the *Hsing-li ta-ch'üan* 8.12.

in the subsequent passage, to move immediately into questions of governance. Using the same logic that speaks of "the spring of spring," Shao establishes four subcategories within each of his major categories of emperor, monarch, king and tyrant. Thus,

> the emperor among emperors uses *tao* to conduct the affairs of *tao*. The monarch among emperors uses *tao* to conduct the affairs of virtue. The king among emperors uses *tao* to conduct the affairs of merit. [And so on up to] the tyrant among tyrants uses force to conduct the affairs of force.[92]

What serves then most literally as an epic calendar turns out to function in several other ways as well. It integrates the measurements of time, from the level of minutes to years to the complete cosmic cycle. It integrates the markers used for this cycle with the four images of heaven—sun, moon, stars, and zodiacal space. And, most important, it integrates time with the practice of government. Thus these discussions conclude with the following passage:

> The times have decline and growth. Affairs have continuity and change. If one is not a sage, he has nothing with which to fully express it. Therefore Confucius said: "A man good enough as a partner in one's studies (*hsüeh*) need not be good enough as a partner in the pursuit of the Way (*tao*); a man good enough as a partner in the pursuit of the Way need not be good enough as a partner in a common stand; a man good enough as a partner in a common stand need not be good enough as a partner in the exercise of moral discretion (*ch'üan*)."[93] From this one knows: how can the times of a billion generations (*shih*) and the truth/classics/regulation (*ching*) of a thousand million generations be sketched upon the ground and lightly spoken of?![94]

The rise and decline of the world can be expressed in images and numbers. Their progress is inevitable, unalterable. But because the sage knows them, he can govern (*ching*) their changes, judge circumstances, and exercise power. He cannot reverse the cosmic decline, but he can do his best to apply the sage's moral concerns to the deteriorating circumstances that heaven-and-earth present him with. It is precisely the ability to contemplate things (*kuan-wu*) that allows him to make this crucial link between things and values.

[92] 6.14b. On emperors, etc., see 5.10a.

[93] *The Analects* 9:29, translated by D. C. Lau (Penguin, 1979). *Ch'üan* is a steelyard. In the commentary literature of Han and T'ang, through which Shao must have read the passage, this *ch'üan* is opposed to *ching* "classic/that which is always true" and connotes the weighing of new situations as they present themselves on the spot rather than the following of norms set in advance. See James Legge, *The Analects of Confucius* (Taiwan reprint, n.d.), p. 226n. Yet the original intention of Confucius seems to have been the more general exercise of power that *ch'üan* also indicates.

[94] 6.14b.

In sum, Shao uses number to do five closely related things. First, number is the level of reality prior to images; its mathematical structure governs the progress from *t'ai-chi* to two modes to four images and on to the ten-thousand things. Number thus takes yin and yang, the logic of the previous level, as its subject matter, especially as these manifest in the eight trigrams. In this way Shao restructures *hsiang-shu* (images and number) by giving priority to number.

Second, number expresses the relationships of images in a simpler, more precise way. As we have seen, the system of images is like a great tree: "It is like the way a root has a trunk, a trunk has branches, a branch has leaves. The bigger they are, the fewer they are. The finer they are, the more they are. Unite them and it makes one. Spread them out and they make ten-thousand."[95] But though this schema unites the ten-thousand into one, to get from leaf to leaf one must trace back to the branch that each has in common, perhaps as far as the trunk, and then back out again. With number, however, one can move immediately anywhere within its system. The way that diagrams convey complex information all at once is the clearest example of this.

Third, number expresses the consistency of the world. Paralleling the way images provide Shao with a framework for positioning the ten-thousand things, number provides him with a consistent way to order time and space (the epic cycles, the progress of the year, the eight directions, etc.). This consistency is demonstrated by the way that 3 times 4 is the same as 2 times 6.[96]

Fourth, growing from these powers, number allows Shao to explain how one can obtain foreknowledge. The production of the world follows the sequence laid down by the production of the images. That sequence can be represented diagrammatically, for example in the *hsien-t'ien-t'u*—the mathematics of diagrams is so consistent that one may travel through it both forwards and backwards. Therefore it is possible to use these mathematical structures to examine what has not yet come into being.

Fifth, in all these ways number demonstrates that the structure of heaven-and-earth is knowable. Not only is this structure objective and apparent, it implies a cycle of values and governance, which can also be known by studying number.

Shao's use of number may be readily distinguished from two other uses, those of European natural science and of Pythagoreanism. First, Shao does not base his numbers on observations of natural regularities—what a Newtonian would mean by *kuan-wu*—nor is he drawn to number because of its calendrical successes. Thus, as Mitukuni Yosida has pointed

[95] 7A.24b.
[96] 7A.12a.

out, "Shao's unique attempt to define the universe numerologically was very much in the style of Han mathematical astronomy, but . . . his cycles were analogical rather than based directly on observed celestial periods."[97] In the same way, Shao's large numbers suggest the technical manipulations of mathematicians.[98] But he works in imitation of their forms, rather than within them. As Michael Freeman has said, nowhere does Shao rely on any operation more complex than simple arithmetic.[99] Thus in this instance *kuan-wu* is not contemplating with the eye; it is contemplating with the mind. And what one sees are the numbers of the *hsien-t'ien*. For, as Shao says, "The *hsien-t'ien* learning is the mind."[100] This is a topic to which we will return in the final section of this chapter.

Shao may also be easily differentiated from numerologists like the Pythagoreans. Early Pythagoreans claimed that things *were* number. These numbers manifested in solid geometry. Thus the pyramid, by its four points, was the elementary form of fire, the cube of water, and so on. Shao, on the other hand, shows how number governs the activities—the function and order—of yin and yang and establishes the relationship of the trigrams. Furthermore, number itself derives from the more profound level of coherence Shao calls spirit. In the next section we will examine the limitations of number and Shao's response to them. Thus we will begin our return to the issues raised at the beginning of this chapter: how literati may know heaven-and-earth by contemplating the things that constitute it, and how they can derive certainty of values from this contemplation.

Spirit and Principles

We have seen a variety of ways in which number expresses the order of the universe. Indeed, "the numbers of the *I* plumb the beginning and ending of heaven-and-earth."[101] But number emerges from the deeper level of spirit.[102] Shao uses the term "*li*," or principles, to represent this most fundamental orderliness.

Despite number's marvelous efficacy, Shao goes to some lengths to warn against its misuse, as in occult practices.

---

[97] Mitukuni Yosida, "The Chinese Concept of Nature," in *Chinese Science*, ed. Shigeru Nakayama and Nathan Sivin (Cambridge: MIT Press, 1973), p. 84.

[98] As well as his use of the word "*yen.*"

[99] Michael Freeman, "From Adept to Worthy," p. 481.

[100] 7B.13a.

[101] 8A.31b.

[102] Although Shao claims that "spirit gives birth to number" (8B.23a), he does not explain just how this occurs. Presumably, as we move from the unitary *t'ai-chi* to the manifest things of the world, the highly abstract coherence of number emerges somehow from inchoate spirit.

The *tao* of heaven-and-earth is simply straightforwardness, that is all. One should use straightforwardness to seek it. If one relies on cleverness and number, going along a shortcut, this is twisting heaven-and-earth and giving in to human desires.[103]

In place of this, Shao recommends the proper way to address such matters:

[When speaking about *tao*,] if words issue forth from genuineness and integrity (*ch'eng*), then your mind will not labor but be at ease. After a while people will come to believe your words. If you compose falsehoods and rely on number, you may for a time deceive people. In the long run you must be defeated.[104]

That is to say, "Cleverness and number can be set forth in a morning. But at some time they will be exhausted. Only perfect integrity is as long-lasting as heaven-and-earth."[105] In sum, the use of number may degenerate into practices that are deceptive, soon exhausted and selfish.

In contrast to the clarity of number, spirit by its very nature escapes our attempts to pin it down. It points to hidden processes of heaven-and-earth that are not susceptible to the precise articulation that Shao can provide for the realms of number or image.[106] Therefore most of Shao's definitions are couched in negatives:

There is no place that spirit is and no place it is not.[107]

Hidden in heaven, hidden in earth, arriving without going, not controlled by yin and yang—this is spirit.[108]

Yet for all that, spirit is not chaotic. Indeed, it possesses a self-existing orderliness that Shao uses the word *li* or "principles" to express:

The images and numbers of heaven can be extended.[109] As for [heaven's] spiritual workings (*shen-yung*), it cannot be measured. Heaven can be fully expressed by principles. It cannot be fully expressed by physical forms (*hsing*). The techniques of astronomy [110] use physical forms to fully express heaven—is this possible?![111]

[103] 8B.31a.
[104] 8B.29b.
[105] 8B.30a.
[106] In all these ways Shao's use of the term *shen* is consonant with other eleventh-century *tao-hsüeh* thinkers. See Graham, *Two Chinese Philosophers*, pp. 112–18, and Ira Kasoff's discussion of Chang Tsai's equally unsystematic treatment of such a realm, *The Thought of Chang Tsai*, pp. 53–60 (heaven) and pp. 60–65 (spirit).
[107] 8B.16b, playing on *Hsi-tz'u* A4.
[108] 8B.27b.
[109] In the sense that they extend on the model of 1–2–4–8 and thus can be extended to allow us to know new things.
[110] Literally, "of the *hun-t'ien* or egg-shaped theory of the cosmos."
[111] 8A.16b. Compare 8B.22b.

By *li* Shao means something very much like the English word "principles." The most striking characteristics of *li* are their inaccessibility to measurement, their moral dimension and their omnipresence. We can begin to understand the nature of principles through a series of contrasts with other terms. Above, Shao has opposed them to *hsing* or physical forms. In the following passage on the calendar, he contrasts them with *fa* or models. Ou-yang Hsiu, in his preface to the *Hsin T'ang-shu* essay on the calendar, argues against the application of number to the study of heaven-and-earth. Though number builds consistent and systematic patterns, heaven-and-earth keeps changing, so that the calendars of Han are now out of date. Though Shao is popularly known as a calendar-maker, we have seen that his "calendar" is not designed to provide us with the usual sorts of precise measurements. In this passage he seems to be making the same argument as Ou-yang:

> The calendar cannot be free of mistakes. Those today who study the calendar only know the models (*fa*) of the calendar; they do not know the principles (*li*) of the calendar. Lo-hsia Hung could do calculations.[112] Master Kan and Master Shih could examine the heavenly signs.[113] Lo-hsia Hung only knew calendrical models. Yang Hsiung knew calendrical models and also knew calendrical principles.[114]

The word translated here as "calendar" is *li*, which also means "to calculate the motion of the heavenly bodies" or just "to calculate." Shao seems to have all these meanings in mind when he opposes *fa* and *li* (principles). Yang Hsiung knew *li-fa*—models to follow and rules to invoke in measuring the calculable activities of heaven-and-earth. Yet he also knew *li-li*—the principles of heaven-and-earth that cannot be measured by form or number. As Shao remarks,

> The numbers of the world emerge from principles. If one goes against principles, then one enters (engages in) technique. People today use number and so enter technique; therefore they do not enter (arrive at, conform to) principles.[115]

---

[112] Lo-hsia (fl. ca. 140–104 B.C.E.) is said to be the earliest exponent of the *hun-t'ien* or celestial sphere theory of the universe, in which "The heavens are like a hen's egg and as round as a crossbow bullet; the earth is like the yolk of the egg, and lies alone in the centre" (Chang Heng [78–139 C.E.], quoted in Needham, *Science and Civilisation*, vol. 3, p. 217). For Shao's views on Lo-hsia, see 8A.17a.

[113] These are "two of the greatest, and earliest, astronomers in Chinese history, Shih Shen of the State of Chhi [Ch'i] and Kan Te of the state of Wei. Their work must be placed between about -370 [370 B.C.E.] and -270 [270 B.C.E.]. It was they, together with a third astronomer, Wu Hsien, who drew up the first star-catalogues. . . ." Needham, *Science and Civilisation*, Vol. 3, p. 197. For Shao's views of these two, see 8A.17b.

[114] 8A.17b. Yang (53 B.C.E.–18 C.E.) "saw the mind of heaven-and-earth," says Shao, ibid., alluding to the *T'uan-chuan* of hexagram #24 Fu.

[115] 7B.19b.

Regarding the learning that arrives at principles: if you have not arrived at integrity, you will not reach it. Regarding the learning of principles in things: if there is something you do not comprehend, you cannot use force to penetrate it. With forced penetration there is subjectivity. If there is subjectivity, then you lose principles and enter technique.[116]

Shao is distinguishing here between two types of knowing. The first is true learning or *hsüeh*, which we examined briefly at the beginning of this chapter. It has principles as its object. The second is mere knowledge about the world and is developed by what Shao calls "techniques" (*shu*). Confusion arises when literati talk about "learning the principles in things." Most literati think that they can master the world by force of knowledge and by manipulation. Shao however argues that this brings only limited benefit. Worse, it cuts one off from real knowledge of things: it generates an attitude of selfishness that leads to the distorted vision discussed above.

The English word "principle" thus also suggests the morality that is essential to Shao's conception of *li*:

The Buddha discards [the relationships of] ruler-minister, father-son and husband-wife. How is this the principle that is so of itself?![117]

To follow principles is to act normally (constantly). To be outside principles is to act aberrantly.[118]

Finally, Shao argues that principles are present in everything: "There is no affair great or slight that does not have the principles of heaven and of humanity."[119] They are hidden and difficult to know, yet they bring knowledge superior to all others:

There are many today who talk about reading books. But there are few who are able to. If you attain the true delight of heaven's principles,[120] what book can you not read? What obstacle can you not break through? What principles can you not master?[121]

Everyone knows that things can be seen with the eye. Shao has argued that images and numbers can be seen with the mind. But he suggests a

---

[116] 8B.29a. The first sentence is also found by itself in 8B.25b. Again: "If you forcibly seize it and demand to get it, this is going against the principle of heaven. If you go against the principle of heaven, distress and disaster will necessarily occur" (8B.31b).

[117] 8B.38b. The term is "*tzu-jan chih li.*"

[118] 8B.26a.

[119] 8B.31b.

[120] Though the words are the same, this is not the Ch'eng brothers' "*t'ien-li,*" the pattern to which everything should conform, but merely the principle that characterizes heaven's process.

[121] 8B.34a.

still more subtle way to contemplate things (*kuan-wu*). If we use principles, we can see them fully and directly, become a sage, and attain to the world's highest knowledge:

> Now, what is meant by contemplating things is not using the eye to contemplate them. It is not contemplating them using the eye but contemplating them using the mind. It is not contemplating them using the mind but contemplating them using principles.
>
> All things of the world have principles in them, all have nature in them, and all have destiny in them. The reason we call it principles is that they can be known after investigating them. The reason we call it nature is that it can be known after fully developing it. The reason we call it destiny is that it can be known after fully attaining it.[122]
>
> These three are the world's true knowledge. Even a sage cannot go beyond it.[123]

On the first level of contemplation, we use our senses—compasses and squares, likes and dislikes, the usual methods of assessing the phenomenal world. On the second, we use our mind to reflect on these perceptions, using images and number to order them. But how does one contemplate using principles? We know that such contemplation goes beyond the conscious use of eye or mind, and we know that by means of principles, the spiritual workings (*shen-yung*) of heaven can be fully expressed.[124] This suggests that principles exist beyond the possibility of measuring, such that the kind of knowing appropriate to them cannot itself be known in any conventional way. Shao certainly never describes what it might be. Our definition of *li*, then, needs to stress its aspects of immeasurability and profundity, the necessarily mysterious quality that goes with the level of reality Shao calls "spirit."

What does this use of the term *li* say about the way we should understand number? First of all, Shao states that "the numbers of the world emerge from principles."[125] While these two levels of reality are distinct, they are no more in tension with each other than are number and images. But number can be abused for selfish purposes—unless one understands that it is rooted in spirit.[126] Then one sees what cannot be measured: the learning of integrity or authenticity (*ch'eng*) that is a crucial part of sagehood.[127]

By principles, then, Shao does not mean specific individual principles,

---

[122] In reference to the discussion of principle, nature and destiny in *Shuo-kua* 1.
[123] 6.26a. A similar passage is found in 7B.23a.
[124] 8A.16b.
[125] 7B.19b.
[126] "Spirit, then number" (7B.23b). "Spirit gives birth to number" (8B.23a).
[127] For an extended discussion of the importance of *ch'eng*, see 8B.25a–26a.

each applying to one thing (*wu*) or category (*lei*). Rather, "principles" indicate a coherence or intelligibility that is precisely not susceptible to such articulation. This is certainly different from the use of the same term *li* by the Ch'eng brothers to indicate the pattern that all things should conform to, as the next chapter will demonstrate.

We have seen in the previous sections how the things (*wu*) of heaven-and-earth are ordered. We must now return to human beings, specifically to the human mind. How is that mind related to the three levels of order we have just examined? What is the special power of "things," that Shao should place such emphasis upon contemplating them? These two questions will lead us to a final appreciation of Shao Yung's view of heaven-and-earth and man's role within it.

MIND AND THINGS

We can begin with Shao Yung's definition of mind:

> Mind is *t'ai-chi*. The human mind should be like stopped water—then it will be settled. Settled, it will be still. Still, it will be enlightened.[128]

The stilled mind is thus equated with the very root of existence. But mind operates at other levels as well. Moving upward through Shao's three levels of order from *t'ai-chi* to spirit and principles, we find in the following passage that mind seems to contain the principles of heaven-and-earth.[129] It is also the source of diagrams, from which number and image arise. Finally, the ten-thousand things all arise in it.

> The *hsien-t'ien* learning is a model/method/law of the mind (*hsin-fa*). Thus the diagrams all arise within. The ten-thousand transformations and the thousand affairs all come into being in the mind. Although the diagrams are without writing, I speak all day without ever departing from them. Indeed, the principles of heaven-and-earth and the ten-thousand things are fully expressed in their midst.[130]

The *hsien-t'ien* learning is a *hsin-fa*—a model, method, and law of the mind. It is a model in that mind possesses the same orderliness as the diagrams. It is a method in that literati can train their own minds by studying the diagram. It is a law in that the real, unchanging structure of the world is present in both *hsien-t'ien* and the mind. As one of Shao's poems remarks:

---

[128] 8B.25a.

[129] But Shao never directly addresses this issue that so engaged Ch'eng I and Chu Hsi.

[130] 7A.34b. Mind, then, is *t'ai-chi* in the sense that everything arises in it and the ten-thousand transformations are born therein.

Man is born after heaven-and-earth.
His mind existed before heaven-and-earth.
Heaven-and-earth emerge from me.
What more is there to say about it?[131]

Not only do the diagrams arise in the mind, the possibilities of all trans-formations are also born there. When he contemplates the diagrams, Shao finds that his speech emerges congruent with them as well. Thus *t'ai-chi*, diagrams, and mind can endlessly produce things. Indeed, the prin-ciples of all things are fully present in all three. Therefore "if the mind is one and undivided, it can respond to the ten-thousand things. This is why the superior man empties his mind and is thus unmoved."[132]

What are things, that the sages' responsiveness to them should be so crucial? As we have seen, most fundamentally, we human beings are nat-ural things of heaven-and-earth. We saw earlier that Shao states: "From this we know that I am also a man, and men are also I. Men and I are both things."[133] We have also seen at some length that the order of the world—from objects to images to number to principles—is also complete in things. This is why Shao places such importance on knowing their *hsing* or true nature, rather than being misled by our projections. And most recently we have discussed how the *hsien-t'ien* learning is complete in the mind. Thus mind, *t'ai-chi*, and things are all congruent.

Things have a two-fold value. First, because mind is difficult to observe and *t'ai-chi* is hidden, it is best to begin our studies by contemplating things. The outer orderliness, which is more accessible and can be ex-pressed with image and number, leads us to the principles that exist at a more subtle level. Second, since things contain the order of heaven-and-earth, they offer a real, "object-ive" basis for ultimate values. There is not a separate source for such values outside them, thus no need to look else-where. If literati know things, they will know the proper place in heaven-and-earth for everything. They will also know how to act, since they can see beyond their selfish particularities and identify with the processes of heaven-and-earth.

These views culminate in the following long passage, where Shao shows how man, as sage/thing, does not differ from heaven-and-earth and the ten-thousand things. Indeed, it is precisely because man is a thing that he can know things so well. In particular, he can infer knowledge of

---

[131] *I-ch'uan chi-jang chi*, 19.12b.

[132] 8B.29a. For a discussion of the place of mind in, *inter alia*, eleventh-century thought, see Irene Bloom, "On the Matter of the Mind: The Metaphysical Basis of the Expanded Self," in *Individualism and Holism*, ed. Donald Munro, (Ann Arbor: Center for Chinese Studies, 1985), pp. 293–330.

[133] 6.27a.

everything from his own human circumstances. Further, his body, speech, and mind can also act as the body, speech, and mind of heaven.

> In this way, men are also things, and the sage is also a man. There is a thing of one thing. There is a thing of ten things. There is a thing of a hundred things. There is a thing of a thousand things. There is a thing of ten-thousand things. There is a thing of a million things. There is a thing of a billion things. Isn't man the thing of a billion things?
>
> There is a man of one man. There is a man of ten men. There is a man of a hundred men. There is a man of a thousand men. There is a man of ten-thousand men. There is a man of a million men. There is a man of a billion men. Isn't the sage the man of a billion men?
>
> From this one knows that man is the perfection of things and that the sage is the perfection of man. One can only call the perfection of things the "thing of things." One can only call the perfection of man the "man of men." Now, the thing of things means the perfect thing. The man of men means the perfect man. Take a perfect thing and combine it with a perfect man, and if it is not the sage, then what kind of man do you mean? If he is not sagely, then I do not believe it.
>
> Why? Because he can use one mind to contemplate the ten-thousand minds, use one person to contemplate the ten-thousand people, use one thing to contemplate the ten-thousand things, use one generation to contemplate the ten-thousand generations. And because his mind can represent the intentions of heaven, his mouth can represent the words of heaven, his hands can represent the work of heaven, his person can represent the affairs of heaven. And because above he can know the seasons of heaven, below he can fully express the principles of earth, in the middle fully express the circumstances of things, and over-all illuminate human affairs. And because he can order and adjust heaven-and-earth, participate in cosmic creation, evaluate past and present, and put men and things in their proper relation. . . . [134]

These are bold claims. They go well beyond noticing a few qualities that human beings might have in common with the ten-thousand things. Indeed, the sage/man/thing can use his personal qualities of body, mind, or generation to understand the general qualities of all minds, all things, in all times. Still more actively, he can use these qualities to act as heaven. And still more exaltedly, he can adjust heaven-and-earth, participate in cosmic creation, and put men and things in their proper relation.

Shao goes on to explain that all this is so because the sage and heaven share a single *tao*:

> The *tao* of *tao* is fully expressed by heaven. The *tao* of heaven is fully expressed by earth. The *tao* of heaven-and-earth is fully expressed by the ten-

[134] 5.5a–6a.

thousand things. The *tao* of heaven-and-earth and the ten-thousand things is fully expressed by man. Someone who can know how the *tao* of heaven-and-earth and the ten-thousand things are fully expressed by man can then fully express the people.[135]

Because heaven has the ability to fully express things, it is called august heaven. Because a man has the ability to fully express the people, he is called a sage. If august heaven differs from the ten-thousand things, it is not what is called august heaven. If the sage differs from the people, he is not what is called a sage. Because the ten-thousand people and the ten-thousand things are the same, the sage surely does not differ from august heaven. Since this is so, the sage and august heaven are one *tao*.

The sage and august heaven are one *tao*, so the ten-thousand people and the ten-thousand things can also by this be one *tao*. The ten-thousand people of one generation and the ten-thousand things of one generation can also by this be one *tao*, so the ten-thousand people of the ten-thousand generations and the ten-thousand things of the ten-thousand generations can also by this be one *tao*. This is clear (*ming*, bright, illuminating).

Now, the full expression of things by august heaven and the full expression of people by the sage both have four mansions in them. The four mansions of august heaven are what are called spring, summer, autumn, and winter. Yin and yang rise and fall in their midst. The four mansions of the sage are what are called the *Book of Change*, the *Book of Documents*, the *Book of Poetry*, and the *Spring and Autumn Annals*. Rites and music decay or flourish in their midst.[136]

In heaven, earth, humanity, and the ten-thousand things, there is only one *tao*. That one *tao* manifests equally in the natural world and in human culture. In heaven, yin and yang rise and fall amidst the four seasons. For the sage, rites and music decay and flourish amidst the Four Classics. The literatus who can contemplate things realizes how all knowledge is unified. By learning the nature of things, he learns his own nature and that of heaven-and-earth. Thus the ordering powers of natural process become human powers as well. "It is not just this generation that calls it most spiritual and most sagely. 'Knowledge does not go beyond this.' "[137]

---

[135] The term *chin*, "fully express," indicates how a category within Shao's hierarchy of stages can give full expression to the possibilities of the stage just prior to it. Thus earth can give full expression to the *tao* of heaven, etc. Understanding this, Shao argues, gives one the power to fully express, or set the field of possibilities for, the people.

[136] 5.7a–8a.

[137] 6.26b, quoting *Hsi-tz'u* B3.

CHAPTER FIVE

Ch'eng I and the Pattern of Heaven-and-Earth

IN 1050, when Ch'eng I was seventeen, he sent a long memorial to the Emperor Jen-tsung, criticizing contemporary society. Part of this memorial reads as follows:

> Your ignorant and worthless subject Ch'eng I, sincerely risking death and repeatedly saluting, offers this memorial to Your Majesty the Emperor. . . .
>
> What your subject has studied (*hsüeh*) is the *tao* of the world's Great Mean.[1] Sages take it as their nature and are sages. Worthies follow it and are worthies.[2] [The sage-emperors] Yao and Shun used it and were Yao and Shun. Confucius transmitted it and was Confucius. As *tao* it is utterly vast, but its practice is utterly easy. Through the Three Dynasties[3] there was no one who did not follow it. Since Ch'in (221–206 B.C.E.) it has declined without revival. The likes of Wei (220–264) and Chin (265–419) have far departed from it. Han (206 B.C.E.–220 C.E.) and T'ang (618–906) achieved a modest prosperity, but their practice was impure. From olden times many have studied it, but examining their attainments [we see] that they are few indeed. . . .
>
> One does not regard one's body as one's own, but acts in response to the times. Advance and withdrawal are without constancy, so one abides only in righteousness. . . . Chu-ko Liang and your subject are examples of "not regarding one's body as one's own, but acting in response to the times."[4] He resonated to the righteousness of Liu Pei's three visits[5] and commiserated with the people

---

[1] *T'ien-hsia ta-chung chih tao*, that is, the supreme principles of the world. The phrase derives from the standard Old Text commentary to the *Shu Ching* (Book of Documents) by K'ung An-kuo (ca. 156–74 B.C.E.). See *Ku-chu shih-san-ching, Shang-shu (Ssu-pu chi-yao)*, 7.1b (page 38). "*Tao* of the Great Mean" is how K'ung glosses the term "*huang-chi*" (supreme principles) from part two of the *Hung-fan* (Great Plan) section of the *Shu*. (This is also, of course, the origin of Shao Yung's title, "*Huang-chi ching-shih shu*.") K'ung in turn may have derived the term "Great Mean" from the *I Ching*. The 14th hexagram, Ta-yu (Great Abundance), consists entirely of yang or strong lines, except for the fifth, the ruler's position, which is yin or weak. The *T'uan-chuan* states: "The weak attains the honored place at the Great Mean. Thus above and below respond to it." (Cf. W/B p. 457.) Is Ch'eng making a veiled criticism of his emperor?

[2] Paraphrasing Mencius 7A30.

[3] The Hsia, Shang and Chou, or China in the second and first millennia B.C.E.

[4] Chu-ko (181–234) was the great strategist and adviser to Liu Pei (162–223), who claimed to be the legitimate heir of Han.

[5] According to legend, Liu Pei was received by Chu-ko only on the third visit to his hermitage.

in their bitter affliction. . . . As for your subject, I live at the time of Your Sagely Brilliance. Thus, anxious over the world's danger and disorder, how could I in righteousness regard [only] my own body as good, without a word to enlighten Your Majesty? Therefore I said, "Advance and withdrawal being without constancy, one abides only in righteousness."

Your subject begs to discuss the affairs of the world. I do not know, does Your Majesty consider the world today to be secure? In danger? Ordered? Disordered? How could one know that it is in danger and disordered without thinking of the way to deliver it! If you say "secure and ordered," then your subject begs to illuminate how this is not so. In all sincerity, how do present conditions differ from sleeping on a pile of firewood that contains a fire—because the fire has not yet broken into a blaze, does one then call it "secure"? The *Book of Documents* says, "The people are the root of the nation. If the root is strong, then the nation is peaceful."[6] I would humbly suggest that the way of a strong root lies in securing the people. I would humbly suggest that the root of the kingly *tao* is benevolence (*jen*). . . .

For two thousand years the kingly *tao* has not been practiced. People living in later times all doltishly say that the times are different and that things have changed, so that it cannot be practiced again. This is the depth of their ignorance. . . . But your subject observes Your Majesty's mind (*hsin*): it is not unanxious about the world. If Your Majesty uses your anxious mind to practice the kingly *tao*, then how can there be any difficulties?. . .

> [Offered by] your doltish subject [Ch'eng] I, entirely overstepping his bounds, in extreme agitation and fear, risking death, kowtowing, with cautious speech.[7]

When he is older, Ch'eng I will be less optimistic about the prospect of imperial power acting on its own to improve literati morals. Yet this memorial suggests significant continuities between the youth of seventeen and the mature thinker. Most obvious is the demand for righteous action in response to ubiquitous moral decay. We can see, too, Ch'eng's enormous self-assurance, deriving in part from his commitment to *tao*—the ancients' touchstone, now unpracticed for two thousand years. As Ch'eng I matured he deepened his connection to that *tao* and shifted the locus of the problem toward the practices of his fellow literati, developing a more precise etiology: the current crisis was due to literatus ambition, greed, desire, that is, to selfishness (*ssu*).

Ch'eng's *I Ching* commentary is, among many other things, a record

---

[6] In *Wu-tzu chih ko* (Songs of the five sons). Cf. James Legge, *The Shoo King or Book of Historical Documents* (Hong Kong, 1865), p. 158.

[7] *Erh-Ch'eng chi* (The complete works of the Ch'eng brothers) (Peking: Chung-hua, 1981), pp. 510–15.

of this social analysis, which he worked and reworked throughout his later years.[8] On its simplest level it addresses elements of literatus life like the family, government service, and the process of learning, which are always addressed in moral terms. A half-dozen examples will suggest both how Ch'eng uses the text and the nature of his views on contemporary society. For instance, the *Hsiang-chuan* to hexagram #10 Lü (Treading) states that "the superior man (*chün-tzu*) uses the distinction between above and below to stabilize the people's aspirations."[9] Ch'eng I himself aspired to sagehood. But in the contemporary world, his commentary argues,

> from ordinary literati to high officials, people aspire daily to honor and glory. Farmers, artisans and merchants aspire daily to wealth and extravagance. Millions and billions of minds compete for benefit. With the world so disordered, how can there be unity?[10]

Ch'eng attacks this greed as particularly out of place in official life. Instead of acting for the public good, officials just reckon their own benefit and harm.[11] The first line statement of Lü reads, "If he treads forward on his accustomed path, there will be no fault."[12] Ch'eng takes this statement to be about advancement into officialdom. He comments:

> If he cannot be at ease with himself in his accustomed poverty, then in his advance he acts from greed, seeking to eliminate his poverty. He does not desire

[8] As he remarks in *Erh-Ch'eng chi, I-shu* (Remaining works of the Ch'eng brothers) 17.174. The preface to the *I-chuan* (Commentary on the *I Ching*) is dated 1099. References to the *I-chuan* are to the most widely used current text, the 1884 *Ku-i ts'ung-shu* copy of the 1351 *Chi-te-t'ang* woodblock edition (Taipei: Shih-chieh, 1972); this text has been checked against the punctuated version contained in *Erh-Ch'eng chi*. A reference of the form "*I-chuan* 48.3" will indicate page 48, column 3. In fact, as A. C. Graham points out, the *I* commentary is "the only full-length work written in person by either of the Ch'engs." See *Two Chinese Philosophers* (London: Lund, Humphries, 1958), p. 143. But note also Hoyt Tillman's cautions regarding this point in his *Utilitarian Confucianism* (Cambridge: Harvard University Press, 1982), pp. 81–82.

The most useful essay on Ch'eng's *I Ching* studies is Toda Toyosaburō, "Izen ekiten kō," in his *Ekikyō chushaku shikō* (An outline history of *I Ching* commentaries) (Tokyo: Fugen, 1968), pp. 530–57. See also Lin I-sheng, *I-ch'uan I-chuan ti ch'u-shih che-hsüeh* (The this-worldly philosophy of Ch'eng I's *I Ching* commentary) (Taipei: Commercial Press, 1978). In the *Chin-ssu lu*, Chu Hsi and Lü Tsu-ch'ien's topically arranged anthology of their Northern Sung masters, approximately one-sixth of all selections come from Ch'eng's commentary. Wing-tsit Chan's translation of this work is therefore especially helpful to students of Ch'eng's *I*. See his *Reflections on Things at Hand* (New York: Columbia University Press, 1967).

[9] Cf. W/B, p. 45.

[10] *I-chuan* 48.3. Cf. Chan, trans., *Reflections*, p. 206.

[11] *Erh-Ch'eng chi* 19.260.

[12] Cf. W/B, p. 45.

to have a positive effect. Once he has advanced, he will necessarily be extremely arrogant. Therefore if he goes forward there will be fault.

The worthy is at peace treading his accustomed path. His circumstances delight him. His advance will have a good effect.[13]

Ch'eng's commentary on the *I Ching* reflects how eleventh-century China provided enormous opportunities for literatus advancement into real power—as politicians, within a vigorous economy, as litterateurs, as members of influential families, etc. We can gauge as well the enormous pressures they were under, from each other, their families, the state, and merchants, all in competition for scarce resources. Ch'eng portrays this society as fraught with ambitious men making an unending series of wrong decisions. For him the solution is simple: one must choose righteousness (*i*) over personal benefit (*li*). The difference between the great Shun and the famous bandit Chih is merely that.[14] For "the worthy knows only righteousness, and that is all."[15] Or as his memorial had put it, "Advance and withdrawal being without constancy, one abides only in righteousness."[16]

Righteous behavior is essentially acting without selfishness. Selfishness invades every aspect of human existence, and human emotionality is especially prone to it. Even kindness (*en*) can lead to difficulties when it arises inappropriately. Hexagram #37 Chia-jen means "family." Its second line is yin or weak. Ch'eng's commentary discusses a particular form that this weakness may take:

In the blood relationship of father and son, men usually let feelings conquer decorum and kindness snatch away righteousness. Only the man who stands firm (*kang*)[17] is able not to lose the correct pattern (*li*) through his selfish love. Thus in the hexagram "Family," firmness is essentially considered good, as in the first, third, and top lines.[18]

Indeed, the top line of this hexagram reads "If there is sincerity and sternness, in the end it will be auspicious." The *Hsiang-chuan* to this line—which Ch'eng I assumes to have been written by Confucius—adds: "The

---

[13] *I-chuan* 48.6. Cf. Chan, trans., *Reflections*, p. 184.

[14] *Erh-Ch'eng chi* 17.176. Here Ch'eng is reworking Mencius's distinction between the two men on the basis of benefit and goodness (7A.25).

[15] *Erh-Ch'eng chi* 2A.18.

[16] Note that Ch'eng I's own career pattern accords with these principles. He declined repeated offers of official posts, acceding only at the age of fifty-four. For brief summaries see Chan, *Reflections*, p. xxx; J. P. Bruce, *Chu Hsi and his Masters* (London: Probsthain, 1923), pp. 41–45; and Wing-tsit Chan's biography in Herbert Franke, *Sung Biographies* (Wiesbaden: Steiner, 1976), pp. 174–79.

[17] For a discussion of *kang* as the solid or yang line, see chapter 1.

[18] *I-chuan* 163.7. Cf. Chan, trans., *Reflections*, p. 173.

auspiciousness of sternness means [looking] back at oneself." Ch'eng comments:

> The line statement says that to regulate the family there must be sternness and strictness, and Confucius also repeatedly warns us to be strict first with ourselves. If sternness and strictness are not first practiced in oneself, then people will be resentful and will not submit. Thus when it says "If there is sternness it will be auspicious," it means being able to "[look] back at yourself."[19]

There is a relentless quality to this self-discipline. For example, commenting on line three of hexagram #7 Shih (Army), he says, "[Mencius] never considered Tseng Tzu's filial piety excessive.[20] For whatever a son can personally do is what ought to be done."[21] In the same way, there is no "time off" outside this practice. Ch'eng I reports the following:

> Once Lü Yü-shu[22] came from Kou-shih in the middle of the sixth month.[23] I peeked at him when he was at leisure and found that he was always sitting formally with dignity. He was earnest and sincere indeed.[24]

What is more, one's selflessness must be so thorough as to lack the slightest self-consciousness. "Although you may treat the affairs of the world impartially (*kung*), if you do it with any selfish intention, that's selfishness (*ssu*)."[25] Indeed, "as soon as someone intends to be impartial, that's a selfish mind."[26] Thus Ch'eng I demands a severe and constant vigilance of himself and recommends the same to all others. He applies the *Book of Change* to this project as well.

This impression of Ch'eng as a fierce moralist is not incorrect. But by neglecting the basis on which his morality rests, it is ultimately as incomplete and narrow as it makes him out to be. That basis is the unity of human beings with heaven-and-earth and all things. Like the problems of human society, this issue engaged Ch'eng when he was still very young. Here is his earliest surviving attempt at a solution.

A RECORD OF RAISING FISH (WHEN TWENTY-TWO)

Before the study was a stone pool. My family bought young fish to feed the cats, but when I saw their frothing I could not bear it, so I selected some to

---

[19] *I-chuan* 165.9. Cf. Chan, trans., *Reflections*, p. 173. However, for Ch'eng's warning against taking this severity too far, see his commentary to the top line of hexagram #35 Chin (Advance [Progress]), *I-chuan* 156.2.

[20] Tseng Tzu was considered the author of the *Hsiao Ching* or *Classic of Filial Piety*.

[21] *Erh-Ch'eng chi* 2A.36.

[22] On Lü (1044–1090), "an outstanding pupil of the Ch'eng brothers," see Chan's note in *Reflections*, p. 64 n. 138.

[23] That is, probably in late July.

[24] *Erh-Ch'eng chi* 18.191. Cf. Chan, *Reflections*, p. 145.

[25] *Erh-Ch'eng chi* 5.77.

[26] *Erh-Ch'eng chi* 18.192.

raise. I got over a hundred and raised them in [the pool]. The large ones were like fingers, the slight ones like slivers. With chin in hand I observed them all day long. When I first released them, how elating—fish attaining their proper place. By the end of the time that I observed them, how pitiful—what feelings resonated within me.

I read the books of the ancient sages and observe their rules and prohibitions. "Close-mesh nets should not be placed in ponds."[27] For if a fish's tail is not a foot long, it should not be killed; the market should not sell it nor the people eat it. The humanity (*jen*) of the sages is to care for things like this without injuring them. But if things are to be caught in this way, then what should *I* do, who delight in their life and [in allowing them] to follow their nature? I think about these fish in such circumstances: should they have [to suffer] this hardship? And can't all things be seen by analogy to these fish?

Ah fish, ah fish! Thin hooks and fine nets—I cannot prohibit those elsewhere. Roasting and sucking [your flesh]—I can free you from that here. I know the vastness of rivers and oceans is sufficient to let you follow your nature. I think of putting you there, but I have not yet found the road [that goes there]. I am only able to take some dippers of water to save your life. In saving you I am true to my mind, and many of you have survived. But given the myriad kinds of things between heaven and earth—what of my mind then? Ah fish! Ah fish! What makes my mind feel pity is not fish alone. Thus I wrote "A Record of Raising Fish."

Recorded in summer, 1054.

In the past I wrote the "Record of Raising Fish." That was almost thirty years ago. I saw it by accident in an old basket. I sighed for myself: I was young and had aspiration. I could not bear to discard it. Observing what I knew in the past, following what I have reached today, I am ashamed of my youthful mind—was I not close to throwing myself away? I showed it to my students, that they should take me as a warning.

1079, first month, thirteenth day, written beneath the south window of the western study.[28]

Why was Ch'eng I ashamed? There are three reasons. In part it was the claim for emotionality as the basis for his connectedness with all things. More importantly, this piece expresses his helplessness in the face of a concrete moral issue—there is little he can do here beyond feeling sorry for fish. We will explore these two questions more fully in the next sections of this chapter. As well, this essay is an example of *tso-wen*, writing essays with a conscious aesthetic purpose, which, we will see in chapter 7, Ch'eng strongly condemned as wasteful.

[27] Mencius, 1A.3. The principle is that if fish are allowed to grow and breed before being caught, then there will be enough for everyone to eat.
[28] *Erh-Ch'eng chi*, p. 578 (*Wen-chi* 8).

It is instructive first, however, to compare this essay, written at age twenty-one, with Ch'eng's memorial to the emperor Jen-tsung, written four years earlier. Both are passionate expositions. But otherwise the scale and tone of the two pieces appear to be diametrically opposed. The memorial discusses the full extent of the empire's socio-political problems with remarkable self-assurance. It is addressed to the reigning emperor; once it left Ch'eng's hands it became an official document, to be lodged in the imperial archives. It is populated by sages like Confucius and Shun and heroes like Chu-ko Liang, and it deals with the people of China as victims of national disorder. It proposes a solution: the emperor must practice the kingly *tao*—and "I would suggest that the root of the kingly *tao* is benevolence (*jen*)."

The second essay discusses a fish pool next to the family study. Though it also quotes from ancient writings, it has no explicit persona other than Ch'eng I and his fish, in danger of being fed to the cats. Addressed to no one in particular, it survived among old papers. The essay leaves Ch'eng I uncertain about what he might do for the myriad things of heaven-and-earth. In this case, the sages' answers are not even adequate. They discuss fish from a narrowly human perspective, providing instructions so that people will always have enough to eat. But Ch'eng himself cannot bear to eat these fish! Thus he must discover "what *I* should do, who delight in their life."

The great achievement of the mature Ch'eng is the resolution of these concerns into a complex moral philosophy. In particular, he will conjoin his resonance with fish, commitment to global ethics, and concern for human society. Thereafter he will not discuss such issues without reference to the intimacies of the human mind, the totality of heaven-and-earth, and their natural moral imperatives. For "what makes my mind feel pity is not fish alone."

The remainder of this chapter explores how Ch'eng I uses the *I Ching* to engage these questions. The first section addresses his conception of *li*, usually translated as "principle" but here as "the pattern." This is a complex demonstration, but when we return to the *Book of Change* at the end of it we will see that "the pattern" finds its clearest and most perfect written expression in the *I Ching*. Next we will tackle the question of *hsüeh* or access: how do you know the pattern? The answer again lies in the *I* as both a guide to action and a guide to seeing the pattern in everything around one. Finally we discuss constancy and change and the implications of truly knowing *li*.

LI—THE PATTERN

In the introduction we encountered a young Ch'eng I with enormous aspirations. These aspirations raise a host of questions, of which the most important is the functionally identical pair "How am I united with heaven-and-earth and all things?" and "What is the basis for moral action?" In this section, we will see how Ch'eng articulates his mature vision of unity and its natural moral imperatives in terms of *li*, "the pattern."[29]

For *li* is the unitary pattern of heaven-and-earth, by virtue of which each thing attains its proper moral function. It is essential to realize the inseparability of this unity and this morality. We might suppose that the second is implied by the first, but Ch'eng I would say that for things to be part of heaven-and-earth and to possess a way of proper action is one and the same. As noted above, Ch'eng is often regarded as a moralist who demands submission to rules.[30] Instead, we could see him as teaching a way of acting that grows effortlessly from one's insight into heaven-and-earth.

What is the nature of Ch'eng I's unity? The fish story shows that as a youth he experienced a loving concern for all things in heaven-and-earth. The mature Ch'eng, while insisting on this connectedness, never emphasizes its emotional roots.[31] Rather, everything in the world is interconnected because a single pattern runs through it all. This pattern includes distinctions of kind and role like tyrant and sage, exalted and humble, ruler and minister, etc. But it is ultimately unitary: there is only one pattern to heaven-and-earth. Ch'eng I compares *li* to a network of roads, and we might imagine it like the crackle glaze that entirely covers certain Chinese tea bowls: every area is distinctly patterned, yet the particular patternings run together and form a whole. But while the tea bowl's patterns are relatively stable, the configuration of heaven-and-earth is in constant flux.

This conception of unity differs from others common in the mid-eleventh century, which Graham has characterized by their assumption that

[29] *Li* is, of course, also important to other mid-eleventh century thinkers, though in differing ways, and to Buddhists and others both before and after them. See Glossary for a brief discussion. Graham, *Two Chinese Philosophers*, p. 8, summarizes some stages in that term's development from its first millennium B.C.E.. meaning of "the patterning in jade." The present chapter—and all Western studies of the Ch'engs—owe Graham an enormous scholarly debt. See also Wing-tsit Chan, "The Evolution of the Neo-Confucian Concept *Li* as Principle," *Tsing Hua Journal of Chinese Studies*, 5.2 (1964), pp. 132–49.

[30] For Ch'eng's awareness of the inadequacy of a rule-governed solution and his advice against merely imitating the behavior of the sage Yao, see *Erh-Ch'eng chi* 18.187. This issue is directly addressed in the discussion of constancy and change, below.

[31] But note that his brother often expresses his heart-felt connection to the life-force that is present all around him. We can see this simply by looking at three contiguous entries in the *Chin-ssu-lu* (Taipei: Commercial Press, 1967), pp. 15–16: "Observe the disposition of living things in heaven-and-earth." "The will to life of the myriad things is most worthy of observation." And: "What fills the breast is the heart/mind of commiseration." Cf. Chan, trans., *Reflections*, p. 21.

all things are one in that all emerge from a common source, imperceptible yet continuous with them, like the underground spring from which the stream flows and divides, or the buried root from which the tree grows and branches out. This viewpoint is associated with a tendency to nature mysticism of the sort which Taoism and Zen Buddhism inspired in Chinese poetry and painting, a sympathy with all vitality and growth, the sense of a mystery active in the generation of things and within one's own heart.[32]

Ch'eng I's pattern has no single source nor secret origin to be discovered in one's mind, nor grounding in the cultural tradition, as we have seen Su Shih argue. It entails no increasingly subtle layers of reality to be successively penetrated, as Shao Yung insists. It is present in everything, not as its essence or the embodiment of a transcendent spiritual force but simply as the way a thing participates in the functioning of heaven-and-earth. Thus Ch'eng I's simplest definition of the pattern is *"suo-i jan,"* "that by which [it's] like this" or "that by which [something works] this way."[33]

These issues intertwine in Ch'eng's comments on hexagram #52 Ken (Stopping [Keeping Still/Mountain]). The *T'uan-chuan* glosses Ken as "coming to rest" (*chih*). In his commentary to this passage Ch'eng I says:

> Now, if there is a thing, there must be a rule (*tse*).[34] A father comes to rest in compassion; a son comes to rest in filial piety. A ruler comes to rest in *jen*; a minister comes to rest in reverence.[35] Of the myriad things and the multiple

---

[32] *Two Chinese Philosophers*, p. xvii. Here Graham mentions Chou Tun-i and Chang Tsai and refers us to examples from Ch'eng Hao (pp. 109ff). In addition, note the story of Chang Tsai's unwillingness to eat bamboo shoots because he did not want to cut off incipient growth (Chan, trans., *Reflections*, p. 248 n. 42, quoting the *I-Lo yüan-yüan lu*). Chou Tun-i of course would not cut the grasses before his study window (*Erh-Ch'eng chi* 3.60). See also Donald Munro, "The Family Network, the Stream of Water, and the Plant: Picturing Persons in Sung Confucianism," in *Individualism and Holism*, ed. Donald Munro (Ann Arbor: Center for Chinese Studies, 1985), pp. 259–91, for a persuasive discussion of the problem of unity in Ch'eng-Chu thought as well as a discussion of Chu Hsi's combination of the two perspectives.

[33] See for example *Erh-Ch'eng chi* 19.247, 15.151, 15.157. It is important not to mistake this pattern for something independent of the patterning to which it refers, as Ch'eng I's students and Chu Hsi seem to have done. Willard Peterson, in "Another Look at Li," *Bulletin of Sung-Yüan Studies* 18 (1986), pp. 13–32, lists various good reasons not to translate the *li* of Ch'eng I and Chu Hsi as "principle." To these I would add the fact that Ch'eng I speaks of "seeing" *li* as we see the patterning in jade. When Ch'eng I wishes to speak of principles, he uses the word "*i*" (otherwise "righteousness/meaning"). See *Erh-Ch'eng chi* 15.167, where *i* and *li* mean something like "component principle" and "systemic pattern"; and *Erh-Ch'eng chi*, p. 1125 (Ch'eng's preface to the *Spring and Autumn Annals*). Peterson himself translates *li* as "coherence." But "coherence" is not Ch'eng I's *li*; it is only a quality of the pattern, like "unity" or "goodness."

[34] Paraphrasing *Shih Ching* #260.

[35] Paraphrasing the *Ta Hsüeh*; see Ch'eng's edition of that text in *Erh-Ch'eng chi*, p. 1130 (*Ching-shuo*).

affairs, each has its [proper] place. If it gets its place, it is peaceful. If it loses its place, it is disorderly. That by which the sages could cause the world to be well governed is not that they could set rules for things. They only rested each in its proper place, that is all.[36]

Several important notions are contained here in a condensed form. Within the pattern are precise roles that prescribe definite behavior. These are not made by men, not even by sages. These differences of role are not disruptive. On the contrary, if everyone found his place in the world, utter harmony would result.

We can best explore these issues by examining a celebrated phrase, "*li i erh fen shu.*"[37] This statement means both that "the pattern is unitary, its divisions multiple" and that "the pattern is unitary, but social roles differ." It refers to the way in which the pattern unifies seemingly disparate things yet maintains their distinctions, and to how types and hierarchies can exist amidst ultimate unity.[38] This simultaneous affirmation and transcendence of differences is explored in Ch'eng's commentary to hexagram #38 K'uei (Opposition). K'uei means something like "a setting apart." It is slightly stronger than "differ" but not as strong as "oppose." In his commentary Ch'eng I discusses "the way the sage unites differences" by "extending the sameness that is in the pattern of all things." The *T'uan-chuan* to that hexagram reads:

Heaven and earth are set apart but their affairs are the same. Male and female are set apart, but their aspirations comprehend [each other's]. The myriad things are set apart, but their affairs are ordered by types (*lei*). The timely uses of K'uei are great indeed!

Ch'eng comments:

Extend the sameness in the pattern of things to illuminate the timely use of K'uei—this is the way the sage unites differences. It is commonly known how sameness is the same. A sage however can illuminate the fundamental sameness in the pattern of things [even though the things themselves are set apart]. Thereby he can take the world as being the same, and harmonize and unite the myriad types.

[The *I Ching*] uses heaven and earth, male and female, and the myriad things to illuminate this. Heaven is high and earth below; their substances are set apart. Yet yang descends and yin rises, and they mutually unite and realize the transformation and nurturing of affairs. In this way they are the same. The

---

[36] *I-chuan* 236.6.

[37] *Erh-Ch'eng chi*, p. 609 (*Wen-chi* 9). Cf. commentary on line four of hexagram #31 Hsien (Stimulus [Influence]), *I-chuan* 138.9.

[38] For a discussion of this issue in terms of three dominant metaphors of Ch'eng-Chu thought, see Donald Munro, "The Family."

different makeups of male and female are set apart. But in their aspiration to mutually seek each other, each comprehends the other. Living things have myriad differences that set them apart. But in attaining the harmony of heaven-and-earth and in receiving the *ch'i* of yin and yang, they form corresponding types.

Though things differ, the pattern is fundamentally the same.[39]

Distinctions are real, as between high and low, father and son, ruler and minister. The unitariness of the pattern does not obscure these differences but rather confirms their particular nature. Here Ch'eng I is not only arguing against those who would set up one *tao* for heaven-and-earth and another for man,[40] but also against Buddhist claims that all distinctions are without basis,[41] Taoist claims that everything is equal,[42] and Mohist demands for universal love without gradations.[43]

Ch'eng offers several explanations for the unity of differences, but all refer ultimately to what he regards as "natural," self-evident facts about the world. On one level, everything is composed of the same yin and yang *ch'i*, which must be harmoniously balanced for them to exist. On another level, "opposites" like male and female are naturally—sexually—drawn together, despite strife between them. Finally, the things of the world naturally—by their apportionment of yin and yang—form types (*lei*) with each other. Such types are not merely a means to classify things by groups; more fundamentally they manifest the orderliness that naturally obtains in heaven-and-earth.

Fen (distinctions and roles) are multiple, but the pattern emphasizes how their differences are sublated.[44] This is true equally in heaven-and-earth, in human relations, and among all living things. The fiercely contending forces of normal literati experience, which subvert the social and physical orders, have deviated from the pattern. Thus Ch'eng's views presuppose a powerful ultimate harmony. Indeed he sees the true functioning of society as similar to the functioning of yin and yang. The two main topics of his *I Ching* commentary are therefore the actions of the superior man (*chün-tzu*) and physical processes like the progress of the year, the interactions of yin and yang, or natural cycles of growth and decline. In his view, the distinctions and imperatives built into things are inherently

[39] *I-chuan*, 167.1.

[40] That is, against Yang Hsiung (*Erh-Ch'eng chi* 18.183), Liu Mu (*Erh-Ch'eng chi* 18.223), and Wang An-shih (*Erh-Ch'eng chi* 22a.282).

[41] See, *inter alia*, discussions by the brothers beginning *Erh-Ch'eng chi* 2A.23.

[42] Specifically Chuang Tzu's notion of the equalization of things, *Erh-Ch'eng chi* 19.264.

[43] See Ch'eng I's "Letter in reply to Yang Shih discussing [Chang Tsai's] 'Western Inscription,' " *Erh-Ch'eng chi*, p. 609 (*Wen-chi* 9), in Chan, *A Source Book in Chinese Philosophy* (Princeton: Princeton University Press, 1963), p. 550.

[44] *Aufgehoben*, that is, both maintained and yet, at a higher level, transcended.

moral in the same way that high and low are part of the physical world.[45] Just discover the pattern and act accordingly: "That by which the sages could cause the world to be well governed is not that they could set rules for things. They only rested each in its proper place, that is all." There is no need to be clever or to invent new ways of behaving—quite the opposite.

This is true because the pattern is constant, even as the world itself is constantly changing. If we realize the pattern here and now, we have seen something that has always existed and always will exist. What made the sages of antiquity sages was only indirectly that they "took the *tao* of the world's Great Mean as their nature," as Ch'eng had argued at age seventeen. Rather, by birth or learning they were able to see the pattern, which we can equally see today. Wisdom like that embodied in the *I Ching*, without transmission for a thousand years, is thus recoverable.[46]

It is useful here to address two issues of a more technically philosophical nature that tend to arise when Ch'eng I's thought is introduced into a Euro-American context. The first concerns the use of *li* to define things. The second involves finding a philosophical language in which to explain how the pattern is both one and many. Regarding the first, it is important to stress that Ch'eng's conception of the pattern is not intended to define what things are.[47] He does not think in terms of isolated entities but rather of the way things function and interact.[48] Indeed, says Ch'eng,

"Thing" (*wu*) means "activity" (*shih*). If you completely investigate the pattern in activities, there will be nothing you don't understand.[49]

Thus Ch'eng treats "things" as processes that take place, as a set of relationships between things.[50] In his system, therefore, it makes little sense

[45] *Erh-Ch'eng chi* 18.225.

[46] Related to this is Peterson's point that *li* explain how it is possible to know things ("Another Look at *Li*," pp. 24ff). Thus Ch'eng I often uses the pattern as a way of affirming either that something is the case ("There is such a pattern.") or that something is possible. See Graham, *Two Chinese Philosophers*, pp. 27ff.

[47] As many writers have supposed. See Russell Hatton's useful critique, "A Comparison of *Li* and Substantial Form," *Journal of Chinese Philosophy* 9 (1982), pp. 45–71, where the ideas of Fung Yu-lan and others are criticized. Willard Peterson's discussion of the *li* of common household objects is also somewhat misleading in this regard ("Another Look at *Li*," pp. 15f.).

[48] As Graham has pointed out, in general, "the *li* accounts not for the properties of a thing but for the task it must perform to occupy its place in the natural order," that is to say, the moral order (*Two Chinese Philosophers*, p. 18).

[49] *Erh-Ch'eng chi* 15.143.

[50] In this regard it might be useful to recall the arguments of Hall and Ames that understanding Confucius's sense of *i* ("righteousness") entails a philosophy of events, not of entities. See David L. Hall and Roger T. Ames, "Getting it right: On saving Confucius from the Confucians," *Philosophy East and West* 34 (1984), pp. 3–23.

to ask what the pattern of a chair is. He does not use the pattern to explain the existence of things in the world, like the meta-physics of Shao Yung, but rather how moral action is natural and obvious.[51] Moreover, even in regard to activities, Ch'eng is as much concerned with showing how the whole of the pattern can be seen *in* filial piety as he is with defining the particular pattern *of* filial piety. That is, he wishes to show how, from acting in a filial manner, one can come to know the whole of the pattern of heaven-and-earth.

The second philosophical question is related to this through the passage *"li i erh fen shu."* As we have seen, there is only one *li*, only one pattern to heaven-and-earth, but there are also many *li*, many local instances within the unitary patterning. Regarding the former, Ch'eng remarks:

> It's like later people explaining the *I*: they say that Ch'ien [the first hexagram] is the *tao* of heaven and K'un [the second hexagram] is the *tao* of earth. This is nonsense. If you speak of their substance, then "Heaven is honored, and earth is humble."[52] But if you speak of their *tao*, how is there any difference?[53]

More explicitly:

> Within heaven-and-earth, the pattern of the myriad things is without difference (literally, "has no place that is not the same").[54]

Yet Ch'eng also speaks of "the hundred *li*,"[55] addressing them individually, as particular patterns within "the pattern."[56] Thus, in his commentary to hexagram #24 Fu, Ch'eng remarks that "The first line . . . lacks the pattern of being able to give aid."[57] "*Tao*" of course works the same way: in the passage above, Ch'eng I remarks that it is nonsense to speak of the *tao* of heaven as distinct from the *tao* of earth. But he himself in his

[51] Indeed, it cannot address these issues of existence except with great awkwardness. See Chu Hsi's attempt, one hundred years later, to deal with the *li* of a chair, as discussed in Hatton, "A Comparison of *Li*." Even here, Chu speaks only of the *use* of a chair. Thus, when Ch'eng I says that "a single plant, a single tree, all have the pattern" (*Erh-Ch'eng chi* 18.193), he is arguing less for the individual pattern of each thing than that the pattern is present everywhere, even in seemingly insignificant animate objects. As Graham notes (*Two Chinese Philosophers*, pp. 16–17), only rarely does Ch'eng refer to the *li* of individual things. Of the passages that Graham mentions in this regard, most, it seems to me, are primarily arguments for the presence of the pattern in every individual thing.

[52] Quoting the opening words of the *Hsi-tz'u-chuan*.

[53] *Erh-Ch'eng chi* 18.183.

[54] *I Shuo* (Discussions of the *Book of Change*), *Erh-Ch'eng chi*, p. 1029.

[55] See for example *Erh-Ch'eng chi* 2A.32, 2A.34, 15.167ff.

[56] In this case English requires that we offer a plural form of "pattern" to accommodate these multiplicities. But this is a grammatical inconvenience, not, I think, a conceptual barrier.

[57] *I-chuan*, 107.9.

I Ching commentary often refers to the *tao* of one thing or another, as in "the *tao* of the superior man" and "the *tao* of danger."[58] Thus *tao* and the pattern operate equally on two levels: they order the whole, which is unitary, and also the specifics, which are multiple.[59]

This coexistence of one and many may be clear. But the precise nature of their interrelationship is harder to grasp. Ch'eng I himself compares this situation of many *li* to a network of roads, each of which is connected with the others:

> In examining things and investigating the pattern, it's not that one must fully investigate [all] things in the world. Just fully investigate it in one matter; in the others you can extend it by inference. As for filial piety, investigate the pattern of how it is filial piety. If there's a matter that you cannot investigate, then investigate another, either doing the easy first or doing the difficult first, according to your depth. It's like a thousand roads and ten-thousand paths: all of them can take you to the capital, so just finding one way (*tao*) to enter is fine. The fact that you can investigate it is just because the myriad things are all one pattern. As for any one thing or any one matter, however small, they all have this pattern.[60]

But Ch'eng makes a further claim regarding the relationship of whole to parts. Not only is the pattern present everywhere, it is in every instance complete. Here are four examples.
In heaven:

> In what is called "the pattern of heaven" (*t'ien-li*), the hundred patterns are all present, complete. Fundamentally not the slightest thing is missing.[61]

In human beings:

> Taking something close like our bodies, the hundred patterns are all completely present.[62]

Again, and by way of transition to a wider field:

> "The myriad pattern is complete within me."[63] This is true not only of human beings. All things are like this.[64]

---

[58] As in the case of hexagram #24 Fu. See *I-chuan* 105.1, 105.2, 106.9ff.

[59] The same is true of *jen*, which is both the single nature of all human goodness and a particular virtue like righteousness or wisdom. See the long passage that begins on *Erh-Ch'eng chi* 15.154, where Ch'eng remarks that "You must distinguish its being within *tao* from its being [one of] the Five Constant [Virtues]."

[60] *Erh-Ch'eng chi* 15.157. See Graham's discussion, *Two Chinese Philosophers*, p. 58.

[61] *Erh-Ch'eng chi* 2A.32. The sources do not indicate whether this remark is from Ch'eng I or Ch'eng Hao.

[62] *Erh-Ch'eng chi* 15.167.

[63] Mencius 7A4.

[64] *Erh-Ch'eng chi* 2A.34 (Ch'eng Hao?).

In everything:

> The mind of a single person is the mind of heaven. The pattern of a single thing is the pattern of all things. The revolution of one day is the revolution of one year.[65]

An analogy might help us understand what Ch'eng I is saying. Think of the way in which the complete human genetic code or pattern is present in every cell of our bodies, even though the genetic makeup of that cell determines that it will be a liver or blood or nerve cell in form and function. Then imagine this relationship obtaining between all things, which make up one body with heaven-and-earth.[66] Finally, note that heaven is itself just the pattern, so there is no separate repository where *li* could reside apart from all things. Of course the whole of the pattern is fully present and available, complete, in any thing. Where else could it be? And how could anything exist in isolation from it?

The unitariness of the pattern also confirms the young Ch'eng's relationship with fish, though on other than emotional grounds. More philosophically, this means that the nature (*hsing*) of all living things is in some sense identical. Ch'eng I says it like this:

> Dogs, oxen, and men know what to avoid. Their nature is fundamentally the same, but being limited by their form, they [animals] cannot change.[67] It's like sunlight in a crack—whether [the crack is] square or round, the light is one. Only what is bestowed [by way of individual ability or *ts'ai*] differs for each.[68]

From here it is only a step to one of Ch'eng I's fundamental claims about human beings:

> Human nature is just the pattern. As for the pattern, from Yao and Shun to commoners, it is one.[69]

Not only is it one, it is good:

> Human nature has nothing [in it] that is not good.[70]

Our nature, being the pattern, is thus the same as that of heaven-and-earth.

What prevents us from knowing this? It is only our "ability" (*ts'ai*),

[65] *Erh-Ch'eng chi* 2A.13.

[66] *Erh-Ch'eng chi*, p. 1179 (*Ts'ui-yen*), though these may be the words of Chang Tsai put into the mouths of the Ch'engs.

[67] As humans can transform themselves through study.

[68] *Erh-Ch'eng chi* 24.312. Cf. Graham, *Two Chinese Philosophers*, p. 57. See, too, *Erh-Ch'eng chi* 17.180 for related views of animals.

[69] *Erh-Ch'eng chi* 18.218.

[70] *Erh-Ch'eng chi* 18.204.

which we receive at birth with our nature. This *ts'ai* is more or less impure, obscured by our allotment of *ch'i*.[71] Those with purer ability can see the pattern more clearly. The rest of us must transform ourselves in ways we will consider in the subsequent section of this chapter. The essential task, however, is to overcome the selfishness that comes along with having a human body.[72] Ch'eng I reserves the term *jen*, Confucius's word for the highest human virtue, to the state of selflessness. Of course he identifies *jen* with *li*.[73]

Thus, not only does Ch'eng use "the pattern" to address issues of unity and morality, he also uses it to express the most difficult terms that he inherited from the classics, the sage-lore of antiquity. The two following passages are good examples:

The pattern, human nature, the decree (*ming*): the three have never differed. If one penetrates the pattern, then one plumbs one's nature; if one plumbs one's nature, one knows the decree of heaven. The decree of heaven is the *tao* of heaven.[74]

Penetrating the pattern, plumbing your nature, and arriving at the decree are only one thing. As soon as you have penetrated the pattern, you've plumbed your nature. As soon as you've plumbed your nature, you've arrived at the decree.[75]

We began this section with a pair of functionally equivalent questions that Ch'eng I inherited from his youth: "How am I united with heaven-and-earth and all things?" and "What is the basis for moral action?" The pattern shows that the answer lies neither in the power of an emperor nor in powerless individual sympathies. Instead, when literati realize their fundamental connection to everything in heaven-and-earth, they have a real and unshakable basis from which to act; that basis is always, by its nature, moral.

The *I Ching* is important to this project because it reveals the pattern through the medium of a written text. It works on two levels. At the first, its hexagram and line statements tell beginning students how to act. Ch'eng's commentary brings out these lessons, clarifying various moral choices literati might face. But reading the *I* also teaches literati how to

[71] *Ibid*. This is equally Chang Tsai's solution to how human beings, who are fundamentally good, can act otherwise. Chang referred to this as the *ch'i-chih chih hsing*, "the physical nature." The word "*li*" is not very useful in explaining this. See, for example, Ch'eng's awkwardness in *Erh-Ch'eng chi* 18.207.

[72] "In general it is the pattern that, having a body, people are selfish" (*Erh-Ch'eng chi* 3.66). See also Munro's discussion of impartiality, "The Family" pp. 279ff.

[73] " '*Jen*' is the correct pattern of the world." *Erh-Ch'eng chi*, pp. 1136ff. (*Ching-shuo*).

[74] *Erh-Ch'eng chi* 21B.274. This triad, of course, derives from *Shuo-kua* 1.

[75] *Erh-Ch'eng chi* 18.193.

read the world. Most narrowly, this is so because the things of the world and the *I* are both made up of combinations of yin and yang. More profoundly it is so because of the unitary nature of the pattern. For both reasons the *I* is suitable for addressing everything, "from heaven-and-earth, the obscure and bright, to insects, vegetation, and minute things."[76] But the *I* does not merely accommodate or mirror the world, it embodies its structure. We find in the *I* the same complex layers, envelopes and dynamic interrelationships of patterning that exist in the world. For all these reasons, studying the *I* is a superb way to learn to see the pattern. Ch'eng I, then, uses the *I Ching* to show how matters of unity and of morality—or heaven-and-earth and human action—are really two aspects of the same thing. Thus the major theme of his commentary is the coincidence of the yin-yang pattern with that of the superior man.

Hsüeh—Learning

The process of learning to see the pattern is called *hsüeh*. For Ch'eng this involves a thoroughgoing investigation of oneself and of the world. Though human beings contain within themselves the pattern of all things, only a broad study of self and other will reveal this. Learning, then, is the gradual deepening of a knowledge that is available everywhere one might look for it. In this section we will first discuss the foundation and practice of *hsüeh* and then examine the particular usefulness of the *I Ching* to it.

"Becoming a sage" is another way of expressing the goal of learning. When someone asked: "What is the difference between the sage and the *tao* of heaven?" Ch'eng responded: "There is no difference."[77] His early thoughts on the nature and possibility of achieving sagehood, written at the age of twenty-two or twenty-three, are as follows:

> Someone asked: "In the school of the Sage [Confucius] there were three thousand followers. Only Yen Tzu was said to love learning. It is not that the three thousand scholars did not practice until they comprehended the *Book of Documents*, the *Book of Poetry* and the six arts. What then did Yen Tzu alone love to learn?"
> Ch'eng I said: "Learning the *tao* of becoming a sage."
> "Can one become a sage through learning?"
> He said: "Yes."

[76] *Erh-Ch'eng chi*, p. 394 (*Wai-shu* 7). The preface to Ch'eng's commentary remarks that "As a writing it is vast and great, minute and complete" (*I-chuan*, 1.2, quoting the *Hsi-tz'u-chuan* B8). It is so vast that "when realized in man, it is called *hsing*," while "the person of *jen* calls it *jen*" (*Erh-Ch'eng chi* p. 1029 [*I-shuo*], quoting the *Hsi-tz'u-chuan* A4).

[77] *Erh-Ch'eng chi* 18.209. Ch'eng's strong aspiration to sagehood is apparent in both his youthful essays. Indeed, as his uncle Chang Tsai remarks, "The two Ch'engs from their fourteenth or fifteenth years zealously wanted to learn sagehood" (*Chin-ssu-lu*, p. 346).

"What is the *tao* of learning . . . ?"

"The *tao* of all learning is to 'rectify one's mind' and 'nourish one's nature (*hsing*),' that is all.[78] When you are centered (*chung*), correct (*cheng*)[79] and authentic (*ch'eng*), then you are a sage."[80]

The young Ch'eng I then goes on to discuss the discipline of developing these qualities. Like Mencius, he claims that *jen*, righteousness and all other virtues are already present within the human mind. These days, however, people seek learning outside themselves, in strenuous memorization or literary pursuits. "Thus few arrive at *tao*. In this way the learning of today differs from what Yen Tzu loved."[81]

Ch'eng's enterprise is somewhat paradoxical: all that is required is that we recognize what we already are, yet that recognition is unusually difficult to achieve. Thus he remarks: "The words of the Sage are as far away as heaven and as near as earth."[82] On the one hand Ch'eng argues that the pattern, with which one's behavior must accord, is the most obvious thing in the world.[83] It is our very nature, it is present in everything around us, it is complete in our mind. His commentary to the Ken hexagram therefore states that each thing need only "come to rest in its proper place." Yet, on the other hand, students are asked to address a number of the most troubling aspects of the human condition. Most obvious is human selfishness. The flavor of discipline that this entails runs all through Ch'eng's teachings; we have seen how it requires constant effort and vigilance.

The relationship between nature and culture reflects this paradox. In a relative way, the right cultural environment can aid one's progress in learning to see the pattern. Indeed, learning was easier in the past, when even commoners were familiar with the language and contents of the *Book of Documents* and *Book of Poetry*.[84] Yet culture as such is not a repository or embodiment of the way, as Su Shih for example maintained. Even the Classics are not essential. Ch'eng directs his students to the *Great Learning*, the *Analects*, and Mencius.[85] He also views his own commentaries to the *Book of Change* and the *Spring and Autumn Annals* as reviving a tradition that had been lost for a thousand years.[86] But while individual paths to *tao* may be obscured, the pattern itself is always there,

[78] These are prominent themes in the *Ta-hsüeh* and *Chung-yung*.
[79] *Chung* and *cheng* are key terms from the *T'uan-chuan*. See chapter 1.
[80] *Erh-Ch'eng chi*, p. 577 (*Wen-chi* 8).
[81] *Ibid.*, p. 578.
[82] *Erh-Ch'eng chi* 18.205.
[83] *Erh-Ch'eng chi* 18.185.
[84] *Erh-Ch'eng chi* 18.200. For similar sentiments, see also *Erh-Ch'eng chi* 21A.268.
[85] *Erh-Ch'eng chi* 22A.277 and 285.
[86] See their respective prefaces, particularly *I-chuan* 1.7 and *Erh-Ch'eng chi*, p. 1125.

always available. Thus even while Ch'eng worries that "the learning of the Sage [Confucius] would have almost expired if it weren't for Tzu-ssu and Mencius," he returns at once to the true subject matter of that learning: "How could *tao* ever expire? It is just that men do not follow it. *Tao* is not destroyed. Yu and Li did not follow it."[87]

Any pursuit other than this learning is a destructive diversion. The contemporary literatus environment, which values things like elegant essays and strong calligraphy, therefore makes learning difficult.[88]

> [Someone] asked: "Does composing essays harm *tao*?"
>
> [Cheng I] replied: "It does. When you engage in *wen* (elegant literature), if you don't concentrate your intention on it, then you will not become skillful. If you do, then your will (*chih*, your ambition) will be confined to this. So how would you be able to have the same greatness as heaven-and-earth?"[89]

The process of learning, then, is a matter of directly seeing the unitary pattern. Here is how Ch'eng I explains it:

> That people are troubled and wearied by things and their thought processes obstructed is merely that they don't get the essentials. What is essential lies in being clear about the good. Being clear about the good lies in examining things and investigating the pattern. If you investigate until you arrive at the pattern in a thing, then gradually, after a long time, you will be able to investigate all things under heaven—it's only the unitary pattern.[90]

This is so because

> things and I are one pattern. Just be clear about that [out there] and you will know this [in here]. This is the way to join inner and outer.[91]

Things and I are one pattern. The pattern however is infinitely varied. How can literati learn its unity? Only by practicing its specifics:

> [Someone] asked: "In the 'Record of Conduct' [of Ch'eng Hao] you say 'Fully developing your nature and arriving at your destiny must be rooted in filial piety and brotherly respect.' I don't know how filial piety and brotherly respect can be used to fully develop one's nature and arrive at one's destiny."
>
> [Ch'eng I] said: "Later people have spoken of nature and destiny (*hsing-*

---

[87] Reigned 878–842 and 781–771—famous wicked kings of Chou. *Erh-Ch'eng chi* 17.176. Thus it is better to work with a teacher than read books (*Erh-Ch'eng chi* 2A.26 [Ch'eng Hao?]). Some classics, notably the *Tso-chuan* and *I-li*, are only partially reliable in any case (*Erh-Ch'eng chi* 20.266).

[88] See Ch'eng Hao's complaints about today's youth, *Erh-Ch'eng chi* 1.8. Essays (*wen*) and calligraphy, of course, are prerequisites to literati examination and/or social success.

[89] *Erh-Ch'eng chi* 18.239.

[90] *Erh-Ch'eng chi* 15.144. See also 15.181.

[91] *Erh-Ch'eng chi* 18.193. Cf. 15.157.

ming) as separate things. Nature and destiny and filial piety and brotherly respect are just matters of a single system (*i-t'ung*). From within filial piety and brotherly respect you can fully develop your nature and arrive at your destiny. Even sweeping and answering questions are part of a single system along with fully developing your nature and arriving at your destiny. These have no root and branch, no fine and coarse. Yet later people have spoken of them as if nature and destiny were high and far off.[92]

There is no hierarchy or root and branch of patterns—it is just the unitary pattern, a single web extending throughout heaven-and-earth. Everything we do either conforms to it or not. Filial piety is an outstanding example of the pattern; we must practice it if we wish to be in accord with the pattern. But because the pattern is ultimately one, it is wrong to imagine that we first learn the pattern of sweeping, and then that of filial piety, and then that of writing essays, and only then how the unitary pattern is present in everything. Nonetheless, there is an appropriate order in which to study each of various things. This is not some ontological primacy but simply another aspect of the pattern of growing up, whereby human understanding gradually matures. In the following passage Ch'eng I explains how both aspects of learning—specific moral acts and the unitary principle—proceed at once.

> Someone asked: "When investigating things, is it necessary to investigate every thing, or just investigate one thing and the myriad patterns will all be known?"
> [Ch'eng I] said: "How could you penetrate everything in that way? As for only investigating one thing and then comprehending the multiple pattern, even Yen Tzu did not dare to speak like this. What's necessary is to investigate one thing today and tomorrow investigate another. When the accumulation of practice is great, then suddenly there will be thorough comprehension."[93]

This process of accumulation is a gradual deepening of one's total understanding rather than merely a collection of one portion of the pattern after another. Thus Ch'eng I complains about two incorrect methods of learning:

> [Someone] asked: "Why is it that Han Confucians could not penetrate a single classic, even when their heads had turned white?"
> [Ch'eng I] said: "What use is the Han method of [reading] the classics? It merely takes line-by-line exegesis as its task."[94]

[92] *Erh-Ch'eng chi* 18.224.
[93] *Erh-Ch'eng chi* 18.188.
[94] *Erh-Ch'eng chi* 18.232.

In learning to write essays, if you learn one thing you've learned [only] one thing, if you learn two things you've learned [only] two things.[95]

The process of true learning entails a deepening of what you already un-derstand to be the case, until it becomes more and more real and unde-niably true. A child may have some understanding of filial piety, but only continued practice will realize its truth. Ch'eng I says:

When I was twenty, my interpretation of the meaning of the Classics was no different from today. Yet when I think about today, I feel that their flavor nat-urally differs from when I was young.[96]

Thus it is necessary to investigate many things. For although the pattern is completely present in the mind of each human being and can be seen in everything around us, still in practical terms we seem to need broad ex-perience in order to come to understand its nature.

Ch'eng's *I Ching* commentary constitutes a major record of his own investigation of things, of the pattern. Literati can use it to perfect both aspects of Ch'eng I's learning: it will teach them how to act in specific situations by showing what that pattern is, and eventually they will learn to see the pattern whole. To this end, says Ch'eng, they should first study the individual hexagrams. Only when they have understood these can they understand the general principles of the text. This means that they should not read the *Hsi-tz'u-chuan* before having mastered the hexagram and line statements.[97] In the same way, we will not be able to see how Ch'eng understands either the *I* or the pattern unless we work with the details of his commentary—an abstract summary of his thought cannot communicate the intricacies of interpenetrating layers of pattern, the res-onance of yin-yang process with the actions of the superior man, the im-plications of such matters for literati action, nor Ch'eng's assumption of the harmonious interaction of heaven, earth, and humanity. We will therefore examine with some care the opening passages of Ch'eng's com-mentary to the Fu hexagram. (The complete commentary can be found in the Appendix.)

HEXAGRAM #24 FU (RETURN)

HEXAGRAM STATEMENT: Fu. [The trigram] Chen below, [the trigram] K'un above.

[95] *Erh-Ch'eng chi* 2A.20 (Ch'eng Hao?).
[96] *Erh-Ch'eng chi* 18.188.
[97] For these ideas see *Erh-Ch'eng chi* 19.248 and 2A.13.

COMMENTARY: The *Hsu-kua*:[98] "Things cannot be finally exhausted. 'Stripped away' [hexagram #23 Po] above, it reverts below.[99] Thus it is met by Fu." Things do not have the pattern of being completely stripped away. Thus, when stripping reaches its extreme, comes return. When yin reaches its extreme, yang is born. When yang is stripped to the extreme above, it returns and is born below. Exhausted above, it reverts below. This is how Fu follows Po.

"Things do not have the pattern of being completely stripped away"— that is, every process in the world is cyclical, waxing and waning. There are no ultimate dead ends. "Thus, when stripping reaches its extreme, comes return. . . . This is how Fu follows Po."

Here Ch'eng has emphasized the cycle of birth, growth, exhaustion, and rebirth. In the next paragraph, he applies this pattern to the hexagram configuration and the progress of the year, addressing both in terms of yin-yang balances:

As a hexagram, one yang is born below five yin. Yin reaches its extreme and yang returns. In the tenth [lunar] month, when the flourishing of yin has reached its extreme, there is the winter solstice. Then one yang returns and is born within the earth. Therefore it is "return."

This pattern of development applies equally to the social, that is, moral world of the superior man:

Yang is the *tao* of the superior man. Yang declines to the extreme and then returns again. The *tao* of the superior man declines to the extreme and then grows again. Therefore it has the meaning of returning to the good.

This is the central meaning of Fu: the pattern whereby anything—yang, the superior man, the good—returns. The dominant themes, both here and throughout the *I-chuan*, are yin-yang and the superior man. Thus Ch'eng grounds the *I* text in both the most general aspect of change— universal process—and in that which is nearest at hand—the literatus actor.[100]

Ch'eng now turns to the hexagram statement. Addressing its first half, he discusses the gradual growth of yang: its vulnerable early stages, its invincible momentum, and its ultimate flourishing.

---

[98] "The Ordered Hexagrams," Wing 9 (W/B "The Sequence"), with which Ch'eng always begins his remarks.

[99] The Po hexagram consists of five yin lines below a single yang line; Ch'eng, following most previous readers, takes it as the "stripping away" of yang. In the Fu hexagram, yang returns below five yin lines, which it will gradually supplant.

[100] For Chu Hsi's complaints about both these points, see *Chu Tzu yü-lei* 67.6a, 8b; 117.7b. Wing-tsit Chan summarizes these in *Reflections*, p. xxxiv. Chu's criticisms are addressed in chapter 6.

HEXAGRAM STATEMENT: Fu. Successful. Going out and going in are without distress. Friends come and it is without fault.

COMMENTARY: "Fu, successful"—having returned, it is successful. The yang *ch'i* returns and is again produced below. It gradually succeeds, and produces and nourishes the myriad things. The *tao* of the superior man having returned, success can gradually enrich the world. Therefore in Fu there is the pattern of successful flourishing.

This passage demonstrates how patterns exist within each other. The larger pattern in question is that of Return. Because the yang *ch'i* and the *tao* of the superior man have returned, "success can gradually enrich the world. Therefore in Fu there is the pattern of successful flourishing."

"Going out and going in are without distress." "Going out and in" means being produced and growing. When it returns and is produced inside, it is "going in." When it grows and advances outside, it is "going out." It mentions "going out" first because it sounds better [in Chinese to say "go out/go in" than "go in/go out"]. The production of yang is not from the outside; it comes about within. Thus it says "going in."

When things are first produced, their *ch'i* is most subtle. Thus there is often difficulty at the beginning.[101] When yang is first produced, its *ch'i* is most subtle. Thus it often snaps off. What is produced by the spring yang is split by the yin cold. If one observes the grasses and trees at dawn and dusk then this can be seen.

Shao Yung's "contemplation of things" emphasizes grasses and trees (*ts'ao-mu*) as categories of existence. Ch'eng I instead sees grasses and trees acting in ways whose patterns are part of the larger pattern of universal process. Yet both Shao and Ch'eng insist that their insights into what was commonly understood by "earth" (e.g., spring vegetation) are of the same kind as their insights into "heaven" (the seasons and the moral nature of things).

"Going out and going in are without distress" means that when the subtle yang is born and grows there is nothing to harm it. Since there is nothing to harm it, it and its kind gradually advance and will be successful. Therefore "it is without fault." "Fault" in regard to *ch'i* is to deviate [from the proper balance]. In regard to the superior man it is to be blocked and not attain to fully realizing the pattern. When yang is just returning, even if there is distress, it could surely not arrest its return. There could be only a hindrance, for the qualities of the hexagram mean "without distress"—returning to the goodness of *tao*.

---

[101] See Ch'eng's discussion of hexagram #3 Chun, *I-chuan*, pp. 18ff.

To teach literati what the pattern is, Ch'eng I talks about specific things (grasses and trees in early spring) and specific events (the winter solstice). These things are important, however, only insofar as they constitute patterns. As patterns of activity, "flourishing," "splitting," or "returning" are invariable. That is, the pattern called "flourishing" has a definite shape, such that every time it will unfold in the same way. Here the pattern is one of growth, despite any obstacle: "even if there is distress, it could surely not arrest the return." Arresting the return is another pattern. We must therefore be extremely careful to identify the pattern correctly.

> One yang, when it is first born, is of the utmost subtlety and surely cannot yet overcome all the yin and bring forth the production of the myriad things. It must await the coming of the other yang. Only after that can it succeed in producing things and be without deviation, so that "friends come and it is without fault." The three yang—the ch'i of tzu, ch'ou and yin[102]—produce and develop the myriad things. This is the success of the many yang.
>
> If the tao of the superior man has declined and then returned, how can it simply conquer the inferior men? It must await the gradual flourishing of its friends and kind, and then they can join their strength to conquer them.

The pattern is unvarying: if it is Return, nothing will stop it. But within this pattern is a subtler aspect—the way the pattern develops over time. The ultimate triumph of yang and the superior man is not immediate.

Ch'eng's statements may present problems for modern readers. Are his insights profound and universal, or has he merely provided a list of some fairly obvious patterns of development? It depends on what one expects from the commentary, that is, how it is applied. Ch'eng, for example, is concerned to demonstrate the unitariness underlying all phenomena, not only in general terms but in specific instances. If that is not a real issue for modern readers, it will be harder to appreciate his accomplishments.

> HEXAGRAM STATEMENT, (continued): Reverting and returning to tao. In seven days comes the return. It is beneficial whatever one does.

> COMMENTARY: It means that the tao of decline and growth alternately return. After the decline of yang, in seven days there comes a return. [Hexagram #44] Kou is the first waning of yang. After seven changes it makes Fu, so it says "seven days," meaning seven changes.[103] [The hexagram statement of #19] Lin

---

[102] These are the Earthly Branches correlated with the eleventh, twelfth and first lunar months. It is in these months that yang begins its return.

[103] Kou is the opposite of Fu, with one broken line in the first place and five solid lines above it. After seven changes, it makes Fu. These "seven changes" begin with the hexagram Ch'ien, which has all solid lines. Starting with the bottom line, one line at a time turns into

says, "In the eighth month there is inauspiciousness," which means that the growth of yang is overtaken by the growth of yin in the eighth month.

When yang advances, yin retreats. When the *tao* of the superior man grows, the *tao* of the petty man declines. Therefore "it is beneficial whatever one does."

Ch'eng does not share Shao's interest in calendar-making.[104] But the clearest and largest-scale example of the development he is discussing is in fact the movement of the year. Once again, the patterns of heavenly process and of the superior man are the same.

Ch'eng I's *I Ching* commentary surrounds the literatus with patterns of appropriate behavior. These are especially apparent in his commentary to the line statements, which Ch'eng sees as variations on the fundamental theme of the hexagram. Because it speaks in terms of patterns, the *I* can function as a guide to all matters, from self-cultivation to family affairs to how to serve in government and when to withdraw. In Ch'eng's reading it is not particularly a book of divination, nor a demonstration of Wang Pi's non-being.

But this is only one part of using the *I*. Another involves seeing the pattern. This means coming to know the vast nature of heaven-and-earth and thereby gradually eliminating the selfish, partial quality of one's mind. Ch'eng's commentary makes clear how complex this is by exploring the layers, envelopes, and interrelations of patterning and the multiplicity of elements in which it is embodied. For example, Fu is first of all the return of yang and of the superior man. Because of this, it also has within it the pattern of flourishing. In turn this must develop gradually, as like elements gather with it. Their pattern is revealed in the interactions of superior and inferior men, flourishing and decline, stripping away and returning, the times of the year, going out and going in, hindrance and unobstructedness, action and compliance, activity and tranquillity, firm and soft, etc. Articulating this pattern is enormously complex, but a literatus who can see it clearly knows the true nature of heaven-and-earth.

SHIH—THE TIMES

So far the literatus has studied patterns—in texts, in his life and in the world around him. But even if he has the broad acquaintance of many patterns, how does he know which of those patterns characterizes his

---

its opposite; after six changes, Ch'ien has become K'un. The seventh change brings a solid line back. This is Fu.

[104] Indeed for Shao, hexagram #19 Lin is notable not for its association with the eighth month and the impending decline of yang but for the fact that it is composed of two yang lines below four yin. Thus it is the hexagram that follows Fu, as yang *continues its growth*. As Fu represents the first month, Lin represents the second.

present circumstances? In the same sense, when he consults the *I Ching*, how does he know which hexagram to read?

This is the problem of *shih*, "the times," "timeliness," "circumstances." It arises as part of a larger problem of constancy and change. The student learns various patterns, which are constant: Fu is always Fu, flourishing will always flourish. Yet he lives in a world of constant change, where the pattern is never the same moment to moment: sometimes it is flourishing, sometimes it is obstructed. If one correctly understands Fu but incorrectly imagines that *current* conditions are flourishing, then one will surely decline.

The same problem arises in ethics. Ch'eng I knows that there is no set of rules for behavior that applies to every situation. The pattern, though constant and unchanging, is not in this sense "constant principles." This distinguishes his approach from a didacticism that leads only to conformity, which, he says, "makes everything the same. . . . *That* cannot be called harmony."[105] Yet at the same time, he is deeply concerned to establish and to communicate the basis for moral action.

The only solution, says Ch'eng I, is to act in accordance with situations as they occur, that is, to seek the pattern as it develops moment to moment and take the course of action that is proper to it. Thus the phrase "*sui-shih*" (in accordance with the times) appears time and again in his *I Ching* commentary. Indeed, it is Ch'eng's most basic definition of "*I*," with which the preface to his *I Ching* commentary begins:

> *I pien-i yeh, sui-shih pien-i i ts'ung tao yeh.*
>
> *I* is "change," changing in accordance with the times so as to follow *tao*.[106]

For

> the way of the superior man is to accord with the times and act. Following what is appropriate and according with change cannot consist of rules.[107]

This is the heart of Ch'eng's ethics, and the rest of this section will be devoted to understanding what he means by it. We should begin by considering the dangers that lie in an approach to virtue that attempts to

---

[105] *Erh-Ch'eng chi* 15.171, in reference to Wang An-shih. Cf. *Erh-Ch'eng chi* 15.146 and 177 for similar remarks.

[106] *I-chuan* 1.1.

[107] Commentary to the *T'uan-chuan* of hexagram #17 Sui (Following), *I-chuan* 77.4. Note also that in regard to "the times," he remarks: "To know the times and recognize circumstances—this is the great method of the *I*." (Commentary to hexagram #43 Kuai [W/B Break-through], line two, *Hsiang-chuan*, *I-chuan* 195.10.) Or again: "What those who study (*hsüeh*) the *I* should understand profoundly is whether the times are flourishing or declining, and whether the circumstances are strong or weak." (Commentary on hexagram #26 Ta-ch'u [W/B The Taming Power of the Great], line two, *Hsiang-chuan*, *I-chuan* 114.9.)

create unchanging human values. Ch'eng provides three examples of this. The first two concern the *I*, while the third addresses problems in knowing the Mean. All three grow from attempts to derive a single, unchanging meaning from the Classics.

> When reading the *I*, it is essential to know the times (*shih*). Each of the six lines can be applied by anyone. A sage naturally has the applications of a sage. A worthy naturally has the applications of a worthy. Commoners naturally have the applications of commoners. A student naturally has the applications of a student. A ruler has a ruler's applications, a minister has a minister's applications. Everything is comprehended.
>
> Accordingly [someone] asked: "[The second hexagram] K'un is the affairs of the minister. Does the ruler of men have any application for it?"
>
> The teacher said: "How is it without application? For example, 'His broad virtue supports things.'[108] How could the ruler of men not apply this?"[109]

Thus the *I* is used differently by people in different positions—but all of it can be used at some time by anyone. This is because its patterns are so fundamental that each of them finds application in everyone's life. In another conversation, Ch'eng I clarifies the consequences of disregarding this principle:

> [Someone] asked: "Teacher Hu[110] explained 'nine in the fourth' [i.e., a yang line in the fourth position of the hexagram] as the prince. I'm afraid that is not the meaning of hexagrams."
>
> The teacher remarked: "There's no harm, though. Just look at how it's applied. If it should be the prince, then make it the prince. Since the fourth is near the ruler,[111] then making it the prince isn't harmful either. But don't embrace only one thing. If you seize on one affair, then you will make the 384 lines [of the sixty-four hexagrams] into only 384 affairs and that's all."[112]

The predetermined interpretation of a line reduces the *I* to a code book consisting of no more than 384 possible messages. This turns the myriad pattern into a limited set of rules. To read the *I* merely as an encyclopedia of ethics, even the very best ethics, is to obscure its true nature.[113] Instead

---

[108] Quoting the *Hsiang-chuan* to K'un.

[109] *Erh-Ch'eng chi* 19.249.

[110] Hu Yüan (993-1059) was Ch'eng I's teacher when he wrote the essay "What Yen Tzu Loved to Learn." See chapter 2 for a discussion of his *I Ching* commentary, the first directed specifically to the world of Sung literati action, both public and private. See also Lin I-sheng, *Hu Yüan ti i-li I-hsüeh* (Taipei: Commercial Press, 1974).

[111] Generally defined as the fifth line of the hexagram.

[112] *Erh-Ch'eng chi* 19.249.

[113] As Chan notes, Chu Hsi agreed with this principle—yet accused Ch'eng of contravening it. See *Chu tzu yü-lei*, 67.8a. In Chan, trans., *Reflections*, p. 112. This matter is discussed in chapter 6.

"The *I* takes its meaning by changing in accordance with the times,"[114] just as the student himself acts in accordance with them.

There is a troubling implication to this: the same act may be righteous in one circumstance and unrighteous in another. Thus Ch'eng remarks:

> To pass by one's own door three times and not go in was the Mean in the generation of Yü and Chi.[115] But if they lived in an alley, that would not have been the Mean. To live in an alley was the Mean in the time of Yen Tzu. But if he had passed by his door three times without going in, that would not have been the Mean.[116]

Underlying this is the fundamental problem of change itself, which means that nothing is constant or unmoving.[117] Ch'eng's solution is worked out in his commentary to hexagram #32 Heng (W/B Duration). Its *T'uan-chuan* reads:

> "Heng" means "long-lasting" (*chiu*). . . . "It is beneficial whatever one does": it ends and then has a beginning.[118]

Ch'eng comments:

> In the pattern of heaven-and-earth there has never been anything that could be long-lasting by not moving (*tung*, acting). By moving, "it ends and then begins again." This is how it is long-lasting without becoming exhausted. There has never been anything produced by heaven-and-earth, even the solidity and breadth of the great mountains, that is able not to change. Therefore lasting long is not being set (*i-ting*). If it were set, it could not last long. The constant *tao* lies only in changing in accordance with the times (*sui-shih pien-i*).
>
> Therefore it says, "It is beneficial whatever one does," illuminating how the pattern is like this, fearing that people would get mired in constancy.[119]

True constancy therefore consists in constant readjustment to changing circumstances, continually "beginning again." In this way, "it is beneficial whatever one does"—yet what one is to do is never known in advance.

Thus one does not invoke a constant model in order to know what to do. Instead, proper action comes from identifying the pattern in the

---

[114] Commentary to hexagram #36 Ming-i, line five; *I-chuan* 160.9.

[115] Because these servants of the sage-emperor Shun were so occupied with the affairs of state; see Mencius 4B29.

[116] *Erh-Ch'eng chi* 18.214. The issue of the Mean, which Ch'eng I calls "most difficult to conceptualize," is also discussed in *Erh-Ch'eng chi* 15.164.

[117] As Ch'eng remarks, "The *I* takes its meaning according to the times, for change is without constancy." (Commentary to hexagram #12 P'i (Standstill), line 2, *I-chuan* 57.6.) For a discussion of this passage, see Toda, *Ekikyō chushaku shikō*, p. 539.

[118] Cf. W/B, p. 546.

[119] Commentary on the *T'uan-chuan*; *I-chuan* 141.11.

changes of all things and affairs. There is no ultimate repository of righteousness apart from this world, apart from heaven-and-earth. This also suggests the final sense of "*shih*": the moment when all action takes place. As such it is constantly recurring, offering either another chance to recognize the pattern and so act correctly or another chance for pride, ambition and desire. It requires complete attention both to one's own mind and to the larger situation of which one is a part. Thus Ch'eng remarks:

> The pattern lies in the thing. Righteousness lies in handling the thing.[120]

We may suppose, then, that literati might properly use the *I* on three levels. On the first, one studies one's situation thoroughly, decides what hexagram is pertinent, and then simply applies the lessons of Ch'eng's commentary to the situation at hand. On the second, one knows the *I* and the patterns it points to so well that the correct hexagram (and pattern) simply occurs spontaneously. On the third, one embodies the principles of *sui-shih pien-i* so thoroughly that it is no longer necessary to look at or think of the *I* texts. In no case does Ch'eng recommend divination.[121]

SEEING THE PATTERN

Being able to see the pattern constitutes what Ch'eng I calls "true knowing." This transformative knowing is impossible to forget or deny or act against. Such knowledge makes according with the pattern effortless and pleasurable. Nothing is as important as this. For someone who sees the pattern, the self-interested, narrow demands of family, society, and emperor have ultimately no power over what one chooses to do: one just choicelessly, spontaneously follows the pattern. In doing so one serves the *true* interests of family, society, and empire, since each of these is, of course, part of the pattern too. In what follows we will explore the arguments Ch'eng makes to support these points.

While being able to see the pattern may seem mysterious to us, Ch'eng I insists that it is perfectly clear.

> To say that [righteousness] exists is to say that it is apparent (*hsien*). Yet by themselves people do not see [it]. It's obvious, right in the midst of heaven-and-earth.[122]

If your mind is at ease, he says,

---

[120] Commentary on Ken, *T'uan-chuan*; *I-chuan* 236.4.

[121] Though he does not deny its effectiveness. See *Erh-Ch'eng chi* 2A.51 and our discussion in chapter 7.

[122] *Erh-Ch'eng chi* 18.185. Cf. Graham, p. 14.

you will naturally see (*chien*) the pattern. It is very clear, like a level road. For example, the *Classic of Poetry* says:

> The road (*tao*) of Chou is like a whetstone,
> And straight as an arrow.[123]

Certainly this was baffling to Ch'eng I's students. In the following, someone asks him about a famous passage from the opening lines of the *Doctrine of the Mean*:

[The student] asked: " 'Nothing is more visible (*chien/hsien*) than the hidden, nothing is more apparent than the subtle.' What is this?"

[Ch'eng I] said: "People only take what they hear or see with ear or eye to be apparent or visible. They take what is not visible or audible as hidden and subtle. Thus they do not know that the pattern is indeed most apparent.

"It is like the man of old who, playing the *ch'in*, saw a mantis fighting a cicada. The listeners thought there was the sound of killing [in his music]. Killing was in his mind. The people heard his *ch'in* and knew it. Isn't that 'apparent'?

"When someone has something that is not good in him, he tells himself that people do not know it. But the pattern of heaven-and-earth is most clear and cannot be concealed."

[The student] said: "Is this like the 'four knowings' of Yang Chen?"[124]

[Ch'eng I] said: "Yes. In this way, when one speaks of me and another person, there is definitely a distinction. When one speaks of heaven-and-earth, it is only one knowing.[125]

Here Ch'eng suggests that we can know the world by reading the pattern the same way that we know men's minds by listening to their music. Like the pattern, music is intangible, but its communication is immediate and unerring. What we have in our minds is therefore not truly private, insulated from the rest of heaven-and-earth. Rather everything we think, as much as everything we do, resonates throughout heaven-and-earth. As such, it is all immediately apparent to someone like Ch'eng I. We are separate people, but there is only one heaven-and-earth. Thus, as Ch'eng says, there is only one knowing.

This knowing has enormous consequence.

[123] *Erh-Ch'eng chi* 18.205, quoting *Shih Ching* #41. Cf. Chan, trans., *Reflections*, p. 97.

[124] Of the later Han. He was known as "the Confucius of West-of-the-Pass." The rebel leader Wang Mi visited him at his house, hoping to recruit Yang to his cause.

At midnight [Wang Mi] offered ten catties of gold to Chen. Chen did not accept. Wang Mi said: "In the middle of the night there is no one who will know."

Chen replied: "Heaven knows. Spirit knows. I know. You know. How can you say no one will know?"

Wang Mi was ashamed and left.

From *Hou Han shu* 54.1760 (Peking: Chung-hua, 1965).

[125] *Erh-Ch'eng chi* 18.224.

[T'ang] T'i asked: "After the student has been able to see the *tao*-pattern, if he believes earnestly and acts strenuously, will it also [aid] his seeing?"

[Ch'eng I] said: "There is more than one [level of] seeing. But after seeing takes place even belief is inessential."

He asked again: "Isn't it so that having seen the *tao*-pattern everything is as it ought to be (*tang-jan*)?"

"Right. Wherever the pattern is, east is just east, west is just west. Why do you need belief?"[126]

Knowledge that was previously only intellectual now assumes the power to transform our actions. We become like someone bitten by a tiger:

> True knowing and ordinary knowing differ. I once saw a farmer who had been wounded by a tiger. Someone mentioned that a tiger had wounded a man—everyone was startled, but the farmer's complexion changed, different from everyone. That a tiger can wound people—even every three-foot-high youth knows that. But he has not experienced true knowing.
>
> True knowing must be like the farmer's. Thus when someone knows what is not good and still does it, this is not having experienced true knowing. If he had truly known, he certainly wouldn't do it.[127]

In general we know what we should do. But this does not constitute true knowing unless it compels us to act. While we may be prevented from accomplishing what is right, with true knowing there is never any hesitation or doubt about what we ought and want to do: "That people are unable to be like this is just that they haven't seen the real pattern."[128]

At this point the discipline of learning begins to drop away, and one experiences true delight in following the pattern. It is a major turning point. Talking about it, Ch'eng I remarks:

> People often say that knowing not to do something improper requires effort. But knowing not to bore through a wall (to steal) does not depend on effort. There are deep and shallow [degrees] of this knowledge.
>
> The ancients said that delighting in following the pattern was what was called a superior man. If you make an effort, it is only knowing how to follow the pattern, it is not taking delight. Only when you have reached delight, that is, when following the pattern is a delight, and not following the pattern is not delightful, when it is therefore painful not to follow the pattern, then you will naturally not need to make an effort.[129]

[126] *Erh-Ch'eng chi* 22A.296. Cf. Graham, *Two Chinese Philosophers*, p. 55.
[127] *Erh-Ch'eng chi* 2A.16. Cf. *Erh-Ch'eng chi* 15.188.
[128] *Erh-Ch'eng chi* 15.147.
[129] *Erh-Ch'eng chi* 18.186. Cf. 2A.16, where Ch'eng I or Ch'eng Hao states that a joyful

In sum:

> If someone can know and see [the pattern], how will he be unable to act? Whatever ought to be done, he need not rouse his will before acting. If he must rouse his will before acting, then he has a selfish mind.[130]

True action is selfless, beyond desire or dislike. Here Ch'eng's youthful confidence reemerges transformed into choicelessness. Using images of life and death—the mauling of a tiger, the murder of an insect—he describes a point of view from which selfishness is inconceivable and personal ambition irrelevant. This perspective inverts the value system of most literati. Commenting on the first line statement of hexagram #22 P'i (Adornment [Grace]), Ch'eng remarks:

> What the superior man considers valuable is commonly considered shameful. What is commonly thought valuable, he holds cheap.[131]

Because the pattern is so-by-itself, it cannot be manipulated for selfish ends.

> "The decree of heaven, how majestic and unceasing"[132] just means that the pattern naturally continues itself unceasingly. It's not that men enact it. If men could enact it, even if they could manage it ten million ways, it would necessarily expire sometime. It merely acts without being enacted (*wei-wu-wei*). Therefore it does not expire.[133]

Seeing the pattern, then, is the basis of all true action, personal, familial or governmental. Institutions can aid or hinder one's development, but Ch'eng I himself pays little attention to these matters.[134] This perspective transforms the ground of the literatus's relationship with imperial power. Service with the emperor is no longer the fulfillment of one's aspirations

---

mind is the clearest proof of attainment. In *Erh-Ch'eng chi* 2A.8 Ch'eng I remarks that following propriety (*li*, ritual) is effortless for him.

[130] *Erh-Ch'eng chi* 17.181. Cf. Chan, trans., *Reflections*, p. 63.

[131] *I-chuan* 98.11. We might expect Ch'eng to praise a son who rescues his family from poverty by passing the imperial examinations. But Ch'eng advocates this only if the son can undertake the examinations free of any concern for whether he passes or not. See *Erh-Ch'eng chi* 18.194; and Chan, trans., *Reflections*, p. 199. For evidence of the radical nature of this advice, relative to contemporary moralists' discussions of family economics, see Patricia Ebrey, *Family and Property in Sung China* (Princeton: Princeton University Press, 1984), pp. 44–46.

[132] *Shih Ching* #267.

[133] *Erh-Ch'eng chi* 18.227. Compare: "The pattern of heaven is present, complete. Fundamentally not the slightest thing is missing. It does not exist because of [the sage-emperor] Yao; it does not perish because of [the tyrant] Ch'ieh" (*Erh-Ch'eng chi* 2A.43; Ch'eng Hao?).

[134] For a good selection of remarks, mostly on social hierarchy, see Chan, trans., *Reflections*, chapter 9, "Systems and Institutions," pp. 218–37.

to glory. Instead it becomes a matter of correspondence between two minds with similarly great perspectives. Seeing the pattern, one may freely resist the emperor's might: what power has he over you? Ruination or death is unimportant. However much one wishes to bring order to the empire, and however much the empire requires it, it is pointless and disastrous to compromise one's vision. Thus, should one be prevented from putting such principles into action, it is simply one's fate.

Ch'eng I discusses these circumstances in the context of hexagram #47 K'un (Difficulties [Oppression/Exhaustion]). The *Hsiang-chuan*, drawing on the images associated with the component trigrams, states:

> The pool is without water: K'un. The superior man fulfills his aspirations by knowing fate (*ming*).[135]

Ch'eng comments:

> A pool without water—the image of fatigue. When the superior man comes upon the times of exhaustion and, taking every precaution, still cannot avoid it, it is fate. He should determine what *is* his fate so as to be able to fulfill his aspirations. When he knows what his fate should be, then poverty, cold,[136] calamity, or disaster will be unable to move his mind.[137] He will only act righteously, that is all.[138]

[135] Cf. W/B, p. 182.
[136] With the connotation of being shut out of government.
[137] Paraphrasing Mencius 2A2.
[138] *I-chuan* 211.11.

CHAPTER 6

Chu Hsi and Divination

THE CONTEXT

In 1175 Chu Hsi wrote a letter to Chang Shih (1133–1180) describing what was to become the basis of his entire approach to the *I Ching*:

> I recently had an idea about how to read the *I*. When the sages created the *I* it originally was to cause people to engage in divination, in order to decide what was permissible or not in their behavior, and thereby to teach people to be good. . . . Thus the hexagram and line statements are based simply on the images [the hexagram configurations and their symbolic correlations].[1]

The two major aspects of Chu's *I Ching* studies are foreshadowed here: his theory of divination and his theory of interpretation. Chu claimed that the original meaning of the *I* was to be found not in its various layers of text but in the oracular function of the hexagrams, which were devised by the primordial sage Fu-hsi. The hexagram and line statements, written by the later sages King Wen and the Duke of Chou, were merely a means of access to the *I*'s original oracular intention. This, in turn, implied that if Southern Sung literati were to take the *I* seriously they would have to understand how the *practice* of divination could be incorporated into the quest for sagehood. Using the *I*, for Chu, meant not only reading it but performing divination, as it was originally intended to be used. When done properly, he said, divination "enables everyone from kings and dukes to the common people to use it for self-cultivation (*hsiu-shen*) and ordering the state (*chih-kuo*)."[2]

Chu's approach to the *I* may be taken as a paradigm of his "reconstitution" of the Confucian tradition. He had a clear sense of looking back on a legacy of wisdom, extending from the very origins of Chinese civilization to his Northern Sung predecessors. But, like Confucius, his relationship to the past was more than that of a transmitter. He was a syn-

---

[1] *Chu-tzu wen-chi* (The collected works of Chu Hsi) (*Ssu-pu pei-yao* ed.), *chüan* 31. Quoted and dated by Ch'ien Mu, *Chu-tzu hsin hsüeh-an* (A new scholarly record of Chu Hsi) (Taipei: San Min, 1971), 5 vols., vol. 4, p. 28.

[2] *Chu-tzu ch'üan-shu* (The complete works of Chu Hsi) (Taipei: Kuang-hsüeh, 1977 reprint), 27:12a. "Self-cultivation" and "ordering the state" are two of the eight stages of the *Great Learning* (Ta-hsüeh). See Wing-tsit Chan, *A Source Book in Chinese Philosophy* (Princeton: Princeton University Press, 1963), pp. 86–87.

thesizer (as he has so often been called) in the true sense of the word. He not only systematized the newly revived Confucian tradition, but by selecting, rejecting, recombining and adding elements he also transformed it.

In regard to the *I Ching*, Chu insisted upon the importance of divination (which along with sacrifice had been one of the ritual bases of early Chinese political culture[3]) and the necessity of using it in the process of self-cultivation. This was a reappropriation of the original function of the *I* in the context of the specific intellectual and religious needs of the Southern Sung, as Chu understood them. As we have seen in chapter 2, by the time of the Southern Sung there was a growing disenchantment with politics as the focus of Confucian moral activity (*te-hsing*). The failure of the Northern Sung political reforms and the threat of military subjugation by northern tribes persuaded Chu Hsi and many of his contemporaries that the prerequisite to solving the problems of the Sung was the inner cultivation of moral character by the literati class. This was a return to the fundamental Confucian notions that moral power (*te*, or "virtue") is superior to physical coercion ("laws and punishments") as a foundation of government,[4] and that without humanity or humaneness (*jen*) proper behavior (*li*) is meaningless.[5]

In the Northern Sung, the "external" measures of institutional and political reform had been tried and had failed. Through Chu Hsi's efforts, the debate over the source of values and the question of whether one can know the Way had been won by the Ch'eng school, according to which values are inherent in the heaven-endowed moral nature and can be known and put into effect by means of self-cultivation. For Chu Hsi self-cultivation was the ultimate criterion of literati learning.[6] The problems now to be faced concerned practice: how to know the Way and how to put it into effect. This was a socio-political problem as well as a religious one, for access to a Way rooted in heaven-and-earth and human nature afforded literati a source of moral authority independent of the state. Thus we find Chu Hsi concentrating on the inner life of the individual, on the *Great Learning*'s premise that "self-cultivation is the root" of social and political order.[7] Chu's fundamental problematic, the basis of all his

---

[3] See David N. Keightley, "The Religious Commitment: Shang Theology and the Genesis of Chinese Political Culture," *History of Religions* 17 (1978), pp. 211–25.

[4] *Analects* 2:1, 2:3.

[5] *Analects* 3:3.

[6] See Peter K. Bol, "Chu Hsi's Redefinition of Literati Learning," in *Neo-Confucian Education: The Formative Stage*, ed. Wm. Theodore de Bary and John W. Chaffee (Berkeley and Los Angeles: University of California Press, 1989).

[7] See Daniel K. Gardner, *Chu Hsi and the Ta-hsüeh: Neo-Confucian Reflection on the Confucian Canon* (Cambridge: Harvard University Council on East Asian Studies, 1986); and Conrad Schirokauer, "Chu Hsi's Political Career: A Study in Ambivalence," in *Confu-*

intellectual concerns, was the possibility and the difficulty of attaining sagehood by means of self-cultivation. It is in this context that we must situate his approach to the *I Ching*.

The problem of attaining sagehood in Chu Hsi's system is connected with his theory of mind. We shall, therefore, briefly examine this complex topic before we look more closely at Chu's approach to the *I Ching*.

The Problem of Mind

According to Chu Hsi, mind or heart (*hsin*) is composed of *ch'i*, the psycho-physical substrate of all things, in which inheres *li*, the principle, coherence, order, or pattern underlying the cosmos. The *li* of the mind is human nature (*hsing*), which is inherently good. The *ch'i* of the mind is the clearest, most refined form of *ch'i*, but the degree of this clarity varies from person to person. The sage is a person whose mind is composed of perfectly clear *ch'i*; it is free of the obstruction or cloudiness ordinarily caused by the mind's physical endowment (*ch'i-chih*). Thus the sage possesses complete knowledge of the moral pattern inherent in all things, including his own mind. He therefore has perfect self-knowledge and fully manifests the goodness of human nature. By acting as an exemplar of human virtue the sage can exert a transforming influence on society.

Every person has, theoretically, the potential to become a sage. While those of us with murkier endowments of *ch'i* have less chance of becoming sages than those born (by chance) with clearer endowments, still each of us knows *li* to some extent.[8] Our knowledge of *li*, partial as it may be, is not essentially different from the sage's perfect knowledge. To become a sage is therefore a matter of purifying our *ch'i*, or "transforming the physical endowment" (*pien-hua ch'i-chih*) by means of various intellectual and spiritual practices. These methods of self-cultivation include:[9]

---

cian Personalities, ed. Arthur F. Wright and Denis Twitchett, (Stanford: Stanford University Press, 1962), pp. 162–88. For the *Great Learning* see Chan, *Source Book*, p. 87. On the matter of intellectual changes between Northern and Southern Sung see Robert P. Hymes, *Statesmen and Gentlemen: The Elite of Fu-chou, Chiang-hsi, in Northern and Southern Sung* (Cambridge: Cambridge University Press, 1986). Hymes argues that a development parallel to the one outlined here was the shift in literati political thought and action from a national frame of reference to a more local one (see especially pp. 121–22, 132–35).

[8] On the role of chance in the appearance of sages, see *Chu-tzu yü-lei* (Chu Hsi's Classified Conversations), comp. Li Ching-te, 1270. (Taipei: Cheng-chung, 1970 reprint), *chüan* 4, p. 129.

[9] See T'ang Chün-i, "The Development of the Concept of Moral Mind from Wang Yang-ming to Wang Chi," in *Self and Society in Ming Thought*, ed. Wm. Theodore de Bary (New York: Columbia University Press, 1970), pp. 93–120, and Donald J. Munro, *Images of Human Nature: A Sung Portrait* (Princeton: Princeton University Press, 1988), pp. 81–97.

1. Abiding in reverent composure (*chü-ching*), an attitude that orients and unifies one's activity, underlying and making possible the following:
2. prudence in solitude (*shen-tu*), or extreme care taken to heighten awareness of psychic phenomena (ideas, feelings, intentions) in their incipient (*chi*) phases, at the point when the unexpressed (*wei-fa*) mind first expresses itself;
3. self-examination (*hsing-ch'a*), to distinguish the good psychic phenomena from the evil or selfish ones;[10]
4. preserving and nourishing (*ts'un-yang*) the good psychic phenomena, and the innate moral mind and nature of which they are the direct expressions;
5. conquering the self *(k'o-chi)*,[11] or eliminating the bad psychic phenomena, such as selfish desires;
6. quiet-sitting (*ching-tso*), or meditation, conceived as a quiescent phase in a daily cycle of activity and stillness, when one collects oneself without banishing thoughts; a relatively (but not totally) inactive period that nourishes creative activity;[12]
7. investigating things and extending knowledge (*ko-wu chih-chih*), that is, "completely fathoming the patterns of things and events,"[13] both externally and within oneself, eventually to arrive at a cognitive "interpenetration" (*kuan-t'ung*) of all things, conceived as an enlightenment experience; and
8. practice (*hsing*), to put into effect one's knowledge, in effect to validate one's self-cultivation.

Chu Hsi's treatment of the *I Ching* is best understood as an effort to facilitate the individual's efforts at self-cultivation, in terms of both the inner dimension (particularly items 3, 4, and 5 above, which fall roughly under the "rectification of mind" category of the *Great Learning*) and the practical problems entailed in moral activity, or practice. Like Ch'eng I, he felt that the *I* could help people to learn the moral pattern (*li*) according to which heaven-and-earth functions, and to adapt their personal and social activity to that pattern. But he also felt that in order to do so one needed to undergo an existential transformation by the various means listed above, and that the sages who founded the cultural tradition were necessary participants in this process. Thus his work on the *I* was an attempt to make available, not only to literati but also to common people,

[10] The capacity to distinguish good and evil was said to be an innate characteristic of the human mind, corresponding to "wisdom," one of the Five Constant Virtues (or Four Virtues in *Mencius* 2A.6). See Donald Munro, *The Concept of Man in Early China* (Stanford: Stanford University Press, 1969), pp. 49–58.

[11] Cf. *Analects* 12:1.

[12] See Okada Takehiko, *Zazen to Seiza* (Sitting-meditation and quiet-sitting) (Tokyo: Ofusha, 1966).

[13] Chu Hsi, *Ta-hsüeh chang-chü* (The *Great Learning* in chapters and verses), in *Ssu-shu chi-chu* (Collected commentaries on the *Four Books*) (*Ssu-pu pei-yao* ed.) 2a.

the wisdom and transformative moral power of the sages who created the
I.[14] In terms of using the *I Ching*, divination was the crucial means by
which access to this power could be attained.

Chu Hsi's Work on the I

Chu wrote two books on the *I*: a commentary, entitled *Chou-i pen-i*
(Original meaning of the Chou-i), and a shorter book on the theory and
practice of divination, the *I-hsüeh ch'i-meng* (Introduction to the study of
the I).[15] The *Chou-i pen-i* was completed in 1177 and revised sometime
after 1186.[16] As the title suggests, it was an attempt to move beyond the
later accretions of interpretation embodied in the Ten Wings, and to penetrate to the original meanings intended by the three sages responsible for
the earliest layers of the *I*: Fu-hsi (the hexagrams), King Wen (the hexagram statements), and the Duke of Chou (the line statements). Despite
Chu's belief that Confucius had written all of the Ten Wings (he did not
accept Ou-yang Hsiu's arguments to the contrary[17]), he questioned the

[14] The ability to "transform" (*hua*) others was a traditional hallmark of the Confucian
sage. See, e.g., *Mencius* 7A.13, "the superior person transforms where he passes."

[15] In addition there are numerous essays and letters in his *Collected Works* (*Chu-tzu wen-
chi*) concerning the *I*, and a surprisingly large section of his *Classified Conversations* (*Chu-
tzu yü-lei*) is devoted to the *I* (approximately 11 percent of the total number of pages).

The *Chou-i pen-i* has been reprinted and is available in numerous editions, the *I-hsüeh
ch'i-meng* in somewhat fewer. The editions of the *Chou-i pen-i* used here are the Imperial
Academy edition (Taipei: Hua-lien, 1978 reprint); and Li Kuang-ti, ed., *Chou-i che-chung*
(The *I Ching* Judged Evenly), 1715 (Taipei: Chen Shan Mei, 1971 reprint), 2 vols. The
latter, in which Chu's commentary is collated with Ch'eng I's, also contains the edition of
the *I-hsüeh ch'i-meng* used here (vol. 2).

Other editions of the *Pen-i* are: *Chou-i Pen-i* (Taipei: Kuang-hsüeh, 1975); Yen Ling-feng,
ed., *I Ching chi-ch'eng* (Complete Collection of the *I Ching*) (Taipei: Ch'eng-wen, 1976),
vol. 28; and Wang Yün-wu, ed., *Ssu-k'u ch'üan-shu chen-pen* (Rare Editions from the Imperial Library), 6th series, vols. 1 and 2 (two different editions). The *Pen-i* can also be found
in various inexpensive "popular" editions, sometimes unattributed.

Other editions of the *Ch'i-meng* are: *Chu-tzu i-shu* (Chu Hsi's Surviving Works) (Taipei,
1969 reprint), vol. 12; Hu Kuang, comp., *Hsing-li ta-ch'üan shu* (Great Compendium on
Nature and Principle), 1415 (Ssu-k'u ch'üan-shu chen-pen, 5th series, reprint), ch. 14-17;
and Li Kuang-ti, comp., *Hsing-li ching-i* (Essential Meanings of Nature and Principle), 1715
(*Ssu-pu pei-yao* ed., reprint), *chüan* 4.

[16] See Ch'en Chen-sun (fl. 1211–1249), *Chih-chai shu-lu chieh-t'i* (Annotated Bibliography of Chih-chai Library) (*Kuo-hsüeh chi-pen ts'ung-shu*, vol. 3), *chüan* 1; Wang Mou-
hung, *Chu-tzu nien-p'u* (Biography of Chu Hsi), 1706 (Taipei: Shih-chieh, 1966 reprint), p.
280; *Ssu-k'u ch'üan-shu ts'ung-mu t'i-yao* (Summaries of Works in the Imperial Library)
(*Kuo-hsüeh chi-pen ts'ung-shu* ed.), vol. 1, *chüan* 3, pp. 27–28; and Toda Toyosaburō,
Ekikyō Chūshaku Shikō (Outline History of *I Ching* Commentaries) (Tokyo: Fugen, 1968),
pp. 581–93.

[17] See above, chapter 2. Note, though, that Chu follows Ou-yang's approach to the Classics in terms of bypassing the exegetical tradition in an attempt to recover the original mean-

value of these later texts as interpretive aids. The appendixes, he said, reflect Confucius's own ideas about the pattern of the Way (*tao-li*).[18] Confucius's intentions in writing them were different from those of the three earlier sages, and should therefore not be relied upon to uncover the original meaning of the basic text.

Accordingly, Chu's edition of the *I*, with his commentary, was printed with all the appendixes intact and separate from the earlier layers of the text.[19] It had been the general practice ever since the ascendance of Wang Pi's (226–249) interpretation of the *I* to collate the *T'uan*, *Hsiang*, and *Wen-yen* commentaries (comprising five of the Ten Wings) with the hexagrams to which they applied. For Wang Pi, this collation facilitated "using the Wings to support the basic text," a hermeneutic principle that he inherited from Fei Chih (ca. 50 B.C.E.–10 C.E.) and Cheng Hsüan (127–200), the earliest prominent *i-li* (meaning and principle) commentators.[20] When Wang Pi's commentary was later enshrined in the *Chou-i cheng-i* (Correct meaning of the *I Ching*) as the official interpretation of the T'ang Dynasty (618–906), this arrangement of the text acquired yet higher status. The most prominent *i-li* commentator of the Northern Sung, Ch'eng I, followed Wang Pi's arrangement. It was, by this time, a standard feature of the *i-li* approach—partly because of Wang Pi's authoritative status, but mostly because the arrangement supported both the technical and the philosophical hermeneutics of the *i-li* school, according to which the meaning of the *I* is best sought in the text, not directly in the hexagrams themselves.

---

ings. Recall that Ou-yang wrote a commentary on the *Classic of Poetry* entitled "The Original Meaning of the Poetry" (*Shih pen-i*).

[18] *Tao-li* will be translated here either as "pattern of the Way" when the emphasis is on the unity of *li*, or as "moral principle(s)" when the emphasis is on the multiplicity of its manifestations. Chu uses the term in these two senses, which correspond to Ch'eng I's claim that "the pattern is unitary, its manifestations are multiple" (*li-i erh fen-shu*).

[19] Nevertheless, this arrangement was not retained in all later editions. Of those mentioned in note 15, the Imperial Academy edition, the *Chou-i che-chung*, and vol. 2 of the *Ssu-k'u ch'üan-shu chen-pen* (6th series) all use the Wang Pi arrangement of the text (see below). The Kuang-hsüeh edition, the *I Ching chi-ch'eng*, and vol. 1 of the *Ssu-k'u ch'üan-shu chen-pen* (6th series) use Chu Hsi's arrangement. According to Wang Mou-hung, the practice of ignoring Chu's arrangement dates back to some of his students shortly after his death (*Chu-tzu nien-p'u k'ao-i*, p. 280, n. 3).

[20] See T'ang Yung-t'ung, "Wang Pi's New Interpretation of the *I-ching* and the *Lun-yü*," trans. Walter Liebenthal, *Harvard Journal of Asiatic Studies* 10.2 (1947), pp. 124–61; and G. E. Kidder Smith, Jr., *Cheng Yi's (1033–1107) Commentary on the Yijing* (Ph.D. dissertation, University of California at Berkeley, 1979), pp. 24–29.

To recapitulate the discussion in chapter 1, *i-li* (meaning and principle) and *hsiang-shu* (image and number) are the two traditional interpretive approaches to the *I Ching*. The *i-li* approach bases interpretation on the textual layers of the *I*, while the *hsiang-shu* approach is based on hexagram structure, imagery, symbolism and numerology.

Chu was by no means the first Sung commentator to return to the structure of the "Old *I*." Several such editions had appeared in the Northern Sung, and Chu's friend Lü Tsu-ch'ien had also published one. In Chu's colophon to Lü's edition he wrote:

> Confucius wrote the Appendixes, "lifting one corner to show the whole outline" [paraphrasing *Analects* 7:8]. But after various scholars divided up the Classic with the appendixes, students relied on these texts in choosing their interpretations. Eventually they could no longer grasp in their minds the whole Classic, and hastily seized upon the "one corner" of the Appendixes as the correct explanation. In this way each line of each hexagram refers to merely one event, and the use of the *I* incorrectly becomes limited, lacking the means to "connect all situations under heaven." This being the case, I am uneasy with it.[21]

In the following section we shall see how Chu Hsi attempted to improve on earlier commentators' use of the *I* "to connect all situations under heaven."

Chu's second book on the *I*, the *I-hsüeh ch'i-meng* (Introduction to the study of the *I*) was published in 1186. In a letter to Lu Tzu-mei he described his purpose in writing it:

> I have recently written a little book on divination. My reason for writing it is that those who have discussed the *I* in recent years have been either completely vague in regard to image and number (*hsiang-shu*), or else so literal and fragmented that we cannot delve into it. Therefore I have extended just the numerological sections of the Sages' discussions of image and number in the appendixes to the Classic, to infer their intentions. I consider this to be sufficient in terms of theory to examine the Sage's original referent in creating the *I*, and in terms of practice to enhance the practical usefulness of ordinary people's "contemplation of the changes and pondering of the prognostications."[22]

As this letter suggests, the *Introduction* is basically a divination manual, relying heavily on *hsiang-shu*, and specifically on Shao Yung. The first of its four chapters is a detailed study of the numerological and cosmological symbolism of the Ho-t'u (Yellow River Chart) and the Lo-shu (Lo River Diagram). These are numerological diagrams that had been associated with the *I Ching* ever since the Han dynasty (206 B.C.E.–220 C.E.). The Ho-t'u, in particular, was said to have been used by Fu-hsi as a model for

---

[21] *Chu-tzu wen-chi* 82:20b, quoting *Hsi-tz'u* A 11 (cf. Wilhelm/Baynes, p. 316). Primary references to the *Hsi-tz'u* in this chapter are given according to Chu Hsi's slightly rearranged version of the text, which was followed by James Legge and Richard Wilhelm in their translations. Alternate page references are given to the Wilhelm/Baynes translation (3d ed., 1967) for the convenience of the reader.

[22] *Chu-tzu wen-chi* 36:5b, quoting *Hsi-tz'u* A2 (cf. Wilhelm/Baynes, p. 290).

the hexagrams of the *I* (although the connections between the two are extremely vague). According to K'ung An-kuo (fl. 130 B.C.E.), quoted by Chu Hsi in the *Introduction*:

> The Ho-t'u came out of the Yellow River on a dragon-horse when Fu-hsi ruled the world. He accordingly took its design as a model in drawing the eight trigrams. The Lo-shu was the design arrayed on the back of a spirit-tortoise at the time when Yü controlled the flood. In it are the numbers up to 9. Yü accordingly followed its classifications in setting up the Nine Regions [of China].[23]

Chu Hsi accepted the tradition of the historical origins of these diagrams, and believed them to have been revealed to the sages by heaven; hence the need to "fathom their pattern" (*ch'iung-li*), in particular their numerological principles. This he does, at great length, in the first chapter of the *Introduction*. Nevertheless, as we shall see in the following section, he preferred another version of the myth recounting the creation of the *I* that gave a somewhat more active role to Fu-hsi.

In the second chapter of the *Introduction* Chu explores the yin-yang patterns by which the trigrams and hexagrams of the *I* may be generated by the successive recombination of solid and broken lines. Here he also discusses the Fu-hsi and King Wen sequences of the trigrams, as well as Shao Yung's *Hsien-t'ien* (Preceding heaven) diagram. In the third chapter he discusses in detail the milfoil divination procedure, which he had reconstructed from the fragmentary version in *Hsi-tz'u* A9. (His version of this procedure has remained standard to this day.)[24] And in the final chapter he explains how to derive a second hexagram from the one determined by the yarrow stalks, and how to interpret the transformation from the first to the second as a prognostication. Clearly, this book was intended to be a practical manual of divination, to be used by those learning the Way of the sages.

The ultimate purpose of performing divination, like everything else in Chu's system, was to contribute to self-cultivation. As we shall see below, the oracular power of the *I* was considered to be like the "spiritual" (*shen*) capacity of the perfectly clear mind of the sage to know the future.

[23] *I-hsüeh ch'i-meng*, p. 1207. This is an amplification of the statement in *Hsi-tz'u* A11, "The River gave forth the Chart, and the Lo gave forth the Diagram. The sages took them as models" (cf. Wilhelm/Baynes, p. 320). One or both of the charts are also briefly mentioned in the *Shu Ching* (Book of Documents, "Ku-ming" chapter) and the *Ta-Tai li-chi* (Record of ritual of the elder Tai, "Ming-t'ang" chapter). Sung traditions tracing the transmission of these charts from the Han to the Sung seem to be merely conjectural. See James Legge, trans., *The I Ching*, 1899 (New York: Dover Publications, 1963 reprint), p. 15; A. C. Graham, *Two Chinese Philosophers* (London: Lund Humphries, 1958), pp. 157–75; and Imai Usaburō, *Sōdai Ekigaku no Kenkyū* (Research on Sung dynasty studies of the Book of Change) (Tokyo: Meiji, 1958), pp. 146–241.

[24] It is the one given in the Wilhelm/Baynes translation of the *I*, 3d ed., pp. 721–24.

This transcendent clarity of mind could be cultivated by a person working to become a sage. But the extreme difficulty of interpreting the text of the *I* made this a highly problematic endeavor, fraught with pitfalls.

INTERPRETING THE *I*

The premise of Chu Hsi's interpretive theory is the myth, taken as a historical datum by Chu Hsi, of Fu-hsi's creation of the *I*. The myth, as told in the *Hsi-tz'u*, goes as follows:[25]

> In ancient times, when Pao-hsi [Fu-hsi] ruled the world, he looked up and contemplated the images (*hsiang*) in heaven; he looked down and contemplated the patterns (*fa*) on earth. He contemplated the markings of the birds and beasts and their adaptations to the various regions. From near at hand he abstracted images from his own body; from afar he abstracted from things. In this way he first created the eight trigrams, to spread the power (*te*) of [his] spiritual clarity and to classify the dispositions of the myriad things.[26]

According to Chu, the primordial sage Fu-hsi created the *I* in the form of hexagrams that he derived from patterns in nature. There was no text associated with it until the troubled time of King Wen (the founder of the Chou dynasty in the eleventh century B.C.E.), who felt that people were no longer capable of interpreting the hexagrams directly. While he was imprisoned by the wicked last king of the Shang, King Wen therefore composed the hexagram statements to help elucidate the oracular meaning of the hexagrams. His son, the Duke of Chou, later wrote the line statements as further clarification. Chu Hsi's point in his letter to Chang Shih (quoted at the beginning of this chapter) is that these texts were not the original locus of meaning. They were intended merely as clarifications of the graphic and oracular meanings of the hexagrams. Therefore a correct interpretation of the text must make sense in the same way.[27]

---

[25] By "myth" I mean a sacred story symbolizing some fundamental value or belief of a particular social group. A myth may or may not have a historical basis.

[26] *Hsi-tz'u* B2 (cf. Wilhelm/Baynes, pp. 328–29). For Chu's discussion of the relationship between this myth and the one involving the *Ho-t'u* (Yellow River Chart), see *Chou-i che-chung*, p. 1207 (Chu's reply to Yüan-shu).

[27] The range of meanings of the term "image" (*hsiang*) in *I Ching* lore includes the concrete objects after which Fu-hsi modeled the hexagrams, the hexagrams and trigrams themselves as line diagrams, their yin-yang meanings, and the various symbolic correlations elaborated in the *Shuo-kua* and occasionally mentioned in the hexagram and line texts. The term is an extremely important one in the *Hsi-tz'u*, occurring nearly forty times. For example, in A11 and A12 it is argued that the imagery of the *I* conveys concepts that cannot be expressed in words, and that this is the key to the profundity of the *I*. For discussions of *hsiang* see Hellmut Wilhelm, *Heaven, Earth, and Man in the Book of Changes* (Seattle: University of Washington Press, 1977), pp. 32–35, 190–221; and Gerald William Swanson,

Furthermore, Chu later argued, the "original intention" or purpose of the hexagrams was not philosophical but oracular: they were intended to be used to determine how to act in particular situations, not to express moral principles. Among scholars ever since Wang Pi, though, the *I* had generally been used as textual support for whatever philosophy was being put forth. This, according to Chu, was not only likely to result in specious argumentation, it was also bound to neglect the real access to the "mind of the sage" that the *I* could provide—a connection that could prove invaluable in the extremely difficult process of self-cultivation. Hence Chu Hsi's repeated dictum, "The *I* was originally created for divination."[28]

This principle of interpretation led Chu to emphasize two things in his commentary on the *I* (the *Chou-i pen-i*): the "original meaning" (*pen-i*) and the "original intention" (also pronounced *pen-i*). The original meaning, first, is the literal denotation of the text, referring to the structural features, numerological characteristics, and symbolic associations of the hexagram and its component lines and trigrams. For example, his commentary on Ta-yu (hexagram #14 "Great Possession") begins as follows (the hexagram text is "Great possession; primal success"):

> Great Possession is possession in great measure. Li [the upper trigram] comes to rest over Ch'ien [the lower], fire over heaven. All is illuminated. The 6 in the fifth place is a yin line abiding in respect. It attains the central position, while the five yang lines respond to it. Thus it is a great possession. Ch'ien is strong and Li is bright.[29]

Second, Chu emphasizes the oracular meaning of the text, since divination is the original intention or purpose for which the text was written. Thus his commentary on hexagram #14 continues:

> Abiding in respect and responding to heaven is a Way of success. If the diviner has these virtues, then there will be great goodness and success.[30]

Its original intention is what renders the *I* significantly different from the other Classics, according to Chu. Unlike the *Documents, Odes, Ritual*, and *Spring and Autumn* Classics, the *I* was not used by Confucius

---

The Great Treatise: Commentatory Tradition to the "Book of Changes" (Ann Arbor University Microfilms International, 1974), pp. 148–63, 313–15.

Chu Hsi, as will become clear in this section, argues that the more concrete, graphic images of the *I*—that is, those actually produced by Fu-hsi—are more important than the symbolic correlations and the metaphorical images found in the texts (such as the dragon of hexagram #1, Ch'ien, and the mare of hexagram #2, K'un). See his "*I* hsiang shuo" (Discussion of the Images of the *I*), *Chu-tzu wen-chi* 67:1a–2a.

[28] See for example, *Chu-tzu yü-lei* 66, *passim*.

[29] *Chou-i pen-i* 1:33a.

[30] Ibid.

and the early kings for pedagogical purposes, but only for divination.[31] In a sense the original intention of the *I* is not merely what the author meant, but what he meant for the reader (i.e., the user) to do.[32]

Chu's disagreements with both the *hsiang-shu* and the *i-li* interpretive traditions were basically that they both, in different ways, had partial views of the *I*. The *hsiang-shu* commentators, especially those of the Han, recognized the importance of the graphic imagery and its correlations, but failed to apply it to human affairs. They were, he said, "mired in muck" and "bound by forced associations."[33] The *i-li* commentators, on the other hand, correctly focused on the moral principles (*tao-li*) that could be discerned in or inferred from the text, but they ignored the text's concrete referent (i.e., the configuration and imagery of the hexagrams).[34]

Chu's difference with the *i-li* school can readily be seen by comparing his commentary with Ch'eng I's. Ch'eng focuses on the general concepts embodied in the hexagram and line statements; his discussions of the structural features of the hexagrams are minimal. Compare, for example, his comment on the hexagram text of hexagram #14 with that of Chu Hsi given above:

> The qualities (*ts'ai*) of the hexagram can be considered "primacy and success."[35] As for the virtues (*te*) of hexagrams in general, there are cases of the name of the hexagram itself containing the meaning (*i*), such as "Holding together; auspicious" (hexagram #8 Pi) and "Modesty; success" (hexagram #15 Ch'ien). There are cases where one derives the meaning of the hexagram from the counsel and admonition,[36] such as "Army; perseverance and a strong man;

---

[31] *Chu-tzu yü-lei* 67, p. 2639. See Ssu-ma Ch'ien, *Shih-chi* (Historical Records) (*Ssu-pu pei-yao* ed.), 47:19a, and Ch'ien Mu, *Chu-tzu hsin hsüeh-an*, vol. 4, p. 15.

[32] For a wide range of discussion on intentionality and the "intentional fallacy," see the thematic issues "On Interpretation" of *New Literary History* 3, no. 2 (1972), and 4, no. 3 (1973), especially Quentin Skinner, "Motives, Intentions, and the Interpretation of Texts," *New Literary History* 3, no. 2 (1972), pp. 393–408. Skinner argues that, while motives cannot reveal the meaning of a text, intentions can. It should be noted that Chu Hsi referred to both motives and intentions in regard to the interpretation of the *I*: The sages' motive in creating it was their "anxiety" or "concern" (*yu*) for ordinary people who had difficulty knowing the right thing to do (see, for example, *Chou-i pen-i*, preface, p. 1a, and *Chou-i che-chung*, p. 1024). Motive, however, does not figure directly into Chu's interpretive theory.

[33] *Chu-tzu wen-chi* 67:1a–1b ("I hsiang shuo"), and *I-hsüeh ch'i-meng* (*Chou-i che-chung* ed.), preface, p. 1203.

[34] *I-hsüeh ch'i-meng*, p. 1203, and *Chu-tzu wen-chi* 36:5b.

[35] These are the first two of the "four virtues" (*ssu-te*) of the *I*, as interpreted by Ch'eng I: *yüan, heng, li* and *chen* (translated by Shchutskii as "beginning, penetration, definition, stability" [*Researches on the I Ching*, p. 202]). Chu Hsi interprets these four words as two phrases: "great penetration; benefiting in correctness" (*Chou-i pen-i* 1:1b; cf. Shchutskii, pp. 136, 154, 203).

[36] *Hsün-chai*, the short phrase between the hexagram name and the oracular formula.

auspicious" (hexagram #7 Shih) and "Comrades; in the countryside, success" (hexagram #13 T'ung-jen). And there are cases [such as the present] in which it is expressed in terms of the hexagram qualities, such as "Great possession; primacy and success." Since [the *T'uan-chuan* refers to the virtue of this hexagram as] "firm and strong, cultured and bright; responding to heaven and acting in season," thus it is able to have "primacy and success."[37]

Note that all three of the loci of meaning Ch'eng discusses here are based on the hexagram text; he does not discuss the trigram/hexagram structure in terms of yin-yang theory, as Chu Hsi does (above). Chu consistently begins each discussion of a hexagram or line with an explanation of the yin-yang relationships of the lines and the imagery of the component trigrams. On that basis, he attempts to clarify the relationship between the lines and the statements, drawing particular attention to the oracular pronouncements.

To set Chu Hsi's theory of *I Ching* interpretation in a broader context, let us briefly look at his general theory of interpretation, his "methodology of reading" (*tu-shu fa*).[38] Chu developed what can be characterized as a "systemic" approach to textual interpretation, involving the interrelations of author, text, and reader. There are both objective and subjective elements in this theory.

The first stage of textual interpretation is to apprehend the literal denotation or referent of the text, as intended by the author. To this end Chu said one should apply whatever historical and philological data might be available, using the context and circumstances of the text's composition to explicate it and the author's intended meaning. His use of the traditional accounts of the *I*'s creation by Fu-hsi, King Wen, the Duke of Chou, and Confucius is an example of his concern for recovering its original meaning. Such an approach would help the reader, he said, to avoid projecting his own ideas onto the text. It was important to treat texts as objects (*wu*) external to one's mind so that they could exert a rectifying leverage on it. "How can those who take their own private ideas and read them into the books of the sages and worthies get anything from their reading?"[39] Partiality or self-centeredness was something always to be guarded against. One should read a text with an "equable mind"[40] and total attention, taking care to interpret each passage in its context,[41] without comparing the book with others until after it is completely read.[42]

[37] *Chou-i che-chung*, p. 234.
[38] See Daniel K. Gardner, "Principle and Pedagogy: Chu Hsi and the Four Books," *Harvard Journal of Asiatic Studies* 44:1 (1984), pp. 57–81.
[39] *Chu-tzu ch'üan-shu* 6:5a.
[40] Ibid., 6:4a–4b.
[41] Ibid., 6:5b.
[42] *Chu-tzu yü-lei* 67, p. 2641.

This is the objective aspect of Chu Hsi's methodology of reading: books are to be treated as things, the patterns or principles of which must be thoroughly investigated.

After one has ascertained the intended meaning, according to Chu, a certain subjective involvement with the text is necessary for full understanding. One must extend one's mind into the thing, responding to its pattern and making it one's own:

> One must first read thoroughly, so that all the words seem to come from one's own mouth. Then think cogently, so that all the ideas seem to come from one's own mind. Only then will one be able to get it.[43]
>
> In reading books one's body and mind must enter inside each paragraph.[44]

Ultimately the purpose of reading is not simply to recover the wisdom of the sages but to use it to bring something new into the world. And the emphasis is always on the creative subject, the self:

> Approach the old teachings in order to bring out new views.[45]
>
> In reading books one should not simply look for the pattern of the Way on the page. One must come back and investigate one's own self.[46]

This subjective dimension of Chu's hermeneutics is closely connected with his theory of the coordinate relationship of knowledge (*chih*) and practice (*hsing*):

> The efforts of both knowledge and practice must be exerted to the utmost. As one knows more clearly, he acts more earnestly, and as he acts more earnestly, he knows more clearly. . . . When one knows something but has not yet acted on it, his knowledge is shallow. After he has experienced it, his knowledge will be increasingly clear, and its character will be different from what it was before. . . . Knowledge and practice always require each other. It is like a person who cannot walk without legs although he has eyes, and who cannot see without eyes although he has legs. With respect to order, knowledge comes first, and with respect to importance, practice is more important.[47]

---

[43] *Chu-tzu ch'üan-shu* 6:9b.

[44] Ibid., 6:3a.

[45] Ibid., 6:4b.

[46] Ibid., 6:18b. This is similar in some respects to Paul Ricoeur's idea of the "appropriation" of a text, although Chu Hsi is more sanguine than Ricoeur concerning the possibility of recovering the author's intended meaning. See Paul Ricoeur, "What is a text? Explanation and Understanding," in *Paul Ricoeur: Hermeneutics and the Human Sciences*, ed. and trans. John B. Thompson (Cambridge: Cambridge University Press, and Paris: Editions de la Maison des Sciences de l'Homme, 1981), pp. 158–61. Chu's theory is closer to David M. Rasmussen's theory of the actualization of latent meanings, in *Symbol and Interpretation* (The Hague: Martinus Nijhoff, 1974), pp. 7–17.

[47] Chan, trans., *Source Book*, p. 609 (substituting "practice" for "action"). See also Munro, *Images of Human Nature*, pp. 97–101.

Breadth of study is not as good as essential knowledge, and essential knowledge is not as good as concrete practice.[48]

Thus knowledge and practice are interdependent. Knowledge is not complete until it is acted upon and thereby incorporated into the subject's own will or intentionality. To know the meaning of a text is not merely to absorb it passively. It is an active appropriation of the author's intention into one's own experience. In the case of the *I Ching*, this appropriation takes the form of divination.

Chu Hsi's hermeneutical principle that meaning is part of a broader intentionality that also includes practice is the basis for much of his criticism of previous commentators on the *I*, especially those of the *i-li* school. Ch'eng I, in particular, came in for harsh criticism on this score. Chu's critique typically proceeds as follows:

In the time of high antiquity people's minds were cloudy, and they did not know wherein good fortune and misfortune lay. Therefore the sage [Fu-hsi] created the *I* to teach them divination and to enable them to act on good fortune and to avoid misfortune. . . . At first there were only prognostications and no texts . . . until King Wen and the Duke of Chou composed the hexagram and line texts, enabling people to apprehend the lines and easily contemplate the good fortune and misfortune in the texts. Confucius also feared that people would not understand the reasons [for acting or not acting], so he further explained the lines one by one, saying what makes this line auspicious is its centrality and correctness, and what makes that line inauspicious is improper position. He clearly elucidated this, allowing people to understand easily. For example, the *Wen-yen* [appendix, attributed to Confucius] explains the moral principles (*tao-li*) on this basis [i.e., line by line]. But it is not the case that the sage created the *I* primarily for discussing moral principles in order to instruct people. One must see the sage's original intention; then one can study the *I*.[49]

Basically, the *I* was originally created for divination. Thus its statements must be based on the images and numbers (*hsiang-shu*), and are not products of the sages' own intentions. . . . Those who have discussed the *I* recently have not understood this at all. Thus, although their discussions contain the textual meaning (lit., meaning and principle, *i-li*), they lack the contextual meaning (lit., situational intention, *ch'ing-i*).[50]

This is the crux of the distinction between reading the *I* as a book of philosophy or moral principle and reading it as a divination manual. The hexagram and line texts were not written by King Wen and the Duke of Chou to express their own ideas; they were written to facilitate the oracular use of the hexagrams created by Fu-hsi. Principles can, of course, be

[48] *Chu-tzu yü-lei* 13, p. 353.
[49] *Chu-tzu ch'üan-shu* 27:9b–10a.
[50] Ibid., 27:17b–18a.

inferred from these texts. But those who disregard the concrete referent and the oracular intention are likely to misconstrue the intended meaning and to miss the point of reading the *I*. The point is to apply that moral principle in specific circumstances, or situations (*ch'ing*).

> The *I* was originally a book of divination. Later men took it only as divination, until Wang Pi's use of Lao-tzu and Chuang-tzu to explain it. After that, people only considered it [a book of] pattern/principle and not as divination. This is all wrong.[51]
>
> [Ch'eng] I-ch'uan merely took up his *I* and construed it in terms of metaphorical explanations. But I fear that the sages, indeed, would not have been willing to write such a metaphorical book.[52]
>
> The pattern of the Way [expressed in Ch'eng's] *Commentary on the I* is refined, and its words are extensive, with nothing left out. It fills in the gaps in other people's writings on moral effort (*kung-fu*). How clear and natural! But it is not in accord with the original meaning. The *I* was originally a book of divination. Its hexagram texts and line texts contain everything. How to use it is left to the reader. Mr. Ch'eng can only discuss it in terms of the unitary pattern.[53]

In saying "how to use it is left to the reader," Chu means that the specific behavioral implications of a line are determined by the contextual situation in which it is received in divination. The interpretation must accord with the "resonances of [the subject's] intention" (*i so kan-t'ung*).[54] That is to say, the meaning of the text must be capable of application by any person:

> If we regard [the *I*] as [a book of] divination, then all people—scholars, farmers, artisans, and merchants—will be able to make use of it in all their affairs. If this sort of person divines, he will make this sort of use of it. If another sort of person divines, he will make another sort of use of it.[55]

According to Chu Hsi, the *i-li* approach to the *I*, focusing on the texts attributed to King Wen, the Duke of Chou, and Confucius, uses these texts merely as a point of departure for the moral philosophy of the commentator. It cannot penetrate to the original meaning of the *I* itself because it gives insufficient attention to the original form in which the *I* was created (namely the hexagrams and their graphic and numerological symbolism) and to the intended use of the hexagram and line texts (to aid in the interpretation of hexagrams obtained in divination). Consequently, while the *i-li* commentators generally treated the *I* as a source of moral

---

51 *Chu-tzu yü-lei* 66, p. 2578.
52 *Chu-tzu yü-lei* 67, p. 2628.
53 Ibid., p. 2626.
54 *Chu-tzu ch'üan-shu* 27:14a–b.
55 *Chu-tzu ch'üan-shu* 27:7a.

guidance, their interpretive approach cut them off from the concrete subjective engagement with the *I*, and with the sages who created it, that
would most effectively contribute to the process of self-transformation.
Ch'eng I's commentary, for example, is such an elaborate discussion of
the moral pattern that "people who study it today no longer look at the
original Classic; they merely read the commentary. This is not how to get
people to think."[56]
Thus Chu's disagreement with the *i-li* school turns on an implicit distinction between teaching moral behavior (i.e., the right responses to specific situations) and teaching moral cultivation (i.e., how to transform
oneself into a sagely human being). Ch'eng I, according to Chu, had taken
each of the 384 hexagram lines of the *I* as corresponding to a particular
situation from which a specific moral principle could be learned. For example, he had interpreted the lines of hexagram #1 Ch'ien with reference
to historical events in the life of the Sage-Emperor Shun, events that provided models of behavior which could be emulated. In Chu Hsi's view,
"in this way each line of each hexagram refers to merely one event, and
the use of the *I* incorrectly becomes limited, lacking the means to 'connect
all situations under heaven.' "[57] Chu's own commentary on the *I*, like his
other commentaries, was designed not as a handbook of ethical behavior
but as an aid in one's subjective involvement with the Classic:

> In Mr. Ch'eng's explanations of the Classics, the pattern is contained in the
> explanatory remarks. In my *Collected Comments on the Lun-yü*, I merely elu-
> cidate the phrases, allowing people to get the taste of the text of the Classic.
> The pattern is contained in the text of the Classic.[58]

In other words, Chu Hsi's commentaries were not intended to develop
the specific moral implications and lessons to be learned from the text
and applied to the life of the reader. The reader must learn how to do that
himself. Chu merely tries to be a facilitator for the subject's own engagement with the wisdom and power of the sages.
To illustrate Chu Hsi's hermeneutical approach to the *I* in practice, we
shall look at portions of a long exchange between Chu Hsi and a student
of his, Liu Yung-chih,[59] recorded in the *Chu-tzu yü-lei* (Chu Hsi's classified conversations). It is an instructive dialogue because in it Chu Hsi

---

[56] *Chu-tzu yü-lei*, quoted by Tai Chün-jen, *T'an I* (On the *I*) (Taipei: K'ai-ming Bookstore,
1961), p. 100.

[57] *Chu-tzu wen-chi* 82:20b (from Chu's colophon to Lü Tsu-ch'ien's *I*, cited above), quoting *Hsi-tz'u* A 11 (cf. Wilhelm/Baynes, p. 316). It should be noted that, as we have seen
above in chapter 5, Ch'eng I also criticizes those who connect each hexagram line with a
specific situation (*Erh-Ch'eng chi* 19.249). Chu Hsi apparently felt that Ch'eng failed to
avoid this error himself.

[58] *Chu-tzu wen-chi* 82:20b.

[59] See Chan Wing-tsit (Ch'en Jung-chieh), *Chu-tzu men-jen* (Chu Hsi's disciples) (Taipei:
Hsüeh-sheng, 1982), pp. 318–19.

makes rather fine adjustments in his student's interpretation of a single hexagram line. If we can understand his reasoning here we will probably have understood his interpretive theory.

Liu's question concerns the interpretation of the second line of hexagram #2 K'un. Since he refers to Chu Hsi's commentary on the line it will be helpful to have that before us:

> TEXT: Six in the second place. Straight, square and great. Without practice [*hsi*, repetition] everything is advantageous.
>
> CHU'S COMMENT: The soft [line] is obedient (*shun*) and secure in the correct place. This is K'un's "straightness." The bestowal of definite form is K'un's "squareness." Its virtue [namely obedience, docility] is to combine without limit; this is K'un's "greatness." The 6 in the second place is a soft line moving into the central and correct position; it receives the essence of the way of K'un. Therefore its virtue is straight internally, square externally, and flourishes greatly. Everything will be advantageous without depending on study (*hsüeh-hsi*). If the diviner has these virtues, the prognostication will be like this.[60]

The student, Liu Yung-chih, asks a question that seems to derive in a straightforward way from the sentence in Chu's commentary, "Everything will be advantageous without depending on study":

> Yung-chih asked: "Under 6 in the second place of K'un, does 'straight, square, and great; all is advantageous without practice' mean that the student must use practice, and only later will he reach the point of not having to practice?"
> [Chu Hsi] replies: "It is not like that. When the sages created the *I* it meant only that in the lines of this hexagram there was this image. . . . If a person received this prognostication, then corresponding to this situation there would be this application. It [the passage in question] does not go so far as to mean that the student must practice until he no longer needs to practice. In the case of a student, of course it must be like this. But there was no such intention in the *I* created by the sages."[61]

[60] *Chou-i pen-i* 1:11a; *Chou-i che-chung*, p. 141. To recapitulate the discussion in chapter 1, the terms "central" and "correct" refer to two basic principles of *I Ching* interpretation. The central lines are those in the second and fifth places, i.e., in the centers of the two component trigrams. To be correct, a yin (broken, or soft) line must occupy an even-numbered position (second, fourth, or sixth), and a yang line must occupy an odd-numbered position. See Li Kuang-ti's general introduction to the *Chou-i che-chung*, p. 100; *Chu-tzu wen-chi* 85:8a; and Wilhelm/Baynes, pp. 360–61. In the hexagram K'un, the yin line in the second place is both central and correct, which is why it "receives the essence of K'un." "This," says Chu Hsi, "is the basic substance of the explanation of the K'un hexagram" (*Chu-tzu yü-lei* 69, p. 2765). "Straight internally, square externally" alludes to the *Wen-yen* commentary on K'un (*Chou-i pen-i* 1:12b), which says, "The *chün-tzu* is reverently composed (*ching*) to straighten [himself] internally, and does what is right (*i*) to square [himself] externally." This line was used extensively by the Ch'eng brothers and became a Neo-Confucian formula for moral cultivation. See Chan, *Source Book*, pp. 538–39, 545.

[61] *Chu-tzu yü-lei* 66, p. 2590.

Here Chu Hsi distinguishes the original meaning of the line from its application to a specific divinatory situation. In the above-quoted comment on the text, the last two sentences pertain to one specific application, appropriate only to a student; they do not refer to the Duke of Chou's original meaning. The sages were not thinking only of students when they devised and wrote the *I* (although Chu's commentary appears to incline in their direction). As we saw above, the text must be interpreted so as to be applicable to any person's circumstances: scholar, farmer, artisan, or merchant. Thus corrected, Yung-chih tries again:

> Yung-chih said: However, "all advantageous without practice" has to do with "achieved virtue."[62]
>
> [Chu Hsi] replies: Wrong again. It never says anything about "achieved virtue." It is only that in the lines of this hexagram there is this image. If one receives this prognostication, then it corresponds to this image; it never says anything about "achieved virtue." This is how my theory of the *I* differs from the theories of both former and recent scholars.[63]

Yung-chih seems to be trying Chu's patience. He still has not seen that one must first understand the text's literal referent, namely the hexagram imagery, before one tries to derive a moral principle from it. The principle must be directly implied by both the imagery and the statement. Only by observing what Chu Hsi believed to be the coherence (i.e., the unifying principle or pattern, *li*) of the various levels of the *I* can the reader maintain contact with the intentionality of its sagely authors.[64] Even then one must be aware that Fu-hsi's original intention in creating the divination system was partially dissipated by the later sages, who were more inter-

---

[62] Probably alluding to the *Wen-yen* commentary on hexagram #1 Ch'ien: "The superior person acts in accordance with achieved virtue," or "virtue already achieved" (*Chou-i pen-i* 1:8a; cf. Wilhelm/Baynes, p. 379). Yung-chih's idea here may be that the morally powerful or accomplished person gets things done by the force of his moral example, without resorting to empirically observable methods. Cf. *Analects* 2:1, "He who rules by virtue (*te*) is like the pole-star, which remains in its place while all the lesser stars do homage to it" (Waley's translation, slightly modified, from Arthur Waley, *The Analects of Confucius* [London: George Allen & Unwin, 1938], p. 88). Thus "without practice, everything is advantageous."

[63] *Chu-tzu yü-lei* 66, p. 2590.

[64] Chu Hsi's assumption that there is actually a definite connection between the image and the text is, of course, not supported by modern scholarship, which has shown the *I* to be a very heterogeneous text. (See Arthur Waley, "The Book of Changes," *Bulletin of the Museum of Far Eastern Antiquities* 5 [1933], pp. 121–42, and Ku Chieh-kang, ed., *Ku-shih pien* [Analysis of ancient history], 1931 [Hong Kong, T'ai-p'ing Book Co., 1963 reprint], vol. 3.) It is to Chu's credit, actually, that he recognized and freely admitted the extreme difficulty of making exegetical sense of the *I*. He was compelled to attempt to make sense of it not only by the weight of tradition, but also by his other (faulty) assumption that the *Hsi-tz'u* was written by Confucius and contained fragments of historical information concerning the creation of the *I*.

ested in moral principle than in divination. As he continues in his response to Yung-chih:

> The *I* was created merely as a divination book. . . . If you can understand my theory, then you can understand that Fu-hsi and King Wen's *I* was originally created for this use. Originally it did not contain very many moral principles (*tao-li*). Only then had the original intention of the *I* not been lost. Today, people do not yet understand the sage's original intention in creating the *I*—they first want to discuss moral principles. Even though they discuss it well, they lack the contextual pattern (*ch'ing-li*). [Their writings] simply have nothing to do with the origin of the *I*. The sage [Confucius] has clearly explained, "In antiquity the sages created the *I* by observing the images [in heaven], laying out the hexagrams, and appending the texts to them in order to elucidate good fortune and misfortune."[65] This is abundantly clear. My reason for claiming that the *I* is merely a divination book can be seen in this kind of passage. . . .
>
> People reading the *I* today should divide it into three levels: Fu-hsi's *I*, King Wen's *I*, and Confucius's *I*. If one reads Fu-hsi's *I* as if there were no *T'uan*, *Hsiang*, and *Wen-yen* discussions, then one will be able to see that the original intention of the *I* was to create the practice of divination.[66]
>
> King Wen's mind was not as expansive as Fu-hsi's, and so he was anxious to speak out. Confucius's mind was not as great as King Wen's mind, and he too was anxious to speak out about moral principle. This is how the original intention [of the *I*] was dissipated.[67]

Finally, Yung-chih apparently comes to understand the importance of the intentionality of the sage, although Chu Hsi still qualifies his student's response:

> Yung-chih said: The sage created the *I* merely to clarify the pattern of yin and yang, firm and soft, good fortune and misfortune, growth and decline.
>
> [Chu Hsi] replies: Although that is the case, nevertheless when Fu-hsi created the *I* he only drew the eight trigrams.[68] So when did he ever explain the pattern of yin and yang, firm and soft, good fortune and misfortune? But within [the hexagrams] there is contained this moral pattern. Imagine how a man of antiquity taught people: he did not discuss much, he only discussed methods. In this way he had people rely on them and practice them.[69]

Elsewhere Chu says of the second line of K'un:

> The original intention [of the line] is to teach people to understand that this line has these virtues. If a person prognosticates and receives the situation [to the

[65] *Hsi-tz'u* A2, slightly reworded (cf. Wilhelm/Baynes, p. 286).
[66] *Chu-tzu yü-lei* 66, p. 2591.
[67] Ibid., pp. 2592–93.
[68] Elsewhere Chu says that Fu-hsi went on from the eight trigrams to draw the sixty-four hexagrams. See *I-hsüeh ch'i-meng*, pp. 1234–39, and *Chu-tzu wen-chi* 38:7a.
[69] *Chu-tzu yü-lei* 66, p. 2593.

effect] that all will be advantageous independently of study, then if he is able to be straight, and able to be square, and able to be great, then "all will be advantageous without practice." But [the original intention] is not to try to explicate the way of K'un.[70]

The purpose of the line, in other words, is to teach people to recognize and to actively cultivate the three virtues of K'un in themselves. It does not teach *how* to cultivate these virtues (this would be teaching the "way of K'un")—it only teaches the necessity of doing so. The person receiving this prognostication in actual practice would presumably be receptive to this particular counsel at this particular time.

In Chu Hsi's view, the *i-li* school, by using the *I* as a moral philosophical text rather than a divination manual, implicitly discouraged the practitioner from opening his moral decision-making and action to the "spiritual" (*shen*) influence of the milfoil stalks, and to the transcendent sagely wisdom or heavenly pattern to which they give access.[71] We might say that from Chu Hsi's perspective, the *i-li* approach impeded the subject's participation with the sages in "the transforming and nourishing processes of heaven-and-earth"[72]—the specific process in question here being the subject's own self-transformation. The sage and the ordinary person are, in this sense, "co-creators" of the fully realized human being.

DIVINATION AND SELF-CULTIVATION

Chu Hsi went to considerable lengths to make divination by means of yarrow or milfoil stalks (*achillea millefolium*) accessible to literati. He wrote a detailed critique of the various methods of divination that had been proposed since the Han[73] (all of them presumably based on the fragmentary method outlined in *Hsi-tz'u* A9), and he wrote three versions of what he considered to be the correct method.[74] And as we have seen, he wrote a book on the theory and practice of divination, the *I-hsüeh ch'i-meng* (Introduction to the study of the I).

Chu outlined his understanding of divination and its relevance to self-cultivation in a letter to Lü Tsu-ch'ien. The hexagram and line texts, he said, were originally meant for diviners "to determine good fortune and misfortune, and on that basis [to issue] counsel and admonition." The *T'uan*, *Hsiang*, and *Wen-yen* commentaries were written by Confucius to clarify the moral patterns of the hexagram and line texts "on the basis of

[70] *Chou-i che-chung*, p. 142.

[71] See *Hsi-tz'u* A11 (Wilhelm/Baynes, pp. 316–17) and below for the mechanism by which this access is gained.

[72] *Chung-yung* 22, in Chan, *A Source Book*, p. 108.

[73] "Examining errors in milfoil divination" (*Chu-tzu wen-chi* 66:11b–27b).

[74] In the *I-hsüeh ch'i-meng* (chap. 3), in "The Divination Procedure" (included in the *Chou-i pen-i*), and in "Five Praises of the I" (*Chu-tzu wen-chi* 85:6a–8b).

the intentions of these counsels and admonitions of good fortune and misfortune." However:

Later people saw only Confucius's discussions of the moral pattern, and did not go back to infer the original intentions of King Wen and the Duke of Chou. Because they denigrated divination as unworthy of discussion, their means of discussing the *I* were consequently far from the concreteness of daily use (*jih-yung chih shih*). . . .

Whenever one reads a hexagram and line, according to the prognostication obtained, one empties [or pacifies] the mind to search out what the meaning of the verse refers to, and considers it a decision as to good fortune or misfortune, yea or nay. Then one examines the precursor of the image and seeks out the reason for the pattern, and then extends them to one's affairs. This enables everyone from kings and dukes to the common people to use it for self-cultivation (*hsiu-shen*) and ordering the state (*chih-kuo*). I myself consider this way of inquiry to be like obtaining the bequeathed intentions of the Three Sages [Fu-hsi, King Wen, and the Duke of Chou].[75]

It is clear from this letter that Chu Hsi understood the practice of divination—properly done—to be entirely relevant to self-cultivation. *How* he understood this relevance is the question we must now consider. We shall begin by analyzing the *Hsi-tzu* passage he quotes most often in connection with the "general purpose" (*ta-i*) of the *I* (A11).[76] This will provide us with a broad outline of the *I*'s role in Chu Hsi's system. We shall then examine the two crucial terms in Chu's concept of divination: "responsiveness" (*ying*) and "incipience" (*chi*).

The Master [Confucius] said: What does the *I* do? Just this: the *I*
[1] discloses things,
[2] completes affairs, and
[3] encompasses the Way of all under heaven.
Therefore the sages used it
[4] to penetrate the wills of all under heaven,
[5] to determine the tasks of all under heaven, and
[6] to settle the doubts of all under heaven.

Chu defines five of the six predicates (nos. 1, 2, 4, 5, 6) in this passage in terms of divination. The sixth (no. 3) he explains in terms of the *I*'s correspondence with the world. He clearly specifies that divination involves acting as well as knowing:

The *I* discloses things, completes affairs, and encompasses the Way of all under heaven [1–3]. This is the general purpose of the *I*.[77]

[75] *Chu-tzu ch'üan-shu* 27:12a, and Wang Mou-hung, *Chu-tzu nien-p'u*, p. 72.
[76] For example in *Chu-tzu ch'üan-shu* 27:9b.
[77] *Chu-tzu yü-lei* 66, p. 2575.

"To disclose things and to complete affairs" [1, 2] means to enable people to do divination in order to understand good fortune and misfortune, and to complete their undertakings. "To encompass the Way of all under heaven" [3] means that once the hexagram lines are set out, the Way of all under heaven is contained in them.[78]

The Sage created the *I* to teach others to act when prognostications are auspicious, and not to act when inauspicious. This is the meaning of "penetrating the wills of all under heaven, determining the tasks of all under heaven, and settling the doubts of all under heaven [4–6]."[79]

We might further clarify this set of functions by applying two sets of polarities to it: natural/human and inner/outer.

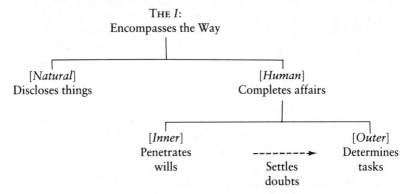

THE *I*:
Encompasses the Way

[*Natural*]
Discloses things

[*Human*]
Completes affairs

[*Inner*]
Penetrates
wills

Settles
doubts

[*Outer*]
Determines
tasks

This array of the *I*'s functions can be unpacked as follows. The hexagrams of the *I* represent the yin-yang fluctuations and transformations of the Way. The *I* as a symbol system "discloses things" by representing natural pattern in graphic form, making it easier to comprehend. But the Way, to be actualized, must also be internalized by the human will and put into effect in human affairs. Moral decisions must be made, based on an integrated understanding of the self and the world. Self-doubt is inevitable at this point, and the *I* provides a method by which doubts can be settled and intentions trained to issue spontaneously in a proper direction. Divination is this method.

Responsiveness (ying)

Divination, in Chu Hsi's view, is a way of learning to "respond" (*ying*) to "incipient" (*chi*) change, both in external events and in the mind. "Responsiveness," or "moral responsiveness," is the ability to respond intui-

[78] *Chou-i pen-i* 3:13b; *Chou-i che-chung*, p. 1022.
[79] *Chu-tzu yü-lei* 66, p. 2575.

tively, spontaneously, and in a morally correct manner to the changing pattern (*li*) of situations and events. It is a responsive harmony with the social and natural environment, a way of fitting into the pattern of change, of attaining harmony with the Way (*tao*).

Responsiveness is one of the key characteristics of the mind of the sage. The sage has this capacity because his mind is clear and free-flowing, unobstructed by murky *ch'i*; he can therefore detect and respond to the subtlest patterns in things. This clarity and sensitivity of mind is called *shen-ming* "spiritual clarity," which we will discuss in a moment.

Ch'eng Hao had spoken of the importance of moral responsiveness in his "Letter on Stabilizing Human Nature" to Chang Tsai:

> The constant pattern of heaven-and-earth is that its mind pervades all things, yet it has no mind. The constant pattern of the sage is that his dispositions accord with all phenomena, yet he has no dispositions. Therefore, in the education of the *chün-tzu*, there is nothing like being completely broad and impartial, and responding in accordance with things as they come.[80]

Chu Hsi defined the last two phrases in terms of three phases of mind— silence, stimulation, and penetration:

> "Extremely broad and impartial" means "silent and unmoving." "Responding in accordance with things as they come" means "stimulated and then penetrating."[81]

The phrases he uses here as definitions come from *Hsi-tz'u* A10:

> The *I* is without thought and without activity. Silent and unmoving, when stimulated it then penetrates all situations under heaven. If it were not the most spiritual thing under heaven, how could it be like this?[82]

Chu acknowledges that this passage refers not to the human mind but to the *I*. He adds, though, "The mystery of the human mind, in its activity and stillness, is also like this."[83]

Thus Chu Hsi uses the oracular function of the *I* as a source of insight into the nature and functioning of the human mind—specifically into the central problem of the relationship between the still substance of the mind (its pattern) and its active functioning (its physical nature). While Ch'eng

[80] *Erh-Ch'eng chi*, p. 460 (*Wen-chi* 2). See also Chan, *Source Book*, pp. 525–26, and *Chu-tzu ch'üan-shu* 45:12b.

[81] *Chu-tzu ch'üan-shu* 45:13a. See also David Yü, "Chu Hsi's Approach to Knowledge," *Chinese Culture*, 10:4 (1969), pp. 1–14. On the phases of the mind in Chu Hsi's thought, see Thomas A. Metzger, *Escape from Predicament: Neo-Confucianism and China's Evolving Political Culture* (New York: Columbia University Press, 1977), pp. 85–98.

[82] *Chou-i pen-i* 3:13a, or *Chou-i che-chung*, p. 1019 (cf. Wilhelm/Baynes, p. 315).

[83] Ibid.

I saw the *I* as a repository of moral pattern, a source of values grounded in heaven-and-earth, Chu Hsi saw the *I* as an analogue of the mind of the sage that can be used to "rectify" the ordinary mind.

Another good statement of the idea of moral responsiveness is found in a comment by Chu Hsi on the following passage from the *Hsi-tz'u*:

> The virtue of the milfoil is round and spiritual. The virtue of the hexagrams is square and wise. The meanings of the six lines change in order to inform. With these the sage purifies his mind and retires into secrecy. He suffers good fortune and misfortune in common with the people. Being spiritual, he knows the future. Being wise, he stores up the past. Who is comparable to this? [It was] the ancients, with broad intelligence and astute wisdom, those who were spiritually martial and yet non-violent.[84]

Chu Hsi comments:

> "Round and spiritual" means the unboundedness of transformation. "Square and wise" means that affairs have definite patterns. . . . The sage concretely embodies the virtues of the three [milfoil, hexagrams, and lines] without the slightest worldly tie. When there is nothing happening, then his mind is silent, and no one can see it. When there is something happening, then the operation of his spiritual wisdom responds when stimulated (*sui kan erh ying*). This means he understands good fortune and misfortune without divination. "Spiritually martial and yet non-violent" means he apprehends pattern without recourse to things.[85]
>
> This refers to the basis on which the sage created the *I*. The milfoil is active, the hexagrams are still, and the lines fluctuate without limit. Before their drawing, this pattern was already contained in the mind of the sage. But before its stimulation by things, it [his mind] was "perfectly still and unmoving," and no incipient sign could be named. With the appearance of things and his response to them, he felt anxious for the world [and thus created the *I* for the benefit of later generations].[86]

The *Hsi-tz'u* passage above posits a certain correspondence between the *I* and the sage, based on their common qualities *shen* (spirit) and *chih* (wisdom). *Shen* is a notoriously difficult word to translate in this context. In the compound *kuei-shen* it means "spirits" of departed ancestors or of natural objects like mountains and rivers. (*Kuei* are similar but not as benign; hence *kuei-shen* is usually translated "ghosts and spirits.") *Shen* as it is used in the *Hsi-tz'u* is defined by A. C. Graham as "not a personal

---

[84] *Hsi-tz'u* A 11 (cf. Wilhelm/Baynes, pp. 316–17).

[85] *Chou-i pen-i* 3:13b; *Chou-i che-chung*, p. 1023.

[86] *Chou-i che-chung*, p. 1024. Elsewhere he says, "The learning of the sages is to base one's mind on fully investigating principle, and to accord with principle by responding to things." *Chu-tzu wen-chi* 67:19b, "Kuan-hsin shuo" (Treatise on the examination of the mind). Cf. Chan, *Source Book*, p. 604.

spirit but a daemonic power or intelligence which is active within the operations of heaven and earth and which emanates from the person of the sage."[87] It is the capacity of certain forms of ch'i to "penetrate immediately through things without being obstructed by their forms."[88] Graham has used "psychic" as a translation of the adjectival form of shen. Here we shall use the more traditional translation "spirit/spiritual," in part because "psychic" lacks an adequate nominal form. But "psychic" does convey some of the epistemological connotations of shen that shed light on Chu Hsi's concept of divination. For example, in the Hsi-tz'u it is said that the milfoil stalks are "shen (spiritual/psychic) things"[89] through which the I responds "like an echo"[90] to the charge put by the diviner. Likewise the sages, by virtue of their ability "to know incipiencies"[91] "are shen and thus know the future."[92] Their shen enables them "to hurry without haste, and to get there without moving,"[93] i.e., to transcend the ordinary conditions of cause-and-effect activity, and to know things by nonempirical means.

Shen enables the sages and the milfoil to detect the patterns underlying the transformation of ch'i. As a characteristic of ch'i itself shen refers to the coherence of certain phenomena in which coherence is not empirically observable by the ordinary mind. According to Chu Hsi (quoting Chang Tsai): "Ch'i has [the two modes] yin and yang. When it proceeds slowly, it is transformation (hua). When it is unified and unfathomable, it is shen."[94]

For the mind manifesting this "spiritual" quality to the highest degree (i.e., the mind of the sage), responsiveness to incipient activity is spontaneous because there is no obstruction between external phenomena and the mind. It is appropriate to the stimulus and the occasion, or "timely." Thus it is objective, or true to the pattern of the external thing as it is, unswayed by private motivations. And it is morally correct because (par-

[87] Two Chinese Philosophers, pp. 111–12.
[88] Ibid., p. 113.
[89] Hsi-tz'u A11 (cf. Wilhelm/Baynes, pp. 317, 320).
[90] Ibid., A10.
[91] Ibid., B5.
[92] Ibid., A 11.
[93] Ibid., A10.
[94] Chou-i pen-i 3:21a. This has interesting implications for the history of Chinese science. With the unfathomability of certain functional modes of ch'i built into the conceptual system, it is difficult to see how anomalies (in Thomas Kuhn's sense) could ever threaten the integrity of the basic cosmological paradigm. The notion of shen functioned as a great shock absorber to the system, enabling it to remain intact for a very long time, but obviating the need to adapt to new discoveries about the natural world. For an illustration of this, see Mark Elvin's discussion of Fang I-chih (1611–1671), in The Pattern of the Chinese Past (Stanford: Stanford University Press, 1973), pp. 225–34. For a more extended discussion of the role of anomalies in traditional Chinese cosmology, see John B. Henderson, The Development and Decline of Chinese Cosmology (New York: Columbia University Press, 1984).

adoxically) it is also subjective: the mind responds in accordance with its innate heavenly pattern, which is continuous with the pattern of the external object. These are the characteristics of the mind of the sage attributable to its *shen-ming*, its "spiritual clarity."

Since the milfoil stalks of the *I* are also *shen* (an assumption that is never questioned), they too can respond to incipient change spontaneously and appropriately. This is the *I*'s function as an instrument of divination, to detect change and to indicate a proper response to it. While the sage does not need divination (since he already possesses the spiritual clarity of mind that makes possible knowledge of the future and perfect moral responsiveness), the ordinary person can make use of the *I*—and through it the sages—in his effort to achieve on his own the sagely capacity for moral responsiveness.[95]

Incipience (chi)

Both the milfoil and the mind of the sage have the capacity to detect the otherwise imperceptible stirrings of change in phenomena. These infinitesimal changes are called "incipiencies" (*chi*). Divination is an instrument or technique for the detection of these incipient changes.

The purpose of detecting incipient change is twofold. On the most basic level, one uses divination to determine the course of events in complex or doubtful situations, so as to make correct decisions regarding one's own activity. By responding to incipient change one seems to be "knowing the future," but actually the character and direction of future events (i.e., their pattern or principle, *li*) are already present in incipient form. On another level one uses divination to develop one's own ability to respond to events as they occur. Ultimately, the person working to attain sagehood seeks to learn and internalize the "spiritual" capacity of the milfoil (and the mind of the sage) by making his mind as pure and unobstructed as the mind of the sage. The goal is moral responsiveness: to respond to incipient changes spontaneously and correctly, i.e. in accord with the dynamic pattern of the Way, as the sage does without recourse to divination. Divination, therefore, can be used as an aid in the moral and psychophysical purification or "rectification" of the mind.

Chu Hsi's claim that divination is the detection of incipient change is found in his commentary on chapter 24 of the *Doctrine of the Mean*. The topic of this chapter is *ch'eng* "integrity, authenticity, genuineness," which is both a moral and a metaphysical concept. The text of the chapter is as follows:

---

[95] For further discussion of Chu Hsi's concept of *shen* in regard to the *I*, see below, "The Limitations of Divination."

It is characteristic of absolute integrity (*ch'eng*) to be able to foreknow. When a nation or family is about to flourish, there are sure to be lucky omens. When a nation or family is about to perish, there are sure to be unlucky omens. These omens are revealed by the milfoil and tortoise and in the movements of the four limbs. When calamity or blessing is about to come, it [integrity] can surely know beforehand if it is good, and it can also surely know beforehand if it is evil. Therefore he who has absolute integrity is like a spirit.[96]

In his commentary Chu Hsi says of the various types of divination and foreknowledge mentioned here:

These are all premonitions of pattern (*li chih hsien-chien che*). But only one whose integrity is absolutely perfect, and who hasn't the slightest selfish artifice left in his mind's eye, is able to examine the incipiencies (*ch'a ch'i chi*) therein.[97]

Even if the indications of good fortune and misfortune by the milfoil and tortoise are very clear, the person who is not perfectly sincere will be unable to perceive them.[98]

Thus divination is a matter of "examining incipiencies," an ability possessed only by one with utmost integrity or genuineness (*ch'eng*).

"Integrity" and "incipience" are discussed in several pithy chapters of Chou Tun-i's *T'ung-shu* (Penetrating the *Book of Change*), on which Chu Hsi wrote a commentary. The references to incipience in these discussions concern mental activity, not external phenomena, and there is no explicit mention of divination. Nevertheless, there are suggestions here of the use of divination as a potential aid in achieving self-knowledge and rectifying the mind, and we have just seen the connection between incipience and divination in the comments quoted above. In the *T'ung-shu*, Chou Tun-i says:

In integrity there is no activity. In incipience [there is] good and evil.

Chu Hsi comments:

Incipience is the imperceptible beginning of movement. It is that according to which good and evil are distinguished. With the first sign of movement in the human mind, heavenly pattern will certainly appear there; yet human desires have already sprouted amidst it.

Integrity has no activity, and so it is simply good. In movement there is activity, and so there is good and there is evil.[99]

---

[96] *Chung-yung* 24, trans. Chan, *Source Book*, p. 108, slightly modified.

[97] *Chung-yung chang-chü*, in Chu Hsi, *Ssu-shu chi-chu*, p. 17b.

[98] *Chu-tzu yü-lei* 64, p. 2503.

[99] Chang Po-hsing, comp., *Chou Lien-hsi chi* (Chou Tun-i's Collected Works) (*Ts'ung-shu chi-ch'eng* ed.), p. 81 (*T'ung-shu*, chap. 3). Cf. Chan, *Source Book*, pp. 466–67. In Chu's "Hsin-shuo" (Treatise on the Examination of the Mind) he relates the incipient move-

This defines the context of the moral struggle and the human predicament as Chu Hsi saw it. The ontological foundation or substance (*t'i*) of the cosmos is absolutely good, in the sense that it is logically prior to the differentiation of good and evil. It is fully contained in the human mind, and it theoretically can be known through self-examination. But the psycho-physical activity of knowing gives rise to evil, which obscures the fundamental goodness of human nature. Evil, therefore, is a quality of function (*yung*), not of substance.[100] Although good is ontologically prior to evil, evil is real and presents an inevitable obstacle to self-knowledge. Thus Chu Hsi (quoting Ch'eng Hao) could say:

> Good and evil both are [aspects of] heavenly pattern [i.e., of its function or operation]. But what is called evil is not originally evil.[101]

The "incipient" phase of mental activity is the point at which the mind has just been stimulated (*kan*), but no response (*ying*) has yet appeared. As Chou Tun-i says, "Movement with yet no form, between being and nonbeing, is incipience."[102] It is the juncture between the still substance of the mind and its active function. According to Chu Hsi, this incipient phase of mind is the critical point at which either evil human desires or the original goodness of heavenly pattern and human nature can become actualized in the world. It is also the point on which foreknowledge and divination focus:

> The primary and unmanifest [ground] is the substance of the actual pattern (*shih-li*). The apt yet unpredictable response is the functioning of the actual pattern. Between activity and stillness, substance and function, suddenly in the space of an instant there is the beginning of the actual pattern and the auspicious and inauspicious omens of the multitudinous phenomena.[103]

The moment of incipient mental activity at the "birth of a thought"[104] is the point at which the creative pattern of heaven manifests itself. At that moment, if one can attend to it, knowledge is not limited by empirical, spatio-temporal conditions, for the ground of those conditions is itself present and can be known. Knowledge of incipient activity is tantamount to foreknowledge, or oracular knowledge, since the character and

---

ment of the mind to its "precariousness": "What is meant by the precariousness of the human mind is the budding of human selfish desires." *Chu-tzu wen-chi* 67:19a, trans. Chan, *Source Book*, p. 603.

[100] That is, in Western philosophical terminology, evil is not a primary quality of the world, but it is a secondary quality and as such is real.

[101] *Chu-tzu wen-chi* 67:17a. Cf. Chan, *Source Book*, p. 598.

[102] *Chou Lien-hsi chi*, p. 87 (*T'ung-shu*, chap. 4).

[103] Ibid.

[104] Ibid., p. 82.

direction of future events is present in incipient form. Furthermore, there is a moral incentive to pay attention to the incipient phase of mind, and a sense of urgency in Chu Hsi's exhortation to do so:

Incipiencies, or the subtle indications of activity, lie between desiring to act and imminent activity, where there is both good and evil. One must understand them at this point. If they reach the point of becoming manifest, then one cannot help anything. . . . The point of subtle incipience is extremely important.[105]

At that moment, one must exhaustively examine [oneself] and recognize what is right and wrong. At first there will be tiny, brief, subtle indications. When one has exhaustively examined oneself for a long time, one will gradually see their full extent. As it is heavenly, there is a moral pattern. The gaps in it determine the incipient, subtle indications and differentiate good and evil. If one can analyze it in this way, then things will be investigated and knowledge perfected. With perfected knowledge, intentions will be made sincere. With sincere intentions, the mind will be rectified, the self will be cultivated, the family will be regulated, the state will be well governed, and all under heaven will be at peace.[106]

In terms of Chu Hsi's system of self-cultivation, the incipient phase of mental activity is when one must cognitively distinguish one's good feelings, ideas, and intentions from the bad ones (e.g., selfish desires). This is self-examination (*hsing-ch'a*).[107] One must then follow through on that discrimination by actively preserving and nourishing (*ts'un-yang*) the good mental phenomena and conquering or subduing (*k'o*) the evil ones.[108] A student of Chu Hsi's summarized the implications of incipience for moral cultivation as follows:

Master Chou said: "In integrity there is no activity; in incipience there is good and evil." This clarifies the unexpressed substance of the human mind, and refers to the beginnings of its expressed phase. He probably wanted students to extend their [self-]examination to the subtle signs of germinal activity, to understand how to decide which to extirpate and which to adopt, so as not to lose [contact with] the original substance [or ontological ground]. . . . Students should be able to examine the predilections and aversions of what is expressed [by the mind], right at the time of the incipient subtleties of germinal activity. What comes out straight [i.e., as true, direct expression of integrity and human nature] is the pattern of heaven; what comes out deviant is human desire. . . . We should take advantage of and find guidance in what comes out

---

[105] Ibid., p. 83.

[106] Ibid., p. 82. These are the eight stages of the *Great Learning* (*Ta-hsüeh*).

[107] Item 3 in the list of methods of self-cultivation given above, under "The problem of mind."

[108] Items 4 and 5 above, "The problem of mind."

straight, and extinguish what comes out deviant. When this effort is perfected, then the expression of our mind will spontaneously come out on course, and will ensure our possession of heaven's decree. . . .

The Teacher [Chu Hsi] replied: "This explanation has got it."[109]

In summary, Chu Hsi understood *I Ching* divination to be an instrument for the detection of incipient psycho-physical activity, both in external events and within oneself. Incipience is the critical point at which the pattern of the Way begins to manifest itself, but has not yet become actualized in concrete phenomena. Divination focused internally can contribute to self-knowledge; focused externally it allows one to harmonize one's activity more effectively with the flow of events. One can also more effectively exercise control or mastery (*chu*) over events in their incipient phase.

In Chu Hsi's system, therefore, the *I* could contribute to self-cultivation in the following ways:

First, it could enable one to "settle doubts" about one's behavior by indicating which course of action would be auspicious and which inauspicious. This, of course, was the most basic function of the *I*, the one most directly implied by Fu-hsi's original intention: "The Sage created the *I* to teach others to act when prognostications are auspicious, and not to act when inauspicious."[110] In terms of the methods of self-cultivation outlined at the beginning of this chapter, this corresponds with "practice" (*hsing*).

Second, on a deeper level, the *I* could serve to heighten one's sensitivity or moral responsiveness (*ying*) to one's environment by teaching one how to detect, interpret, and respond to incipiencies external to oneself. In other words, moral responsiveness is the internalized capacity to choose correct courses of action. This involves self-knowledge as well as knowledge of external events, for moral responsiveness to the social and natural environment must be based on an integrated understanding of self and world. The cognitive aspect here corresponds with "investigating things and extending knowledge" (*ko-wu chih-chih*).

Third, the *I* provided a means of acquiring self-knowledge (corresponding with "self-examination," *hsing-ch'a*), i.e., learning to become aware of one's ideas, intentions and feelings in their incipient phases, by means of divination, and fourth, morally purifying these mental phenomena by learning—with the guidance of the sages' interpretations of the hexagrams—how to distinguish the good ones from the bad, and how to "preserve and nourish" (*ts'un-yang*) the former and "conquer" or extirpate the latter (*k'o-chi*).

---

[109] *Chou Lien-hsi chi*, pp. 83–85.
[110] *Chu-tzu yü-lei* 66, p. 2575.

Thus Chu Hsi defined the legitimate uses of the *I Ching* in the context of the pursuit of Confucian sagehood, and more specifically in the context of "rectifying the mind." While in the Northern Sung the *I*, along with the Four Books, had begun to receive greater philosophical attention than it had previously,[111] Chu Hsi refocused attention on the practical use of the *I* as a manual of divination, reinterpreting this ancient ritual in terms of his theory of mind and incorporating it into his religious-philosophical system.

Chu Hsi's thoroughness was unsurpassed: virtually no aspect of the cultural tradition was left out of his synthesis. But this same thoroughness also compelled him to deal with potential abuses of divination, an examination of which will help us further pin down his conception of the *I Ching*.

The Limitations of Divination

Chu Hsi's understanding of the limitations of divination is connected with his view of "ghosts and spirits" (*kuei-shen*). Divination in ancient times had been understood as a means of communicating with the spirits (*shen*) of departed ancestors. This conception undoubtedly persisted in Chu Hsi's time, for he occasionally used this terminology in reference to divination. However, he did not conceive *kuei* and *shen* to be conscious, personal beings, and it would certainly be a mistake to personalize his conception of divination on the basis of this terminology. Ghosts and spirits, according to Chu Hsi, were impersonal manifestations of *ch'i*. They had no personal will—they operated according to the natural pattern of yin and yang. They were therefore susceptible (at least theoretically) of being understood:

> By the time we have attended thoroughly to ordinary daily matters, the patterns governing spiritual beings will naturally be understood.[112]

[111] See Gardner, *Chu Hsi and the Ta-hsüeh*, pp. 12–14.

[112] *Chu-tzu ch'üan-shu* 51:2a, trans. Chan, *Source Book,* p. 644 substituting "ghosts and spirits" for "spiritual beings." Such a view of *kuei-shen* was by no means new to the Sung, but had been current (at least in skeptical circles) since the Han. See, e.g., Wang Ch'ung (27–100?), *Lun-heng* (*Ssu-pu pei-yao* ed.), 20:9a–16a, 21, 22; and Alfred Forke, trans., *Lun-Heng*, 1907 (New York: Paragon, 1962 reprint), vol. 1, pp. 173–249, 532–37. A similar view of ghosts and spirits was held by Ch'eng I, who had variously defined them as "traces of the creative process" (*I-ch'uan I-chuan* 2, p. 82), "functions of heaven-and-earth" (quoted by Chu Hsi, *Chung-yung chang-chü* 8b), and "products of the creative process" (*Hsing-li ta-ch'üan shu* 28:1a). Ch'eng also believed divination to be a "valid" (*yu-li*) operation that would yield a valid response unless the questioner approached it with a "selfish mind." See Lü Tsu-ch'ien, comp., *Chou-i Hsi-tz'u ching-i* (Essential interpretations of the *Chou-i Hsi-tz'u*), in *Ku-i ts'ung-shu* (*Pai-pu Ts'ung-shu chi-ch'eng* ed.) 1:19b, and the discussion in chapter 7, below.

200 of 288 · Chapter Six

> *Shen* is stretching out (*shen*), and *kuei* is bending back (*ch'ü*). For example, the moment when wind and rain, thunder and lightning, are first manifest is *shen*. And when wind stops and rain passes, thunder stops and lightning ceases, this is *kuei*.[113]

Despite this thoroughly naturalistic and rationalistic conception of *kuei* and *shen*, it is clear that what Chu Hsi is referring to by these terms are the spirits of the dead. For this reason we are justified in translating them "ghosts and spirits." He says, for example:

> *Kuei* and *shen* are nothing more than the waxing and waning of yin and yang, such as the nourishment of shelter and comfort[114] and the darkness of wind and rain. In the human being, the vital essence (*ching*) is the yin soul (*p'o*), and the yin soul is the container of *kuei*; the psycho-physical substance (*ch'i*) is the yang soul (*hun*), and the yang soul is the container of *shen*. The vital essence and psycho-physical substance combine to make a [living] thing.[115] How then can there be a [living] thing without a *kuei* and *shen*? "The roaming of the yang soul constitutes a change [namely death]."[116] When the yang soul has roamed then we know that the yin soul has descended [into the earth].[117]

Thus when Chu Hsi speaks of *kuei* and *shen* he refers to the souls (*hun* and *p'o*) of living things after death, in accordance with common belief. But he insists on interpreting them in naturalistic, or impersonal, terms. This reflects a somewhat ambivalent attitude toward *kuei* and *shen*. There was, of course, classical precedent for this in Confucius's well-known reticence concerning spirits and certain other topics:

> The Master did not discuss uncanny events, feats of strength, disorders, or spirits (*shen*).[118]

---

[113] Ibid. Note that Chu is here giving a naturalistic (i.e., impersonal) explanation of phenomena which were commonly personified as spirits. We cannot explain for sure why the beginning of a storm is "stretching out" and the end is "bending back." The terms are probably used metaphorically to a certain extent, although still with a concrete referent. The point is that *kuei* and *shen* are names for certain functional modes of *ch'i*, or phases of natural processes. The traditional etymologies of *kuei* and *shen*, relying on phonetic associations, were similar: *kuei* was glossed as *kuei* "return," and *shen* as *shen* "extend, go out." See, for example, Wang Ch'ung, *Lun-heng*, 20:9b. Chu Hsi refers to these definitions in *Chou-i pen-i* 3:4b, commenting on *Hsi-tz'u* A4 (Wilhelm/Baynes, p. 294), where he says: "The yin essence and yang *ch'i*, collecting to form things, are the extending of *shen*. The *hun*'s floating and *p'o*'s sinking, alternating to make [life and death] transformations, are the returning of *kuei*."
[114] Cf. *Lao Tzu* 51.
[115] Cf.*Hsi-tz'u* A4.
[116] *Hsi-tz'u* A4.
[117] *Chu-tzu ch'üan-shu* 51:2b.
[118] *Analects* 7:20.

Be reverent towards ghosts and spirits, but keep them at a distance.[119]
If we are not yet able to serve man, how can we serve ghosts (*kuei*)?[120]

While we ourselves cannot say much about Confucius's belief in ghosts and spirits (except that it is unlikely that he doubted their existence), Chu Hsi's views are more accessible. He distinguished the term *kuei-shen* from *shen* alone. *Kuei-shen*, he said, refers to observable, functional modes of *ch'i* (as just described); *shen* refers to the "mysterious functioning" (*miao-yung*) of *ch'i*[121] (as described above, under "Responsiveness"), which only the sage can apprehend. As we have seen, *shen* in this sense refers to aspects of the world that are beyond *ordinary* human understanding, but for the sage are ultimately intelligible according to the fundamental pattern of yin-yang transformation. This is why ordinary people need to rely on divination, while the sage does not. *Kuei* and *shen* (ghosts and spirits) were not quite as mysterious as this, despite prevailing beliefs:

> Whenever people talk about ghosts and spirits they consider them uncanny. But since there is such a pattern of the Way in the world, we cannot say that they do not exist, just that they are not regular (*cheng*) aspects of the creative process. They might be irregular cases of yin-yang *ch'i*, but they should not frighten or delude. The explanation for Confucius's not discussing uncanny events is that he had an understanding of the matter and just did not talk about it. When Nan-hsien [Chang Shih] says they do not exist, he is wrong.[122]

Although in *Analects* 7:20 (above) no distinction is made between "the uncanny, feats of strength, disorders, and spirits," Chu Hsi, on the basis of his rationalized conception of *kuei-shen*, introduces a qualification. He says that the first three items

> are not regular (*cheng*) aspects of the pattern, and are definitely what the Sage did not talk about. [But] ghosts and spirits are "traces of the creative process."[123] Although they are not irregular (*pu-cheng*) [apparently contradicting the preceding quote], nevertheless they are not the endpoint of fathoming the pattern. There are things that are not easily understood; therefore he [Confucius] did not lightly discuss them with others.[124]

Chu Hsi's contradictory statements on whether ghosts and spirits were "regular" aspects of the pattern of the Way should not obscure the fact

[119] *Analects* 6:20.
[120] *Analects* 11:11.
[121] *Chu-tzu ch'üan-shu* 51.7b, ct. Chan, *Source Book*, p. 644.
[122] *Chu-tzu ch'üan-shu* 51.5a.
[123] Quoting Ch'eng I, *I-ch'uan I-chuan* 2, p. 82.
[124] Comment on *Lun-yü* 7.20, in *Ssu-shu chi-chu* 4:5a.

that he consistently describes them in terms of the pattern of yin-yang change. And he uses this qualified and rationalized notion of *kuei-shen* to explain divination:

> Divination is actually questioning the ghosts and spirits by means of the milfoil and tortoise, which are objects with spiritual consciousness.[125] We therefore make use of them for their hexagrams and omens.[126]

Here Chu seems to be using *kuei-shen* as an instance, or perhaps as a metaphor, of *shen* in its general sense as the free-flowing, responsive quality of *ch'i*. He may also be co-opting popular beliefs concerning the involvement of ghosts and spirits in divination. By using a de-personalized conception of *kuei-shen* to explain divination, he was able to assimilate and adapt the popular conception to his own theory and to connect divination concretely with his theory of mind.

> *Kuei* and *shen* are merely *ch'i*. That which bends and stretches back and forth is *ch'i*. Within heaven-and-earth there is nothing that is not *ch'i*. The *ch'i* of mankind and the *ch'i* of heaven-and-earth are always in contact, with no gap, but human beings themselves cannot see it. When the human mind moves, it must pass through *ch'i* and mutually stimulate and penetrate this bending and stretching back and forth. In such cases as divination there is always the mind itself as a particular thing. But to speak of it as a matter greater than your [individual] mind [i.e., to describe divination in terms of a general principle], when there is movement there must be a response.[127]
>
> The method of divination instituted by the former kings was to be extremely dignified and extremely reverent, and to pacify the mind in order to listen to the ghosts and spirits. If one is concentrated there will be a response. If one is double-minded there will be an error.[128]

Chu Hsi's naturalistic interpretation of *kuei-shen* can be understood as an attempt to make ghosts and spirits "respectable." They had to be, of course, because Confucius had specifically said, "Respect [or be reverent towards] ghosts and spirits, but keep them at a distance."[129] The problem was how to define the proper distance.

Chu's reluctance to accept ghosts and spirits uncritically reveals the limitations he placed on the use of divination. Divination was a valid

---

[125] *Shen-ling*, like *kuei-shen*, is a function of *ch'i*. See *Chu-tzu ch'üan-shu* 51:3a.

[126] Chu Hsi's comment on *Shu Ching*, "Hung-fan" chapter, in *Ch'in-ting Shu-ching chuan-shuo* (Official commentaries on the Book of Documents) (*Yü-tsuan ch'i-ching* ed.), 11:5a; *The Chinese Classics*, trans. James Legge, 2nd ed. 1893 (Hong Kong: Hong Kong University Press, 1960 reprint), vol. 3: *The Shoo King*, p. 335, n. 20.

[127] *Chu-tzu ch'üan-shu* 51:2b–3a.

[128] Ibid., 27:15b.

[129] *Analects* 6:20.

practice for literati only when it was employed seriously in the process of self-cultivation. It could be used to acquire knowledge of the self and external events; it could be used to purify oneself spiritually by making critical self-judgments concerning one's ideas and intentions; and it could be used as a guide to moral practice. But divination had its limitations. In his comment on Confucius's statement about ghosts and spirits, for example, Chu said:

> People should be properly reverent towards ghosts and spirits, and yet keep them at a distance. If they can see this distinction in the pattern of the Way, then they must follow through on it. As for people who believe in and serve the Buddha in order to seek happiness and profit, this is not distant enough.
>
> As divination has been used since Fu-hsi, Yao, and Shun, it is valid [lit., "there is a pattern to it"]. When people today have doubts about their affairs, and reverently use divination to decide them, what is wrong with it? But if they still have doubts about affairs that they have conducted according to moral principle, and go ahead and inquire through divination, then this is not distant enough.
>
> People themselves have the human Way [by which] to properly conduct their affairs. If today they are not willing to go the limit themselves, and just go on flattering the ghosts and spirits, then this is not wise.[130]

The point here is that supplication and divination are not substitutes for self-cultivation. The proper use of divination is to settle doubts that remain *after* one has "gone the limit oneself" or "exhausted oneself" in the attempt to seek the Way by one's own effort. One should avail oneself of the extraordinary spirituality and wisdom of the sages' *I* only when necessary. Once the moral pattern is understood, according to Chu, "affairs can easily be decided," and there is no point in divining.

> As Shun said to Yü [quoting from the *Shu Ching*], "My will was settled earlier. [Chu omits: I consulted and deliberated, and all were in agreement.] The ghosts and spirits were [Chu adds: necessarily] in accord, and the tortoise and milfoil both [Chu adds: necessarily] went along."[131]

Chu Hsi's preface to the *Chou-i pen-i* also contains an illuminating passage on the limitations of using the *I* as a divination text. It is essentially

130 *Chu-tzu ch'üan-shu* 14:28b.

131 *Chu-tzu yü-lei* 66, p. 2575. Chu is quoting the *Shu Ching*, "Ta-Yü mo." See Legge, *Shoo King*, p. 63, and Ts'ai Ch'en (1167–1230), comp., *Shu-ching chi-chuan* (Collected commentaries on the Book of Documents) (Taipei: Shih-chieh, 1967 reprint), p. 14. The reason for indicating Chu's omissions and additions to the text is that they seem to support the suggestion that he was depersonalizing the common view of divination. It should be noted, of course, that this is a student's transcription of an oral conversation on the *I*, in which Chu Hsi was undoubtedly quoting the *Shu* from memory.

a piece of advice to potentially over-enthusiastic or uncritical students and readers, cautioning them to understand the proper use of the *I* as one part of the overall, multifaceted program of moral cultivation. It refers to an earlier passage of the preface, which discusses constant change in terms of unformed *ch'i* gradually evolving into particular "unified" patterns. Chu cautions:

> There are times, certainly, when there has not yet begun to be unification, and so a [corresponding] hexagram has not yet begun to have a definite image. There are situations, certainly, which have not yet begun to be fathomable, and so a [corresponding] line likewise has not yet begun to have a definite position. To take such a time and seek a hexagram for it is to limit oneself to the changeless; it is not [the way of] the *I*. To take such a situation and explain a line [with reference to it] is to be obstructed and unpenetrating; it is not the *I*. To know what are said to be the meanings of the hexagrams, lines, texts and images and not to know that there is a function for the hexagrams, lines, texts and images is also not the *I*.[132]

What Chu Hsi wants users of the *I* to avoid is the formulaic mapping of changing phenomena onto an overly deterministic, inflexible structure, and the over-reliance on the *I* that might distract them from the real necessity of self-cultivation. Some situations, he says, are simply not yet subject to understanding and resolution. To try to force an understanding of such cases is to try conceptually to pin down something that is really indeterminate, to "limit oneself to the changeless" in a situation in flux. The emphasis here is on the failure to accept the reality of change and the over-estimation of the role the *I* can play in one's life.

Thus, an important aspect of "knowing the incipiencies"[133] of changing events is to know when they have not yet begun to take form; to know when the pattern of the Way is *not* intelligible. This is an exceedingly fine, yet extremely important, distinction. For the incipiencies themselves—*after* they have taken form—are empirically unobservable to the ordinary person. How is one to know them, and yet avoid anticipating them? The difference between responding to incipiencies and anticipating them is the difference between participating in the cosmic process[134] and projecting one's private ideas onto it. One participates with the *I*—and thereby with change—not simply by reading the text but by using it.

> Apprehend [the *I*] in the circulation of [your] essence and spirit, and in the movement of [your] mental functions. Join your virtue with heaven-and-earth;

---

[132] *Chou-i pen-i*, preface, p. 2a.

[133] *Hsi-tz'u* B5 (cf. Wilhelm/Baynes, p. 342).

[134] Or "assisting in the transforming and nourishing processes of Heaven and Earth" (*Chung-yung* 22).

join your brightness with the sun and moon; join your timing with the four seasons; join your good fortune and misfortune with the ghosts and spirits.[135] Only then can you say that you know the *I*.[136]

The only documented case of Chu Hsi's personal practice of *I Ching* divination provides a good example of its use in deciding a course of action. In 1195, as the "False Learning" controversy was heating up,[137] Chu wrote a lengthy memorial which his students feared would have drastic consequences. Chu at that time was sixty-four and not in good health. Some of his students begged him to retire, but he would not listen to them. His friend and student Ts'ai Yüan-ting (1135–1198) suggested he put the question to the milfoil. He did so, obtaining hexagram #33 T'un (Withdraw [Retreat]), changing to hexagram #37 Chia-jen (Family). He then burned the memorial and retired for the last time, taking the new honorific name T'un-weng, "Old Man Who Has Withdrawn."[138]

[135] Cf. *Hsi-tz'u* A6 (Wilhelm/Baynes, p. 302).

[136] *Chou-i pen-i*, preface, p. 2a.

[137] See James T.C. Liu, "How Did a Neo-Confucian School Become the State Orthodoxy?" *Philosophy East & West*, 23 (1973), pp. 483–505; and Conrad Schirokauer, "Neo-Confucians Under Attack: The Condemnation of *Wei-hsüeh*," in *Crisis and Prosperity in Sung China*, ed. John W. Haeger (Tucson: University of Arizona Press, 1975), pp. 163–98.

[138] Wang Mou-hung, *Chu-tzu nien-p'u*, p. 216. Although this is the only specific instance of Chu's divination we know of, he does mention in a letter that his family uses site divination (*p'u-ti*) to select burial sites (*Chu-tzu wen-chi* [Ssu-pu pei-yao ed.], extra collection [*pieh-chi*] 3:4a).

CHAPTER SEVEN

Sung Literati Thought and the *I Ching*

OUR PREVIOUS CHAPTERS have discussed various ways in which four Sung literati sought to ground values in the natural world. Each man set out to demonstrate the coherence of heaven, earth, and humanity, that is, to show that there was one common and universal foundation to all things. If we are careful in our use of the terms, we could say that each offered a particular solution to the longstanding question of integrating culture with nature. As well, each prescribed a transformative method of *hsüeh* whereby literati might learn to apprehend these values for themselves, thereby establishing a basis for their moral autonomy. The first part of this chapter defines these men's commonalities by contrasting them to other Sung ways of conceptualizing the world's coherence.

Within this commonality, our four men show important differences. We will subsequently explore two of these, which concern the role of number as a way to understand the nature of heaven-and-earth, and the value of the cultural tradition to the practice of *hsüeh*. After noting disagreements between Shao, Ch'eng, and Su, we will see how Chu Hsi attempts to resolve these issues, excluding in the process certain of his predecessors' views. In contrast to Chu's narrowing of Sung thought, we suggest a broader and more inclusive coherence, of which Chu Hsi himself forms a part.

In conclusion we will reexamine the *I* as it functioned for these men in three ways: as a text transmitted by the sages, as a model of universal process, and as a practice (either of *hsüeh* or divination or both) that was intended to conjoin the first two. That is, we will see the *I Ching* as a work of culture that links men to many things: to the minds of the sages, to nature and universal process, and thus to the ground of value and the roots of morality.

THE UNDERSTANDING OF COHERENCE

To understand these four men it is useful to contrast their thought with two earlier models of Sung thinking. One is the intellectual world prior to Ou-yang Hsiu, and the other is that of Ou-yang himself. The notion of coherence is an economical way to structure this quick survey—it will show us how things fit together and how knowledge is organized. We will also see how each type of coherence implies a particular style of *hsüeh* or learning.

First is the example of Sung itself, which imposed a centralized state upon a diverse realm. In its first decades the Sung state reflected its administrative unity in three great encyclopedias designed to collect all significant knowledge. These are the *Wen-yüan ying-hua* (First blossoms from the garden of literature, 982–986), which continued the great anthology of literature called the *Wen-hsüan*; the *T'ai-p'ing yü-lan* (Imperial reader from the T'ai-p'ing period, 983), containing whatever an emperor might need to know to administer the realm; and the *T'ai-p'ing kuang-chi* (Extensive notes from the T'ai-p'ing period, 978), with a miscellany of other writings. These encyclopedias arranged broad knowledge of things and affairs into systematic categories, but they did not attempt to reduce the diversity of historical experience to basic principles nor to establish the coherence of things. Instead they prepared their reader for specific practical applications of the knowledge they contained. In these ways they extended an earlier approach to knowing the world apparent in T'ang models like the *T'ung-tien* (Comprehensive standards). Such collections of authoritative past materials assumed that precedents were the best foundation for the present conduct of administration. Thus they set out to conserve the traditions they surveyed.

The civil service examinations encouraged an analogous attitude toward learning. Insofar as the exams required only the mastery of forms, rather than the mastery of ideas, they demanded a simple reproduction of the past. And the rote memorization of texts was itself a kind of collecting of specific items. Both these attitudes imply a sense of *hsüeh* in keeping with that word's original meaning of "to follow a model" or "to imitate." The outward acquisition of culture was sufficient for success. These skills, rather than a concern for the common good, could gain men access to the exercise of political power.

In contrast, Ou-yang Hsiu saw an integrated moral and political order in antiquity. Its coherence, when properly inferred from the record of the sages' past practices, was a true basis (*pen*) on which men of Sung could themselves re-create such order. But though the sages' practices were perfect examples of correct action, Sung was separated from antiquity by centuries of real historical change. Thus literati in the present could share only the intentions (*i*) of the sages, not their institutions. This way of thinking was new in several ways. Like the Sung encyclopedias it rested on concrete examples from a particular time and place, yet it said that such models could not be literally reproduced in the present. Furthermore, it did not accept the authority of Han and T'ang historical experience, which must instead be judged against the standards of the Classics. It required men to be able to integrate past ideas if the results were to be integrative in the present.

This implied a new sense of what it meant to engage in *hsüeh*. *Hsüeh* now required finding the place from which one could view the totality of the sages' intentions. The literatus must still collect much information, but that information became valuable—that is, had direct application to present-day issues of transforming society—only when it had been made to reveal the sages' vision. The goal of learning now was to produce literati who saw the world in these terms, who could act like men of the past with "perfect fairness and great righteousness,"[1] benefiting all people in the empire. *Hsüeh* also became potentially divorced from the realm of examination preparation, since it involved primarily the commitment to transform politics and society. But just as men of the present should be like the sages of the past, so those sages were also only men themselves. They had no mystical qualities, arcane knowledge of heaven, no mysterious *tao*; they were distinguished from other men only by their practical moral insight into socio-political organization. Thus, in Ou-yang's words, Mencius "only taught men to plant mulberries and raise chickens and pigs. He thought that nurturing the living and sending off the dead was the basis of the kingly *tao*."[2]

The four men we study developed a sense of the world's coherence that differed from Ou-yang Hsiu's in one crucial measure: they insisted that the ultimate coherence was that which existed between human beings and heaven-and-earth. Such a view went beyond concepts that Ou-yang could accept in four respects. First of all, Ou-yang argued that antiquity must be the basis for learning, i.e., for reaching conclusions about values. While values are not immediately apparent and must be inferred from the evidence of the sages' past practices, the materials from which he derived them were empirical—texts and public affairs, human acts and responses. Our four men, however, all claimed that the ultimate basis for all learning is the natural world of universal process, whose order is opaque and somewhat mysterious to most literati. This basis exists independently of culture, history or men's conceptions of it. Values that are certain could be derived from it.

Second, Ou-yang insisted that in order to ground themselves in antiquity, literati must overcome their partiality (*ssu*). He was not, however, interested in questions of *hsing*, that is, in inquiring if human beings had their own grounding within. Our four thinkers insisted that all people by their natures possess something that is essential to attaining knowledge of true values. Thus their reason for overcoming selfishness was to be-

---

[1] Ou-yang Hsiu, *Ch'üan-chi*, p. 414.
[2] Ibid., p. 482.

come aware of what one already is, and of one's remarkable connection to all things. Once that is realized, then people's actions would be spontaneously correct.

Third, Ou-yang's ground was a way of maintaining that there could be something constant throughout all changes. But he recognized that change made old forms outmoded. This notion of change is one of discontinuity, of something that cuts one off from the past. It requires one to infer principles, rather than simply copying and implementing. Our four men, with the probable exception of Shao Yung, made change the ground on which all action occurred. But change was not merely what separated them from the ancient past. It made everything new, different even from what had happened only moments before. They concluded that only in the present did one have access to decisions regarding action. However important one's training with ancient texts, however meticulous one's judgments of past historical acts, however crucial the examples of the sages, still one must respond to changing circumstances in the moment. This meant that action could not be governed by rules, nor prescribed in advance.

Finally, as we have seen, the reality of change pushed Ou-yang to look to ancient texts. Our four men surely valued the text of *I Ching*, and each devoted months and pages of analysis to it. They valued the principles they found in it even more, and we have devoted much of this book to elucidating these. But most of all, they valued the ground from which all principles arose, whether that be called *tao*, the pattern, or heaven-and-earth. Texts, in other words, must be transcended; only someone of middling ability stays stuck in them. True authority comes from the degree of one's access to the ultimate ground. Thus Chu Hsi argued that the student of the *I* must work his way back from the *T'uan* commentary of Confucius to the laconic hexagram statements of King Wen, back further to the bare hexagrams recorded by Fu-hsi, and ultimately to the same unmediated reading of the world that Fu-hsi himself engaged in.

A new kind of learning followed. This *hsüeh* was not only about a place to stand and view the whole, and thus to act to transform society. The learner was himself transformed. Whereas Ou-yang's learning gave one authority to order all under heaven, here one could bring the order of heaven into practice oneself. This gave literati the potential of ultimate moral autonomy, beyond the court or any other institution. The source of this *hsüeh* thus moved away from culture toward what we have been calling nature. Chinese philosophers have usually seen the natural world as the ultimate grounding of their thought. In practice, however, they have often treated other elements as more immediately germane. These four men moved the natural background to the foreground, and they read their cultural traditions in terms of it.

NUMBER

Thus far we have spoken of commonalities. Discussing number will point to a major difference between Shao Yung's and Ch'eng I's conceptions of the coherence of heaven-and-earth. This difference is useful in suggesting the breadth of eleventh-century thought. But it will also demonstrate that Shao and Ch'eng, agreeing on what really mattered—how to be, how to act—did not overly concern themselves with their common differences.

The conventional view of the relationship between Shao and Ch'eng is that Ch'eng admired Shao's personal moral stance but had nothing to do with his numerology.[3] There is a certain truth to this. For example, someone wrote to Ch'eng after Shao's death, saying that of Shao Yung's friends only Ch'eng I remained, and might he hear of Shao's learning (*hsüeh*) from him? Ch'eng replied: "I lived with [Shao] Yao-fu in the same lane for more than thirty years. There was nothing in the world that we didn't talk about. Only I never heard a word about number."[4]

A disciple had written that "The meaning (*i*) of the *I* fundamentally arises from number." Responding, Ch'eng clarifies his objections: it is *li*, the pattern, that is the source of all meaning. Number is merely derivative. He writes:

> To say that meaning arises from number is wrong. You have the pattern, and only then do you have images (*hsiang*). You have images, and only then do you have number.[5]

This, of course, is the inversion of Shao's scheme of development, which sees image emerging from number. But Ch'eng does not mean *hsiang* to refer to Shao's "four images of heaven and four images of earth." Instead, *hsiang* seems to indicate a preliminary stage of each thing's coming into being—a philosophical topic that Ch'eng is not normally given to discuss, as A. C. Graham has noted.[6] The passage from Ch'eng I continues:

> The *I* relies on images to illuminate the pattern, and it follows images in order to make number known. If you attain its meaning, then image and number will be amidst it. If you are going to plumb the hidden subtleties of image and exhaust the minutiae of number, this is certainly seeking what flows away and pursuing the ends of things [rather than going to the source]. This is what the occultists (*shu*) cherish. It is not what Confucians engage in.[7]

---

[3] See, for example, A. C. Graham, *Two Chinese Philosophers*, Appendix 2, especially pp. 152–55 and 162.

[4] *Erh-Ch'eng chi*, p. 444 (*Wai-shu* 12).

[5] *Erh-Ch'eng chi* 21A.271.

[6] See his *Two Chinese Philosophers*, pp. 19–20, regarding Ch'eng's remarks on hexagram #50 Ting (Cauldron).

[7] *Erh-Ch'eng chi* 21A.271.

In contrast to these views of number, one of the Ch'eng brothers writes about the purity of Shao's commitment to the Way:

> These days those who trust to *tao* and are not confused by heterodoxy are only [Shao] Yao-fu of Loyang and Tzu-hou [Chang Tsai] of Ch'in.[8]

Again:

> I have had contact with many men. There are three [whose teachings] are not adulterated (*tsa*): Chang [Tsai] Tzu-hou, Shao Yao-fu and Ssu-ma [Kuang] Ch'ün-shih.[9]

And Ch'eng I himself writes:

> In regard to people's learning today, many indeed have heard much or studied hard. But in the end all go into Ch'an learning. There is none among them well grounded and free of delusion like Tzu-hou [Chang Tsai] and [Shao] Yao-fu. And I'm afraid that even their disciples have not avoided it.[10]

But the conventional view of Shao and Ch'eng's relationship makes three incorrect assumptions. The first is that Shao's morality is separable from his larger system. As we have seen in chapter 4, Shao himself argues the opposite point, that his morality derives precisely from his understanding of heaven-and-earth. The second is that Ch'eng's world has no place for number or divination. This is simply not true. Instead we will see that both men are extraordinarily attuned to the interconnectedness of all phenomena, but that each conceptualizes the relationship between things in different ways—that is, each sees a different coherence in heaven-and-earth. Third, though Ch'eng Hao seems to have enjoyed drinking and discussing poetry with Shao,[11] Ch'eng I found him insufficiently fastidious and lacking in a seemly solemnity:

> As for his moral conduct, he is simply impolite and disrespectful. He makes a game of things. Even if it's the pattern of heaven, he still makes a game of it. As he says, for example, in his "Biography of Mr. No-name,"
>
> > He asked heaven-and-earth about it,
> > And heaven-and-earth did not reply.
> > He played with the pellet[12] at his leisure,
> > Going and coming.[13]

[8] *Erh-Ch'eng chi* 4.70.

[9] *Erh-Ch'eng chi* 2A.21.

[10] *Erh-Ch'eng chi* 15.171. And compare 2A.32, where Ch'eng Hao calls him a "heroic literatus" (*hao-chieh chih shih*).

[11] See, for example, the passages beginning in *Erh-Ch'eng chi*, p. 673 (*Wen-chi, I-wen*), and Ch'eng Hao's five poems written with and for Shao on p. 481 (*Wen-chi 3*).

[12] "*Nung-wan*"—there is bound to be a specific referent here, but we have been unable to identify it. What pellet does Shao have in mind?

[13] *Erh-Ch'eng chi* 2A.45. This quotation is unattributed in the *Erh-Ch'eng chi*, but its attitudes seem clearly those of Ch'eng I.

The basis for their friendship must lie elsewhere then. Let us begin our investigation of it with Ch'eng's objections to divination, which, as we might expect, are moral:

> In antiquity "divination was used to resolve doubts."[14] Divination today is not like that. It is to determine the length of one's life and calculate one's success, that is all. Ah! I feel this [deeply].[15]

Yet Ch'eng I was indeed convinced of the efficacy of both divination, under certain stringent conditions, and number, with limited applications. In regard to divination with the *I Ching* he remarks:

> When someone today does divination, the stalks are in his hands, the affair is in the future, and the [prognostications of] fortunate or unfortunate (*chi-hsiung*) are in the text. These three must be conjoined (*ho*, "in agreement"). If the words of the text are not conjoined with the pattern, then naturally it will not prove effective.[16]

Divination is effective because everything in heaven-and-earth is of one pattern. To return to a story we examined in chapter 5, this one pattern is why you can hear the sound of killing in *ch'in* music when the performer is watching a mantis and cicada fight.[17] Explaining how this conjunction works, one of the Ch'eng brothers remarks:

> That divination can create a state of responsiveness (*ying*) [between stalks, the diviner, and the external situation] and that sacrifice can be efficacious is just a single pattern. Though the stalks and turtle lack feeling (*ch'ing*), once they have formed hexagrams, there is "auspiciousness" and "inauspiciousness" there. There is nothing that does not have this pattern [i.e., there is no situation in which this is not so].
>
> If on the basis of the existence of this pattern you ask a question, the response [of the *Book of Change*] will be like an echo. If you ask a question of the hexagrams and images with a selfish mind, then it will not respond, since there is no pattern for this. The pattern of today and the pattern of previous days—which has already been set—are only one pattern. Therefore it responds. The efficacy of sacrifice is the same. The pattern of the ghosts and spirits is out there, I face them with this pattern, and therefore it is efficacious. It is not permitted to [divine] a second or third time[18] because there is only one pattern.
>
> Prescribing medicine to cure an illness—this is also only a single pattern. This

[14] Paraphrasing the *Tso-chuan*, Huan 11. Here Ch'eng uses the phrase "*pu-shih*," which meant originally "to make cracks [in a turtle shell or ox plasteron] and cast stalks [to determine a hexagram]." By Sung times, however, the compound simply meant "divination."

[15] *Erh-Ch'eng chi* 25.326.

[16] *Erh-Ch'eng chi* 15.161.

[17] *Erh-Ch'eng chi* 18.224.

[18] See for example hexagram #4 Meng (Youthful Folly), where this issue is discussed.

medicine cures [the conditions of] such-and-such *ch'i*; if you have this disease, take it and it will respond (*ying*). If the pattern did not tally with it, then the medicine would not (cor)respond.[19]

There is only one pattern and only one *ch'i* or psycho-physical force. Everything is connected within these, and like things respond (*ying*) to each other. Medicine works because of this correspondence, and sacrifice as well. The *Book of Change* as a divination text also echoes the pattern as it exists. (Ch'eng never explains how this is so—like Chu Hsi and others, he seems to have simply taken it for granted.) In chapter 5 we saw Ch'eng remark on the "four knowings" of Yang Chen: "When one speaks of me and another person, there is definitely a distinction. When one speaks of heaven-and-earth, it is only one knowing."[20] This "one knowing" rests on the oneness of the pattern. Yet only someone who is without a selfish mind is able to tune in to it.

Ch'eng, however, goes further, affirming the possibility of knowing things through mathematical inference:

[Someone] asked: "Shao Yao-fu's ability to use number to infer the length of life and beginning and ending of things—is there such a pattern [i.e., are such things possible]?"

[Ch'eng I] replied: "There certainly is."

He also asked: "Some say that human life only reaches the number 120 [years]. Is this so or not?"

[Ch'eng I] said: "It certainly is. This is a round number—it doesn't necessarily have to be like that. Horses and cows are of the category (*lei*) that reaches thirty years, cats and dogs to twelve, swallows to six. And there are some that don't live that long."

He also asked: "And what about examining someone's 'shape and form' (*hsing-se*) or investigating by inference from the numbers of the day on which someone was born?"

[Ch'eng I] said: "One can also examine 'shape and form.' But it will prove effective only if one is most refined."[21]

Having affirmed his belief that it is possible to determine a variety of things by mathematical inference, Ch'eng proceeds in the subsequent passages of the *I-shu* to suggest how this might be so:

The numerological methods of Shao Yao-fu came from Li Ts'ai-chih.[22] Only with Yao-fu did inference by number become adequate to the pattern.[23] . . .

[19] *Erh-Ch'eng chi* 2A.51.
[20] *Erh-Ch'eng chi* 18.224.
[21] *Erh-Ch'eng chi* 18.197.
[22] For a brief discussion of him, see chapter 4, note 43.
[23] *Erh-Ch'eng chi* 18.197.

When you have the pattern, you have *ch'i* (psycho-physical force). When you have *ch'i*, you have number. Number is that which operates (*hsing*) the ghosts and spirits (*kuei-shen*); it is the function (*yung*) of *ch'i*.[24]

Number, then, is implicated with the processes or functioning of *ch'i*. It somehow "operates" the natural forces, though Ch'eng does not clarify this for us. After all, he is only seriously concerned with moral action and its basis, the pattern. Thus number, however efficacious, tells him very little of real significance. For Shao, of course, number is perhaps the best way to know where one stands, and thus what one needs to do.

The passage we have just discussed continues, addressing matters we are more used to hearing about from Shao:

> [The *Hsi-tz'u-chuan* A8 says] "The number of the great expansion (*ta-yen*) is fifty." Number begins with one and is completed with five. Do the small expansion on it and it makes ten; do the great expansion on it and it makes fifty. Fifty is the completion of number. Completed, it does not move. Therefore one reduces it by one to use it [in divination, as one starts with fifty stalks but puts one aside].[25]

Ch'eng, then, contradicts the conventional views of neither *ch'i* nor numerology. All he opposes is their improper application.

We are now ready to examine the differences in how Shao and Ch'eng understand the coherence of heaven-and-earth. The best place to start is extremely simple. Ch'eng I says:

> The mind of a single person is the mind of heaven. The pattern of a single thing is the pattern of all things. The revolution (*yün*) of one day is the revolution of one year.[26]

Shao Yung surely agrees with Ch'eng that each man's mind is indeed the mind of heaven. But he would have to insist that the pattern of a single thing is only *part* of the pattern of all things and certainly that a day is never a year. Ch'eng I's point here is that the order of the whole is fully and perfectly reflected in the order of any one thing. Because the order of heaven-and-earth is immanent in each part of it, true values can be derived anywhere, just by looking at wherever one happens to be. From this perspective, a day and a year simply mark off different amounts of time. The revolution of the day is only the revolution of the year on a smaller scale.

Shao's whole world, however, depends upon hierarchical distinctions

---

[24] *Erh-Ch'eng chi*, p. 1030 (*Ching-shuo* 1).

[25] Ibid. For a discussion of the 49 stalks, see *Hsi-tz'u-chuan* A8 or Wilhelm/Baynes, p. 721.

[26] *Erh-Ch'eng chi* 2A.13.

between the building blocks of heaven-and-earth. It is the only way that he knows to ground his other historical, political and moral distinctions. Thus, although for him, too, the whole of the order of heaven-and-earth is accessible from any one thing, this is true not because the part contains the whole but because one can trace the connectedness of each thing step-by-step to everything. The proper action of a literatus depends on this knowledge. In particular, one must be able to identify the shape of current events and know what one is responding to. But more generally, Shao teaches literati to identify with heaven-and-earth, to recognize their small but crucial place in this large schema. If they can see the world from that perspective, they will act properly, Shao seems to say. It is not necessary to prescribe specific actions.

A pair of quotations will highlight these differences. Recall how Shao Yung accounts for the origin of heaven and of earth through a series of cycles:

> Heaven is born of movement. Earth is born of stillness. One movement and one stillness interact and the *tao* of heaven-and-earth fully expresses them. Yang is born at the beginning of movement. Yin is born at the peak of movement. A yin and a yang interact and the functioning of heaven fully expresses them.[27]

Ch'eng I on the other hand says:

> *Tao* is one yin and one yang.[28] Movement and stillness are without a beginning, and yin and yang are without an origin. If you are not someone who knows *tao*, how could you recognize this?[29]

Shao's heaven and his earth come into being at a specific moment in the cosmic cycle. Similarly yin and yang are born at the apogee of stillness and movement. For Ch'eng I neither yin nor yang can have an origin, since they are, like *tao*, beyond time, beyond creation or destruction. They are implicit in *tao* in such a multitude of ways that it is simply wrong-headed to assign them fixed positions. If you are not someone who lives steeped in that ineffability, "how could you recognize this?"

Each man also has a distinct sense of the nature of time and its application to realizing values. For Shao the regularity of the units that mark the passage of time is a clear embodiment of the order he finds in heaven-and-earth. It is on the basis of this order that Shao is able to know the future. Furthermore, from the perspective of his 129,600-year cycle, the passage of time is an essentially moral journey, from birth to flourishing through decay to annihilation. For Ch'eng, time is just a matter of the

[27] *Huang-chi ching-shih shu* 5.1b.
[28] Paraphrasing a famous passage in *Hsi-tz'u-chuan* A4.
[29] *Erh-Ch'eng chi*, p. 1029 (*Ching-shuo* 1).

moment (*shih*), the constantly recurring opportunity every literatus has to either accord with the pattern or diverge from it into some variety of selfishness.

The following conversation between Ch'eng and Shao makes sense when read against these differences. It concerns knowledge—what it is necessary to know, and how one knows it.

> Shao Yao-fu said to Master Ch'eng: "Although you are very bright, the affairs of the world are numerous indeed. Are you able to know them all?"
>
> The Master said: "There are certainly many that I do not know. But what do you mean by 'not know'?"
>
> At that moment there was some thunder, and Yao-fu said: "Do you know where thunder arises?"
>
> The Master said: "I know, but you don't."
>
> "What do you mean?" Yao-fu said in astonishment.
>
> The Master said: "I already know it, so why would I use number to infer it? If I don't know something, then I depend on inference to know it."
>
> Yao-fu said: "Where do you think it arises?"
>
> The Master said: "It arises in the place it arises." Yao-fu, with a start, praised it as a good response.[30]

Why does Shao Yung praise Ch'eng's tautology? We may not be able to fully plumb his Zen-like answer, but at the very least it will lead us into some important differences between the two men. We should first review Shao Yung's epistemology. To understand one's place in the world, and thus what one should do, one needs to know the status or position of each thing within its larger network of relationships. Thus Shao's own treatment of thunder places it in the hierarchy of the four images of heaven and the four images of earth:

> The sun is heat. The moon is cold. The stars are day. The zodiacal spaces are night. Heat, cold, day, and night interact, and the changes of heaven fully express them.
>
> Water is rain. Fire is wind. Earth (*t'u*) is dew. Stone is thunder. Rain, wind, dew, and thunder interact, and the transformations of earth (*ti*) fully express them.[31]

"Knowing where thunder arises" entails knowing this set of interactions. More generally, knowing depends on understanding the complete hierarchy that unfolds from *t'ai-chi* through spirit to number to image and ultimately to the ten-thousand things of the world. If one knows this schema, then one can "infer by means of number."

For Ch'eng, knowing means knowing what to do; and one knows what

---

[30] *Erh-Ch'eng chi* 21A.269.
[31] *Huang-chi ching-chih shu* 5.2a.

to do because one is aware of the pattern. This knowledge is direct, unmediated by the structures of number. Indeed, it cannot be inferred by number. It does not depend on a hierarchy of stages, especially one of *t'ai-chi*, number, images, and things. Instead, the pattern is a great network, present everywhere, that incorporates both the training of children and the attainment of sagehood into a single enterprise. Ch'eng remarks:

> Sweeping and answering questions are part of a single system (*i-t'ung*), along with fully developing your nature (*hsing*) and arriving at your destiny (*ming*). These have no root and branch.[32]

In these terms, where thunder arises is irrelevant, and a tautology is indeed a satisfying answer. But why might Shao have been impressed with Ch'eng's answer? Here is our best, though still uncertain, attempt to answer that question.

For both men the whole of heaven-and-earth resonates together, and everything occurs in its proper place. Though each defines this place through different means, both are convinced of its natural rightness. Despite his complex analysis of thunder, Shao accepts Ch'eng's remark that he still does not know where it arises. For Shao seems to have momentarily forgotten the ultimate point of his own system, which is to demonstrate the coherence of heaven-and-earth. Ch'eng simply reminds him that everything, at least in the world of nature, arises as and where it ought.

But Ch'eng goes on elsewhere to attempt a more imperialist move on Shao's teachings. He claims that they are ultimately based on the pattern, at the same time that he scolds Shao for engaging in occult practices (*shu*):

> The learning of Yao-fu takes its meaning first of all from the pattern. Whether he is discussing image and number (*hsiang-shu*) or the pattern of heaven-and-earth, it must emerge in fours. Nonetheless, from this he can infer the pattern, saying, "When I attain this great thing [the pattern], then the ten-thousand things emerge from me. There is nothing that is not in place." For this it is not necessary that he have occult methods (*shu*). What is important is that it is difficult to use [his ideas] to "order the nation and all under heaven."[33]

Ch'eng I finds Shao's work convincing because so much of it is assimilable to a way of thinking based on the pattern. Shao's love of fours, of course, is irrelevant to the pattern, so Ch'eng argues that it is therefore also irrelevant to Shao's truth!

The ground of these agreements has implications for the major analytical tool in most Chinese discussions of *I Ching* schools. This is the distinction between the *i-li* and *hsiang-shu* approaches, which we have

[32] *Erh-Ch'eng chi* 18.224.
[33] Paraphrasing the first section of the *Ta-hsüeh* (Great Learning). *Erh-Ch'eng chi* 2A.45.

treated briefly in chapter 1 and more fully in chapter 6. *I-li* stresses the content of the hexagram and line statements as the key to the *I*'s meaning, while *hsiang-shu* attends primarily to the configuration and relationship of the trigrams and hexagrams. By this measure, Shao Yung and Ch'eng I's *Book of Change* are at opposite ends of the spectrum. The customary "attitude of disciples" would make Shao and Ch'eng into philosophical opponents. Instead each agreed profoundly on fundamental principles: grounding in heaven-and-earth, from which humanity is ultimately inseparable; access to its coherence through a transformative *hsüeh*; and acting as a sage, independent from human institutions yet utterly interdependent with the ten-thousand things of heaven-and-earth. Thus both the heart of their philosophical assumptions and the results of their practice are very close indeed. It is as if each spoke the same language but imputed a different grammar to it, structuring the same phenomena in profoundly different ways.

We would expect the difference between *i-li* and *hsiang-shu* methods to imply major differences in philosophical content. The evidence of Shao and Ch'eng, however, shows how the two can lead to similar results. It suggests that in some instances the customary distinction between the two schools primarily serves the convenience of later morphologists of the *I* traditions. This in turn suggests that Chu Hsi's eventual synthesis of the two approaches might not have been as philosophically difficult as it first appears.

To close this discussion, we might note that both Shao and Ch'eng also agree that the *I* is more than a text. It represents the *tao* of universal process, which exists independently of any writing. On this basis Shao considers Mencius the ideal reader of the *I*, even though nowhere does Mencius mention the book. Shao remarks:

> In regard to knowing the *I*, it is not necessary to cite discussions and commentary, as if only this constituted "knowing the *I*." Mencius wrote a book without ever mentioning the *I*, yet the *tao* of the *I* is present in it. But there are very few men who see this. Being able to use the *I* is what is meant by "knowing the *I*." Mencius, for example, could be said to be very good at using the *I*.[34]

And as one of the Ch'engs remarks: "From the *Mencius* one can observe the *Change*."[35]

CULTURE

Late-eleventh-century literati who rejected the New Policies and accepted that man is more than a political and social actor were forced to choose

---

[34] *Huang-chi ching-shih shu* 8B.31a.
[35] *Erh-Ch'eng chi*, p. 366 (*Wai-shu* 3).

between the positions of Su Shih and Ch'eng I. Su offered them the opportunity to engage literature, calligraphy, or music with the same seriousness with which they sought to order all under heaven. That is, he offered them the opportunity to engage in *wen* as a means of bringing *tao* into practice. Ch'eng denied them this.

[Someone] asked: "Does composing *wen* (*tso-wen*, writing with an aesthetic purpose) harm *tao?*"

[Ch'eng I] replied: "It does. When you engage in *wen* (*wei-wen*), if you don't concentrate your intention on it, then you will not become skillful. If you do, then your will (*chih*, your ambition) will be confined to this. So how would you be able to have the same greatness as heaven-and-earth? The *Book of Documents* says, "Play with things and you destroy the will.""[36] Engaging in *wen* is indeed playing with things. Lü Yü-shu has a poem that says:

> Learning like Yüan-k'ai [Tu Yü] and you just become an obsessive.
> *Wen* like [Ssu-ma] Hsiang-ju and you're just an entertainer.
> Stand alone within the Confucian gate, without a single thing
> Other than just transmitting the mind-fasting attained by Yen Tzu.[37]

"This poem is very good.

"Those who engaged in learning in the past were devoted only to nourishing their feelings and nature. They did not study other things. Those today who do *wen* are only devoted to writing to please the ear and eye of men. If you're devoted to pleasing men, isn't that being an entertainer, or what?"

[The interlocutor] asked: "Did the ancients study (*hsüeh*) how to do *wen?*"

[Ch'eng I] replied: "When people see the Six Classics, they think that the sages made *wen* (wrote with aesthetic concerns). They do not know that the sages just recorded what occurred in their breasts, which became *wen* of itself. This is what is meant by 'Those who have virtue necessarily have words [in which to express their understanding].' "[38]

[The interlocutor] asked: "Why were [Confucius's two disciples] Yu and Hsia praised for their *wen-hsüeh?*"

[Ch'eng I] replied: "When did Yu and Hsia ever take up a brush to study writing compositions? It's as it says, 'Contemplate the *wen* of heaven to detect the changes of the seasons. Contemplate the *wen* of humanity to transform all under heaven.'[39] How are these the *wen* of compositions?"[40]

[36] "Hounds of Ao." Cf. James Legge, *Shoo King*, p. 348. I owe this and the following identifications in this passage to Wing-tsit Chan, trans. *Reflections on Things at Hand*, pp. 64–65, whose translation I have closely followed here.

[37] According to Chuang Tzu, Confucius's disciple Yen Hui was able to "fast" his mind until *tao* came to dwell in it (see his chapter 4). Note that in saying so, Chuang Tzu is making Yen Hui out to be a Taoist. Lü and Ch'eng are able to co-opt this reference to their own purposes, however.

[38] *Analects* 14:5.

[39] Quoting the *T'uan-chuan* to hexagram #22 Pi (Adornment [Grace]). Cf. W/B p. 495.

[40] *Erh-Ch'eng chi* 18.239.

Here Ch'eng I and his student are using the word *"wen"* in three of its several contemporary meanings.[41] At one extreme it is "adornment," the elegance for which certain literary works are prized. At the other extreme it is the apparent structure or pattern of things. In this latter sense it is close to the term *li* before Ch'eng and his brother endowed it with more profound philosophical meanings. Bounced between these two, *wen* is "writings," which tend in the direction of adornment yet can be made to address the most basic of moral concerns. Ch'eng's interlocutor seems to confuse this scale, allowing "writings" of the sages and Confucian disciples to be confused with "elegance for its own sake," simply because the Classics are so beautifully expounded. Ch'eng argues that their beauty is purely a by-product of their authors' clarity of mind.

At the end he brings in the *I Ching*, quoting the *T'uan-chuan* of hexagram #22 Pi (Adornment [Grace]).[42] Here Ch'eng argues that the only meaning of *wen* worth serious consideration is as these patterns of heaven and humanity. In this sense the *I Ching* is not "literature" at all. It is, rather, "pattern." It is therefore "cultural" only secondarily; that is, it was produced by certain people in a certain cultural setting, written in hexagrams and Chinese characters. Ch'eng himself reads it in Northern Sung China—but none of this touches its essence or shapes its significance. What a literatus writes is just a manifestation of his understanding of the pattern; it is valuable if he is attuned to it and useless or damaging if he is not.

Su's view is very different. Though anything of value derives from *tao*, Su insists upon man's crucial mediating role in its creation. All institutions—of governance, literature, painting—have histories. Only by understanding their historical developments can one work one's way back upstream toward *tao* and thus embody the whole tradition. And only then can one respond appropriately in the present, as ruler, writer, or artist, thereby broadening the very tradition in which one participates.

Su is clear that *wen* as writing could point literati to *tao* because writing could manifest something that was very close to *tao*. Such *wen* was effective not because of a prescribed content but because it evoked an ineffable experience in its reader, drawing him toward *tao*. As such it was of potentially enormous power. In this way Su's vision confirmed literati's attraction to writing. It also preserved the value of past culture and even the structure of a canon, but in reference to something that was not definable, that allowed for change, and that was independent of the state.

However, the term *wen* means more than literature, adornment, and patterning. It also means "culture," and in the mid-eleventh century there

---

[41] For a brief discussion of *wen*, see Glossary.

[42] Wilhelm/Baynes, p. 96. The phrase "contemplate the *wen* of heaven" also occurs in the *Hsi-tz'u-chuan* A4, where it describes how Fu-hsi created the *I Ching* hexagrams.

was considerable concern for the preservation of *ssu-wen*, "our culture" in the sense of "our cultural tradition." As we have seen from his study of the *I*, Su is committed to cultural artifacts as the crucial evidence of those who have brought *tao* into practice and as the necessary texts for those who would learn how to do the same. Men thus stand between *tao*, or nature, and specific works, or culture.

For Ch'eng I the crucial aspect of human existence is acting properly. This view limits *ssu-wen* or culture to two related meanings. It is both the environment that supports literati in acting well and that environment which in turn arises from their doing so. Such an environment is surely textual and social, yet its most important quality is its foundation in heaven-and-earth. Literati must preserve and purify it, but for Ch'eng I man is not a creator. As we saw in chapter 5, in his commentary to hexagram #52 Ken Ch'eng remarks:

> That by which the sages could cause the world to be well governed is not that they could set rules for things. They only rested each thing in its proper place, that is all.[43]

In this way Ch'eng's sense of culture is severely subordinated to his sense of nature. The category "culture" has no autonomous existence. When he recommends a broad investigation of the world, it is only so that students might attain the basic insight into heaven-and-earth.

This gives a particular flavor to his reading of texts, the primary cultural repository of learning. He says:

> The student (*hsüeh-che*) should take the *Analects* and *Mencius* as the foundation. Once he has researched these, then he can illuminate (*ming*) the Six Classics without research.[44]

That is, with a good basis in the main teachings, the rest will follow by itself. This passage also appears in the *Reflections on Things at Hand*. In his English translation, Wing-tsit Chan has appended two lines from Chu Hsi's *Yü-lei* that might have been composed as an uneasy clarification of Ch'eng's remark:

> With the *Analects* and *Mencius*, the work [required of the student] is less and what is obtained is relatively greater. With the Six Classics, the work is greater and what is obtained is relatively less.[45]

Chu is concerned with maintaining the importance of the Classics in their own right, not simply as the confirmation of basic principles derived elsewhere. As we will see below, culture is for him a real category of human

---

[43] *I-chuan* 236.6.

[44] *Erh-Ch'eng chi* 25.322.

[45] *Chu-tzu yü-lei*, p. 428 (our translation). This remark opens the section on the *Analects* in the *Yü-lei*. Chan's translation is on page 103 of the *Reflections on Things at Hand*.

endeavor, not merely epiphenomenal to heaven-and-earth. Knowing the foundation is still the goal of all learning, but all except sages must work extensively with bequeathed texts. If you want only the main points, says Chu, "then there are a lot of parts you could cut out of the *Mencius!*"[46]

Just as Chu attempts to synthesize the positions taken by both Su and Ch'eng on culture, so he wishes to subsume the positions on number taken by both Ch'eng and Su. It is to these views of his that we now turn.

CHU HSI

Chu Hsi's treatment of the *I Ching* was part of his exhaustive reevaluation and systematization of virtually the entire Chinese cultural tradition. As such, it was situated in the context of long-running debates that were at once social, political, and religious. In particular, Chu surveyed the eleventh-century masters and set out what he regarded as definitive resolutions to matters they had discussed. Questions such as the proper focus of advanced education, the nature and function of the civil service examinations, and the role of literati vis-à-vis government were inseparable from fundamental religious-philosophical topics such as *tao*, the nature and destiny (*hsing-ming*) of human beings, and the relationship of humanity with heaven. As a result of his victory in these debates, twelfth-century thinkers placed increased emphasis on the concepts of human nature and mind, and on the practice of moral cultivation.

Chu's study of the *I* speaks significantly of the role of number and the cultural tradition in these moral-metaphysical questions. The key figure linking all three concerns is Fu-hsi, the first mythic sage, who originally created the hexagrams. The prominence of Fu-hsi in Chu Hsi's writings and conversations on the *I* is quite striking. As we have seen in chapter 6, Chu used one of the myths of Fu-hsi's creation of the *I* as a basis for his interpretive theory.[47] "The *I* was originally created for divination (*I che pen wei pu-shih erh tso*)," he said repeatedly.[48] This basic historical fact, according to Chu, was the essential clue to the "original intention" and the "original meaning" of the *I*.

But the significance of Fu-hsi's creation of the *I* went well beyond its connection with the correct method of interpretation. Fu-hsi's creation

---

[46] *Chu-tzu yü-lei*, p. 435. This passage was brought to our attention by Chan, trans., *Reflections*, p. 105.

[47] *Hsi-tz'u* B2 (Wilhelm/Baynes, p. 328). It should be realized that King Wen and the Duke of Chou also had a hand in creating the basic text of the *I*, as did Confucius in allegedly writing the Ten Wings. While Chu's references to "the sages' creation of the *I*" sometimes include these later sages, his basic hermeneutic principle is that the later strata of the text must be read as clarifications of Fu-hsi's intention, and the "original meaning" of the later textual levels points back to Fu-hsi's creation.

[48] See especially *chüan* 66 of his *Classified Conversations* (*Chu-tzu yü-lei*).

was, in Chu Hsi's system, the first manifestation of the Confucian *tao* in the world. This is evident from Chu's redefinition of the *tao-t'ung*, or "succession of the Way," the lineage of sages to which he considered himself heir. Previous Confucians since Mencius had considered Yao (roughly five hundred years later than Fu-hsi) to be the progenitor of the "way of the sages." But Chu Hsi declared Fu-hsi to be the first sage.[49] And while Fu-hsi was credited with a number of important pre-agricultural inventions, such as traps and nets for hunting and fishing, clearly his chief contribution to the tradition, in Chu Hsi's estimation, was his creation of the *I*.

Chu's reformulation of the *tao-t'ung*, especially his selection of the Northern Sung thinkers from whom he claimed to have inherited the Way, was one of the major features of his intellectual system. What was it about Fu-hsi's creation of the *I* that warranted such a prominent position in this tradition? Most significant was the particular method by which it was accomplished. Fu-hsi, motivated by his humane concern for people of later ages, contemplated the moral principles inherent in natural patterns (the "ought" inherent in the "is")[50] and translated them into abstract, numerological symbols that could be used as a device to guide behavior. Fu-hsi was able to see this unity of the natural and moral pattern without engaging in learning (*hsüeh*). He could do so because he embodied the "mind of the sage," the mind possessed by all people but ordinarily obscured by impure *ch'i*. Yet Chu Hsi frequently draws attention to Fu-hsi's "contemplating above and examining below, seeking from afar and selecting from the near at hand,"[51] and specifically points out that Fu-hsi did not create the *I* by intuition alone.[52]

[49] Earlier figures, such as Shen-nung, the Divine Farmer, were also known by Mencius, but apparently were not included in the "way of the sages" (*sheng-tao*). Chu places Fu-hsi at the head of the tradition in the preface to his *Ta-hsüeh chang-chü* (The Great Learning in Chapters and Sentences), in *Ssu-shu chi-chu*, p. 1a. For more extended discussions see Wing-tsit Chan, "Chu Hsi's Completion of Neo-Confucianism," in his *Chu Hsi: Life and Thought* (Hong Kong and New York: The Chinese University Press and St. Martin's Press, 1987), pp. 121–30; and Joseph A. Adler, *Divination and Philosophy: Chu Hsi's Understanding of the I-ching* (Ann Arbor: University Microfilms International, 1984), pp. 73–81.

[50] Chinese philosophers have persistently argued, against the drift of modern Western philosophy since David Hume, that values *can* be derived from facts. See A. C. Graham, "Taoist Spontaneity and the Dichotomy of 'Is' and 'Ought,' " in *Experimental Essays on Chuang-tzu*, ed. Victor H. Mair (Honolulu: University of Hawaii Press, 1983), pp. 3–23; A. C. Graham, "What Was New in the Ch'eng-Chu Theory of Human Nature?" in *Chu Hsi and Neo-Confucianism*, ed. Wing-tsit Chan (Honolulu: University of Hawaii Press, 1986), pp. 138–57; and Joseph A. Adler, "Descriptive and Normative Principle (*li*) in Confucian Moral-Metaphysics: Is/Ought from the Chinese Perspective," *Zygon: Journal of Religion and Science*, 16:3 (1981), pp. 285–93.

[51] A paraphrase of *Hsi-tz'u* B2 (Wilhelm/Baynes, p. 328). See, e.g., *I-hsüeh ch'i-meng*, section 2, in *Chou-i che-chung*, p. 1223, and ibid., p. 1207 (Chu Hsi's reply to Yüan-shu).

[52] *I-hsüeh ch'i-meng*, section 2, in *Chou-i che-chung*, p. 1224.

How could this have been achieved by the Sage's thinking and deliberation? The natural existence of particular allotments [lit., "numbers"] of ch'i found shape in the models and images.[53]

Fu-hsi derived the *I* from the self-existing world around him by a process that may be considered a mythic paradigm of *ko-wu*, the "investigation of things."[54] The values transmitted by the cultural tradition, which began with the *I*, are in this way abstracted from and confirmed by the pattern (*li*) of heaven-and-earth.

In placing so much emphasis on Fu-hsi, his creation of the *I*, and his original intention in creating it, Chu Hsi was tying his particular vision of the Confucian tradition to the primordial origins of Chinese culture. The *I* stood there at the beginning: the product of the first sage, a symbolic expression of the continuity of heaven-and-earth and human values, of nature and culture, cosmology and ethics, *wen* and *li*. The *I* was the perfect symbol of the integrated order that Sung literati since Ou-yang Hsiu had been seeking. Fu-hsi, in a sense, prefigured Chu in the comprehensiveness of this vision. Fu-hsi created a numerological symbol system comprehending heaven-and-earth and human affairs, whose elements Chu Hsi integrated in his systematic treatment of moral-metaphysical, cultural, and numerological questions. Chu seems to have seen in Fu-hsi an incipient reflection of his own synthesis.

Chu's attempt to integrate the practice of divination into his larger system is a good example of his vision of the cultural tradition. His "rationalized" conception of divination—i.e., his reinterpretation of divination as a function of mind and impersonal *ch'i* rather than personal ghosts and spirits—recalls a similar process that had occurred much earlier in the Confucian tradition. This was Confucius's philosophical reinterpretation of ancestral sacrifice in terms of ritual propriety (*li*) and filial piety (*hsiao*).[55] Divination and sacrifice had been the dual basis of the religious state in Shang times (16th–11th century B.C.E.).[56] Chu Hsi's treatment of divination restored it, in a sense, to its former parity with sacrifice by giving it a role in the project of achieving sagehood. The related, ancient concept of *shen* (spirit), with a wide range of meanings, was similarly given a role in this discourse. Chu's systematization of the cultural tradition was nothing if not comprehensive.

Chu's Northern Sung predecessors, both within and outside the *tao-*

[53] *Chou-i che-chung*, p. 1203. Here Chu is speaking of the Ho-t'u and Lo-shu, another myth of the *I*'s origin that he is able to incorporate in his overall understanding of the text.

[54] *Hsi-tz'u* B2 (Wilhelm/Baynes, p. 328), discussed above in chapter 6.

[55] It also recalls Hsün Tzu's interpretation of sacrifice in terms of human emotions rather than spirits, in chapter 19 of his book. See Burton Watson, trans., *Hsün Tzu: Basic Writings* (New York: Columbia University Press, 1963), p. 110.

[56] David N. Keightley, "The Religious Commitment: Shang Theology and the Genesis of Chinese Political Culture," *History of Religions*, 17 (1978), pp. 211–25.

hsüeh camp, were of course major figures to be dealt with in this new synthesis. This is not the place to summarize his evaluations and interpretations of the various strands of Northern Sung thought. We can, however, characterize his relations with Northern Sung approaches to the *I Ching*. Chu regarded the *I Ching* tradition generally in terms of the two traditional interpretive approaches: the "image and number" (*hsiang-shu*) school, which focused on the graphic and numerological elements, including the many charts and diagrams (*t'u*) associated with the *I*; and the "meaning and pattern" (*i-li*) school, which sought the meaning of the *I* in its textual layers. Shao Yung was considered to be the chief Northern Sung exponent of the *hsiang-shu* approach (although Chou Tun-i ran a close second). And Ch'eng I's commentary on the *I* had quickly gained prominence as a definitive *i-li* interpretation. Chu Hsi and Lü Tsu-ch'ien drew heavily on Ch'eng's commentary in compiling their anthology of Northern Sung masters, the *Chin-ssu lu* (*Reflections on Things at Hand*).[57] On the other hand, Chu said of Shao Yung's major work, the *Huang-chi ching-shih shu*, that "it had nothing to do with the *I*."[58]

It is somewhat surprising, then, that Chu was highly critical of Ch'eng I's approach to the *I* (see chapter 6),[59] and that despite his criticisms of Shao Yung's *magnum opus* he made considerable use of Shao's ideas regarding the *I* and its associated diagrams. He was especially impressed with Shao's Preceding Heaven Chart (*hsien-t'ien-t'u*), also known as the Fu-hsi sequence of hexagrams. Chu felt that this symmetrical, binary sequence was an image (*hsiang*) of the "natural pattern" (*tzu-jan chih li*) of the *I*. It was therefore a demonstration of the *I*'s correspondence with heaven-and-earth, which was one of the bases of the *I*'s efficacy as an oracle. The significance of "natural pattern" also extended to other charts and diagrams associated with the *I*, e.g., the Ho-t'u (Yellow River Chart) and Lo-shu (Lo River Diagram), which were said to have been revealed in high antiquity to Fu-hsi and Yü, respectively. These two diagrams, as well as the Fu-hsi sequence of hexagrams and the alternative King Wen sequence, are discussed at length, with copious references to and quotations from Shao Yung, in Chu Hsi's *Introduction to the Study of the I*.

The *i-li* or "textual interpretation" (*wen-i*) specialists, on the other hand, were "scattered and dispersed."[60] Wang Pi, for instance, based his

[57] Approximately 17 percent of its selections were taken from Ch'eng's *Commentary on the I* (*I-chuan*). See Wing-tsit Chan, trans., *Reflections on Things at Hand*, pp. 322–23.

[58] *Chu-tzu ch'üan-shu* 53:64b. Cf. *Chu-tzu wen-chi* 67:1a and *I-hsüeh ch'i-meng* (*Chou-i che-chung* ed.), preface, p. 1203.

[59] While Chu's evaluation of Ch'eng's approach to the *I* is predominantly negative, he does have conciliatory words for Ch'eng in a postface to an edition of Ch'eng's *Commentary on the I*. He says that only Ch'eng was able to base his teaching on Fu-hsi, King Wen, and Confucius, who had different methods (*fa*) but the same way (*tao*). *Chu-tzu wen-chi* 81:18a–b.

[60] *I-hsüeh ch'i-meng*, p. 1203.

interpretation on Lao Tzu and Chuang Tzu rather than on the original meaning of the *I*.[61] Su Shih also was far from the original meaning; he used the *I* simply to support his own philosophical system, which was a badly flawed one. Su's claim that human beings cannot directly know their natures or the *tao* excluded him entirely from Ch'eng I and Chu Hsi's project, for it undercut their basic conception of the moral nature and sagehood.[62]

Thus Chu criticized both of the traditional approaches to the *I*, and attempted a synthesis of the two. His basic criticism of the *hsiang-shu'* approach was that it was often arbitrary and did not serve well as a guide to moral behavior. The *i-li* approach, on the other hand, was properly concerned with moral behavior, but it tended to be divorced from the original form and the original meaning of the *I*, often treating it merely as a reflection of the commentator's own ideas. Chu's approach was to make use of *hsiang-shu* to the extent that it clarified the cosmological basis of the *I* and its structural, numerological, and symbolic levels, but only to apply these patterns to the task of achieving sagehood. We might say, then, that he used *hsiang-shu* methods for *i-li* purposes.

This carefully selective use of the *I Ching* tradition and his Northern Sung predecessors attests once more to the coherence of Chu Hsi's own vision. He used the *I Ching* to show that the study of the Way as defined by himself and his selected intellectual ancestors was grounded in an integrated network of cosmic pattern and moral principle, a network that was understood in its entirety by the creators of Chinese culture. The *I* therefore functioned to legitimize Chu's system, as it did for most traditional Chinese thinkers. But Chu went beyond this ubiquitous and facile use of the *I*. His system allowed individuals to learn to realize the inherent goodness of their natures and thereby become sages. This process, according to Chu, was the necessary means of building a humane state. What was new in Chu's use of the *I Ching* was to show how it contributed a means by which individuals could connect in a concrete, experiential way with the wisdom of the primordial sages contained in their own minds, thereby grounding the Sung state in human nature and in the creative origins of Chinese culture.

USING THE *I CHING*

We can distinguish three aspects under which Sung literati understood the *I Ching*. The first is as a text transmitted by the sages. The second is as a representation of universal process. The third is as a practice, either of

---

[61] *Chu-tzu yü-lei* 66, p. 2578.

[62] See Chu's critique of Su's commentary on the *I*, in *Chu-tzu wen-chi* 72:16a–23b, and the discussion by Peter K. Bol, "Chu Hsi's Redefinition of Literati Learning."

hsüeh or divination or both, that can make the representations of that universal process available for literati use.

As a Text

Sung literati commonly shared two beliefs about the *I Ching* as a text: it was a record of the sages' profound insights, and it was a book about heaven-and-earth. Both these beliefs were problematical to Ou-yang Hsiu. In order to discredit the latter, he attacked the former, denying that Confucius wrote all of the Ten Wings and linking what remained of the text with the disreputable practice of divination. He could not dispose of it entirely, but he found very little useful in it. The best he could say was that it was concerned with "the patterns of order and chaos, rise and fall, success and failure."[63] Hu Yüan was successful at recovering more of the *I*. In particular, he wrote extensively on the hexagram and line statements, which he applied stringently to matters of governance, literati behavior, and the family. At the same time he denied the relevance of *hsing-ming* or matters of heaven-and-earth to these affairs.

Each of the four men of this book found his own way to preserve both the sage's involvement and the relevance of heaven-and-earth. At one extreme Su Shih emphasized the role of the men who translated the workings of *tao* into a written form (*wen*) accessible to later men. Thus the traditional account, in which Fu-hsi initiated a project that was only completed by Confucius, accords well with Su's own understanding of the gradual elaboration by human beings of the cultural tradition, and of how insight is developed and transmitted. Men, after all, broaden the Way, not vice versa. At the other extreme is the position of Shao Yung and Ch'eng I: that which gave the *I* value was precisely that which no man could have invented, for the sages had discovered an order that transcends individual human consciousness. As we have seen, Chu Hsi attempted to synthesize these positions. For him the *I* was a part of the Confucian cultural tradition. As such it was both the reflection of the real order of heaven-and-earth and the product of human sages.

We know very well the Sung practice, ever since Ou-yang Hsiu, of rejecting the received commentaries in favor of a direct reading of the Classics, fearing that commentaries would interpose a distorting lens between the reader and the sagely authors of antiquity. Our four men carried this a step further. They feared that even the Classics might prevent readers from apprehending things for themselves. Thus they recommended reading the things of the world as the basis for reading the Classics. Each suggested supplements or correctives to philosophical texts. Shao Yung

---

[63] *Ch'üan chi*, p. 129, "*I* huo wen," first section.

created diagrams, of which he remarked "though they are without writing, I speak all day without ever departing from them. Indeed, the principles of heaven, earth, and the ten-thousand things are fully expressed in their midst."[64] Su Shih claimed that *tao* was unknowable, *a fortiori* inexpressible. Instead he practiced poetry, prose, and calligraphy that demonstrated how his *wen* brought *tao* into practice. Ch'eng I and Chu Hsi insisted that students must go beyond the words of any text. Ch'eng, for example, ends the preface to his *I Ching* commentary with this instruction: "What I have transmitted is the texts. Grasping the meaning from the texts is up to the reader."[65] Chu Hsi urged students to appropriate meaning for themselves, thereby potentially realizing the mind of the sages. (He was, however, much less optimistic than Ch'eng that such a reading would be successful.)

Why then did these four men concern themselves so much with the Classics? First, to speak negatively, the Classics were cultural objects that they could not ignore if they wished to speak for and to all literati. More positively, the Classics were their patrimony, however much Shao and Ch'eng attempted to ground them outside historical time. Rather than being the objects of antiquarian or philological inquiry, the Classics were instead the most acute, profound, and vast account of issues such as human nature and natural process. All four men were also able to find in the *I* particular evidence that the greatest human minds of the past had thought as they themselves did now. Their final solution, however, was to read the Classics as evidence that the Classics could, and must, be transcended.

These men found enormous latitude to remake that cultural tradition from within. The response to this remaking is worth noting, however. Su and Ch'eng were among the first literati in Sung times to have disciples and schools, and Chu perfected that institution. These disciples were not as bold as their masters, and treated their teachers' insights as canonical themselves. In this context, the function of "the Classics" was filled by the canonized teachings of the iconoclastic teacher.[66] All but Su seem to have encouraged this, for all four men, including Su, viewed their overturning of received tradition as the recovery of the true tradition. Still, some students went too far and misunderstood the nature of the new orthodoxy, imagining it to entail the aping of their teacher. One of Ch'eng's lesser students complained that

---

[64] *Huang-chi ching-shih shu* 7A.34b.

[65] *I-chuan* 2.8.

[66] For a discussion of this phenomenon, see Wm. Theodore deBary, *Neo-Confucian Orthodoxy and the Learning of the Mind-and-Heart* (New York: Columbia University Press, 1981), pp. 9–13.

"the teacher wants to make everyone the same (*t'ung*) as him."

The teacher did not answer.

A disciple said: "What the teacher wants to make the same—it's not making them the same as himself, he really wants sameness in *tao*."[67]

With the exception of Su, these men also viewed multiple interpretations of the *I* as evidence of other men's faulty understanding—we have seen, for example, Chu Hsi's criticisms of the other three. For them, there really was only one *I*, which each man claimed to understand. For all but Su we could also say that this was so because there was only one structure to heaven-and-earth. Our modern notion that multiple readings grow from the fundamental indeterminacy of texts would not have made sense to any of them.

As Universal Process

As universal process, the *I* was felt capable of representing everything taking place in heaven-and-earth. Of course, the manner in which these universal processes were expressed differs from man to man. Ch'eng I states that "The meaning of the *I* is the *tao* of heaven-and-earth."[68] Shao Yung remarks that "The *I* possesses 384 lines. These are the true *wen* (pattern, text) of heaven."[69] And we have seen many, many other ways of addressing this question.

Nonetheless, our four men agreed that universal process constitutes a set of relationships among all things, and that this relationship is dynamic. The *I* is, indeed, a classic (*ching*) of change (*i*). We have spent several chapters discussing the relationships that each man saw pertaining among things. Here we will discuss their notions of change. We should begin by noting that for these men, change does not mean reform and that, apart from yin and yang, they had little theory of change as such. Change is above all the arena in which one is constantly presented with new situations demanding an immediate response—since appropriate behavior cannot be derived from a set of rules. Thus Chu Hsi might be speaking for all four men when he says, "Apt yet unpredictable response is how the pattern functions."[70]

Shao Yung seems at first the exception. There is an apparent rigidity to his system that perhaps prompted Joseph Needham's famous remark that

the *Book of Changes* was a system for *pigeon-holing novelty* and then doing nothing more about it. Its universal system of symbolism constituted a stupen-

[67] *Erh-Ch'eng chi*, p. 444 (*Wai-shu* 12).
[68] *Erh-Ch'eng chi*, p. 1028 (*Ching-shuo* 1).
[69] 7A.23a.
[70] *Chou Lien-hsi chi*, p. 87, commenting on chapter 4 of Chou Tun-i's *T'ung-shu*.

dous *filing-system*. It led to a stylization of concepts almost analogous to the stylizations which have in some ages occurred in art forms, and which finally prevented painters from looking at Nature at all.[71]

Certainly our men have little interest in novelty in its own right—not even Su Shih. But even Shao's system has both a synchronic and diachronic aspect: it is about relationships between existing categories of things, but it also describes how new things come into being to assume their places in this orderly world.

At one point Shao discusses a passage from *Hsi-tz'u* B7 on constancy and change. It reads:

> As a text, the *I* cannot be kept at a distance. As *tao*, it constantly shifts its abode. It changes and moves without dwelling [anywhere]. It flows circling through the six empty places.

Shao explains that "the six empty places are the six line positions [of the hexagram]. They are empty in order to await the matters that 'change and move.' "[72]

Elsewhere Shao has referred to these six as representing the six bifurcations by which one moves from one to sixty-four.[73] These are set. But what emerges through them is ever new. And that emergence can occur only because the positions "are empty in order to await the matters that 'change and move.' " Shao is, in other words, well aware of the difference between categories of order, on the one hand, and that which fills those categories, on the other. His own work is most famous for its attention to the former, but all his moral teaching is directed at the individuals who must fill the roles that the cycles of heaven-and-earth prepare for them. While they can do nothing to alter the largest pattern of rise and decline, their ability to see into the nature of heaven-and-earth and become sages themselves is at the heart of Shao's teaching.[74]

Moreover, the rigidity of Shao's system stands in sharp contrast with the spirit of his poetry, which is attuned to the spontaneous movement of things and which wonders at their continuous, harmonious production. Here is a poem from his series of "Autumn Reminiscences":

[71] Joseph Needham, *Science and Civilisation in China* (Cambridge: Cambridge University Press, 1956), vol. 2, p. 336.

[72] 7B.21a.

[73] 7A.24b, as discussed in chapter 4.

[74] Mao Huai-hsin has argued that Shao's system of change is also a system of progressive history ("Shao Yung ti jen-sheng-kuan yü li-shih che-hsüeh," *Chung-kuo che-hsüeh* 12 [1984], pp. 161–75). But the present discussion suggests that there is a significant gap in Shao's thought between the largest cosmic developments, which are set, and the level on which individuals operate, making moral decisions. A truly progressive history must be conceived to somehow join these two.

A butterfly circles the cold chrysanthemum.
A cricket calls by empty steps.
With a dog lying before the gate,
Without a guest coming throughout the day.
Clear waves flow tranquilly mid-stream.
White clouds rest quietly in clumps.
How does heaven's harmony arise?
From time to time I drink a cup of wine.[75]

As a Practice

In conclusion we should return to the *I*'s usefulness to Sung literati. All
four men we have examined here saw it as providing a means to move
from a text to the universal process it embodies via the practice of *hsüeh*.
But each understood this differently. For Su Shih the *I* illustrates the universal but cumulative process of bringing culture into being, elaborating
upon the past, transforming it, and continuing it. The *I* is *wen* that is
grounded in *tao*, the one source whence all things ultimately arise. As a
text created over time by ancient sages, it is a manifestation of their *tao*
of joining fundamental unity with the dualistic variations of social life. It
follows for Su that men can think of the *I* in two ways. First, they can
take the sixty-four hexagrams and associated texts as practical guides to
sorting out their own circumstances and determining a course of action
that will allow them to act for the common good and avoid endangering
themselves. As Su says, they will be able to "make few their errors." Su
does not argue against the value of having external standards, as long as
the text or institution is the product of men who made the connection to
tao.

It is possible, however, to aim higher and act as a sage oneself—which
leads to the second way men can think about the *I*. Su sees the sages as
men who worked back through the accumulated layers of culture, text,
and experience of their predecessors to arrive at the intuition of the unity
of the ultimate source of all things. This movement through the world of
man's culture, a journey back in time through the historical tradition, is
an exploration of ever more profound and inclusive patterns of commonality. It culminates in a leap into that mysterious state where one experiences unity yet realizes one cannot "hold it fast." There one acts, speaks
and writes without hesitation or calculation in response to the situation
of the moment. The *I* is proof that men who have attained this moral
autonomy can in fact produce works that serve as normative guides for

[75] *I-ch'uan chi-jang chi* (*Su-pu ts'ung-k'an* ed.), "Ch'iu-huai san-shih-liu shou" 28: 3.42b.

their times and the future. In the *Hsi-tzu-chuan* Su finds statements he believes describe this process in some detail.

We have, then, two seemingly contradictory views. In the first, we are told that there are guides to the moral life that we can follow. In the second, we are told that the real model for a moral man is the cultivation of his ability to be morally autonomous. But the contradiction is only apparent. Su has given an account of how men in the present can create classics (*ching*, constants) for their own day. He supposes that few men will achieve this, but those who do can bring into being works that the rest can live by. His vision thus allows him to believe it possible to hold together two sets of concerns that have, in fact, become separate. Su Shih, like his contemporaries, was aware of the disjunction between past and present. Sung men could no longer read the Classics as the ancients had. They could not accept them as normative without having to infer from them the meanings and values they believed could guide men's minds. In Su's account of how the sages created classics and how he creates literary works, the works of the present are informed by the author's threading of the past. Thus the nagging awareness that he saw the ancients quite differently from how they saw themselves, this painful burden of self-consciousness, is at least ameliorated by the conviction that at some level the culture of the present can be made to contain the cultural traditions of the past.

But there is a far deeper problem. By Su Shih's time it was simply impossible to maintain that cultural accomplishments were of value, merely by virtue of their being *wen*. The separation between *wen* and *tao*, between culture and value, could not be overlooked. What we see in this greatest of literary men is an attempt to show that the two can in fact be held together without reducing either. *Tao*, as the ultimate source, will not be reduced to a doctrine; it will remain ineffable and mysterious, beyond man's control. Culture, as the ongoing elaboration and transformation of past traditions, will continue as well, the creation of the new and unique now given license. And yet, Su would have it, it is possible to achieve unity with *tao* while returning to the realm of man's culture to act in a morally responsible fashion, that is, to create things that can truly serve as models to guide others to a harmonious and benevolent society. The *I Ching* is a text that demonstrates how constancy, discerned by sages in the past, is available in the present; how *wen* leads one back to *tao*; and how new cultural forms can emerge constantly from *tao*.

Shao Yung saw the *I* as the materials that, prior to his own work, best expressed the orderliness existing on several levels in heaven-and-earth. As images, the *I* provided the markers whereby one might keep track of the ten-thousand things, both in their relationship to each other and as they came into being. As number, it captured the still more fundamental relationships of cosmic cycles. The text also acknowledged the levels of spirit (*shen*) and principle (*li*), which were necessarily not subject to articulation. And it was the *locus classicus* of *t'ai-chi*, the great ultimate of heaven-and-earth.

But once he has obtained these terms, Shao provides them with special technical meanings, and the hexagram and line statements are in any case nearly useless to him. The *I* system, too, can only suggest his own. Once his is established, he reapplies it to the *I* so as to reorder the sixty-four hexagrams into the binary sequence. Nonetheless, he still shares many of the assumptions of the others: the *I* sets out the orderliness of heaven-and-earth, it represents universal process, it encompasses everything, and on its basis we can determine significant matters in the present world. The practice of "contemplating things" that it teaches is the way to sagehood.

Ch'eng I's primary exposition of the *I Ching* took the form of a commentary on the hexagram and line statements. While Su and Chu also commented on these, their more philosophically important writings on the *I* addressed the *Hsi-tz'u-chuan* or consisted of separate essays. It is worth considering why and how an *I Ching* commentary meets Ch'eng I's needs so well. We have discussed Ch'eng's understanding of the pattern as a huge network uniting all things of heaven-and-earth. The goal of learning or *hsüeh* is to see that pattern whole in each thing or event one encounters, to see it so plainly that it is impossible to go against it through selfish action. The student's progress in this endeavor is through the investigation of the pattern in the many things of his life—in obedience if a small child, in texts when he can read, in social interactions at all stages. In each, he has the opportunity to see his true nature, to realize it, and so to realize the pattern.

For Ch'eng I the *I Ching* is the literatus's world in microcosm; it thus offers him a chance to speak to all these moral issues. Indeed, a reading of the *Reflections on Things at Hand*, one-sixth of whose selections are from Ch'eng's *I-chuan*, can give the impression that Ch'eng uses his *I Ching* commentary merely as an opportunity to advise literati on the moral aspect of everything they do. But, as we have seen, despite the centrality of proper action to his teachings, Ch'eng resolutely condemns a simple mapping of *I* text to life situations. For what is powerful about his conception of the pattern is that it is ultimately unitary as well as multiple. His commentary works to show how that is true, moving back and forth between the most particular, the most general, and the most rarefied examples. An *I Ching* commentary is the ideal literary genre to present this type of complex intermingling. His *I-chuan* is in this sense less the exposition of a philosophy than its demonstration. It is thus something that cannot be summarized, excerpted, or adequately conveyed in an abstraction of its main points. Such an abstraction is bound to reify the pattern, and thus prevent a full realization of the *I* as a practice.

The prominence of divination in Chu Hsi's approach to the *I* is its most notable feature. It is, of course, related to his treatment of Fu-hsi, whose version of the *I* was simply a system of hexagram divination. A precise characterization of Chu's personal attitude toward divination is difficult. As we have seen in chapter 6, he regarded divination as an aid in the process of self-cultivation, and much of his written work on the *I* only makes sense as an attempt to guide students in its proper use. But he was uneasy about its possible misuses. He said it should only be used when one's own spiritual and intellectual resources were exhausted. The extent to which he himself practiced divination is open to question. Only one case is documented, and that was done at the suggestion of Ts'ai Yüan-ting, whose other interests included the symbolic and numerological lore of the pitch-pipes.[76] It is, of course, possible that divination was so commonplace among Sung literati that it rarely deserved mention. However, it is more likely that Chu felt himself capable of knowing what to do in most cases without resorting to divination. A sage, of course, had no need for divination, although Chu never called himself a sage.

Let us reflect now from a more philosophical perspective on the meaning of divination in Chu Hsi's system. Recall the parallelism between the mind of the sage and the *I*: both are "spiritual" and "wise," and both are capable of detecting incipient change. The idea that the sage can detect incipiencies and thus "see the future" while ordinary people must occasionally resort to divination reflects the essential tension in Chu Hsi's thought between two aspects of mind: the "moral mind" or "mind of the Way" (*tao-hsin*) and the "human mind" (*jen-hsin*).[77] While mind is essentially indivisible, one must distinguish these two aspects. The mind of the sage is guided by the moral mind according to the pattern of heaven (*t'ien-li*). The mind of the ordinary person is generally guided by human desires (*jen-yü*) and must be "rectified" or clarified through self-cultivation. This means "causing the moral mind always to be master of one's person, and the human mind always to listen to its commands."[78] Divination is a way of "listening" to the mind of the sage, which is essentially equivalent to the moral mind inherent in every person. The sages who created the *I* and wrote its texts thus symbolize the inherent perfectibility

---

[76] See Huang Tsung-hsi, *Sung-Yüan hsüeh-an* (A scholarly record of the Sung and Yüan dynasties) (*Ssu-pu pei-yao* ed.), *chüan* 62.

[77] *Chung-yung chang-chü* (Commentary on the Doctrine of the Mean), in *Ssu-shu chi-chu*, preface, p.1a–1b. The terms come from the *Shu Ching* (Book of Documents), "Counsels of the Great Yü." See James Legge, trans., *The Chinese Classics*, 2d ed. (Hong Kong: Hong Kong University Press, 1960 reprint of 1893 original), vol. 3, pp. 61–62.

[78] *Chung-yung chang-chü*, preface, 1b.

of every human being. And divination, like Fu-hsi's creation of the *I*, is a paradigm of knowing, of "fathoming the (dynamic) pattern" (*ch'iung-li*) in which human life is embedded, and responding to the pattern by fitting one's activity to it.

Furthermore, divination is a form of *experiential* knowing, at least to the extent that the subject incorporates the oracular counsel into his or her life. This is why Chu Hsi argues so vehemently against using the *I* merely as a book of moral principles, which can be *read* without being *learned*. By carrying out or enacting (*hsing*) the sagely wisdom of the *I*, one is not merely reading or learning *about* the pattern of heaven-and-earth. Rather one is internalizing the pattern and thus transforming one-self into a sage. This is the kind of personal moral transformation that Chu Hsi felt was the necessary basis for the political restoration and moral revitalization of Sung culture. While Ch'eng I had also intended literati to pattern their activity after the *I*, Chu thought that Ch'eng's failure to insist on the divinatory context allowed for a merely abstract understanding of the text, when what Chu believed was necessary (all the more so in his own time than in Ch'eng's) was concrete, subjective engagement with the *I*. The *I* was unique among the Classics in providing a practical method by which to effect this experiential learning.

We might summarize these remarks as follows. First, the *I* describes the place of human beings within universal processes, showing them a constant source of values amidst the multiplicity of change. In this way, the *I* is important evidence that the world is coherent and that its order is accessible to human consciousness. Second, the *I* also provides a means to realize this order—"realize" in the sense both of "understand" and "actualize." It does this by being at once a guide to action, a representation of such an order as it exists in both heaven-and-earth and the sage's mind, and a practice of self-cultivation. Third, such a practice allows literati to participate in the workings of universal process to the best of their abilities. A poor student will follow its forms. But a good student will embody its changes, recognizing true values without dependence on textual, social, or political authorities. He will thus be able to mediate between nature and culture.

The *I Ching* was invoked in most of the major intellectual arguments of the eleventh and twelfth centuries. This is not only evidence of its flexibility and capacity to express subtle and varied relationships. It also suggests how literati concerns with such matters as politics, religion, philosophy, literature, and morality were felt to be inseparable from each other, and from the changes of heaven-and-earth.

The Fu Hexagram

THIS APPENDIX contains six translations of hexagram #24 Fu (Return). The first is from the Wilhelm/Baynes text.[1] The second is a reconstruction by Richard Kunst of the original *I Ching* as it may have existed in the early first millennium B.C.E.[2] These are followed by the complete commentaries on the Fu hexagram of Wang Pi,[3] Su Shih,[4] Ch'eng I,[5] and Chu Hsi.[6] Shao Yung, of course, did not write a commentary.

Commentaries are hard to read through because they were not designed to be read from beginning to end. Instead one was meant to consult them in response to a particular need—divination, the clarification of a political principle, self-cultivation. These needs create texts that are by our standards fragmentary, consisting of sixty-four or more individual essays. Furthermore, the general principles that inform them are only obliquely argued out in the commentary itself. Prefaces are usually more accessible, as are essays like the *Hsi-tz'u-chuan* or Wang Pi's *Chou-i lüeh-li* (see chapter 1). These are therefore usually the best place to begin.

But to truly understand the commentator we must read his commentary. And there are other things we can learn about textual interpretation only by comparing several commentaries. These include the variety of legitimate modes of apprehending the *I* text, the number of ways to give a coherent reading of a hexagram, the numerous acceptable means to constitute the relationship of the six lines, etc. These differences reveal the relative lack of constraint the *I Ching* text places on its commentators and the corresponding extent to which the commentaries depend on their authors' larger vision of the world. Yet even men with similar worldviews use the *I* in very different areas of their thought, as this book has demonstrated.

---

[1] Pp. 504–08.

[2] *The Original "Yijing": A Text, Phonetic Transcription, Translation, and Indexes, With Sample Glosses* (Ann Arbor: University Microfilms International, 1985), p. 287.

[3] From *Ku-chu shih-san-ching* (The old commentaries on the *Thirteen Classics*)(*Ssu-pu chi-yao* ed.), p. 19.

[4] *Su Shih I-chuan*, 3.57–59.

[5] *I-ch'uan I-chuan* 104.10–108.7. Kidder Smith would like to thank Professor Cheng Tsai-fa for his careful reading of an earlier version of this translation.

[6] *Chou-i pen-i* 1:48–49a, and *Chou-i che-chung*, pp. 304–5, 669–71.

WILHELM/BAYNES

Fu/Return (The Turning Point)

The Sequence [*Hsü-kua*]
Things cannot be destroyed once and for all. When what is above is completely split apart, it returns below. Hence there follows the hexagram of RETURN.

Miscellaneous Notes [*Tsa-kua*]
RETURN means coming back.

THE JUDGMENT [Hexagram statement]
RETURN. Success.
Going out and coming in without error.
Friends come without blame.
To and fro goes the way.
On the seventh day comes return.
It furthers one to have somewhere to go.

Commentary on the Decision [*T'uan-chuan*]
   "RETURN has success." The firm returns.
   Movement and action through devotion. Therefore, "Going out and coming in without error."
   "Friends come without blame. To and fro goes the way. On the seventh day comes return." This is the course of heaven.
   "It furthers one to have somewhere to go." The firm is on the increase.
   In the hexagram of RETURN one sees the mind of heaven and earth.

THE IMAGE [*Hsiang-chuan*]
Thunder within the earth:
The image of THE TURNING POINT.
Thus the kings of antiquity closed the passes
At the time of solstice.
Merchants and strangers did not go about,
And the ruler
Did not travel through the provinces.

THE LINES
Nine at the beginning:
a) [Line statement]
   Return from a short distance.
   No need for remorse.
   Great good fortune.
b) [*Hsiang-chuan*]
   "Return from a short distance": thus one cultivates one's character.

Six in the second place:
a) Quiet return. Good fortune.
b) The good fortune of a quiet return depends on subordination to a good man.

Six in the third place:
a) Repeated return. Danger. No blame.
b) The danger of repeated return is, in its essential meaning, deliverance from blame.

Six in the fourth place:
a) Walking in the midst of others,
   One returns alone.
b) "Walking in the midst of others, one returns alone," and so follows the right way.

Six in the fifth place:
a) Noblehearted return. No remorse.
b) "Noblehearted return. No remorse." Central, therefore he is able to test himself.

Six at the top:
a) Missing the return. Misfortune.
   Misfortune from within and without.
   If armies are set marching in this way,
   One will in the end suffer a great defeat,
   Disastrous for the ruler of the country.
   For ten years
   It will not be possible to attack again.
b) The misfortune in missing the return lies in opposing the way of the superior man.

RICHARD KUNST, *THE ORIGINAL YIJING*

24.0 Treat.
    In going out and coming in there will be no illness.
    A friend will come without misfortune.
    He will turn around and go back on his way.
    He will come and return in seven days.
    Favorable for having somewhere to go.

24.1 If he does not return from far away, there will be no harm or trouble. Very auspicious.

24.2 A happy return. Auspicious.

24.3 Return along the brink of a river.
Threatening, but there will be no misfortune.

24.4 Return alone in the middle of the road.

24.5 Return from a raid to take captives. No trouble.

24.6 He will get lost on his return.
Ominous. There will be a calamity.
If used to mobilize the army, in the end there will be a great defeat, extending to the ruler of the state.
Ominous. For ten years they cannot attack.

WANG PI'S COMMENTARY

HEXAGRAM STATEMENT: Fu. Successful. Going out and going in are without distress. Friends come and it is without fault. Reverting and returning to *tao*. It returns in seven days. It is beneficial whatever one does.

T'UAN-CHUAN: "Fu, successful"—the firm returns. One acts with compliance so that "going in and out will be without distress."

COMMENTARY: "Going in" means reversion. "Going out" means the firm grows. Therefore it is "without distress." "Distress" is like sickness.

T'UAN-CHUAN (continued): "Friends come—it is without fault."

COMMENTARY: "Friends" means yang.

T'UAN-CHUAN (continued): It reverts and returns to *tao*. In seven days comes its return.

COMMENTARY: From the time when the yang-*ch'i* begins to be totally stripped away[7] until the coming of its return is always seven days.

T'UAN-CHUAN (continued): The heavens revolve.

COMMENTARY: According to the revolutions of heaven, reverting and returning does not take longer than seven days. The return cannot be from far away.

T'UAN-CHUAN (continued): "It is beneficial wherever one goes"—the firm grows.

COMMENTARY: As it goes, the *tao* of the inferior man declines.

T'UAN-CHUAN (continued): Doesn't Fu make apparent the heart/mind of heaven-and-earth?

COMMENTARY: Fu means "reverting to the root." Heaven-and-earth take the root to be their heart/mind. Whatever moves [at some point] ceases and is tranquil. [Yet] tranquillity is not the opposite of movement. Speech ceases and it is quiet. [Yet] quiet is not the opposite of speech. In

[7] The preceding hexagram #23 Po means "stripping away." It consists of five yin lines below one yang line. The notion is that yang has gradually retreated and that only the top line is still yang.

this way, although heaven-and-earth are great—they richly contain the ten-thousand things, thunder occurs, the winds circulate, bringing ten-thousand transformations—silence and utter nothing, these are their root. Thus when movement ceases amidst the earth, only then is the heart/mind of heaven-and-earth apparent. If they took being (having, existence) as their root, then the different categories [of things] could not preserve their existence.

HSIANG-CHUAN: Thunder is amidst the earth. Fu. The former kings closed the passes on the solstice. Merchant travelers did not proceed. Rulers did not inspect their domains.

COMMENTARY: "Domains" are "affairs." The winter solstice [lit. "winter arrives"] is the return of yin. The summer solstice is the return of yang. Thus Fu is to arrive at silence and great tranquillity. The former kings are those who acted on the rules of heaven-and-earth. When movement returns [to the root], it is tranquil. When action returns, it ceases. When affairs return, it is without affairs.

FIRST LINE: Not far and returning. Without reaching repentance. Primally auspicious.

COMMENTARY: One is situated at the very beginning of the return. The initial return is not speedy. Consequently if one arrives at confusion and inauspiciousness, one [can still] return from not far off. There is some regret, but one comes back. If one uses this in self-cultivation, disasters and difficulties are far away. If one uses this in tending to affairs, it is very close to the mark. Therefore it is primally auspicious.

HSIANG-CHUAN: "Returning from not far" in order to cultivate oneself.

LINE TWO: Beautiful return. Auspicious.

COMMENTARY: It attains its [proper] position, situated in the center (*chung*, the Mean). It is the closest to the first. Above are no yang lines to cast doubts on its kinship [to the first line]. Yang means acting in accordance with *jen*. Being above the first line and being in compliance with it is what is meant by "having *jen* below one." Having situated oneself in the central position, being kin with *jen* and rejoicing in its closeness: this is the beauty of return.

HSIANG-CHUAN: The auspiciousness of the beautiful return is that it has *jen* below it.

LINE THREE: Frequent return. Danger. No fault.

COMMENTARY: "Frequent" has the quality of stumbling. [The line] is situated at the end (top) of the lower body (trigram). Although it is surpassed by the confusion of the top line, it is already far from return: this is its stumbling. Stumbling yet seeking to return—it has not reached confusion [like line six]. Thus although it is dangerous, it is without fault. It is appropriate to be quick in returning to *tao*. Stumbling, then in fact returning: though the meaning is "without fault," if it happens again it will be difficult to preserve [oneself].

HSIANG-CHUAN: The "danger of the frequent return": the meaning is "without fault."

LINE FOUR: Proceeding centrally, returning alone.

COMMENTARY: Both above and below the fourth line are two *yin* lines, and it is situated in their midst. Stepping into its position, it responds (*ying*) to the first line. It alone attains that whereby one returns—complying with *tao* and reverting. Nothing will conflict with it. Therefore it says, "Proceeding centrally, returning alone."

HSIANG-CHUAN: "Centrally proceeding, returning alone," whereby one follows *tao*.

LINE FIVE: Nobly returning. Without repentance.

COMMENTARY: It dwells in the noble and proceeds in the center. Dwelling in the noble, it is without resentment. Proceeding in the center, it is able to examine itself. Though it is not sufficient to reach the "auspiciousness of the beautiful return," if one protects one's nobility by returning, regret can be avoided.

HSIANG-CHUAN: "Nobly returning, without repentance." It is central, whereby one can examine oneself.

LINE SIX: Confused return. Inauspiciousness. There are calamities and errors. If one were to set troops in motion, it would end in great defeat, bringing inauspiciousness to the country's lord. Even in ten years it could not be corrected.

COMMENTARY: It takes its place at the very last line of "return." This "confusion" is a confusion in one's seeking to return. Therefore it says "confused return." It is difficult to use it to set troops in motion. There can be conquests, but in the end there must be a great defeat. Using it within the state goes against the ruler's *tao*. One will return only after a great defeat. Evaluating these conditions, although one returns for ten years to repair it, one still cannot correct it.

HSIANG-CHUAN: The "inauspiciousness of being confused in returning" is that it opposes the ruler's *tao*.

SU SHIH'S COMMENTARY

Fu-Returning. Chen (thunder) below and K'un (earth) above.

HEXAGRAM STATEMENT: Fu (Returning). Success. Coming in and going out without ill. A friend comes—no distress. Coming back and returning to its *tao*. On the seventh day it returns. It is beneficial to go somewhere.

T'UAN-CHUAN: "*Fu*. Success." The firm [yang] comes back. It is active but proceeds by according. Thus "coming in and going out without ill (*chi*)."

COMMENTARY: [The change] from [hexagram #2] K'un to Fu [in the *hsien-t'ien* sequence] is called "coming in." From Fu to [hexagram #1] Ch'ien is called "going out." "*Chi*" means "ill."

T'UAN-CHUAN (continued): "A friend comes—no distress. Coming back and returning to its *tao*. On the seventh day it returns." This is heaven's course.

COMMENTARY: It says "seven" because [the six lines of] K'un and the [one] yang line make "seven."

T'UAN-CHUAN (continued): "It is beneficial to go somewhere." The firm [yang] increases. In Fu (Returning) do we not see the mind of heaven-and-earth?

COMMENTARY: Seeing the direction of its intent we call it "mind." Seeing that it has truly become so we call it "actuality" [*ch'ing* or human emotional response]. Whenever a thing is about to perish but returns (*fu*), it can only do so because heaven-and-earth permit it. Therefore when yang is diminishing, five [yang lines] remain [as in hexagram #44 Kou, the inverse of this situation], but it is not enough [to stop the decline of yang]. When it is "increasing" [as here in the Fu hexagram], at first it is one [line], yet that is more than sufficient. How could this be [merely] human effort? The *[Tso] Commentary* says, "That which Heaven is overthrowing cannot be supported."[8] Nor can what it supports be overthrown. To oppose heaven does not bode well. There certainly will be great "distress."

HSIANG-CHUAN: Thunder [Chen trigram] within the earth [K'un trigram]. Fu. The Former Kings shut the passes on the solstice. Merchants did not travel. Lords did not inspect territory.

COMMENTARY: Fu is the very moment of change (*pien-i chih chi*). When a sage is at a moment of change he is tranquil, waiting for it to settle [into the new situation]. He may not try to accomplish something through intervention (*yu wei*). Therefore it uses [the phrase] "shut the passes on the solstice" to make this clear. Below "merchants did not travel" and above "lords did not inspect territory."

YANG FIRST LINE: Not having gone far, it returns. No need for remorse. Great good fortune. The Image reads: "Having not gone far, it returns," because he has cultivated his person.

COMMENTARY: Leaving where he lives but going back again, or losing what he has but getting back again, is called Fu (Returning). He must have left, and then there can be going back. He must have lost, and then there can be getting back. There is no going back without having left;

---

[8] *Tso chuan*, Ting 1, *The Chinese Classics*, trans. Legge, vol. 5, p. 745.

there is no getting back without having lost. This is why there is no "returning" for a sage. A yang first line means he has once seen himself to be in error. However, there has begun to be a "return." Confucius said, "The son of the Yen clan [Yen Hui], is he not quite close? If there is something not good he always knows. If he knows he never returns to practice [it] (*fu hsing*)."[9]

YIN SECOND LINE: To consider beautiful the return. Good fortune. The Image reads: The "good fortune" of "beauty returning" is due to submitting to the benevolent.

COMMENTARY: "To consider beautiful" refers to the yang first line. [Here the second line,] with a yin [line] occupying the yin [position], is the perfection of non-competition. [This second line] retiring, considers [the first line] beautiful, so that the one returning [i.e., the first line] gains credibility. This is called "to consider beautiful the return."

YIN THIRD LINE: Frowning (*p'in*) at the return. Danger. No distress. The Image reads: The danger of "frowning at the return"; the meaning is "no distress."

COMMENTARY: With a yin [line] occupying the yang [position], it does not have the strength to resist, yet within it does not wish [to submit]. Therefore it "frowns" at the return of the yang first line. For one who externally agrees but internally is not content there is no distress when in danger. *P'in* means "frowning."

YIN FOURTH LINE: Proceeding in the middle, alone at the return. The Image reads: "Proceeding in the middle, alone at the return" in order to follow *tao*.

COMMENTARY: [This fourth line, which is] "alone," and the yang first line respond to each other.

YIN FIFTH LINE: In favor of the return. No distress. The Image reads: "In favor of the return"—no regret. Within he examines himself.

COMMENTARY: When one anticipates troubling problems before they have arrived, there will be "no regret." At this fifth line yin is flourishing. Yet internally he calculates that ultimately he will be unable to resist the yang first line. Therefore, he attaches himself to the [fourth line which is] "alone at the return" of the yin fourth line to entrust himself to it [for protection].

YIN SIXTH LINE: Missing the return. Misfortune. There are calamities. If the armies are set in motion, there will be a great defeat in the end, and the state and ruler will be unfortunate. For ten years it will not be possible to attack. The Image reads: The "misfortune of missing the return" is due to having gone contrary to the ruler's *tao*.

COMMENTARY: When he rides the end of the peak of the flourishing [of

---

[9] *Hsi-tz'u-chuan* B4.

yin], employing it unceasingly, while unaware that the yang first line has already returned, it is called "missing the return." "Calamities" manifest heaven's punishment. The return of the yang first line is [due to] heaven. All the multitude agrees, but he alone "misses" it. Employ [the one in this sixth position against] the enemy, and he will bring disaster to his state. Employ him in the state, and he will bring disaster upon himself. Reaching the peak of flourishing, there must be decline. Repeated victories, therefore "defeat." In the end the "state" is "defeated" and the "ruler" unfortunate." That even "for ten years" he will not return makes clear his errors in employing the people and in his extent of warfare.

CH'ENG I's COMMENTARY

Fu. [The trigram] Chen below, [the trigram] K'un above.

COMMENTARY: The Hsü-kua:[10] "Things cannot be finally exhausted. 'Stripped Away' [hexagram #23 Po] above, it reverts below. Thus it is met by Fu." Things do not have the pattern of being completely stripped away. Thus, when stripping reaches its extreme, comes return. When yin reaches its extreme, yang is born. When yang is stripped to the extreme above, it returns and is born below. Exhausted above, it reverts below. This is how Fu follows Po.

As a hexagram, one yang is born below five yin. Yin reaches its extreme and yang returns. In the tenth [lunar] month, when the flourishing of yin has reached its extreme, there is the winter solstice. Then one yang returns and is born within the earth. Therefore it is "return."

Yang is the tao of the superior man (chün-tzu). Yang declines to the extreme and then returns again. The tao of the superior man declines to the extreme and then grows again. Therefore it has the meaning of returning to the good.

HEXAGRAM STATEMENT: Fu. Successful. Going out and going in are without distress. Friends come and it is without fault.

COMMENTARY: "Fu, successful"—having returned, it is successful. The yang ch'i returns and is again produced below. It gradually succeeds, and produces and nourishes the myriad things. The tao of the superior man having returned, success can gradually enrich the world. Therefore in Fu there is the pattern of succeeding.

"Going out and going in are without distress." "Going out and in" means being produced and growing. When it returns and is produced inside, it is "going in." When it grows and advances outside, it is "going out." It mentions "going out" first for reasons of euphony. The produc-

10 "The Ordered Hexagrams," Wing 9, W/B "The Sequence."

tion of yang is not from the outside. It comes about within. Thus it says "going in."

When things are first produced, their *ch'i* is most subtle. Thus there is often difficulty at the beginning. When yang is first produced, its *ch'i* is most subtle. Thus it often snaps off. What is produced by the spring yang is split by the yin cold. If one observes the grasses and trees at dawn and dusk, then this can be seen.

"Going out and going in are without distress" means that when the subtle yang is born and grows there is nothing to harm it. Since there is nothing to harm it, it and its kind gradually advance and will be successful. Therefore "it is without fault." "Fault" in regard to *ch'i* is to deviate [from the proper balance]. In regard to the superior man it is to be blocked and not attain to fully realizing the pattern. When yang is just returning, even if there is distress, it could surely not arrest its return. There could be only a hindrance, for the qualities of the hexagram mean "without distress"—the goodness of returning to *tao*.

The one yang, when it is first born, is of the utmost subtlety and surely cannot yet overcome all the yin and bring forth the production of the myriad things. It must await the coming of the other yang. Only after that can it succeed in producing things and be without deviation and have friends come and be without fault. The three yang—the *ch'i* of *tzu*, *ch'ou* and *yin*[11]—produce and develop the myriad things; this is the success of the many yang.

If the *tao* of the superior man has already declined and then returned, how could it just conquer the inferior man? It must await the gradual flourishing of its friends and kind, and then they can join their strength to conquer them.

HEXAGRAM STATEMENT (continued): Reverting and returning to *tao*. In seven days comes the return. It is beneficial whatever one does.

COMMENTARY: It means that the *tao* of decline and growth alternately return. After the decline of yang, in seven days there comes a return. [Hexagram #44] Kou is the first waning of yang.[12] After seven changes it becomes Fu, so it says "seven days," meaning seven changes.[13] [The hexagram statement of #19] Lin says, "In the eighth month there is inauspiciousness," which means that the growth of yang is overtaken by the growth of yin in the eighth month.

---

[11] These are the Early Branches correlated with the eleventh, twelfth and first lunar month. It is in these months that yang prepares and executes its return.

[12] Kou is the opposite of Fu, with one broken line in the first place and five solid lines above it.

[13] These "seven changes" begin with the hexagram Ch'ien, with all solid lines. Starting with the bottom line, one line at a time turns into its opposite. After six changes Ch'ien has become K'un. The seventh change brings a solid line back. This is Fu.

Yang advances and yin retreats. The *tao* of the superior man grows, and the *tao* of the petty man declines. Therefore "it is beneficial whatever one does."

T'UAN-CHUAN: "Fu. Successful." The firm reverts. In acting, to behave compliantly. This is "going out and going in are without distress. Friends come and it is without fault."

COMMENTARY: "Fu, successful" means that "the firm reverts" and so it is successful. The decline of yang-firm has reached its extreme, and it has reverted. Once it has reverted, it gradually grows and flourishes and is all-successful.

"In acting, to behave compliantly. This is 'going out and going in are without distress; friends come and it is without fault.' " Using the qualities of the hexagram to express how this is so: the lower [trigram] acts and the upper complies. This is "in acting to behave compliantly." The yang-firm reverts and acts compliantly. This is to attain "going out and going in without distress, friends come and it is without fault." The coming of friends is also compliant action.

T'UAN-CHUAN (continued): "Reverting and returning to *tao*. In seven days comes the return." The heavens proceed (*hsing*, revolve). "It is beneficial whatever one does." The firm grows. Doesn't Fu make apparent the mind of heaven-and-earth!

COMMENTARY: Its *tao* reverts and returns, going and coming, alternately declining and rising. "In seven days comes the return"—the revolutions of heaven are like this. That decline and growth follow each other is the pattern of heaven. The *tao* of the yang/firm/superior man grows. Therefore "it is beneficial whatever one does." One yang returns below— this is the mind of heaven-and-earth, which gives birth to things. Previous scholars[14] all took tranquillity as that which makes apparent the mind of heaven-and-earth. They did not know that the sprouts of action are in fact the mind of heaven-and-earth. How could those who do not know *tao* recognize this?

HSIANG-CHUAN: Thunder is within earth.[15] The former kings closed the passes on the [winter] solstice. Merchants and travelers did not proceed. Rulers did not inspect the regions [of their domains].

COMMENTARY: Thunder is the sound of the mixing of yin and yang. [Yet] in its subtlety this yang cannot yet come forth. "Thunder is within earth" is the times (*shih*, circumstance) of yang's first return. When yang is first born below it is very subtle; it is peaceful and tranquil. Only afterwards can it grow.

---

[14] That is, Wang Pi. See his remarks on this passage, translated above.

[15] Thunder is the primary association of Chen, and earth of K'un, the two trigrams that constitute Fu.

The former kings complied with heaven's *tao*. Since the solstice is the first production of yang, they were peaceful and tranquil in order to nourish it. Therefore they closed the passes to keep merchants and travelers from being able to proceed. Rulers did not inspect the four regions. They observed the image of "return" and complied with heaven's *tao*. In the individual person it is also like this. One should be peaceful and tranquil in order to nourish one's yang.

LINE ONE: Nine at the first. Not far, and returning without reaching repentance. Primally auspicious.

COMMENTARY: Fu is yang reverting and returning. Yang is the *tao* of the superior man, so return has the meaning of reverting to the good. The firm-yang first returns and occupies the first position of the hexagram—the earliest to return. This is "not far and then returning." One errs, and after that there is a return. If one did not err, then how could there be a return? Only if the error does not go far and one returns will it not reach repentance. This is greatly good and auspicious.

"*Ch'i*" (reaching) should be pronounced like *chih* (respect) or *ti* (to resist).[16] The *Yü-pien* (Jade Book)[17] says it is *shih* (to go to), with the same meaning. "Without *ch'i* repentance" means "not reaching [the point of] repentance." When [line five of] the K'an hexagram [#29] says "Peace will be brought about, no fault" it means "reaching peace."

[Confucius's disciple] Yen Tzu made no apparent error. Confucius said "He is almost perfect."[18] This is precisely "not reaching repentance." Since the error had been corrected before it took shape, how could there be repentance? But since he was unable to [attain] the Mean without making effort and have what he desired not transgress what is right,[19] this is having errors. However, he was bright and firm, and therefore "there was not a single thing which was not good that he did not know of,"[20] and knowing, did not hurriedly reform. Therefore he did not reach repentance, which is just "not far, and returning."

Ch'i: Lu Te-ming (556–627) pronounces it *chih*.[21] In the *Yü-p'ien*, the *Wu-ching wen-tzu* (The characters of the Five Classics) and the *Chün-ching yin-pien* (Distinctions of pronunciation in all the Classics), see under the *i* (clothing) radical.

---

[16] Using modern Mandarin of course turns this sentence into nonsense. In Sung, we can suppose, all these words could be pronounced the same.

[17] A dictionary of the Classics by Ku Yeh-wang (519–581), based on the *Shuo-wen* and much expanded in T'ang and Sung times.

[18] Here Ch'eng is quoting *Hsi-tz'u-chuan* B4.

[19] Referring to Confucius at age 70; see *Analects* 2:4.

[20] *Hsi-tz'u-chuan* B4.

[21] See his *Chou-i yin-i* (Pronunciation and meaning of the *Book of Change*).

HSIANG-CHUAN: "Returning from not far" so that he can cultivate himself.

COMMENTARY: Returning from not far is the *tao* by which the superior man cultivates himself. The *tao* of learning (*hsüeh*) is no other than this: just know what is not good and speedily reform in order to pursue the good, that is all.

LINE TWO: Six at the second. Beautiful return. Auspicious.

COMMENTARY: The second, though a yin line, occupies a central (*chung*) and correct (*cheng*) place and is close with the first.[22] Its aspirations obey yang, and it is able to be next to *jen* (humaneness). The first yang returns—it is a return to *jen*. The second is close to it, which is how it is beautiful and auspicious.

HSIANG-CHUAN: The "auspiciousness of the beautiful return" is from being next to *jen*.

COMMENTARY: That the return is beautiful and auspicious is because it can be next to *jen*. *Jen* is being impartial in the world, the root of goodness.[23] The first [line] returns to *jen*. The second is related with and next to it. This is how it is auspicious.

LINE THREE: Six at the third. Repeated return. Danger. No fault.

COMMENTARY: The third line puts unsettled yin in the place of extreme movement. This return is made repeatedly and cannot be firm. In returning, settledness and firmness are valued. Repeatedly returning and repeatedly erring/losing (*shih*) is to be unsettled in one's return. Returning to the good and erring/losing it numerous times is the *tao* of danger. The Sage (Confucius) opened up the *tao* of becoming good. He approved of returning to it and considered numerous losses of it dangerous. Therefore he said: "Danger. No fault."

One cannot take repeated loss/erring as a caution against returning [to the good]. Repeated loss is dangerous. How could numerous returns be at fault? The excess is in the loss, not in the return.

HSIANG-CHUAN: The "danger of repeated return"; the meaning is "without fault."

COMMENTARY: Although repeated return and loss are dangerous, the meaning of returning to the good is "without fault."

LINE FOUR: Six at the fourth. Proceeding centrally, alone returning.

COMMENTARY: The significance of this line deserves a careful going over. The fourth line proceeds in the center of many yin, and it alone is

---

[22] That is, occupying the middle of the lower trigram, it is "central." Being a yin line in an even line position, it is "correct." It is yin resting just over a yang line, which also tends to auspiciousness. For further discussion of these principles, see chapter 1.

[23] The first of these is Ch'eng's standard definition of *jen*; see, for example, *Erh-Ch'eng chi* 15.153. The second phrase, *jen* as the "root of goodness," is a quotation from the *Wen-yen*, seventh of the Ten Wings.

able to return. It is naturally placed in correctness and responds to the yang-firm line below.[24] Its aspiration can be said to be good indeed.

It says nothing about auspiciousness and inauspiciousness. Now, the fourth is the soft residing among the many yin. The first line is at the point of great subtlety, insufficient to assist others. It is without the pattern (*li*) of being able to give aid. Therefore the Sage spoke of it alone being able to return and did not wish to say that it alone followed *tao*. This is necessarily inauspicious.

[Someone] said: "If so, then why did he not say 'without fault'?"

[Ch'eng] said: "Because it is yin residing among yin, the most soft and weak. Although it has the aspiration to obey yang, in the end [yang] is still incapable of giving aid. It is not 'without fault.' "

HSIANG-CHUAN: [The *I*] speaks of it alone as returning because it follows the good *tao* of the yang/firm/superior man.

LINE FIVE: Six at the fifth. Sincere returning, without repentance.

COMMENTARY: Six at the fifth possesses the virtues of centrality and compliance. It occupies the position of the ruler and is able to be sincere in returning to the good. Therefore it is without repentance. Although it is fundamentally good, there are also cautionings in its midst. When yang's return is so subtle, with the soft dwelling in the place of honor and the return below without aid, it cannot yet reach success and auspiciousness. It can be without repentance, that is all.

HSIANG-CHUAN: "Nobly returning, without repentance." It is central in order to complete itself.

COMMENTARY: It realizes itself by the *tao* of the Mean (center). The fifth, with yin dwelling in the place of honor, occupies the center and embodies compliance. It is able to make its aspirations sincere. Since it realizes itself by the Mean (center), it can be without repentance. "Realize oneself" means realizing the virtue of one's centrality and compliance.

LINE SIX: Six at the top. Confused return. Inauspicious. There are calamities and errors. If one were to set troops in motion, it would end in great defeat, bringing inauspiciousness to the country's ruler. Even in ten years one could not correct it.

COMMENTARY: With yin-soft dwelling at the end-place of Fu, in the end it is confused and does not return. Confused and not returning—its inauspiciousness is obvious.

"There are calamities and errors." "Calamities" are heavenly calamities, coming from without. "Errors" are one's own excesses, from what one does oneself. Since the confusion and not returning to the good are

[24] As a yin line in the first position of the upper trigram, it responds (*ying*) to the yang line in the first position of the lower trigram.

within oneself, all actions are in error. Though calamities arrive from without, they are still provoked.

When one is confused about/astray from *tao* and does not return, no activities are possible. Thus if you apply it to putting troops in motion, "it will end in great defeat." If it is used to rule the country, it will be the "inauspiciousness of the ruler." "Ten years" is the last number.[25] "Even in ten years one could not correct it" means that even in the end one is unable to act. Since one is confused about/astray from *tao*, *when* would one be able to act?

HSIANG-CHUAN: The "inauspiciousness of being confused in returning" is that it contradicts the ruler's *tao*.

COMMENTARY: Returning, one unites with *tao*. Since one is confused about the return, one is in contradiction with *tao*, and one's inauspiciousness is obvious. "Bringing inauspiciousness to the ruler of the country" means that one "contradicts the ruler's *tao*."

Human rulers reside above and govern the multitudes. They should pursue the world's good. If then they are confused in returning, it is contradicting the ruler's *tao*. Not just the rulers of men: whenever someone is confused in returning, it is in every case contradicting *tao* and inauspicious.

CHU HSI'S COMMENTARY

Return. Success.
Going out and coming in without distress.
Friends come without blame.
The Way reverts and returns.
On the seventh day comes the return.
It is beneficial wherever one goes.

COMMENTARY: Return. The yang is reborn below. Po (hexagram #23 Splitting Apart) having been completed [i.e., the single yang line at the top reverting to yin], it then becomes pure K'un, the hexagram of the tenth month [November-December, in the Fu-hsi sequence of hexagrams]. Yet the yang *ch'i* is already coming alive at the bottom. Only when it has collected for another month does the yang substance begin to form and come back. Therefore the hexagram of the eleventh month [December-January] is Fu. Since the yang has gone and returned, it is a way of success. With Chen as the inner [lower trigram] and K'un as the outer [upper trigram], there is the image of yang active at the bottom, moving harmoniously upward. Thus the prognostication: When there has been going out and coming in there will be no distress, and the coming of

[25] Because "ten" is the final single-figure digit in Chinese.

friends will also bring no distress. From the first birth of one yin line in the Kou [hexagram #44] of the fifth month to this seventh line, the single yang coming back, it is the naturalness of the revolution of heaven.[26] Thus its prognostication is "The Way reverts and returns," until the seventh day, on which [the yang] comes back. Since at this point the virtue of firmness increases, its prognostication is "It is beneficial wherever one goes." "The Way reverts and returns" is the idea of going and coming back, coming and going back. The seven days are the period in which what is predicted will come back.

NINE AT THE BEGINNING: Return from not far away, without reaching the point of repentance. Primally auspicious.

COMMENTARY: The single yang reborn at the bottom is the ruler of Fu. If one rests at the beginning of an affair, erring but not by much, one will be able to return to goodness, without reaching the point of need for repentance. This is a way of goodness and auspiciousness. Thus the prognostication.

SIX IN THE SECOND PLACE: Fortunate return. Auspicious.

COMMENTARY: The soft line is harmonious, central, and correct, next to the nine at the beginning and able to submit to it. This is the good fortune of Fu, an auspicious way.

SIX IN THE THIRD PLACE: Repeated return. Danger. No fault.

COMMENTARY: The yin line in a yang position is not central and not correct. Occupying the position of extreme activity, its return is not established. The image of frequent error and frequent return. Frequent error means danger, but the return is without fault. Thus the prognostication.

SIX IN THE FOURTH PLACE: Proceeding centrally, returning alone.

COMMENTARY: The fourth place is in the middle of all the yin lines. By itself it corresponds with the first line. It is the image of the individual who is able to follow the good while acting in a group. At this moment the yang ch'i is very subtle, as yet insufficient for action. Therefore, there is no mention of auspiciousness. But the normativeness of principle does not involve auspiciousness and inauspiciousness. As Tung [Chung-shu] said, "The man of humanity is correct and proper, and does not scheme for profit. He is clear about the Way and does not calculate rewards." The six in the third position of Po (hexagram #23) and this line [both] illustrate this.

SIX IN THE FIFTH PLACE: Nobly returning, without repentance.

COMMENTARY: Harmoniously abiding in respect in the central position, just at the moment of return. The image of noble return. A way without repentance.

[26] This refers to the Fu-hsi sequence of hexagrams, starting with Kou at the top and reading clockwise, counting the months.

SIX AT THE TOP: Confused return. Inauspicious. There are calamities and errors. If one were to set troops in motion, it would end in great defeat, bringing inauspiciousness to the country's lord. Even in ten years one could not correct it.

COMMENTARY: With a soft yin line resting at the end of Fu, the end is confused. The image of not returning. An inauspicious way. Thus this prognostication.

T'UAN-CHUAN: "Return. Success." The firm turns back.

COMMENTARY: The firm turning back brings success.

T'UAN-CHUAN: Movement and harmonious action. Therefore, "Going out and coming in without distress. Friends come without blame."

COMMENTARY: This refers to the character (virtue) of the hexagram.

T'UAN-CHUAN: "The way reverts and returns. On the seventh day comes the return." This is the course of heaven.

COMMENTARY: Yin and yang ebb and flow, like the turning of heaven.

T'UAN-CHUAN: "It is beneficial wherever one goes." The firm is on the increase.

COMMENTARY: This refers to the substance of the hexagram. Once it is born, it gradually increases.

T'UAN-CHUAN: In Fu one sees the mind of heaven-and-earth.

COMMENTARY: Below the accumulated yin a single yang is reborn. "The mind of heaven-and-earth to give birth to things"[27] is incipient in extinction. Reaching this point [in the cyclical process], its return can be seen. In human beings it is activity at the peak of stillness, goodness at the peak of evil, the original mind beginning to reappear just at the point of vanishing. Master Ch'eng discussed this in detail. Likewise, Master Shao said in a poem:

> At midnight on the winter solstice
> The mind of heaven is without a stir.
> When the first impulse of yang sprouts,
> Before manifold creation has been born,
> Then the taste of the Subtle Wine is indeed flavorless,
> And the sound of the Great Hum is very faint.
> If you do not believe these words,
> Then go ask Pao [Fu] Hsi.[28]

Perfectly said! Students ought to exert their minds on this.

TA-HSIANG-CHUAN: Thunder within the earth. Return. The Former

[27] Quoting Ch'eng I's comment on this line.

[28] "Song of the Winter Solstice" (*Tung-chih yin*), in Shao Yung, *I-ch'uan chi-jang chi* (Beating time by the I River) (*Ssu-pu ts'ung-k'an* ed.) 18.136a. From *Interpretations of the Central Concept of the I-Ching during the Han, Sung and Ming Dynasties*, trans. Douglass Alan White (Ph.D. Dissertation, Harvard University, 1976), p. 84.

Kings closed the passes on the solstice. Merchants did not travel, and the sovereign did not inspect the realm.

COMMENTARY: Peace and quiet in order to nourish the subtle yang. In the *Yüeh-ling* ["Monthly Commands" chapter of the *Li-chi*] this month is when "one fasts . . . and retires oneself . . . in order to wait for the stabilization of yin and yang."[29]

[29] *Li-chi* (*Shih-san-ching chu-shu* ed.) 17:19a, James Legge, trans., *The Li Ki*, in *Sacred Books of the East*, ed. F. Max Muller, 1885 (Delhi: Motilal Banarsidass, 1964), vol. 27, pp. 304–5.

Glossary

We include here a handful of words that are used in significantly different ways by different figures. We have excluded significant words that are used more or less similarly, like *hsüeh*, and concepts like *chi*, "incipience," that, however difficult, are explained within a single section of a single chapter.

Ch'ing 情   The original meaning of *ch'ing* is "human emotional response." When Ch'eng I or Chu Hsi uses the term it is usually with this meaning, as something that is likely to interfere with one's practice of *hsüeh*. From the sense of "response" derives *ch'ing*'s second meaning, as the "particular circumstances [to which one is responding]" or the character and nature of these responses. Shao Yung combines all of these when he speaks of *ch'ing* as subjective views of particular things. Such a view misunderstands things because human emotion reads them in terms of a particularistic self rather than as part of the network of heaven-and-earth. *Ch'ing* is thus the opposite of what is real about things, which Shao calls "*hsing*," "the nature."

Ou-yang Hsiu and Su Shih, however, regard *ch'ing* in almost the opposite manner, as actual human emotion and human circumstance, and thus as the surest guide to what human beings really want, need and are. *Ch'ing* were thus the basis on which the sages produced the enlighted institutions of the past, when politics and morality were fully integrated.

Hsiang 象   "Image," "figure." The earliest reference of *hsiang*, attested to in the *Hsiang-chuan* commentary, Wings 3 and 4, is to the particular image indexed to each of the eight trigrams, e.g., "mountain" to Ken or "swamp" to Tui. Han *hsiang-shu* practitioners extended the meaning of "*hsiang*" to include every other symbolic association of the trigrams. Since the *Hsi-tz'u-chuan* on, *hsiang* has also referred more generally to the process of symbolization itself. Thus *Hsi-tz'u* A12 speaks of *hsiang* as an alternative to words, as a language capable of expressing things that words are inadequate to. Wang Pi applies this when he turns the literal dragons and mares of the text into principles around which the other materials of a hexagram can be organized. He also argues in his *Lüeh-li* that when one has the *hsiang* one can forget the words, and when one has the meaning one can forget the *hsiang*. K'ung Ying-ta takes this power to symbolize as the essence of the *I*, quoting a passage in *Hsi-tz'u* B3 that says "The *I* is *hsiang*; *hsiang* are representations [also pronounced '*hsiang*']." For him symbolization is the mechanism by which the *I* can speak at once to both the concerns of the sage/ruler and to the processes of heaven-and-earth, thereby demonstrating the parallelism of these two realms.

The *Hsi-tz'u* A11 also talks about the "four images" (*ssu-hsiang*), which grow in turn from the two modes of yin and yang and from *t'ai-chi* and give rise to the eight trigrams. Shao Yung of course builds an elaborate system from these materials, which include the "four *hsiang* of heaven" (sun, moon, stars, zodiacal space) and the "four *hsiang* of earth" (water, fire, earth, stone).

The *hsiang* are unimportant to Ch'eng I. Their function of symbolizing or organizing reality is performed by "the pattern" (*li*). Chu Hsi goes back to the *Hsi-tz'u*: *hsiang* are the pre-linguistic expression of Fu-hsi's insight into heaven-and-earth. As such they are the most profound element of the *I Ching* text.

For further discussion, see chapter 6 footnote 27; Hellmut Wilhelm, *Heaven, Earth, and Man in the Book of Changes*; Gerald Swanson, *The Great Treatise: Commentatory Tradition to the "Book of Changes"*; and Willard Peterson, "Making Connections: 'Commentary on the Attached Verbalizations' of the *Book of Change*."

Hsing 性 From the fourth century B.C.E., *hsing* has been used to mean "human nature" in the sense of that which one cannot alter in someone. But that term is as problematic in Chinese as in English. A. C. Graham, in his *Two Chinese Philosophers*, pp. 45–47, summarizes some eleventh-century views. Among them is one that conflates *hsing* with *ts'ai*, or what we might call one's character or characteristic abilities. Ou-yang Hsiu sees *hsing* this way. Though he does not deny that human beings may possess within themselves something that links them intimately with the essence of heaven-and-earth, he claims that possession to be irrelevant to the real business of life. Whatever one may possess as one's nature, there is nothing one can alter in it anyway. This is what most sharply sets him off from Su, Shao, Ch'eng, and Chu.

Ch'eng I and Chu Hsi identifiy *hsing* with the pattern (*li*). It is what human beings have that is the same as heaven, the basis on which they can know heaven-and-earth and become sages. If one sees his true *hsing*, then matters of *ch'ing* will fall into line of themselves.

For Shao Yung, *hsing* means what things, not just people, really are. It is opposed to *ch'ing*, which indicates understanding distorted by human selfishness. Shao thus uses "*hsing*" not as the basis on which human beings attain sagehood but rather to distinguish correct from partial views.

For Su Shih, *hsing* is unknowable because it is the source of all that human beings have done. It is therefore philosophically prior to anything that can be named, and it is also inexhaustible. Only its products can be named. Thus Mencius, calling *hsing* "good," demonstrated the superficiality of his understanding. For Su, the unknowability of *hsing* parallels that of *tao*. Thus, like Ch'eng and Chu, he places *hsing* and the ultimate source of values on the same plane.

Li 理 Before the Ch'eng brothers transformed *li* into a philosophical term capable of expressing the unity and moral character of all heaven-and-earth, it had long existed as the "pattern" or "abstract principle" of things. Graham, in his *Later Mohist Logic, Ethics and Science*, p. 191, speaks of *li* as "the patterned arrangement of parts in a structured whole, of things in an ordered cosmos, of thought in rational discourse." Chan summarizes the later history of the term in "The Evolution of the Neo-Confucian Concept *Li* as Principle," *Tsing Hua Journal of Chinese Studies* 4 (1964), pp. 123–49. In the mid-eleventh century it was often used much as the term *wen* to indicate the pattern of something. Shao Yung speaks of the ineffable "principles" that characterize the realm in which spirit (*shen*) operates. Su Shih speaks of the "patterns" that one may imagine informing a particular discipline or genre (*lei*) such as calligraphy or painting. Whether or not such patterns are "real," there is still a right and a wrong way to do things. Thus Su speaks of the goal of writing as "to illuminate *li*."

The two Ch'engs made patternings into "the moral pattern of heaven, earth and humanity." That is, they took a term with no more religious-philosophical meaning than the English word "pattern" and transformed it into a way of discussing every major philosophical issue of their time. In this they were followed by Chu Hsi, who, like them, uses the term in both its singular and plural senses.

Shen 神 The original meaning of *shen* is "spirits," probably "ancestral spirits." Graham, *Two Chinese Philosophers*, pp. 111–12, describes its Sung use as "a daemonic power or intelligence which is active within the operations of heaven and earth and which emanates from the person of the sage." Shao Yung definitely uses it in this way. However, he also gives it the more specific meaning of a realm, what we called a "level of reality" in chapter 4. This realm is unknowable by normal means, but it is nonetheless coherent. This coherence is expressed by *li*, "principles."

Chu Hsi uses *shen* in the general sense described by Graham. Following *Hsi-tz'u-chuan* A 11, he also applies the term both to the milfoil stalks that are cast to perform *I Ching* divination and to the sage, whose aspect of *shen* allows him to know the future. For a more detailed discussion, see the section "Responsiveness" in chapter 6.

T'ien-ti 天地 The term "heaven-and-earth" is used by Lao Tzu, Hsün Tzu, the *Hsi-tz'u-chuan*, and many, many others to stand for the realm of natural process and the things that spontaneously (*tz'u-jan*) occur in it, as opposed to human cultural creations. In the eleventh century using it raises the issue of whether human affairs are significantly related to heaven. For Su, Shao and Ch'eng it suggests as well the possibility of grounding human values in the natural world. Yet each of these three used a distinct and different term to indicate the ultimate within his system. Su spoke of *tao*, Shao of *t'ai-chi*, Ch'eng of *li*. (Chu Hsi essentially follows Ch'eng I here, though he speaks most often of "*t'ien-li*.")

Wen 文 Sung figures used the word "wen" in four different ways, which variously derive from its original meaning as "patterned." It is the apparent structure or pattern of things, in this sense close to the pre-Ch'eng "*li*." It is "adornment," the elegant patterning for which certain literary works are prized. It is also the writings themselves, and, by extension, the cultural tradition of which they are the embodiment. Thus we see men speaking of "*ssu-wen*," "this [textually based] culture of ours."

Yin-yang 陰陽 All four men take yin and yang as the most fundamental elements of the processes of heaven-and-earth. Yet all four apply them in different ways. Su Shih uses yin and yang to indicate the stage of existence proximate to *tao*, where unity is lost and the problems of multiplicity begin. Shao Yung sees yin and yang as emerging from heaven's movement, as firm and soft emerge from earth's stillness. In turn they divide into major and minor aspects, correlated with sun, moon, stars and zodiacal space. Ch'eng I constantly refers to yin and yang—they are his most basic terms for defining particular workings of the larger pattern. Their functional equivalent in the social world is the pair "inferior man/superior man," in terms of which Ch'eng defines correct action. Chu Hsi applies yin and yang primarily to the natural world and to the hexagram lines.

Bibliography

Acker, William. *Some T'ang and Pre-T'ang Texts on Chinese Painting*. Leiden: E. J. Brill, 1954.

Adler, Joseph. "Descriptive and Normative Principle (*li*) in Confucian Moral-Metaphysics: Is/Ought from the Chinese Perspective," *Zygon: Journal of Religion and Science* 16 (1981), pp. 285–93.

———. *Divination and Philosophy: Chu Hsi's Understanding of the I-ching*. Ann Arbor: University Microfilms International, 1984.

Bergeron, Marie-Ina. *Wang Pi, Philosophe du non-avoir*. Taipei/Paris: Ricci Institute, 1986.

Blakeley, Barry B. "Notes on the Reliability and Objectivity of the Tu Yü Commentary on the *Tso Chuan*," *Journal of the American Oriental Society* 101 (1981), pp. 208–17.

Bloom, Irene. "On the Matter of the Mind: The Metaphysical Basis of the Expanded Self," in *Individualism and Holism*, ed. Donald Munro. Ann Arbor: Center for Chinese Studies, 1985.

Bol, Peter. "Chu Hsi's Redefinition of Literati Learning," in *Neo-Confucian Education: The Formative Stage*, ed. Wm. Theodore de Bary and John Chaffee. Berkeley and Los Angeles: University of California Press, 1989.

———. "Rulership and Sagehood, Bureaucracy and Society: An Historical Inquiry into the Political Visions of Ssu-ma Kuang and Wang An-shih." ACLS Workshop on Sung Dynasty Statecraft in Thought and Action, Scottsdale, Arizona, January 1986.

Bruce, J. P. *Chu Hsi and his Masters*. London: Probsthain, 1923.

Bush, Susan, and Hsio-yen Shih. *Early Chinese Texts on Paintings*. Cambridge: Harvard University Press, 1985.

Cammann, Schuyler. "The Magic Square of Three in Old Chinese Philosophy and Religion," *History of Religion* 1 (1961), pp. 37–80.

Chan, Hok-lam. *Legitimation in Imperial China: Discussions under the Jurchen Chin Dynasty (1115–1126)*. Seattle: University of Washington Press, 1984.

Chan, Wing-tsit. "Ch'eng Hao and Ch'eng I" and "Chu Hsi," in *Sung Biographies*, ed. Herbert Franke, pp. 169–79 and 282–90. Wiesbaden: Franz Steiner Verlag, 1976.

———. "Chu Hsi's Completion of Neo-Confucianism," in *Chu Hsi: Life and Thought*, pp. 121–30. Hong Kong and New York: The Chinese University Press and St. Martin's Press, 1987.

——— (Ch'en Jung-chieh) 陳榮捷. *Chu-tzu men-jen* 朱子門人 (Chu Hsi's disciples). Taipei: Student Book Co., 1982.

———. "The Evolution of the Neo-Confucian Concept *Li* as Principle," *Tsing Hua Journal of Chinese Studies* 5 (1964), pp. 132–49.

———. *A Source Book in Chinese Philosophy*. Princeton: Princeton University Press, 1963.

Chan, Wing-tsit, ed. *Chu Hsi and Neo-Confucianism*. Honolulu: University of Hawaii Press, 1986.

———, trans. *Reflections on Things at Hand*. New York: Columbia University Press, 1967.

Chang Cheng-lang 張政烺. "Mien-shu 'Liu-shih-ssu kua' pa" 緜書《六十四卦》拔 (Postscript to the silk manuscript of *The Sixty-Four Diagrams*), *Wenwu* (1984) 3, pp. 9–14.

———. "Shih-shih Chou ch'u ch'ing-t'ung-ch'i ming-wen-chung ti *I*-kua," 試釋周初青銅器茗文中的易卦 *K'ao-ku hsüeh-pao* (1980) 4, pp. 403–15. Translated as "An Interpretation of the Divinatory Inscriptions on Early Chou Bronzes," *Early China* 6 (1980–1981), pp. 80–96.

Chang Li-wen. "An Analysis of Chu Hsi's System of Thought of *I*," in *Chu Hsi and Neo-Confucianism*, ed. Wing-tsit Chan, pp. 292–311. Honolulu: University of Hawaii Press, 1986.

Ch'ao Pu-chih 晁補之. Chi-le-chi 雞肋集 (*Su-pu ts'ung-k'an* ed.).

Chen, Chi-yun. "A Confucian Magnate's Idea of Political Violence: Hsün Shuang's Interpretation of the *Book of Changes*," *T'oung Pao*, series 2, 54 (1960), pp. 73–115.

Ch'eng I 程頤. *I-chuan* 易傳 (Commentary on the *Book of Change*). Taipei: Shih-chieh, 1972.

Ch'eng I 程頤 and Ch'eng Hao 程顥. *Erh-Ch'eng chi* 二程集 (The collected works of the two Ch'eng brothers). Peking: Chung-hua, 1981.

Ch'eng Shih-ch'üan 程石泉. *I-hsüeh hsin-t'an* 易學新探 (New studies on the *Book of Change*). Taipei: Wen-hsing, 1979.

Ch'ien Mu 錢穆. *Chu-tzu hsin hsüeh-an* 朱子新學案 (A new scholarly record of Chu Hsi). Taipei: San Min, 1971.

Chou Tun-i 周敦頤. *T'ung-shu* 通書 (Comprehending the *Book of Change*). In *Chou Lien-hsi chi* 周濂溪集 (Collected works of Chou Tun-i), ed. Chang Po-hsing 張伯行. *Ts'ung-shu chi-ch'eng* ed.

Chu Hsi 朱熹. *Chou-i pen-i* 周易本義 (The original meaning of the *Book of Change*). Taipei: Hua-lien, 1978.

———. *Chu-tzu ch'üan-shu* 朱子全書 (The complete works of Chu Hsi). Taipei: Kuang-hsüeh, 1977.

———. *Chu-tzu wen-chi* 朱子文集 (The collected works of Chu Hsi). *Ssu-pu pei-yao* ed.

———. *Chu-tzu yü-lei* 朱子語類 (Chu Hsi's classified conversations). Taipei: Cheng-chung, 1970.

———. *I-hsüeh ch'i-meng* 易學啟蒙 (An introduction to the study of the *Book of Change*). In *Chou-i che-chung* 周易折中 (The *Book of Change* judged evenly), ed. Li Kuang-ti 李光地. Taipei: Chen-shan-mei, 1971.

———. *I-Lo yüan-yüan lu* 伊洛淵源錄 (Record of the origins of the I-Lo schools). *Cheng-i-t'ang ch'üan-shu* ed. 正義堂全書.

Chu Hsi and Lü Tsu-ch'ien 呂祖謙, eds. *Chin-ssu-lu* 近思錄 (Reflections on things at hand). Taipei: Commercial Press, 1967.

Chu, Sherman Hsiao-hai 朱曉海. "*Chou-i* chi-ko chi-pen wen-t'i ti t'i-ts'e" 周易幾個基本問題的擬測 (Reflections on some of the basic problems concerning the *Book of Change*). *Tsinghua hsüeh-pao* n.s., 16.1–2 (1984).

Ch'ü Wan-li 屈萬里. *Han shih-ching Chou-i ts'an-tzu chi-cheng* 漢石經周易殘字集正 (Corrected collection of remaining materials on the *Book of Change* from the Han stone classics). Taipei: Commercial Press, 1961.

———. *Hsien-Ch'in Han Wei I-li shu-p'ing* 先秦漢魏易例述評 (On the methods of interpreting the *Book of Change* in the pre-Ch'in, Han and Wei periods). Taipei: Student Book Co., 1975.

de Bary, Wm. Theodore. *Neo-Confucian Orthodoxy and the Learning of the Mind-and-Heart.* New York: Columbia University Press, 1982.

——— et al. *Sources of Chinese Tradition.* New York: Columbia University Press, 1960.

Ebrey, Patricia. *Family and Property in Sung China.* Princeton: Princeton University Press, 1984.

Egan, Ronald C. *The Literary Works of Ou-yang Hsiu.* Cambridge: Cambridge University Press, 1984.

Elvin, Mark. *The Pattern of the Chinese Past.* Stanford: Stanford University Press, 1973.

Fan Chung-yen 范仲淹. *Fan Wen-cheng kung chi* 范文正公集 (The collected works of Fan Chung-yen). *Ssu-pu ts'ung-k'an* ed.

Fan Tsu-yü 范祖禹. *Fan T'ai-shih chi* 范太史集 (The collected works of Fan Tsu-yü). *Ssu-k'u ch'üan-shu chen-pen* ed.

Forke, Alfred, trans. *Lun-heng.* New York: Paragon, 1962.

Freeman, Michael. "From Adept to Worthy: The Philosophical Career of Shao Yung," *Journal of the American Oriental Society* 102 (1982), pp. 477–91.

Fung, Yu-lan. *A History of Chinese Philosophy*, 2 vols. Princeton: Princeton University Press, 1953.

Gardner, Daniel K. *Chu Hsi and the Ta-hsüeh: Neo-Confucian Reflection on the Confucian Canon.* Cambridge: Harvard University Press, 1986.

———. "Principle and Pedagogy: Chu Hsi and the Four Books," *Harvard Journal of Asiatic Studies* 44 (1984), pp. 57–81.

Goodman, Howard L. *Exegetes and Exegeses of the Book of Changes in the Third Century A.D.: Historical and Scholastic Contexts for Wang Pi.* Ann Arbor: University Microfilms International, 1985.

Graham, A. C. "Taoist Spontaneity and the Dichotomy of 'Is' and 'Ought,' " in *Experimental Essays on Chuang-tzu*, ed. Victor Mair, pp. 3–23. Honolulu: University of Hawaii Press, 1983.

———. *Two Chinese Philosophers.* London: Lund Humphries, 1957.

———. "What Was New in the Ch'eng-Chu Theory of Human Nature?" in *Chu Hsi and Neo-Confucianism*, ed. Wing-tsit Chan, pp. 138–57. Honolulu: University of Hawaii Press, 1986.

Hall, David L., and Roger T. Ames, "Getting it Right: On Saving Confucius from the Confucians," *Philosophy East and West* 34 (1984), pp. 3–23.

Hartwell, Robert. "Historical Analogism, Public Policy, and Social Science in Eleventh- and Twelfth-Century China," *American Historical Review* 76 (1971), pp. 690–727.

Harvard-Yenching Institute Sinological Index Series. *A Concordance to Yi Ching.* Taipei: Chinese Materials and Research Aids Service Center, 1973.

Hatch, George. "Su Hsün" and "Su Shih," in *Sung Biographies*, ed. Herbert

Franke, pp. 885–900 and 900–68. Wiesbaden: Franz Steiner Verlag, 1976.

——. "Su Shih I-chuan," in A Sung Bibliography, ed. Yves Hervouet, pp. 4–9. Hong Kong: The Chinese University Press, 1978.

Hatton, Russell. "A Comparison of Li and Substantial Form," Journal of Chinese Philosophy 9 (1982), pp. 45–71.

Henderson, John B. The Development and Decline of Chinese Cosmology. New York: Columbia University Press, 1984.

Hou Wai-lu 侯外廬. Chung-kuo ssu-hsiang t'ung-shih 中國思想通史 (A comprehensive history of Chinese thought). Peking: Jen-min, 1959.

Hu Wei 胡渭. I-t'u ming-pien 易圖明辨 (Illuminating and differentiating the I Ching diagrams). Taipei: Kuang-wen, 1971.

Hu Yüan 胡瑗. As related by Ni T'ien-yin 倪天隱. Chou-i k'ou-i 周易口義 (An oral interpretation of the Book of Change). Ssu-k'u ch'üan-shu ed.

Huang Tsung-hsi 黃宗羲 and Ch'üan Tsu-wang 全祖望. Sung-Yüan hsüeh-an 宋元學案 (Case studies of Sung and Yüan scholars). Ssu-pu pei-yao ed.

Hymes, Robert P. Statesmen and Gentlemen: The Elite of Fu-chou, Chiang-hsi, in Northern and Southern Sung. Cambridge: Cambridge University Press, 1986.

Imai Usaburō 今井宇三郎. Sōdai Ekigaku no kenkyū 宋代易學の研究 (Researches on Sung dynasty I Ching studies). Tokyo: Meiji, 1958.

Kao Heng 高亨. Chou-i ku-ching t'ung-shuo 周易古經通說 (Comprehensive account of the ancient classic The Book of Change). Peking: Chung-hua, 1958.

Kassof, Ira E. The Thought of Chang Tsai (1020–1077). Cambridge: Cambridge University Press, 1984.

Keightley, David N. "The Religious Commitment: Shang Theology and the Genesis of Chinese Political Culture," History of Religions 17 (1978), pp. 211–25.

——. "Was the Chou-i a Legacy of Shang?" Paper presented to the Association for Asian Studies, Chicago, April 1982.

Kim Yung-sik. The World-View of Chu Hsi (1130–1200): Knowledge about the Natural World in the Chu Tzu Ch'üan-shu. Ann Arbor: University Microfilms International, 1982.

Ku Chieh-kang 顧頡剛, ed. Ku-shih pien 古史辨 (Analysis of ancient history). 1931. Reprint. Hong Kong: T'ai-ping Book Co., 1963.

K'ung Fan 孔繁. "Su Shih 'P'i-ling I-chuan' ti che-hsüeh ssu-hsiang" 蘇軾《毗陵易傳》的哲學思想 (The philosophical thought of Su Shih's commentary on the Book of Change), Chung-kuo che-hsüeh 9 (1983), pp. 221–39.

K'ung Ying-ta 孔穎達. Chou-i cheng-i 周易正義 (Correct meanings of the Book of Change). Ssu-pu pei-yao ed.

Kunst, Richard. The Original "Yijing": A Text, Phonetic Transcription, Translation, and Indexes, with Sample Glosses. Ann Arbor: University Microfilms International, 1985.

Legge, James. The Shoo King or Book of Historical Documents. Oxford: Clarendon Press, 1865.

——. The Yi King. Oxford: Clarendon Press, 1892.

Li Ching-ch'ih 李鏡池. Chou-i t'an-yüan 周易探源 (Seeking the origins of the Book of Change). Peking: Chung-hua, 1978.

Li Kuang-ti 李光地. *Chou-i che-chung* 周易折中 (The *Book of Change*—striking the mean). Taipei: Chen-shan-mei, 1971.

Li Ting-tsuo 李鼎祚. *Chou-i chi-chieh* 周易集解 (Collected explanations of the *Book of Change*). Peking: Pei-ching-shih Chung-kuo shu-tien, 1984.

Lin I-sheng 林益勝. *Hu Yüan ti i-li I-hsüeh* 胡瑗的義理易學 (Hu Yüan's "moral principle" studies of the *Book of Change*). Taipei: Commercial Press, 1974.

——. *I-ch'uan I-chuan ti ch'u-shih che-hsüeh* 伊川易傳的出世哲學 (The this-worldly philosophy of Ch'eng I's commentary to the *Book of Change*). Taipei: Commercial Press, 1978.

Liu, James T. C. "An Early Sung Reformer: Fan Chung-yen," in *Chinese Thought and Institutions*, ed. John K. Fairbank, pp. 105–131. Chicago: University of Chicago Press, 1957.

——. "How Did a Neo-Confucian School Become State Orthodoxy?" *Philosophy East and West* 23 (1973), pp. 483–505.

——. *Reform in Sung China*. Cambridge: Harvard University Press, 1959.

Liu Mu 劉牧. *I-shu kou-yin-t'u* 易數鈎隱圖 (Hooking out the diagrams of the numbers of the *Book of Change*). *Ssu-k'u ch'üan-shu* ed.

Liu Tzu-chien 劉子健. *Ou-yang Hsiu ti chih-hsüeh yü ts'ung-cheng* 歐陽修的治學與從政. Hong Kong: Hsin-ya, 1963. Translated as James T. C. Liu, *Ou-yang Hsiu: An Eleventh-Century Neo-Confucianist*. Stanford: Stanford University Press, 1967.

Lü Tsu-ch'ien 呂祖謙, comp. *Chou-i Hsi-tz'u ching-i* 周易繫辭精義 (Essential meanings of the *Hsi-tz'u-chuan*). *Ku-i ts'ung-shu* ed.

Mao Huai-hsin 昌懷辛. "Shao Yung ti jen-sheng-kuan yü li-shih che-hsüeh" 紹雍的人生觀與歷史哲學 (Shao Yung's view of human beings and his philosophy of history). *Chung-kuo che-hsüeh* 12 (1984), pp. 161–75.

March, Andrew. "Self and Landscape in Su Shih." *Journal of the American Oriental Society* 86 (1966), pp. 377–96.

Matsukawa Kenji 松川健二. *Sō-Min no shisō shi* 宋明の思想詩 (Philosophical poetry of the Sung and Ming). Sapporo: Hokkaido University Press, 1982.

Metzger, Thomas A. *Escape from Predicament: Neo-Confucianism and China's Evolving Political Culture*. New York: Columbia University Press, 1977.

Mitukuni Yosida. "The Chinese Concept of Nature," in *Chinese Science*, ed. Shigeru Nakayama and Nathan Sivin. Cambridge: MIT Press, 1973.

Mungello, David. *Leibniz and Confucianism: The Search for Accord*. Honolulu: University of Hawaii Press, 1977.

Munro, Donald. *The Concept of Man in Early China*. Stanford: Stanford University Press, 1969.

——. "The Family Network, the Stream of Water, and the Plant: Picturing Persons in Sung Confucianism," in *Individualism and Holism*, ed. Donald Munro, pp. 259–91. Ann Arbor: Center for Chinese Studies, 1985.

——. *Images of Human Nature: A Sung Portrait*. Princeton: Princeton University Press, 1988.

Nivison, David S. "Introduction," *Confucianism in Action*, ed. David S. Nivison and Arthur F. Wright. Stanford: Stanford University Press, 1959.

Okada Takehiko 岡田武彦. *Zazen to Seiza* 坐禪と靜坐 (Sitting-meditation and quiet-sitting). Tokyo: Ofusha, 1966.

Ou-yang Hsiu 歐陽修. *Hsin Wu-tai shih* 新五代史 (A new history of the Five Dynasties). Peking: Chung-hua, 1974.

———. *Ou-yang ch'üan-chi* 歐陽全集 (The complete works of Ou-yang Hsiu). Taipei: Shih-chieh, 1971.

———. *Shih pen-i* 詩本義 (The original meaning of the *Book of Poetry*). *Ssu-k'u ch'üan-shu chen-pen* ed.

Ou-yang Hsiu, and Sung Ch'i 宋祁, *Hsin T'ang shu* 新唐書 (A new history of the T'ang). Peking: Chung-hua, 1975.

Peterson, Willard. "Another Look at *Li*," *Bulletin of Sung-Yüan Studies* 18 (1986), pp. 13–32.

———. "Making Connections: 'Commentary on the Attached Verbalizations' of the *Book of Change*," *Harvard Journal of Asiatic Studies* 42 (1982), pp. 67–116.

Phelan, Timothy. *The Neo-Confucian Cosmology in Chu Hsi's I-hsüeh ch'i-meng*. Ann Arbor: University Microfilms International, 1982.

Ricoeur, Paul. "What Is a Text? Explanation and Understanding," in *Paul Ricoeur: Hermeneutics and the Human Sciences*. Cambridge: Cambridge University Press, 1981.

Sariti, Anthony J. "Monarchy, Bureaucracy, and Absolutism in the Political Thought of Ssu-ma Kuang," *Journal of Asian Studies* 32 (1972), pp. 53–76.

Saso, Michael. "What Is the *Ho-t'u*?" *History of Religions* 18 (1978), pp. 399–416.

Schirokauer, Conrad M. "Chu Hsi's Political Career: A Study in Ambivalence," in *Confucian Personalities*, ed. Arthur F. Wright and Denis Twitchett, pp. 162–88. Stanford: Stanford University Press, 1962.

———. "Neo-Confucians Under Attack: The Condemnation of *Wei-hsüeh*," in *Crisis and Prosperity in Sung China*, ed. John Haeger, pp. 163–98. Tucson: University of Arizona Press, 1975.

Schulz, Larry. *Lai Chih-te (1525–1604) and the Phenomenology of Change*. Ann Arbor: University Microfilms International, 1982.

Shao Yung 紹雍. *Huang-chi ching-shih shu* 皇極經世書 (Book of supreme principles ordering the world). *Ssu-pu pei-yao* ed.

Shao Yung. *I-ch'uan chi-jang-chi* 伊川擊壤集 (Collected poems of Shao Yung). *Ssu-pu ts'ung-k'an* ed.

Shaughnessy, Edward. *The Composition of the Zhouyi*. Ann Arbor: University Microfilms International, 1983.

Shchutskii, Iulian K. *Researches on the I Ching*, trans. William L. MacDonald and Tsuyoshi Hasegawa, with Hellmut Wilhelm. Princeton: Princeton University Press, 1979.

Skinner, Quentin. "Motives, Intentions, and the Interpretation of Texts," *New Literary History* 3 (1972), pp. 393–408.

Smith, Kidder. "*Zhouyi* Divination from Accounts in the *Zuozhuan*," *Harvard Journal of Asiatic Studies* 49:2 (1989).

Su Shih 蘇軾. *Ching-chin Tung-p'o wen-chi shih-lüeh* 經進東坡文集事略 (Annotated selections of Su Shih's prose). Peking: Wen-hsüeh ku-chi, 1957.

———. *Su Shih I-chuan* 蘇軾易傳 (Su Shih's commentary on the *Book of Change*). *Ts'ung-shu chi-ch'eng* ed.

———. *Su Tung-p'o chi* 蘇東坡集 (Collected works of Su Shih). *Kuo-hsüeh chi-pen ts'ung-shu* ed.

———. *Tung-p'o t'i-pa* 東坡提拔 (Colophons of Su Shih). *Ts'ung-shu chi-ch'eng* ed.

Suzuki Yoshijirō 鈴木由次郎. "Shushi to Eki" 朱子と易 (Chu Hsi and the *Book of Change*), in *Shushigaku taikei* 朱子學大系 (Outline of Chu Hsi studies), ed. Morohashi Tetsuhi 諸橋哲二 et al., vol. 1, pp. 213–32. Tokyo: Meitoku, 1974.

Swanson, Gerald. "The Concept of Change in the *Great Treatise*," in *Explorations in Ancient Chinese Cosmology*, ed. Henry Rosemont, Jr. Chico: Scholars Press, 1984.

———. *The Great Treatise: Commentatory Tradition to the "Book of Changes."* Ann Arbor: University Microfilms International, 1974.

Tai Chün-jen 戴君仁. *T'an-i* 談易 (On the *Book of Change*). Taipei: K'ai-ming, 1961.

T'ang Chün-i. "The Development of the Concept of Moral Mind from Wang Yang-ming to Wang Chi," in *Self and Society in Ming Thought*, ed. Wm Theodore de Bary, pp. 93–120. New York: Columbia University Press, 1970.

T'ang Yung-t'ung. "Wang Pi's New Interpretation of the *I-ching* and the *Lun-yü*," *Harvard Journal of Asiatic Studies* 10 (1947), pp. 124–61.

Teraji Jun 寺地遵. "O-yō Shū ni okeru tenjin sōkansetsu e no kaigi" 歐陽修における天人相関說への懷疑 (Ou-yang Hsiu's doubts about the relationship of man and heaven). *Hiroshima Daigaku Bungakubu kiyō* 28 (1968), pp. 161–87.

Toda Toyosaburō 戶田豊三郎. *Ekikyō chūshaku shikō* 易經注釋史綱 (An outline history of commentaries on the *Book of Change*). Tokyo: Fūgen, 1968.

———. "Sho Yō to Sho Bobun" 紹雍と紹伯文 (Shao Yung and Shao Po-wen), *Hiroshima Daigaku Bungakubu Gakuhō* (1958), pp. 1–28.

T'o T'o 托托, ed. *Sung-shih* 宋史 (History of the Sung). Reprint. Peking: Chung-hua, 1977.

Tseng Ch'un-hai 曾春海. *Hui-an I-hsüeh t'an-wei* 晦菴易學探微 (An inquiry into Chu Hsi's study of the *Book of Change*). Taipei: Fu-jen University, 1983.

Tseng Kung 曾鞏. *Tseng Kung chi* 曾鞏集 (The collected works of Tseng Kung). Peking: Chung-hua, 1984.

Tseng Tsao-chuang 曾枣庄, "Ts'ung 'P'i-ling *I-chuan*' k'an Su Shih ti shih-chieh-kuan" 從《毗陵易傳》看蘇軾的世界觀 (Examining Su Shih's worldview from the perspective of his commentary to the *Book of Change*), *Ssu-ch'uan ta-hsüeh hsüeh-pao ts'ung-k'an* 6 (1980), pp. 59–60.

Tu, Wei-ming. *Humanity and Self-Cultivation*. Berkeley: Asian Humanities Press, 1979.

Waley, Arthur. *The Analects of Confucius*. London: George Allen & Unwin Ltd., 1938.

———. "The Book of Changes," *Bulletin of the Musuem of Far Eastern Antiquities* 5 (1933), pp. 121–42.

Waley, Arthur. *The Book of Songs*. London: George Allen and Unwin Ltd., 1937.

Wang An-Shih 王安石. *Lin-ch'uan chi* 臨川集 (Collected works of Wang An-shih). Shanghai: Chung-hua, 1959.

Wang Chi-hsi 王基西. *Pei-Sung I-hsüeh-k'ao* 北宋易學考 (An investigation of Northern Sung *I Ching* studies). Taipei: M. A. thesis, Taiwan Normal University, 1978.

Wang Ch'ung 王充. *Lun-heng* 論衡 (Critical essays). *Ssu-pu pei-yao* ed.

Wang Mou-hung 王懋竑. *Chu-tzu nien-p'u* 朱子年譜 (Chronology of Chu Hsi). Taipei: Shih-chieh, 1966.

Wang Pi 王弼. *Chou-i lüeh-li* 周易畧例 (General principles of the *Book of Change*). In K'ung Ying-ta, *Chou-i cheng-i* (*Su-pu pei-yao* ed.).

White, Douglass Alan. *Interpretations of the Central Concept of the I-ching during the Han, Sung and Ming Dynasties*. Ph.D. dissertation, Harvard University, 1976.

Wilhelm, Hellmut. *The Book of Changes in the Western Tradition: A Selected Bibliography*. Seattle: Institute for Comparative and Foreign Area Studies, University of Washington, 1976.

———. *Change: Eight Lectures on the I Ching*. New York: Harper, 1964.

———. *Heaven, Earth and Man in the Book of Changes*. Seattle: University of Washington Press, 1977.

———. "*I-ching* Oracles in the *Tso-chuan* and *Kuo-yü*," *Journal of the American Oriental Society* 79 (1959), pp. 275–80.

Wilhelm, Richard. *I Ging: Das Buch der Wandlungen*. Jena, 1924. *The I Ching or Book of Changes*, trans. Cary F. Baynes. Princeton: Princeton University Press, 3rd edition, 1967.

Wood, Alan Thomas. *Politics and Morality in Northern Sung China: Early Neo-Confucian Views on Obedience to Authority*. Ann Arbor: University Microfilms International, 1981.

Wyatt, Don J. "Chu Hsi's Critique of Shao Yung: One Instance of the Stand Against Fatalism," *Harvard Journal of Asiatic Studies* 45 (1985), pp. 649–66.

Yen, Ling-feng 嚴靈峯. *I-ching chi-ch'eng* 易經集成 (Complete collection on the *Book of Change*). Taipei: Ch'eng-wen, 1975.

Yoshikawa Kōjirō 吉川幸次郎 and Miura Kuniō 三浦国雄. *Shushi shū* 朱子集 (An anthology of Chu Hsi). Tokyo: Asahi Shinbun, 1972.

Yü, David. "Chu Hsi's Approach to Knowledge," *Chinese Culture* 10.4 (1969), pp. 1–14.

Yü Yen 俞琰. *Tu-i chü-yao* 讀易舉要 (Reading the *Book of Change* and abstracting its essentials). *Ssu-k'u ch'üan-shu chen-pen* ed.

About the Authors

Joseph Adler teaches in the Department of Religion at Kenyon College, Peter Bol in the Department of East Asian Languages and Civilizations at Harvard University, Kidder Smith in the Department of History and Program in Asian Studies at Bowdoin College, and Don Wyatt in the Department of History at Middlebury College.

Index

Ability. *See Ts'ai*
Analects, 32–33; commentary by Su Shih, 56
Aristocracy, T'ang and Sung compared, 4
Authentic. *See Ch'eng*

Benevolence. *See Jen*
Bibliographic conventions, ix
Birth order of hexagrams, 109
Book of Change. See I Ching
Book of Documents 書經, commentary by Su Shih, 56
Buddhism, and Ou-yang Hsiu, 29

Calendar: and Ch'eng I, 160; and *I Ching*, 22; and Shao Yung, 129
Chang Lei 張耒, 62–63
Chang Shih 張栻, letter from Chu Hsi, 169
Chang Tsai 張載, 25, 46; and Ch'eng I, 210; commentary by Chu Hsi, 54; issues treated by Su Shih, 72–81; teacher of Ch'eng brothers, 51
Change: and Ch'eng I, 161; and Ou-Yang Hsiu, 29; and Sung literati, 229–30
Change of Chou. See Chou-i
Ch'en Hsiang 陳襄, 25
Ch'en T'uan 陳摶, 110n.43
Cheng 爭 (competition), 70
Cheng 正 (correctness), 185n.60; in interpreting hexagrams, 15–16; used by Ch'eng I, 153
Cheng Hsüan 鄭玄, 174
Ch'eng 誠 (authentic), 195; used by Ch'eng I, 153
Ch'eng brothers, 49–53; and Shao Yung, 132; studied by Chu Hsi, 54; and Su Shih, 72–81
Ch'eng Hao 程顥, 51
Ch'eng Hsiang 程珦, 50
Ch'eng I 程頤: agreement with Chang Tsai, Shao Yung, and Ssu-ma Kuang, 210; Chu Hsi's comments on, 225; and the Classics, 153; commentary on Fu, 156–60, 245–51; comments on social ambition, 138–39; compared with Chu Hsi, 172, 179, 182–84, 222–26; at court with Su

Shih, 51–52; cycles in the natural and moral worlds, 157–60; definitions of *wen*, 220; differing with Shao Yung, 148, 158, 160, 210–18; differing with Su Shih, 153, 219–22; discussion of *chün-tzu* and natural cycles, 146–48; dissatisfaction with Sung literati, 4; and divination and number, 212; and ethics, 161–64; *hsiang* following *li*, 210; and *hsing*, 150; and *hsüeh*, 152–60; *i* and *li*, 139–40; and *I Ching* as a text, 228; *I Ching* commentary as social analysis, 138–42; as *i-li* commentator, 174; and *jen*, 149n.59, 151; and *li*, 142–152, 210; memorial to Emperor Jen-tsung, 136, 142; and moral autonomy, 49–53; nature of time, 215–16; objections to divination, 212; "Raising fish" essay, 140–41; relationship to emperor, 168; seeing the pattern, 164–68; and Shao Yung's numerology, 118; and *shih*, 160–64; true action, 167; and *ts'ai*, 150–51; and unity of differences, 145–47; using *I Ching* to reveal the unitary pattern, 151–52; *wu* as *shih*, 147–48
Chi 幾 (incipience), 189–90, 194–99; preceding *ying*, 196
Ch'i 器 (objects), Shao Yung's view, 106–10
Ch'i 氣 (psycho-physical force), 213; according to Chu Hsi, 171; used by Chang Tsai, 46
Ch'i-chih 氣質 (physical endowment), 171
Chiao 交 (interact), 77
Chih 知(智) (knowledge, wisdom), 193; related to *hsing* by Chu Hsi, 181
Chih-kuo 治國 (ordering the state), 169
Chin 金 dynasty (Jurchens), 53
Chin shih 進士 examination, 27
Ch'in Kuan 秦觀, 64n.12
Ching Fang 京房, 22
Ching-tso 靜坐 (quiet sitting), 172
Ch'ing 情 (human emotion), definitions compared, 255
Ch'iung-li 窮理 (fathom the pattern), 176
Chou 周 dynasty, 10

Chou Tun-i 周敦頤, 7, 25, 46, 225; and Ch'eng brothers, 51; and Chu Hsi, 54; and Su Shih, 72–81; use of t'ai-chi, 105n.21

Chou-i 周易 (Change of Chou), 10

Chou-i cheng-i 周易正義, 25

Chou-i lueh-li 周易畧例 essays, 23

Chu 主 (mastery), 198

Chu Hsi 朱熹, 4, 6, 53–55, 169–205, 177–88; attaining sagehood, 171–72; books on I Ching, 173–76, 175–76; and Ch'eng I, 172, 179, 182–84, 184, 225; ch'i, 171; on chih and hsing, 181; commentary on Fu, 251–54; and Confucius, 170, 173, 180, 183; on creation of I Ching, 177; and divination, 169–205, 224–26, 234–35; editor of Ch'eng brothers works, 54; on Fu-hsi as first sage, 223; grounding in ancient texts, 222; and hsiang-shu, 179, 225; on hsin, 171–72; on hsing, 171–72; and I Ching as a text, 228; I-hsüeh ch'i-meng as divination manual, 175–76; and i-li school, 179, 183–84, 225; on jen and li, 170–72; and kuei-shen, 199–203; letter to Chang Shih, 169–77; letter to Lu Tzu-mei, 175; li, 171–72; literati's moral authority, 170; methodology of reading (tu-shu fa), 180–85; and Ou-yang Hsiu, 54; personal use of I Ching, 205; redefinition of succession of the Way (tao-t'ung), 223; and Shao Yung, 225; study of Ho-t'u and Lo-shu, 175; study of milfoil divination, 176, 188–89; study of yin-yang, 176; synthesis of Shao Yung's and Ch'eng I's approaches, 222–26; on te and "laws and punishment," 170; theory of divination, 169, 182; theory of mind, 171–72; using li to explain existence of things, 148n.51; and Wang An-shih and Ssu-ma Kuang, 46

Chu-k'o 諸科 examination, 27

Ch'u 初 (origin), 88

Chü-ching 居敬 (abide in reverent composure), 172

Ch'ü 屈 (bending back), 200

Chuang Tzu 莊子, 62

Chün-tzu 君子 (superior man), 191

Chung 中 (central, Mean), 185n.60; in interpreting hexagrams, 15–16; used by Ch'eng I, 153

Civil service examinations, in Sung, 4, 26, 207

Classics: officially sanctioned edition, 31; Ou-yang Hsiu's views, 29–31; Sung literati interest in, 228; Tseng Kung's views, 46

Coherence, of heaven, earth, and humanity, 206–9

Confucius, 180, 183; Analects, 32–36, 56; Chu Hsi's return to his ideas, 170, 173; and Ou-yang Hsiu, 31; and Ten Wings, 173; views of ghosts and spirits, 201

Contemplation of things. See Kuan-wu

Conventions, bibliographic, ix

Correct, correctness. See Cheng

Cosmic calendar, of Shao Yung, 123–25

Culture and nature, 153, 206. See also Wen

Cyclic markers, Shao Yung's view, 123

Diagrams. See T'u

Divination: Chu Hsi's theory, 169–76, 182–89, 199–205, 234–35; for detecting incipient changes, 194–95; efficacy of, for Ch'eng I, 212; for learning ying, 191–92; limits of, 199–205; objections by Ch'eng I, 212; shown in I-hsüeh ch'i-meng, 175–76; Su Shih's views, 65; using milfoil, 176

Duke of Chou 周公, 173, 177, 180, 183

Economic growth in Sung dynasty, 3

Emotion. See Ch'ing; Jen-ch'ing

Examination system, 207; comments by Su Shih, 63; emphasis on prose, 28–29; reforms, 27; under Wang An-shih, 59

Fa 法 (patterns), 177

Fan Chung-yen 范仲淹, 5, 25, 27, 28, 32

Farmer wounded by tiger, 166

Fei Chih 費直, 22, 174

Firmness and softness. See Kang-jou

Five phases. See Wu-hsing

Foreknowledge, Shao Yung's view, 101n.4, 110, 118, 119

Four images, of Shao Yung, 108–9, 111–12

Fu-hsi 伏羲, 173, 176–77, 180, 183, 223. See also Hsien-t'ien diagram

Ghosts and spirits. See Kuei-shen

Goodness. See Jen

Hainan Island, 56

Han 漢 dynasty: acceptance of *I Ching*, 12, 22; *hsiang-shu* school, 18; Imperial Academy, 22; political uses of *I Ching*, ix

Han K'ang-po 韓康伯, 38

Han Yü 韓愈, 32, 59

Hang-chou 杭州, 52

Heaven-and-earth. *See T'ien-ti*

Heaven's mandate. *See T'ien-ming*

Hexagram: Chia-jen 家人, 139, 205; Chi-chi 既濟, 70n.25; Chieh 解, 15; Ch'ien 乾, 8, 9, 20, 23, 36n.23, 69n.23, 82n.73, 86n.86, 87n.87, 148, 178, 178n.27, 179, 184, 186n.62; Chun 屯, 70n.25, 71n.36, 158n.101; Feng 豐, 13; Fu 復, 8–9, 11, 14–15, 18, 22, 68–69, 116, 120n.68, 129n.114, 148–49, 156–60, 237–54; Heng 恆, 163; Hsien 咸, 72n.42; Huan 渙, 72n.45; Ken 艮, 11, 72n.44, 144–45, 153, 164n.120, 221; Kou 姤, 18, 159; Ku 蠱, 18, 70n.30, 72n.40; K'uei 睽, 145–46; K'un 困 (Difficulties), 168; K'un 坤 (Primal Yin [The Receptive]), 12–13, 20, 23, 148, 162, 178n.27, 185, 188; Li 離, 15; Lin 臨, 22, 159–60; Lü 履, 138; Meng 蒙, 70n.28, 71n.35, 71n.37; Ming-i 明夷, 163n.114; Pi 賁, 163n.117, 167, 179, 220; Po 剝, 120n.68, 157; Shih 師, 19, 70n.26, 71n.38, 140, 179; Sung 訟, 70n.25, 70n.27; Ta-yu 大有, 178, 179; Ts'ui 萃, 71n.32, 72n.43; T'un 遯, 205; T'ung-jen 同人, 71n.33, 71n.39, 179; Wu-wang 無妄, 69n.24, 71n.34, 72n.41

Hexagram statements, 8, 25, 177. *See also Kua-tz'u*

Hexagrams: birth order, 109; Chu Hsi's view of original intention, 177–78; comparison of Ch'eng I and Chu Hsi, 180; forms in *I Ching*, 8–9; Fu-hsi as creator, 177; and Hu Yüan, 37; interpretation in Ten Wings, 13–24; line statements, 9, 177; rules for relations among lines, 15; Shao Yung's reordering, 116–17

Ho-t'u 河圖 (Yellow River Chart): Chu Hsi's view, 175; Shao Yung's view, 120–22

Hsi-tz'u-chuan 繫辭傳, 19–26

Hsiang 象 (image), 178; definitions by Ch'eng I and Shao Yung, 210; definitions compared, 255–56; emerging from *t'ai-chi*, 105–6; Shao Yung's view, 106–10;

Su Shih's view, 68; and trigrams, 17–18

Hsiang-shu 象數 (image-number) school, 175n.20; Chu Hsi's views, 179, 225; Han origins, 18; and *i-li* school, 217–18; Yü Fan as practitioner, 19

Hsiang-t'ui 相推 (interact), 74

Hsiang-yin 相因 (exist through interaction), 80

Hsien-t'ien 先天 (preceding heaven) diagram, 112–19

Hsin 心 (mind): Chu Hsi's theory, 171–72; Shao Yung's definition, 132

Hsing 性 (human nature): according to Chu Hsi, 171–72; Ch'eng I's views, 150; definitions compared, 256–57; Shao Yung's views, 103

Hsing 行 (practice), related to *chih* by Chu Hsi, 181

Hsing-ch'a 省察 (self-examination), 197

Hsing-chi-tao 行其道 (bring *tao* into practice), 66

Hsing-ming 性命 (human nature and fate), 45; and *jen-shih* and heaven-and-earth, 33–42

Hsing-se 形色 (shape and form), 213

Hsiu-shen 修身 (self-cultivation), 169

Hsü-kua 序卦, 14, 245

Hsüan-hsüeh 玄學 (learning that fathoms mystery), 81

Hsüeh 學 (learning, study): according to Shao Yung, 130; Ch'eng I's views, 152–60; redefined, 28–33, 42; role of, 5; and Shao Yung, 101–5

Hu Yüan 胡瑗, 25, 32, 34, 37–39, 227

Hua 化 (transformation), 193

Huang Ju, 96

Huang Yüeh-chou 黃粵洲, 122n.77

Huang-chi ching-shih shu 皇極經世書, 100n.2; by Shao Yung, 100–101

Huang-chou 黃州, 51, 56

Human affairs. *See Jen-shih*

Human emotion. *See Ch'ing; Jen-ch'ing*

Human goodness. *See Jen*

Hun 魂 (yang soul), 200

I (meaning) 義, 179

I (righteousness) 義, Ch'eng I's views, 139–40

I Ching 易經: and calendar, 22; and Chang Tsai, 46; Chu Hsi's views, 169–72, 175–88; claims of Sung literati, 7; coherence,

I Ching (cont.)
16; commentary by Ch'eng I, 156–60;
commentary by Su Shih, 56, 64–90;
commentary examples, 237–44; composition of, 8–9; created for divination,
178; distinguishing basic text from commentary, 9; doubted by Ou-Yang Hsiu,
34–36; and filial piety, 154–55; forms of
hexagrams, 8–9; and heaven-and-earth,
19–26, 233; as historical document, ix,
vii; and *hsing-ming*, 151; as model of
moral order, 231; multiple sources, 10–
11; myth of Fu-hsi's creation, 177; origins, 10–11, 21; and the pattern, 190;
political uses in Han dynasty, ix; as a
practice, 231–35; prior to Sung dynasty,
7–25; self-cultivation, 198–99; Su Shih
on line interpretation, 68; Su Shih's
views, 67–81; summary of uses, 227–35;
in T'ang dynasty, 174; as a text, 227–29;
traditional view of authorship, 11n.22;
as unitary pattern, 151–52; as a universal process, 229–31; as *wen* grounded in
tao, 231; as world in microcosm, 233–34
"*I huo-wen*" 易或問, 34n.16
I so kan-t'ung 意所感通 (resonances of the
intention), 183
"*I tung-tzu-wen*" 易童子問, 34n.16
I-hsüeh ch'i-meng 易學啟蒙, 175–76
I-li 義理 (meaning-pattern) school, 175,
175n.20, 183–84; Chu Hsi's disagreements, 179, 183–84, 225; differing from
hsiang-shu school, 217–18; earliest com-
mentators, 174; and Wang Pi, 23
Image. *See Hsiang*
Incipience. *See Chi*
Intentional fallacy, 179n.32
Intentionality, 179n.32
Investigation of things. *See K'o-wu*

Jen 仁 (benevolence or human goodness),
Ch'eng I's views, 149n.59, 151
Jen-ch'ing 仁情 (human emotion), 31, 45;
Su Shih's views, 65
Jen-li 人理 (patterns of human behavior),
35
Jen-shih 人事 (human affairs), 33–42;
Ou-yang Hsiu's views, 31
Ju 儒 ("scholar"), 62; defined, 62n.8
Jurchens, 43, 53

Kaifeng, 51
Kan 感 (stimulus), 196
Kan Te 甘德, 129n.113
Kang-jou 剛柔 (firmness and softness), Shao
Yung's view, 107–8, 111
King Wen 文王, 173, 176–77, 180, 183
Knowledge. *See Chih*
K'o-chi 克己 (conquer self), 172
K'o-wu 格物 (investigation of things), 224
Ku-wen 古文 (ancient style prose), essays by
Su Shih, 59
Kua-tz'u 卦辭 (hexagram statement), 8
Kuan 貫 (connect), 69
Kuan-wu 觀物 (contemplation of things),
according to Shao Yung, 106, 131
Kuei-shen 鬼神 (ghosts and spirits), limits
of divination, 199–200
K'ung An-kuo 孔安國, 176
K'ung Ying-ta 孔穎達, 25
Kuo-tzu chien 國子監 (State Academy), 51

Learning. *See Hsüeh*
Leibniz, 116
Li Chih-ts'ai 李之才, 48, 110n.43
Li Kou 李覯, 32
Li 理 (the pattern, principle): Ch'eng I con-
trasts with *tao*, 148–49; Ch'eng I on,
139–40, 142–52, 210; Chu Hsi on,
171–72; definitions compared, 257; Hu
Yüan on, 37; as network of roads, 149;
in relation to *hsiang*, 210; Shao Yung on,
127–32; Su Shih on, 73; unity and
morality inseparable in, 142–52. *See also
I-li* school
Li 禮 (rites, proper behavior), 170
Li-i erh fen-shu 理一而分遜, discussion,
144–47
Liang 兩 (duality), 81n.71
Literati: coherence of human beings and
heaven-and-earth, 208; commonalities,
206–26; importance of, viii; moral
authority according to Chu Hsi, 170;
moral autonomy, 206; understanding of
coherence, 206–9
Literature. *See Wen*
Liu Mu 劉牧, 38; use of *t'ai-chi*, 105
Liu Tsung-yuan 柳宗元, 32
Liu Yung-chih 劉用之, 185
Lo River diagram. *See Lo-shu*
Lo-hsia Hung 落下閎, 129

Lo-shu 洛書 (Lo River diagram), 122n.85, 123n.85; and Chu Hsi, 175
Loyang, 43, 48, 51
Lü Tsu-ch'ien 呂祖謙, 184, 189, 225
Luan 亂 (disorder), 70

Magic square of three. *See* Lo-shu
Mandate of Heaven. *See* T'ien-ming
Mantis and cicada story, 165
Meaning-pattern school. *See* I-li school
Mencius 孟子, 59, 62, 208; as ideal reader of *I Ching*, 218; and Ou-yang Hsiu, 32; recommended by Ch'eng I, 153; Su Shih differs with, 77, 79
Meng Hsi 孟喜, 22
Miao-yung 妙用 (mysterious functioning), 201
Milfoil stalks, 188–89, 194; use by Chu Hsi, 205
Mind. *See* Hsin
Moral order, 30–33, 49–53, 206; and *T'uan-chuan*, 15, 19
Movement and stillness, Shao Yung's view, 107n.31, 108

Nan K'uai 南蒯, 12–13
Naturalness. *See* Tzu-jan
Nature and culture, 153, 206
New policies, 43–44; opposition by Ch'eng I, 219; opposition by Su Shih, 56–57, 62–63, 219; restored as policy, 52–53
Ni 逆 (going against), 88, 109–10, 118–20
Nothingness. *See* Wu
Number. *See* Shu
Numerology: in *hsien-t'ien* diagram, 114–15; used by Shao Yung, 48

Objects. *See* Ch'i; Wu
Occult methods. *See* Shu
Orders of reality, Shao Yung, 105–10
Ou-yang Hsiu 歐陽修, 4, 6, 26–32; approach to *hsing*, 208; and Classics, 29–31; and coherence, 207–8; and constancy in change, 29–30, 209; doubts about *I Ching*, 34–36; on *hsüeh*, 208; and *I Ching* as a text, 227; and *jen-ch'ing*, 31; and Mencius, 32; and ongoing change, 29–30; redefines learning, 28–33; "Treatise on Rites and Music," 29–33; and Wang An-shih and Ssu-ma Kuang, 44

Pao-hsi 包羲. *See* Fu-hsi
Pattern, the. *See* Li
Patterns of human behavior. *See* Jen-li
Pen-i 本意 (original intention), 178
Pen-i 本義 (original meaning), 178
Perspective of reality; according to Shao Yung, 101–2, 104
Pien-hua 變化 (variation and transformation), 74
Pien-i 變易 (change), 161–63
Pien-i chih chi 變易之際 (moment of change), 243
P'o 魄 (yin soul), 200
Practice. *See* Hsing
Principles. *See* Li
Printing, 3
Prognostication. *See* Divination
Psycho-physical force. *See* Ch'i
Pythagoreans, compared with Shao Yung, 127

Reading, Chu Hsi's methodology, 180–85
Responsiveness. *See* Ying
Righteousness. *See* I
Ritual, 28–30

Sages: according to Chu Hsi, 171–73; according to Shao Yung, 133–34; chance of appearance, 171
Self-cultivation: according to Chu Hsi, 170, 172; and divination, 189
Selfishness. *See* Ssu
Shang 商 dynasty, 10
Shao Yung 邵雍, 6, 43, 47–48, 100–135; birth order of hexagrams, 109; and change, 229–31; and Ch'eng I, 148, 158, 160, 210–18; Chu Hsi's views, 225; cosmic calendar, 123–25, 129; cyclic markers, 123; derivation of eight trigrams, 109; development of four images, 108–9, 111–12; discussion of sage, 104, 133–34; foreknowledge, 101, 110, 118, 119; Han precedents for calendar studies, 22; and heaven-and-earth, 100, 101; hexagrams, 116–17; Ho-t'u, 120–22; *hsiang* and *ch'i*, 106–10; *hsien-t'ien* diagrams, 112–19; *hsüeh*, 103–4, 130; *I Ching* as a text, 227–28; issues treated by Su Shih, 72–81; *kuan-wu*, 101–5, 131; *li*, 129–32; mind and things, 132–35; nature of things, 102–3, 106; nature of time, 214–

Shao Yung (*cont.*)
  16; and number, 100, 110–32, 210–18; order of heaven-and-earth, 106; and Ou-yang Hsiu, 129; perspective of reality, 101–2, 104–10; *shen* and *li*, 127–32; *shu*, 130; *t'ai-chi*, 105; *tao*, 134–35; and ten-thousand things, 107–9
Shape and form. *See Hsing-se*
Shen 神 (spirit), 84, 193; definitions compared, 257; emerging from *t'ai-chi*, 105–6; as source of number for Shao Yung, 127
Shen 伸 (stretching out), 200
Shen-ming 神明 (spiritual clarity), 191, 194
Shen-tsung 神宗, 42, 43
Shen-tu 慎獨 (prudence in solitude), 172
Sheng-sheng 生生 (coming into being), 74
Shih 識 (discern), 86
Shih 士 (literati), 4
Shih 時 (the times), Ch'eng I's views, 160–64
Shih Shen, 石申 129n.113
Shih yen chih 詩言志 (poetry speaks of the will), 58
Shih-i 十翼 (Ten Wings), 14–26, 173; commentary by Su Shih, 65; Confucius's authorship denied, 34–36; descriptive table, 14; and Fei Chih, 22
Shu 數 (number): efficacy for Ch'eng I, 212, 213–15; emerging from *t'ai-chi*, 105–6; role in understanding heaven-and-earth, 210–18; Shao Yung's and Ch'eng I's views, 210–18; Shao Yung's approach, 110–32
Shu 術 (occult methods), Ch'eng I's criticism of Shao Yung, 217
Shun 舜, 203
Shun 順 (going with), 88, 109–10, 118–19
Shun 順 (obedient), 185
Shuo-kua 說卦, 17–18
Southern Sung dynasty, 53–55, 170
Spirit. *See Shen*
Spirits. *See Kuei-shen*
Spiritual clarity. *See Shen-ming*
Ssu 私 (selfishness), discussed by Ch'eng I, 139–40
Ssu 似 (semblance), 68
Ssu-ma Kuang 司馬光, 25, 42–48, 59; approval by Ch'eng I, 210; comments on *I Ching*, 45; and Wang An-shih, 43–44; working with Su Shih and Ch'eng I, 43

Ssu-te 四德 (Four Virtues), 179n.35
Ssu-wen 斯文 (our culture), 221
Su Ch'e 蘇轍, 50, 65, 99; funerary biography of Su Shih, 60
Su Hsün 蘇洵, 32, 50, 560; influence on Su Shih, 61n.7, 64n.12
Su Shih 蘇軾, 6, 56–99; on "Bringing Tao into Practice," 81–90; and Ch'eng I, 153, 219–22; and Chu Hsi, 222–26; at court with Ch'eng I, 51–52; at court with Ssu-ma Kuang and Ch'eng I, 43; definitions of *wen*, 220–21; differing with Mencius, 77, 79; and divination, 65; on examination system, 63; on Fu, 242–45; on "How to Act According to *I Ching*," 70–81; on "How to Read *I Ching*," 67–70; and *hsiang*, 68; on *I Ching*, 64–90, 228, 231; *Ku-wen* essays, 59; and *li*, 73; and moral autonomy, 49–53; and Ou-yang Hsiu, 50, 58, 65; role of *tao*, 58, 72–81; social vision of, 70–71; and Wang An-shih, 62–63; water metaphors, 76; and yin and yang, 77–79
Succession of the Way. *See Tao-t'ung*
Sui kan erh ying 隨感而應 (respond when stimulated), 192
Sui-shih 隨時 (accord with the times), 161–64
Sun Fu 孫復, 32
Sung encyclopedia, 207
Sung literati, and *I Ching*, 206–35. *See also* Literati
Supreme ultimate. *See T'ai-chi*

Ta-ch'üan 大全 (great whole), 63
Ta-i 大意 (general purpose), 189
T'ai-chi 太極, according to Shao Yung, 105n.21
T'ai-p'ing kuang-chi 太平廣記, 207
T'ai-p'ing yü-lan 太平御覽, 207
T'ang 唐 dynasty, 24–25, 174; survey of Ho-t'u, 120
Tao 道: according to Shao Yung, 134–35; Ch'eng I on contrast with *li*, 148–49; Su Shih on bringing into practice, 81–90; Su Shih on the role of, 72–81; water metaphors, 76; and yin and yang, 77–79
Taoist interest in *I Ching*, viiin.6
Tao-t'ung 道統 (succession of the Way), 223; redefined by Chu Hsi, 223
Te 得 (apprehend), 73

Te ch'i wei jen 得其為人 (apprehend as a person), 94–95

Te-hsing 德行 (ethical conduct), 60; as factor in examination system, 28

Ten Wings. *See Shih-i*

Things. *See Ch'i; K'o-wu; Kuan-wu; Wu*

Thunder, discussion by Shao Yung and Ch'eng I, 216

Ti 帝 (high god), 75

T'ien-ming 天命 (heaven's mandate), 35

T'ien-ti 天地 (heaven-and-earth): definitions compared, 258; *I Ching* as model of, 19–26; and *jen-shih* and *hsing-ming*, 33–42; *li* and unitary pattern of, 142–52; Shao Yung's and Ch'eng I's views, 214–18; Shao Yung's view, 100, 106

Time, Shao Yung's and Ch'eng I's views, 215–16

Times, the. *See Shih*

"Treatise on Rites and Music," 29–30

Trigrams: associations with *hsiang*, 17–18; Ch'ien 乾, 17; examined in *Shuo-kua*, 16–18; and *hsiang*, 17; K'an 坎, 19n.42; K'un 坤, 17, 19n.42; Shao Yung's derivation of, 109, 112–14; Sun 巽, 18

True knowing, and Ch'eng I, 164

Ts'ai 才 (ability), Ch'eng I's views, 150–51

Ts'ai 才 (qualities), 179

Ts'ai Hsiang 蔡䄵, 93, 94

Ts'ai Yüan-ting 蔡元定, 205

Tseng Kung 曾鞏, 46

Tso-chuan 左傳, early *I Ching* use, 12

Tso-wen 作文 (write compositions), 219

Ts'un-yang 存養 (preserve and nourish), 172

Tsung 宗 (source), 76

Tu-shu fa 讀書法 (methodology of reading), 180–85

T'u 圖 (diagram), used by Shao Yung, 110, 112–22

T'uan 彖 (hexagram statement), 8

T'uan-chuan 彖傳, 14–16

Tung Chung-shu 董仲舒, 122

T'ung 通 (thread together), 69

T'ung-tien 通典, 207

Typographic conventions, ix

Tzu-jan 自然 (naturalness), 38

Wang An-shih 王安石, 42–48; new examination system, 59; and Ssu-ma Kuang, 43–44; and Su Shih, 62–63

Wang Pi 王弼, 21–24, 38, 174, 225; commentary accepted by T'ang, 24–25; commentary on Fu, 240–42

Wei-fa 未發 (unexpressed), 172

Wei-wen 為文 (compose literature), 57, 91, 219

Wen 文 (culture, literature): and bringing *tao* into practice, 90–99; definitions by Ch'eng I, 220; definitions by Su Shih, 220–21; definitions compared, 258; role in interpreting *I Ching*, 218–22; Su Shih's views, 57–64

Wen T'ung 文同, 97–99

Wen Yen-po 文彥博, 56n.1

Wen-hsüan 文選, 207

Wen-shih 文士 (literatus of culture), 56

Wen-tz'u 文辭 (verbal elaborations), 66

Wen-yen 文言, 14

Wen-yüan ying-hua 文苑英華, 207

Wisdom. *See Chih*

Wo 我 (self), 85

Wu 無 (nothingness), 38

Wu 物 (things): according to Shao Yung, 133–35; emerging from *t'ai-chi*, 105–6

Wu Tao-tzu 吳道子, 92–93

Wu-hsing 五行 (five phases), Ou-yang Hsiu's critique of, 35

Yang Chen 楊震, 165, 213

Yang Hsiung 楊雄, 59, 122, 129

Yao 堯, 203, 223

Yao-tz'u 爻辭 (line statements), 9

Yarrow stalks, 188–89. *See also* Milfoil stalks

Yellow River Chart. *See Ho-t'u*

Yen Hui 顏回, love of learning, 103

Yin-yang 陰陽: Chu Hsi's study of, 176; definitions compared, 258; Shao Yung's view, 107–9, 111, 115, 119; Su Shih's view, 77–79

Ying 應 (responsiveness), 189–94; as change of state from *chi*, 196; in interpreting hexagrams, 16

Yu-wei 有為 (accomplish through intervention), 243

Yü 禹, 203

Yü Fan 虞翻, 19, 22

Yung 用 (function), 196